PINK 2.0

Pink 2.0

ENCODING QUEER CINEMA ON THE INTERNET

NOAH A. TSIKA

INDIANA UNIVERSITY PRESS
Bloomington and Indianapolis

This book is a publication of

Indiana University Press
Office of Scholarly Publishing
Herman B Wells Library 350
1320 East 10th Street
Bloomington, Indiana 47405 USA

iupress.indiana.edu

Library of Congress Cataloging-in-Publication Data

Names: Tsika, Noah [date], author.
Title: Pink 2.0 : encoding queer cinema on the internet /
    Noah A. Tsika.
Other titles: Pink two point zero | Pink two point oh
Description: Bloomington : Indiana University Press, [2016] |
    Includes bibliographical references and index.
Identifiers: LCCN 2016022246 (print) | LCCN 2016034865 (ebook) |
    ISBN 9780253022752 (cl : alk. paper) | ISBN 9780253023063
    (pb : alk. paper) | ISBN 9780253023230 (e-book)
Subjects: LCSH: Homosexuality in motion pictures. | Gays in
    motion pictures. | Mass media—Technological innovations.
Classification: LCC PN1995.9.H55 T755 2016 (print) |
    LCC PN1995.9.H55 (ebook) | DDC 791.43/653—dc23
LC record available at https://lccn.loc.gov/2016022246

1 2 3 4 5 21 20 19 18 17 16

Contents

Acknowledgments

Endless thanks go to Indiana University Press, and especially editor Raina Polivka, for making *Pink 2.0* possible. Since the moment I first shared my interest in writing a book about the online distribution and reception of contemporary queer cinema, Raina has been immensely supportive, offering considerable insight at every step on the road to publication, and I am, once again, enormously grateful to her. I am also indebted to Jenna Lynn Whittaker, Janice E. Frisch, Nancy Lightfoot, Mary C. Ribesky, Adriana Cloud, Dave Hulsey, and all members of the production team.

I thank the anonymous readers who evaluated the manuscript with admirable care, helping me see what worked about my arguments and, more importantly, what did not. Indeed, their attention to detail was nothing short of humbling. Michael DeAngelis, whose book *Gay Fandom and Crossover Stardom* has been a scholarly touchstone for me since I was a senior in high school, read and offered incisive comments on the entire manuscript, and I thank him for his invaluable feedback. Michael's contributions to queer theory and film studies have, in many ways, influenced my own scholarship, and *Gay Fandom* in particular—a beautifully written book that I have read countless times—taught me, and continues to teach me, the importance of addressing figures, intertexts, and archival documents that are often overlooked.

I thank another Michael, the critic and historian Michael Bronski, for nearly twenty years of friendship, immeasurable insights, and welcome reminders that Belle Barth is good for anything that ails you. This book, like so many others in the field of queer studies, owes a considerable debt to Michael's groundbreaking 1984 publication *Culture Clash: The Making of Gay Sensibility*—another scholarly touchtone for me.

I thank David Greven, whom I have not yet met, for the encouragement that he provided through an especially thoughtful review of my 2009 book, *Gods and Monsters: A Queer Film Classic*—a review that, in its challenging rigor, remarkable discernment, and sheer comradely generosity, I really needed as the cruelly dismissive and frustratingly obtuse one- and two-star reviews began piling up on Amazon, Goodreads, and other websites where users may anonymously denounce those they dislike. Speaking of that earlier book: I remain indebted to its editors, and, in particular, to the fabulous Thomas Waugh, who continues to inspire me.

I thank those of my teachers at Brown, Cornell, Dartmouth, Michigan, and NYU who encouraged my queer interests even as I had trouble articulating them.

At these schools, a number of brilliant scholars inspired me to do this work: at Cornell, Sabine Haenni and Jared Stark; at Dartmouth, Susan Brison, Mary Desjardins, Amy Lawrence, Angelica Lawson, Kathryn Lively, Brenda Silver, Kate Thomas, and Mark Williams; at Michigan, Bambi Haggins, David Halperin, and Sheila Murphy; at NYU, Jonathan Kahana, Antonia Lant, Anna McCarthy, Dana Polan, and Chris Straayer. The late Robert Sklar gave me the awesome gift of his mentorship—a gift that I take with me, along with Bob's field-defining work and the memory of his face and voice on the day in 2006 when my name appeared in a *Los Angeles Times* article on *Brokeback Mountain* fandom.

Speaking of *Brokeback:* William Handley took a chance on an untested first-year graduate student and advised me through the publication, in his invaluable *The Brokeback Book,* of my study of the film's online reception, and I thank him for his continued support. It was for Moya Luckett's dazzling graduate seminar on film history and historiography that I first conceived of the *Brokeback* study, and Moya has always shared my sense of the importance of queer reception, inspiring me through her own incisive readings of cinema and popular culture.

I thank my parents, Mary Tsika and Ronald Tsika, in whose house and in whose luminous company I wrote parts of this book. I thank everyone at Colgate University, and in particular those involved with the LGBTQ Studies Program, for supporting me during my time as a faculty member there. The students in my Colgate courses on queer cinema deserve special mention for their commitment, curiosity, humor, and insight. I also thank the following individuals, who similarly offered both practical and poetic support: Matt Brim, Edmond Chang, Nick Davis, Amin Ghaziani, Lindsey Green-Simms, Hollis Griffin, David Halperin, Guy Lodge, Alexis Lothian, Tara Mateik, John Mercer, Lisa Nakamura, Sam Penix, Christopher Pullen, Kristy Rawson, Margaret Rhee, Julie Levin Russo, Jim Stacy, my colleagues at the City University of New York's Queens College and the Graduate Center, especially Amy Herzog, and the students in my spring 2015 graduate seminar on media archaeology, especially Stephen Bartolomei, Brian Hughes, and Adam Netsky. My department chair, Richard Maxwell, carefully read portions of the manuscript and offered countless insightful comments, inspiring me to expand my thinking. I extend a special thanks to my Queens College colleague Matt Crain, who shared his considerable expertise on the history of internet advertising, generously reading and commenting on key chapters even as his family expanded with the arrival of a daughter.

Finally, and with an abundance of love and admiration, I thank the elegant Eric Grimm—my husband, my best friend, my BFF Rose—who never met a meme he couldn't queer, and who joins me in living against the grain, generously and joyously.

A Note on Scope and Terminology

This book is about some of the online lives of contemporary queer cinema. It adopts a broad view of the internet as, both metaphorically and materially, a "connective fabric"[1]—a "network of networks, which includes related media and information and communication technologies"—for instance, the geolocation services, mobile operating systems, and input devices that enable an app like Grindr (a significant if understudied forum for the reception of queer cinema, as user profiles patterned on *Brokeback Mountain* attest).[2] This book accepts that "one of the defining features of the Internet is its variable and amorphous topology,"[3] and it seeks to avoid the pitfalls of utopian approaches to "new" media by rejecting uncritical celebrations of cyborgs and the "posthuman" in favor of a sustained critique of the consequential racism, classism, corporate structuring, gender essentialism, sexual politics, and general discursive shortcomings of digital networked technologies. "It is not at all clear that the Internet, our Internet, is in fact the decentralized, open, and democratic tool of connection and communication that technolibertarian rhetoric applauds," warns the computer scientist Paul Dourish.[4] This book offers a similar challenge to those who continue to champion the internet as an inevitable boon to the lives of sexual and gender minorities—a kind of queer utopia where "anything goes," and where "everything is gay." As I write this in 2016, it seems that many of the foundational, oppositional concerns of queer theory are as applicable to contemporary networked environments as to the sociopolitical conditions of the 1980s and early 1990s, when AIDS, *Bowers v. Hardwick,* and Jesse Helms dominated vast swaths of the horizon of queer representability, at least in the United States. Indeed, the questions posed over a quarter-century ago by the queer reading group Bad Object-Choices seem just as urgent now—not only evocative of their immediate cultural climate but also eerily prescient of the injustices and constraints that characterize the commercial internet and associated technologies: "What are the patterns of reinforcement and resistance that define relations between scopic homoeroticism and racism? How can minority queer subjects imagine or produce a place for their own desires and their own desirabilities in a representational regime that appears to define itself through their exclusion and subordination?"[5]

I start from the unpopular assumption that the internet, rather than seeming synonymous with queerness in its allegedly boundary-shattering potential, in fact routinely concretizes the antithesis of what queer theory, in its epochal iterations, actually articulates and advocates.[6] If the oft-repeated claim that internet access is a fundamental human right is homologous with the perhaps equally familiar assertion that (to quote Hillary Rodham Clinton's 2011 International Human Rights Day speech) "gay rights are human rights," so is enforced ignorance of some of the more disturbing operations of internet companies isomorphic with an inability to perceive what "gay rights" might deny or obstruct in the name of local and transnational politics. In examining what happens when the internet takes hold of queer cinema, I attempt to illustrate Manuel Castells's notion that our current network society "works on the basis of a binary logic of inclusion/exclusion"—a corporate logic of limits that is far removed from the landscape of queer theory, and that has profound consequences for the production, circulation, and reception of narrative fiction films.[7] When exponents of queer theory occasionally—and, in my telling, naively or disingenuously—embrace networked activity as a fundamentally queer enterprise, the object of their approbation is often, at least implicitly, the white, Western, normatively bodied, sexually active, middle-to-upper-class gay man, a subject whose status as a sexual minority should neither distract from nor excuse his highly capitalized capacity to influence, and thus constrain, the construction of "queerness" online. Given the extremely high valuation of such a subject, it perhaps easy to understand why various advertising firms, content farms, and social networking services work to limit queer cinema to the dimensions of a gay masculinity that always seems to be "trending." Indeed, the placement of online advertisements for films as diverse as *Burlesque* (Steven Antin, 2010), *The Paperboy* (Lee Daniels, 2012), *Tammy* (Ben Falcone, 2014), *Magic Mike XXL* (Gregory Jacobs, 2015), and *Ricki and the Flash* (Jonathan Demme, 2015) has depended upon the identification of gay men on and through social media.[8] If, in the summer of 2015, you saw, on Instagram, a shirtless, heavily muscled, gay-identified porn or reality television star wearing an official *Magic Mike XXL* hat, announcing the release date of that film, and employing several "proprietary" hashtags, you have some familiarity with how advertisers invest in the fantasy of the gay male tastemaker, using it to determine many of the contours of online film reception. Similarly, when a gay-identified social-media celebrity models Meryl Streep fandom as a means of selling the "fabulous" *Ricki and the Flash*, or Melissa McCarthy fandom as a means of touting *Tammy*, his labors are often the result not simply of corporate sponsorship but also of a persistent sense that queer cinema, however expansive in theory, is best marketed by and for gay men. (That *Tammy* depicts lesbian characters is almost beside the point for those in charge of promoting it to "the LGBT community," while the white, conventionally handsome, "sassy" gay son of *Ricki* is paradigmatic of queer ad campaigns and social-media success, as internet celebrities from Connor Franta and Joey Graceffa to Davey Wavey and Tyler Oakley attest.[9]) Pushback can be found in many places, however—even online, and particularly in parts of the global South. In arguing against "the imagination of a single, seamless global web of connection that is Western, contemporary, and post-industrial,"[10] Jack Linchuan Qiu writes, "While the global network society expands and accelerates, it also exacerbates social exclusion and threatens 'losers' of globalization, digitization, and capitalization with complete historical annihilation."[11] With Qiu's cautions in mind, I have structured this book to reflect the availability of queer alternatives to Western constructions of gay masculinity on the commercial internet, considering, for example, access to and specific uses of information and communication technologies in Nigeria, where locally produced queer cinema has shaped popular understandings of the internet, and vice versa. In no way, then, am I offering "the internet" as a universal, ahistorical phenomenon, even as I define this particular medium in relatively broad terms.

That I consider the internet a medium (not unlike, say, radio or television) is reflected in my decision to refrain from capitalizing the term in these pages (except, of course, when quoting the work of others). Microsoft Word may reprimand me for doing so, and my iPhone may impose capitalization through autocorrect, but I stand by my use of the lowercase *i*, even as I acknowledge that few major publications in the field of internet studies reflect my approach.[12] To capitalize the word "internet" would seem—to this millennial, at least—distinctly campy, on a par with an aged person earnestly complaining, in writing, about children smoking "the Pot" or appearing insufficiently appreciative of "the Cinema." Indeed, the presently popular use of caustic neologisms and retro joke terms like "the net," "the information superhighway," and, especially, "the interwebs," along with the Dubya-derived pluralization of the word "internet," suggests the need to question received wisdom regarding terminology in the field of digital studies. While capitalization seems increasingly suspect for a medium that is no longer new and a networked experience that is not monolithic, it remains, in English, vernacularly appropriate to refer to "the internet" rather than to "internet"; no popular rhetorical shift has yet occurred that would render the latter acceptable (the way that, say, references to an article-free "cinema" have become acceptable, and even far preferable to the now-antiquated and altogether pretentious term "the cinema"). In other words, until Justin Timberlake (in the guise of Sean Parker, the character he plays in David Fincher's 2010 film *The Social Network*) tells us to "drop the 'the,'" we will be referring with impunity to "the internet" even as we concede the medium's broadness. Throughout this book, I capitalize the term "World Wide Web"—the name of a specific invention of Tim Berners-Lee and colleagues at the European Laboratory for Particle Physics (CERN)—as well as the term "Web 2.0" (a designation popularized by, among others, Tim O'Reilly). However, by refraining from capitalizing "internet," I hope to suggest the importance of broadening the scope of the medium's study (to accommodate, say, analyses of Android and iPhone apps that operate irrespective of the Web, as digital "walled gardens") while simultaneously critiquing the medium's limitations (including the normative confinements of closed hypertext environments) and attending to those frameworks and experiences that may lead us, as David Silver puts it, "in directions that were not preprogrammed."[13] In offering this critique, I do not intend to suggest that queer theory is monolithic or uniquely culpable in colluding with new platforms and modes of networked expression. Quite the opposite: it is the very intellectual and affective freedom afforded by queer theory that may allow us to conceive of what to "do" with and on the internet, precisely by problematizing the very "radicalness" so often cited in this theory's (essentialized) name. For if queerness isn't inherently radical—as Lisa Duggan, Roderick Ferguson, Dwight McBride, and many others remind us— then neither is digitality, whatever the technolibertarians may say.

PINK 2.0

Introduction

Questioning the "Queer Internet"

Along with the hegemony of computers comes a certain logic, and therefore a certain set of prescriptions determining which statements are accepted as "knowledge statements."

Jean-François Lyotard, *The Postmodern Condition*

Criticism serves two important functions: it lays bare the conditions of exclusion and inequality and it gestures toward alternative trajectories for the future.

Heather Love, *Feeling Backward*

Queer is always an identity under construction, a site of permanent becoming.

Annamarie Jagose, *Queer Theory: An Introduction*

In April 2014, Brendan Eich tendered his resignation as CEO of the Mozilla Corporation, a software outfit best known for its web browser Firefox. The designer of the dynamic computer programming language JavaScript, Eich was a prominent, if not exactly munificent, supporter of Proposition 8, donating a mere $1,000 to the 2008 campaign to ban same-sex marriage in the state of California. While Eich's relatively meager contribution, exposed to public scrutiny, might well have embarrassed him on its own strictly monetary terms, it was its discriminatory objective that created a firestorm of controversy—one that fed on the ostensibly ironic contrast between JavaScript's status as a versatile, multi-paradigm language and its creator's apparently heterosexist single-mindedness. When, in early 2012, Twitter users first caught wind of Eich's relationship to Prop 8, it became a trending topic, and tweets highlighting the disjuncture between JavaScript's groundbreaking "openness" and Eich's personal "repressiveness" began to proliferate. "Apparently @brendaneich, father of #JavaScript, isn't as versatile as his language," tweeted one user, while the *Los Angeles Times*, operating in an equally facetious mode, posed the question "Has your 4-year-old contribution to an anti-gay marriage law suddenly resurfaced on the Internet?"[1] Other responses were far more sobering, with several gay Mozilla employees and their partners expressing outrage over Eich's appointment as the company's CEO. Hampton Catlin, the computer programmer

1

who created the Sass and Haml markup languages, and who was designing apps for Firefox OS at the time of Eich's resignation, provided a personal interpretation of the controversy, identifying as a gay victim of Prop 8 and an opponent of those who would combat marriage equality.[2] What all of these purportedly pro-gay responses to the allegedly anti-gay Eich have in common, however, is an unquestioning investment in JavaScript as an engine of queerness. In highlighting the affective chasm between a computer programming language and its all-too-human creator, these commentaries only reinforce the clichéd and altogether questionable notion that JavaScript, like other modes of computing—and unlike a few Eichian "bad apples"—is inherently, liberatingly "queer."

Perhaps the most revealing criticism of Eich appeared as a landing page on the free dating website OkCupid, and amounted to a call to boycott Mozilla. In March 2014, users accessing OkCupid via Firefox were greeted with a message asking them to reconsider their choice of web browser. "Hello there, Mozilla Firefox user," read the message. "Pardon this interruption of your OkCupid experience, [but] Mozilla's new CEO, Brendan Eich, is an opponent of equal rights for gay couples." Proceeding to detail OkCupid's fidelity to gay and lesbian users, the message acknowledged the website's stake in marriage equality: "If individuals like Mr. Eich had their way, then roughly 8% of the relationships we've worked so hard to bring about would be illegal. Equality for gay relationships is personally important to many of us here at OkCupid. But it's professionally important to the entire company." That the message consistently uses the word "gay" to stand in for "gay and lesbian" is symptomatic of OkCupid's discursive and interactive limitations—of an antiquated, even offensive rhetoric that it attempts to conceal through its avowed commitment to "equality." At the time that OkCupid issued its anti-Eich message, the website's users were required to select one of only two gender identities ("male" or "female") and one of only three sexual orientation identities ("straight," "gay," or "bisexual"). As a site that then traded in—indeed, required—cisgender identifications, OkCupid was not unlike most major dating websites that cater to (or that at least seek to accommodate) "gay and lesbian" users and that often deploy the term "gay" as a queer catchall, thus signaling a certain, inescapable orientation toward homosexual men.[3] Apart from smacking of a general masculinist bias, such an orientation evokes the popular presumption that gay men are among the most likely individuals to pursue love and sex online.[4] It speaks to the continued need for commercial websites to chase the so-called "gay dollar" even in an age of accelerating "post-gay" protestations.

Under a purportedly queer umbrella, gay men are perpetually positioned as dominant; in marketing terms, they matter the most, motivating and reflecting the consumerist claim that "some queers are better than others."[5] Thomas Waugh has explored the emergence of this claim, pointing out that by the 1970s "the concentrated, profitable market of young, urban gay males was a well-tested commercial reality," one that hinged on the fantasy of "free living, big spending young bachelors with sophisticated tastes."[6] Today, certain discourses of digital exceptionalism are reserved for gay men, or emerge in their name. In the male-dominated tech community, coming out as gay is often, as Alice E. Marwick suggests, celebrated as synonymous with broader, digital-era ideals of openness and transparency; the line between gayness and digital fluency is consistently effaced in the cultures of Silicon Valley, including at the highest corporate levels.[7] If the internet is often (mis)understood as a diffuse, supranational medium, so are corporate constructions of gay masculinity that posit an essentialized base of muscled, cultured, big-spending, sexually active studs. Occasionally, however, such studs are assembled in the service of specific, "exceptional" state formations. Consider, for instance, "Brand Israel," the notorious marketing campaign of the Israeli government that is practically synonymous with the phenomenon of "pinkwashing," and that trades in images of indistinguishable, nearly naked young men—all of them upheld as indices not merely of how "hot" Tel Aviv can be, but also of how far Israel has come with respect to "LGBT rights" (here presented as coextensive with "human rights," as in Hillary Rodham Clinton's 2011 International Human Rights Day speech).[8] Despite strategic uses of the rights-based rhetoric of inclusion, the supremacy of the "G"—of gay men—is practically axiomatic in these campaigns, even after decades of a heavily commodified "lesbian chic" in France, the United States, and other parts of the global North. When, in July 2010, the market research firm Harris Interactive released poll results suggesting that "gay and lesbian adults are more likely and more frequent blog readers" than their straight (and, presumably, queer) counterparts, online responses reliably reduced the phrase "gay and lesbian" to "gay"—a rhetorical move that, far from simply signaling a desire for concision, often worked to normalize internet use as a gay male enterprise. Even lesbian bloggers were complicit in these masculinist strategies. For instance, the lesbian-identified British blog The Most Cake (TMC) argued in response to the poll results that "the internet is the natural medium for gay." Illustrating the blog post with an image of two nearly identical white men—both clad in muscle-accentuating superhero costumes—kissing against a waxen background, TMC invoked the stereotypical gay male fan, naturalizing his online ascendance and celebrating it through the metonymic deployment of Superman. White, gender-normative, sexually active gay guys are, in other words, the "super men" of the internet—something that "everyone knows." The Harris Interactive poll results were, for TMC, thus reflective of queer common sense, almost to the point of appearing redundant: they in fact "confirmed" the lesbian blogger's "long-held suspicions." In her words,

> I didn't need statistics to tell me that gay people are more keen on the internet. I guess the reason I picked up on these survey results . . . was that they chimed

with my own experience. Though my friends on Facebook are probably 50:50 gay/straight, it's the gay ones that are all over it, uploading pictures, statuses, making chats and staging epic flash-mob comment attacks. Gay people know more about youtube [sic], and have almost definitely signed up to an internet dating site (it still counts even if you deleted it).

Further praising Facebook's interface as an especially (and universally) gay-friendly one, the blogger furnishes no fewer than four explanations for the internet's "natural" gayness—and for the gay person's "natural" internet savvy. Rehearsing standard consumerist claims about gay people being "more used to having to look for what they want"—whether sex or queer cinema—she concludes that "having to do a little investigative googling [sic] to find a good music review is not that much of a hurdle" for gay consumers accustomed to the hard work of evading oppression, "hence the fact that gays are a bit more adventurous in delving through the blogosphere."[9] Like so many prominent queer blogs, TMC contributes to the notion that the internet is built on the labors of gay men and in particular on their coded communication methods. As graphical accompaniment to textual explanations of this "gay internet," TMC predictably offers Apple's logo as evocative of the arsenic-laced apple with which Alan Turing committed suicide (or was murdered, as per various conspiracy theories)—a familiar conflation of gay cultural and corporate histories that invariably normalizes whiteness, maleness, and Eurocentrism, even on lesbian-identified blogs.[10] Such accounts rely heavily on anecdotal evidence, falling back on a clichéd, sentimental presentation of the internet as a gay haven and precluding considerations of what gay men actually do online—of their particular practices and inscriptions. More than just a marketing concept, the equation between gay men and the internet has the force of a structure of feeling, emerging as difficult to describe yet somehow commonsensical, despite—or perhaps because of—the obvious limitations placed on internet use around the world, which speak as much to a generalized queerphobia as to structural forms of racism and classism.[11] It is one of the goals of this book to challenge and contextualize typical celebrations of a "queer internet"—to put, in Fredric Jameson's words, "an only too frequently ahistorical experience of the present into something like historical perspective."[12]

Gay essentialism is patently central to a range of efforts to "queer" the commercial internet, and it often depends upon the disavowal of race, class, gender, and nationality as seismic factors in access to and mastery of digital networked technologies. Such tendentious strategies are not new. In investigating the rhetoric of the gay and lesbian tourism industry, Jasbir K. Puar observes a longstanding tendency to exclude queer formations that aren't identifiable with white male bodies. Thus even when "gay and lesbian" categories are invoked, lesbianism is rarely accorded a place in the statistical construction of gay exceptionalism.[13] When it comes to the selling of queer cinema, no consumers are more exceptional—and none are more explicitly beloved of distribution and marketing firms—than white, normatively bodied, middle- and upper-class gay men.[14] At the same time, however, post-gay culture threatens to contradict and contravene these corporate conditions, encouraging key queer filmmakers to identify as "fluid" in their sexual identities—to shun the "gay label" in what ranges from a principled, postmodern critique of rigid identity categories to a rather self-aggrandizing stance that reads as reactionary (as in François Ozon's publicly articulated rejection of homosexuality as monotonous and thus "very sad").[15] Given these increasingly global cultural circumstances, the marketing mandates assigned to and on behalf of gay men are becoming more challenging and contradictory: as an audience category, gay men are frequently essentialized as capable of producing paratexts—as, that is, so technologically adept, "wired," and "connected" as to generate supplementary or interpretive materials that effectively set the tone for online film reception. Yet they are working, in several conspicuous instances, with source texts (including Ang Lee's *Brokeback Mountain* [2005]) that obscure or otherwise complicate conventionally defined gay subjectivities.

Pink 2.0 considers the tension between the logic of market accommodation—the corporate targeting of an ever broader public through "open-ended" narratives (as in the infamously derivative Focus Features ad campaign for *Brokeback*, with its opportunistic references to James Cameron's *Titanic* [1997])—and attempts to secure the gay dollar through the cultivation of gay cultural and sexual exceptionalism. What are some of the gay subjectivities that emerge through these practices? What does queer cinema, as a contemporary category of production, become through its exposure to digital networked technologies and practices? What do purportedly queer-themed online marketing and reception strategies occlude? What subject-positions do they disallow, and why? What are some of the consequences for queer theory as it continues to contend with the digital turn, and where, on an internet that is at once more promising and less expansive than it initially appears, might we locate productions more radical—more suspicious of received knowledge—than, say, an anally oriented *Brokeback* parody?

Classifying Queer Cinema

> Queerness is not yet here . . . The here and now is a prison house. We must strive, in the face of the here and now's totalizing rendering of reality, to think and feel a then and there.
>
> —José Esteban Muñoz, *Cruising Utopia*

The category of queer cinema offers an abundance of practical and theoretical challenges, whether restricted to author-specific identity politics or inclusive of an array of seemingly contradictory texts. When deployed in its narrowest capacity, "queer cinema" refers either to the work of self-identified queer filmmakers or to theatrically exhibited audiovisual narratives that prominently feature self-identified queer characters. It is important to point out, however, that the term "queer" is hardly capacious in these instances, as it typically indexes questions only of gay masculinity or lesbian femininity. "Scholars allow such constraints," writes Nick Davis, "when they pose queer cinema as the exclusive enterprise of gay or lesbian artists and stories, or when they isolate star directors, canonized films, or bracketed historical periods as summative of much broader trends."[16] For filmmaker Pratibha Parmar, whom Davis quotes, this approach suggests that scholars are complicit both in the commodification of queer cinema and in the discursive contraction—the dramatic reduction of terms and experiences for the sake of salability—on which such commodification depends. It is scarcely anachronistic to suggest that queer cinema has its roots in the silent era (as anyone who has seen the gender-troubling 1914 film *A Florida Enchantment*, or any number of even earlier explorations of human behavior, can attest), and Parmar's suspicion that the category had, by the early 1990s, been whittled down to the dimensions of "a marketable, collective commodity produced by white gay men in the U.S." is well worth remembering.[17] Other scholars have focused primarily on the class dimensions of queer cinema, suggesting that a certain bourgeois tameness—part and parcel of the general aesthetic conservatism of films from the specialty distributors Wolfe Video, TLA Releasing, and Strand Releasing—is identifiable only as gay.[18] For David Pendleton, "queer" is a misnomer when applied to such insipid films as *Billy's Hollywood Screen Kiss* (Tommy O'Haver, 1998) and *The Broken Hearts Club: A Romantic Comedy* (Greg Berlanti, 2000), which tend, through their emphatically middle-class trappings, to present male homosexuality as a fixed, normative identity category well suited to the bourgeoisie. (That such films may furnish considerable erotic pleasure, addressing a diversity of sexualized subject-positions within a rubric of gay masculinity, is another, perhaps queerer matter—one that I address in this book.[19]) Pendleton, for his part, favors "formal experimentation" and "outsider status" as the constitutive elements of queer cinema.[20] In so doing, however, he may appear to revert to the very reverence for transgression that Brad Epps, Jasbir Puar, and other scholars have convincingly critiqued as a clichéd, and ultimately unproductive, component of queer theory.[21] Nevertheless, Pendleton's point that "gay cinema is advancing at the expense of queer cinema" is important, particularly as digital platforms embrace and extend the sort of identitarian streamlining that he sees in the production of gay masculinity as a "preferred" market. Indeed, Wolfe Video, TLA Releasing, Strand Releasing, and relative newcomer Breaking Glass Pictures are all well represented on iTunes, YouTube, Netflix, Hulu, Nintendo Wii, and Amazon, where the vast majority of their titles are conspicuously identified as "gay," whatever the styles, identities, and sexual practices they actually index.[22] "The ongoing codification of gay cinema makes it easier to distinguish from queer cinema," argues Pendleton.[23] *Pink 2.0* examines that codification as it operates on the commercial internet.

While it may seem tempting to lay exclusive blame for the dilution of queer cinema upon those digital networked technologies that appear to have inherited a general cultural preference for white, wealthy gay men at the expense of, say, black, working-class transwomen, it is important to critique the specific limitations of queer films themselves, the most commercially successful of which have offered little beyond some familiar figurations of consumerism, normative embodiment, vanilla sex, and fixed identities.[24] It is perhaps equally important, however, to attend to those contexts that rarely receive mention in scholarly accounts and that achieve, at best, an intermittent, partial, and scarcely heralded online presence. Such contexts include nontheatrical film and video, a category that offers vital reminders that nonwhite artists have long contributed to a broadly defined queer cinema, even if their productions have been obscured through various forms of corporate racism and academic inattention. The work of Bruce and Norman Yonemoto—Japanese-American artists who often interrogated the cultural distortions of Hollywood cinema, television advertising, and the gallery-industrial complex—is instructive in this regard, running the gamut from parody and pastiche (as in their 1986 video *Kappa*, which quotes John Huston's 1962 biopic *Freud* while repurposing some of the tropes of gay pornography and exploitation films) to inventive examinations of race and nationality (as in *Green Card: An American Romance* [1982] and *Japan in Paris in L.A.* [1996]). In 2013, Bruce Yonemoto joined Vimeo, the video-sharing platform, where he has since uploaded excerpts of thirty-two of the many works that he produced with his late brother. As of this writing, however, Yonemoto has only twenty-seven followers, and his Vimeo account is hardly readily identifiable with contemporary queer cinema—or even with "queer" as a capacious category of cultural production. Whatever the personal predilections that may emerge through one's browsing history in order to shape future search results, one is unlikely to discover the work of Bruce and Norman Yonemoto when Googling "queer cinema." It is out there, however, if one knows to look for it—available in tantalizing fragments that complicate conventional accounts of media history.

Concern regarding the parochialism of many nominally queer categories and practices has long galvanized scholars, despite or perhaps because of their disregard for nontheatrical film and video. In the early 1990s, Lauren Berlant and Elizabeth Freeman wrote of the "masculine a priori that dominates even queer spectacle" and lamented "the relative weakness with which economic, racial, ethnic, and non-American cultures have been enfolded into queer counterpublicity." Despite its canonization as "queer friendly," the internet appears only to have confirmed and extended what the authors call "the genericizing logic of American citizenship," suggesting the durability of that logic even amid an explosion of dazzling new technologies.[25] As Robert McChesney maintains, the capitalist stranglehold on the internet and other digital communication systems is such that we can no longer expect "qualitatively different and egalitarian" practices but, instead, can only anticipate those that "will look much like what currently exists."[26] Equally disturbing is the internet's capacity to distort and discard systems of thought that resist the binary logic of digital media, as Jacob Gaboury has suggested.[27] Indeed, an awareness of the potentially deleterious effects of popular technologies on certain modes of cognition has long been central to literary and queer theory. Writing in the late 1970s, over a decade before the development of the World Wide Web, Jean-François Lyotard critiqued the tendency of computing to reject, and thus threaten with obsolescence, any form of knowledge that simply "doesn't compute"—whether due to its resolutely nonbinary reasoning or to nuances that no amount of algorithms could possibly approximate. In Lyotard's prescient conception, knowledge "can fit into the new [computational] channels, and become operational, only if learning is translated into quantities of information," the result being that "anything in the constituted body of knowledge that is not translatable in this way will be abandoned."[28] In her 1995 book *Space, Time, and Perversion,* which was published shortly after the U.S. Federal Networking Council passed a resolution firmly defining the term "internet" and opening the medium to commercial use, Elizabeth Grosz observed a certain homology between then-new information and communication technologies, with their promises to facilitate a multiplicity of identifications and interactions, and longstanding taxonomic approaches to male sexuality, with their tendency to celebrate masculinity as a potentially endless yet always phallocentric proliferation of erotic practices. For Grosz, writing at the birth of the commercial internet, "male sexuality, straight and gay, continues to see itself in terms of readily enumerable locations defined around a central core or organizing principle"—a description that recalls the early rhetoric surrounding Tim Berners-Lee's World Wide Web, which tended to posit a balance between expansion and control, proliferation and standardization (via, for instance, Uniform Resource Identifiers). What concerns Grosz, particularly with respect to the implicit and emergent imbrication of gay male sexuality with digital networked technologies, is "the tying of the new to models of what is already known, the production of endless repetition, endless variations of the same."[29] The popular conflation of internet use and gay male sexuality—a conflation with queer cinema as its crux—occurred almost immediately following the commercialization of the internet. 1996 witnessed the debut of PopcornQ ("the ultimate online home for the queer moving image") on the World Wide Web (www .popcornq.com), America Online (at keyword "PopcornQ"), and the Microsoft Network (at Go word "PopcornQ"). The PopcornQ Film & Video Professionals List, an e-group "with an emphasis on the genre of gay, lesbian, bisexual and transgender motion pictures and events," was formed in 2000, but its membership, which eventually grew to 630 users, was dominated by self-identified gay men interested in pursuing "gay projects"; despite the e-group's seemingly inclusive tagline, the term "transgender" was rarely bandied about, and the cinematic examples most frequently cited—the ones said to be the most celebrated and thus worthy of emulation—were no more transgressive than Jonathan Demme's Oscar-winning *Philadelphia* (1993). When considering the symbiotic relationship between queer cinema and the internet in the age of media convergence, then, it is possible to perceive the filmic preponderance of white, middle-class gay men, whom a range of funding and distribution rubrics continue to privilege, as a major part of the problem. This is illustrated most dramatically by Roland Emmerich's whitewashed docudrama *Stonewall* (2015), which, however generative of resistance in the form of condemnatory tweets and think pieces, nevertheless guaranteed the iconographic online dominance of its white, normatively bodied, gay-identified protagonist (played by Jeremy Irvine), its contentious yet widely assimilable avatar.

The chilling inexorability of such a figure of gay masculinity online—the sense of relentlessness that accompanies his ascendency in contexts at least nominally devoted to streaming, excerpting, promoting, and debating queer cinema—is, I argue, an unacknowledged component of what Jaron Lanier refers to as the phenomenon of "lock-in." For Lanier, lock-in "happens when many software programs are designed to work with an existing one. The process of significantly changing software in a situation in which a lot of other software is dependent on it is the hardest thing to do. So it almost never happens."[30] Lanier's concept of lock-in, with its echoes of Nietzsche's "prison-house of language" and Foucault's "episteme," suggests precisely why "gay" continues to function as the default term for "queer," and also why, in illustrating that term—in exhorting users to put a face to a name, as it were—various digital designs make blue-eyed, blond-haired, square-jawed Jeremy Irvine an inevitable icon of contemporary queer cinema, an avatar as inescapable as it is redundant. Simply put, images of Irvine are at home on an internet ruled by a certain kind of advertising; they reflect the idealized base of gay male consumers that lends "queerness" to the corporate imaginary; they fit in with the ads for Gillette, GNC, and Viagra that invariably precede promotional film clips on Out.com, or that crowd the margins of *The Advocate*'s website, reflecting and addressing the whiteness, fitness, fastidiousness, and phallocentrism of a particular gay male constituency. Whatever its historiographic (and aesthetic) shortcomings, *Stonewall* reflects an understanding of how gay liberation made all of this possible—even inevitable. "This is what we need more of around here: clean-cut kids, all-American kids," claims the proprietor of the Stonewall Inn, referring to Irvine's aptly named Danny Winters. "People in New York like a straight-looking boy like you—you could do very well down here," adds a black drag queen, inviting Danny to dominate what he calls "the scene." "Resist the radicalism!" advises a sprucely dressed speaker at the Mattachine Society's special "Gay Is Good" meeting, and Danny has little difficulty conforming to a gay male ideal that many characters (even nonwhite ones) conflate with capitalist legitimacy. ("In its history as a white, middle-class movement," writes Matias Viegener, "gay liberation may be said to have fashioned gay identities suited to the bourgeoisie."[31]) Fittingly, the pop hit "A Whiter Shade of Pale" is the preferred seduction song of Mattachine leader Trevor (Jonathan Rhys Myers); it plays twice in the film, as accompaniment to Danny's efforts to fend off the influence of anything that isn't Mattachine-approved. Later, Danny asserts that "difference" doesn't even begin to describe what separates him from the gender-fluid Ray (Jonny Beauchamp), who loves him, but who must settle for a charitable, chaste kiss on the cheek from this apparent paragon of normativity. In some perverse historiographic sense, however, the film's domineering gayness is appropriate—an accurate reflection of what the Stonewall Inn, as an exclusionary establishment, once meant to many queers of color, as well as of what the Stonewall riots immediately signified in the American imaginary (namely, a gay male affair marked by "boys in chinos and penny loafers," to quote Eric Marcus).[32] For Mark D. Jordan, the riots didn't represent "the birth of gay liberation"; they merely "marked a moment in an ongoing quarrel about how to mirror homosexual lives—about how to make homosexuality visible." Rather than epitomizing a queer openness and indeterminacy, the internet simply and persistently reflects the very tension that, in Jordan's telling, lay at the heart of gay liberation—the struggle "between elite codes of ironic figuration and the passionate earnestness of literal display."[33]

However accurately it indexes an objectionable cultural history, *Stonewall* still occludes the complex contributions of queers of color, consigning them to the plot's hazy, stereotyped periphery. Acknowledging the historical ascendance of white gay men hardly requires an attendant fetishizing of Jeremy Irvine, but the filmmakers have ensured that even oppositional online accounts of their work will need to rely on Irvine's face and figure in order to become intelligible and "spreadable." The fault, then, is not simply with those tech experts who must make various design decisions; it is also with those who must make, market, and distribute films that purport to directly depict, obliquely address, or otherwise register the experiences of sexual and gender minorities. In short, as long as queer cinema continues to seem synonymous with white gay men, then so, perhaps, will its online reception—especially when circumscribed by studios and distributors, as on Focus Features' "Share Your Story" webpage, which helped to popularize *Brokeback Mountain* fandom as a primarily gay male phenomenon, but one that remained strategically amenable to certain formations of straight femininity.[34] To attempt to contribute a queerly nonbinary understanding of human sexuality to the now-defunct "Share Your Story"—to endeavor to "share" a sense of *Brokeback* as registering fluidity rather than the hard-won emergence of an "honest" and inviolate gayness—was to experience exclusion, and implicit condemnation, at the hands of site administrators tasked with shaping the film's reception. Alarmingly, and presumably at the behest of Focus Features and its parent company, NBCUniversal, such administrators labored to limit *Brokeback* fandom to gay men who identified with the equally butch Jack and Ennis, but they also, on occasion, incorporated the voices of women who, like Michelle Williams's Alma and Anne Hathaway's Lureen, had "survived" their marriages to closeted homosexuals. Gayness—specifically, male homosexuality—was thus the discursive stock-in-trade of "Share Your Story," as it remains across a commercial internet that occasionally encounters queer cinema.

On a less immediately accessible level, however, alternatives to such a binary logic may already be available—provided one is willing to look for them. Davis, for instance, advocates a renovation of the very concept of queer cinema itself—a destabilizing project with the potential to "enable a broader base of texts, a more nuanced grasp of its politics, and a more open future."[35] For the purposes of this book, the term "queer cinema" refers to films that, in any number of ways, represent gender and sexual minorities, but it evokes potentialities that its specifically gay-identified constituents rarely reflect. While I generally agree with Davis's warning that "opposing queerness to gayness is as false a position as conflating them," I want to explore the mechanisms through which digital media both manufacture and undermine this opposition.[36] I want, in other words, to critique the commercial internet's capacity to reintroduce the kinds of identitarian binaries that queer theory has long sought to relinquish, while simultaneously respecting the desiring potential—the sheer irreverence and occasional irrationality—of user-generated productions that only *appear* to confine queerness to male homosexuality, or that demonstrate the potentially dazzling expansiveness of a rather pedestrian designation like "gay guy."[37]

The aggressive extrication of "gay" from "queer" represents a persistently popular practice, one that is central to a wide range of cultural productions, including those authored by sexual minorities. Consider, for instance, the second season of the HBO series *Looking* (2014–2015), in which a lead character proudly proclaims, "I'm not queer; I'm gay"—a statement that the series, with its carefully depoliticized, consumerist celebration of gay men as muscled tastemakers adjacent to Silicon Valley, does not appear to critique. If popular representations of sexual minorities often demand imaginative interventions—reading practices that can queerly expand them beyond binary frameworks—then so, perhaps, do digital networked technologies. In her essay "Queer OS," Kara Keeling expresses her yearning for the sort of social operating system that would facilitate "uncommon, irrational, imaginative and unpredictable relationships between and among what are currently perceptible as living beings." What Keeling calls "the cultural logics of new media technologies" are often, more specifically, sexual logics that embed the gay-straight binary at every opportunity.[38] If a number of corporate interests and popular stereotypes have conspired to make "gay"—and with it the wealth, whiteness, normative embodiment, sexual insatiability, cosmopolitanism, and cis-masculinity of the "ideal" homosexual—the dominant online construction in relation to sexual minorities in general and queer cinema in particular, then this dubious streamlining has demonstrable offline consequences. If cinema shapes sexual subjects, then it stands to reason that the medium's increasing online presence—circumscribed as it is by the practices and algorithms that uphold hard, gay-identified cocks over an inchoate queerness, or that routinely interpellate transwomen as gay men—has painful effects on digital natives and digital immigrants alike, siphoning queer cinema through narrow or downright ignorant and reactionary frameworks.[39]

Queer cinema is—or, at the very least, should be—about more than just cock shots. Teresa de Lauretis certainly suggests as much in her 2011 essay "Queer Texts, Bad Habits, and the Issue of a Future": "A text is queer, regardless of the queerness of its authorial persona, if it carries the inscription of sexuality as something more than sex."[40] Keeling, for her part, understands queer "as naming an orientation toward various and shifting aspects of existing reality and the social norms they govern, such that it makes available pressing questions about, eccentric and/or unexpected relationships in, and possibly alternatives to those social norms."[41] Jasbir Puar's point that such terms as "gay," "lesbian," "LGBTIQ," and even "queer" are inadequate—"because they are both excessive and simultaneously too specific"—is well taken, however.[42] Equally urgent is her critique of those who read queerness "as singularly transgressive of identity norms," for not only does such a reading seek to consolidate the sexual exceptionalism of queerness, and in so doing deny the implication of queerness "in ascendant white American nationalist formations"; it also strengthens the exclusionary mechanisms on which exceptionalism depends—exceptionalism being "a founding impulse, indeed the very core of a queerness that claims itself as an anti-, trans-, or unidentity."[43] I agree with Puar that these taxonomic problems are perhaps irresolvable, and I intend to embrace the radical potential of "queer" without occluding its current compromises—including and especially its reduction, in cinema as well as on the internet, to the corporate dimensions of gay masculinity. The term "queer," as I understand it, demands an awesomely expansive—indeed limitless—definition, even if it often falls short of suggesting as much in presently available industrial and user-generated practices.[44] That is because "queer," to quote Peter Dickinson, constitutes "a literary critical category of an almost inevitable definitional elasticity, one whose inventory of sexual meanings has yet to be exhausted and one that challenges and upsets certain received national orthodoxies of writing"—including, I argue, writing on and about the internet.[45] A medium that first massified in the global North, the commercial internet, whose standardized interfaces include identitarian dropdown menus and whose most popular search engines partake of multiple surveillance techniques in order to devise precise and impermeable typologies, simply doesn't do "definitional elasticity"—at least not on its own, corporate terms.

The Gay Male Market

> The values of the marketplace rule the central circles of gay life, perhaps to a disturbing degree, where the body is advertising and "knowing the price of everything" is a main principle of doing business.
>
> John DiCarlo, "The Gym Body and Heroic Myth"
>
> Digital elitism does not reconfigure power; it entrenches it.
>
> —Alice E. Marwick, *Status Update*

"Gay people are a marketing man's dream," proclaimed the Gay European Tourism Association in 2014. "Not only do they tend to have more disposable income and travel more than their straight friends, but reaching out to gay people is relatively easy."[46] While such a proclamation is eminently contestable—Experian Marketing Services reported in 2013 that gay men in Europe and the United States in fact "have *lower* annual household discretionary expenditures than heterosexual men," due presumably to their disproportionate residence in high-cost urban centers—it still centralizes an assumption that an increasing number of advertising and marketing firms take to be an irrefutable truth: that gay men comprise a powerful and lucrative consumer group, one whose online presence and so-called digital skills far exceed those of straight consumers, thus making them more readily "reachable"—and, of course, co-optable as "prosumers" and "produsers"—through web-based promotional campaigns.[47] In 2000, a poll conducted by Harris Interactive declared that gay men were "among the heaviest internet users"—a result that subsequent polls have reproduced with astonishing regularity, to the point of promoting a new, essentialist stereotype of gay men as "web-enabled."[48] Closely monitoring the online transactions of self-identified and suspected gay men, and even assigning gayness to particular internet users in reports to third-party advertisers, have become popular strategies of dataveillance. As Frank Pasquale suggests, "bots can plunder social networks for their wealth of clues to sexual orientation," but "gay" often manages to come out on top—and not just in the surveillance of assumed sexual minorities. After all, as Pasquale admits, "there's money to be made from knowing if someone is gay"—or simply from suspecting as much—and various configurations of white gay men have dramatically increased the data assets of social networking services, especially the Facebook that first emerged as a posh, exclusive alternative to the racialized "ghetto" of MySpace.[49]

In many academic and journalistic circles, there is a persistent belief that the internet is most identifiable, and most valuable, as a vehicle of queerness—and that individuals are at their queerest when operating online. In "How the Internet Made Us Gay," Jack Glascott defines the medium as "egalitarian," claiming not merely that it has been the principal catalyst of a popular "acceptance of gays" but also that it has promulgated many of the gay "styles" with which it is apparently synonymous.[50] The high-toned techno-utopianism of Sandy Stone and Nicholas Negroponte thus fuses with a vernacular sense of the internet as "spreading the rainbow" (though pinkwashing would provide a more apt metaphor here, given the patterns of inequality that such enthusiasm invariably enables). Crucially, the queerness that internet use is said to confer on all users—the sense of unpredictability that it seems to foster, the boundlessness that it allegedly allows—has its roots in a certain fantasy of male homosexuality, which queer theory has occasionally presented as the repressed essence of all of human sexuality. Thus as part of his attempt to trouble the gay-straight binary, Guy Hocquenghem, in *Homosexual Desire*, upholds gay male promiscuity as emblematic of "desire itself"—a model of human eroticism that would be inescapable but for the "Oedipal cloak of morality" that so often shrouds it.[51] The "special" relation to desire that gay men allegedly enjoy becomes open to all internet users—widely practicable online—in accounts that adopt Hocquenghem's bombast, extending it into considerations of various digital platforms. If, in other words, male homosexuality functions for Hocquenghem by "putting sex into everything," then the internet, so closely associated with erotic experience, succeeds in "making all of us gay"—or, rather, in positioning its privileged users in direct relation to the very ideal that Hocquenghem mobilizes.[52] White gay men in the global North have both defined the most conspicuous contours of the internet's queerness and watched as those contours are defined on their behalf, especially by marketers who take the high valuation of male homosexuality seriously indeed. What Dwight A. McBride calls "the gay marketplace of desire" is thus perpetually produced by and for white gay men, even as queer theory, digital media theory, and popular culture claim otherwise, citing a broader, even limitless purview. Responding to claims that his efforts to "politicize desire are tantamount to policing desire," McBride cautions against the reflexive acceptance of queer theory's occasional grandiloquence, noting that "the realm of desire for queer theorists seems ever to represent the possibility for a kind of idealized freedom and liberality"—a possibility that is plainly restricted to a few privileged figures, even (perhaps especially) in the age of the internet.[53]

Broadly speaking, the commercial targeting of gay men has evolved, in the post-Stonewall period, from the coded, connotative strategies of what Michael Bronski terms "window advertising" to the more open, even celebratory focus on "niche communities" that such marketers as Absolut Vodka, American Airlines, General Motors, Macy's, and Orbitz have famously embraced, first through advertising in gay-identified print media, and later by infiltrating gay dating sites and "lifestyle" blogs.[54] Film distribution and marketing companies have similarly sought to solicit the "gay dollar" through practices of audience targeting. In a notable recent example, Warner Bros., having gleaned the "gay appeal" of the studio's male-stripper film *Magic Mike* (Steven Soderbergh, 2012) from various fan-driven online sources, hired a special marketing agency, the Karpel Group, "to generate buzz online and at gay bars and clubs."[55] I myself participated in this process of promoting *Magic Mike* to gay men, willingly highlighting the sex appeal of openly gay actor Matt Bomer, one of the stars of the film, in a piece for the *Huffington Post*'s Gay Voices, which ended up a hyperlinked (and thus potentially discursively constricting) player in the Warner Bros. marketing campaign.[56] I am, in other words, hardly immune to queer critique—hardly a paragon of antinormativity. I stand not outside of but well within many of the production, marketing, and reception strategies that I critique and even condemn in this book—and not simply because my research often turns to the metrics of Google and Facebook, and in the process unavoidably contributes, however marginally, to their corporate success. I hope, however, to follow Kara Keeling's queer mandate to produce work that "acknowledges its own imbrication with and reliance on" proprietary technologies and corporate practices, "while still striving to forge new relationships and connections."[57] Keeling, recalling Tara McPherson's point that our intellectual labors are inescapably shaped by the hardware and software on which they depend, offers a vital reminder of the usefulness of self-awareness and self-critique in queer theorizing. So, too, does Sara Ahmed, who suggests that the transformative potential of queer politics lies not necessarily in "being free from norms, or being outside the circuits of exchange within global capitalism." It lies, in some cases, in the way queerness is imbricated with other, perhaps even queerphobic formations: *"It is the non-transcendence of queer that allows queer to do its work."*[58]

My own, publically oriented, unremunerated form of *Magic Mike* fandom may have been inexcusably implicated in certain corporate, homonormative, and even homonational mandates, marking me as collusive with the continued discursive production of "queer cinema" as something of and for white gay men in the global North.[59] Other fans, however, were operating more illicitly, laboring online in order to extract a wider range of gay-specific meanings from *Magic Mike,* and in ways that often resisted the prescriptions of the Karpel Group, which prominently included efforts to unite straight women and gay men through a "shared" interest in shirtless studs.[60] One YouTube creation, titled "Magic Mike gay scene," consists of nine seconds of the film's central workout sequence, in which an aspiring male stripper receives the sort of expert training that, viewed from a particular angle, looks a lot like gay sex.[61] Furtively captured by a cell phone in a theatrical exhibition space, and subsequently stripped of sound, this nine-second "camrip" shows two nearly naked male characters gyrating in tandem; taken out of its narrative contexts, the gyrating calls to mind (some of) the mechanics of anal sex, with the actor Matthew McConaughey occupying the role of the top, and the actor Alex Pettyfer that of the "power bottom." What for Warner Bros. and the Karpel Group was a film with an "innocent," built-in appeal to straight women and gay men became something else for this YouTube user: an old-fashioned, opportunistic attempt to appeal to one audience "type" without alienating another—and a film whose carefully structured, ultimately platonic same-sex eroticism deserved to be "called out," and, in the process, *brought* out, in all its obvious, carnal "gayness." *Pink 2.0* looks at the latter tactic, with its gay-identified, digitally enabled libidinousness, against the backdrop of official efforts to sell—and, at times, to suppress—contemporary queer cinema.

Since the start of the twenty-first century, digital paratexts have provided some of the most powerful and popular points of access to theatrically released feature films. They have come to include YouTube videos, GIFs, Vines, Tumblr photomontages, Twitter hashtags, and many more formats and platforms. Comprising a complex fabric of easily distributable audiovisual interpretation—a blend of official forms of promotion, fan-driven modes of resistance, and the casual products of "clip culture"—digital paratexts often seem to supersede their ostensible cinematic sources, especially when they go viral, acquiring online viewers in excess of actual ticket, DVD, or Blu-ray buyers. Consider, for instance, "BrokeBack [sic] Love Scene," a user-generated YouTube video that consists of a pirated recording of two male characters experiencing anal sex in Ang Lee's *Brokeback Mountain*.[62] Receiving well over one million views within weeks of its illicit appearance on YouTube, the video generated heated debate in its page's comment section, largely among users who struggled to uphold or debunk the amorous aspects of "butt fucking" at the expense of engaging with *Brokeback's* plot and performances. Thanks to YouTube, and to the unauthorized, extractive practices that flourish on the site, the central sex scene of a contemporary queer film has had a life beyond its original narrative context—a viral life that has inspired extensive commentary on the mechanisms of gay male sex and subjectivity, and that has "infected" other websites, as well, triggering a veritable explosion of fan-produced, "porny" and parodic condensations of *Brokeback Mountain*.

In Gerard Genette's inaugural definition of the term, the paratext functions in supplementary fashion, as a material form that manages to shore up a primary or source text—to "ensure the text's presence in the world, its 'reception' and consumption."[63] For Genette, writing about literary production, the paratext—whether in the form of a pamphlet or a painting—works to confirm the primacy of the book that inspired it. But the paratext is also, more often than not, ambiguous or ambivalent in its relationship to an "original" text. It may be a condensed version of that text—a "clip" or "supercut," in the parlance of contemporary au-

diovisual consumption—or a seeming substitute. Genette explores such complexity, quoting the literary critic J. Hills Miller's conception of the prefix "para" as "a
double antithetical prefix signifying at once proximity and distance, similarity
and difference, interiority and exteriority."[64] Miller goes on to "unpack" the prefix in ways that well describe the function of digital paratexts in the realm of cinema reception, and that speak to the complex, even contradictory negotiations
of gay male subjectivity characteristic of the digital age: "A thing in 'para' . . . is
not only simultaneously on both sides of the boundary line between inside and
out. It is also the boundary itself, the screen which is a permeable membrane
connecting inside and outside."[65] Such language plainly evokes a classic, indeed
foundational, concept in queer theory, that of being "both inside and outside at
the same time"—an approach to human sexuality that dispenses with familiar
binary oppositions, and that disturbs, in Diana Fuss's words, "a symbolic order
based on a logic of limits, margins, borders, and boundaries."[66] It also evokes the
relations of the closet—what Eve Kosofsky Sedgwick describes in terms of the
interplay between "the known and the unknown, the explicit and the inexplicit"—
and addresses the difficulty of defining the paratext's connections to its source.[67]
Indeed, in the digital age, a certain epistemological, chicken-or-egg conundrum
structures our experience of paratexts: which came first—the popularity of
Brokeback Mountain, or that of the pirated, viral YouTube video that presents
the film's showpiece sex scene as a stand-alone piece of "pure gay porn"? Do film
distributors, in their production and circulation of "cine-minded" paratexts,
think first of theatrical exhibition prospects, or do they invariably begin only
with ancillary markets in mind? Does the gay man who illicitly uploads, recuts,
and rebrands a queer film hope to promote interest in that film, or simply support for his own practices of gay identification and cultural revision? It remains
useful to heed Sedgwick's advice about the need to "attend to performative aspects of texts . . . as sites of definitional creation, violence, and rupture in relation to particular readers, particular institutional circumstances."[68] The digital
paratext, disseminated online, has become a key, indeed indispensable means of
comprehending gay-identified films and their gay-identified fans—a powerful,
potentially viral player at the meeting point of corporate profit and personal
piracy.

Pink 2.0: Gay Cartographies in Digital Cultural Production

> [A]ny frame placed around contemporary queer cinema must be a pliable one,
> capable of admitting nuance, contradiction, and compromise.
>
> —Nick Davis, *The Desiring-Image*

As Nick Davis demonstrates, a radically expansive conception of what counts as
queer cinema is bound to yield a dizzying diversity of themes, techniques, modes

of address, and potential interpretations. And yet gay subjectivities continue to constitute conspicuous subjects and objects of queer-identified film production and reception in the digital age. When, how, and why do filmmakers and their fans work to limit the meanings of what might otherwise be read as expansive, polysemic queer films, turning them into digital artifacts that affirm male homosexuality as a fixed identity category? When, how, and why do corporations step in to support or otherwise modify this practice, ensuring that the gay consumer remains recognizable even at the expense of other queer subject-positions? These and other questions signal the central conundrum that this book traces, and that, in my telling, goes by the name "Pink 2.0."

A play on what Lisa Parks describes as "the info-tech world's terminology for new generations of innovation"—on, specifically, the expression "Web 2.0," which Tim O'Reilly helped to popularize as a heuristic device for analyzing digital interactivity—the term "Pink 2.0" attempts to convey, however cheekily, some of the movie-minded ways that male homosexuality has achieved expression online, in both corporate and "resistant" terms, and often at the expense of alternative queer constructions.[69] Taking the color most frequently associated with gayness—a color that, in its "reclaimed" triangular representations, has long symbolized gay pride and gay activism—I fuse it with the numerical designation for a new generation of web design that centralizes communicability, ease of use, social networking, and collaborative content creation. "Pink 2.0" thus represents a way of efficiently communicating gayness through digital encoding and online circulation, but also of getting at the sexual and cultural heart of a contemporary queer cinema that remains, in many of its incarnations and regardless of its occasionally postmodernist protestations, centered on emphatically gay men. I acknowledge the partiality of my approach, which extracts the "G" from the acronym "LGBTQ," cisgenders it, and examines its cultural and sexual specificities, particularly as they are shaped through online practices of queer cinema reception. I also, however, work from the assumption that, as David M. Halperin argues, "gay critical analysis matters"—that there is such a thing as gay male subjectivity, and that gay male cultural practices remain understudied, particularly as their parodic or prurient digital productions come to be seen as indistinguishable from broader patterns of networked content creation.[70] My approach invokes Eve Kosofsky Sedgwick's commitment, in *Epistemology of the Closet,* to "making space for a gay male-oriented analysis"—what Sedgwick elsewhere terms an "antihomophobic inquiry."[71] Sedgwick's influential focus on male homosexuality has often been subsumed under the broader banner of queer theory, however, leading some scholars to question the points at which "gay" and "queer" converge, diverge, and appear equally inadequate or irrelevant. At a 2010 symposium celebrating Sedgwick's life and work, Lee Edelman expressed his concern with "the consequential erasure of a name"—how "queer," somewhat anachronistically applied to 1990's *Epistemology,* can "closet 'gay male,'" mistaking Sedgwick's rigorous historicism for something far less grounded.[72] *Pink 2.0* takes off from a different, perhaps even obverse concern—not with queer theory taking the place of gay male analysis, as in Edelman's provocative observation, but with gay male analysis taking the place of queer theory. This "closeting of names," which, in Edelman's words, *Epistemology* "at once anticipates, performs, and sheds light on," is, on the commercial internet, not the effacing of "gay" but rather the occlusion of "queer"—an occlusion whose consequences for gay male analysis are curious, to say the least. Halperin, for his part, calls for a close "look at the highly distinctive uses gay men make of straight culture"; this book, by contrast, looks at the specifically digital, "spreadable" uses that they make of contemporary queer cinema—of films that, to varying degrees and with differing means and intentions, explore sexual and gender minorities.[73]

By evoking Web 2.0, I hope to convey not just the general "technological imaginary" that shapes expectations about digital media but also the specific historical boundaries that contain and further define my case studies.[74] The films that I scrutinize in this book were all released after 2000 and thus belong to the era of Web 2.0—the era of the interactive, postgraphical internet, when the medium was said to be returning to its "revolutionary," "egalitarian," "gay-friendly" roots following the dot-com collapse.[75] Focusing on roughly the first decade during which queer-identified films could effectively be networked via the Web during all phases of production and distribution, I emphasize how these films have influenced and been influenced by the commercial internet. "Pink 2.0" signifies the gay specificities that have frequently taken precedence in these processes, but it equally describes fan practices that are rarely mentioned in relation to queer cinema—as if only the *Star Wars* and *Star Trek* franchises could possibly yield a preponderance of fan creations, whether in print or online. Indeed, this book applies many of the central approaches of fan studies—from Henry Jenkins's famous focus, in *Textual Poachers,* on the "mix of frustration and fascination" at the center of fandom, to Mel Stanfill's more recent use of "fan" as an analytic, a way of remaining critically alert to the variegated uses to which both films and their audiences are put—to a contemporary queer cinema that has largely been left out of the scholarly conversation on fandom.[76] The digital fan creations that I centralize in this book have been similarly ignored—discarded in favor of the kinds of viral videos said to be statistically relevant. For my purposes, a video viewed only two dozen times on eBaum's World is just as useful an object of study as a video viewed millions of times on a more popular, more contemporary platform like YouTube.

In engaging a wide range of digital sources, this book considers the gay-identified biases that I condense in the term "the gay algorithm"—the commercialized commitment to male homosexuality in the online marketing, distribution, and reception of contemporary queer cinema. Indeed, it is a very gay algorithm—in fact, a series of gay algorithms—that produces Pink 2.0, a broad set of online designs that invite the user to identify male homosexuality as a subject and an object of queer cinema. Google's autosuggestions provide clues to the operations of Pink 2.0, allowing gayness to rise algorithmically at the expense of other queer constructions. Autosuggestions—also known as autocompletes—are, according to Google, functions not simply of "the search activity of users" but also, and even more significantly, of "the content of web pages indexed by Google."[77] The popular assumption that these "algorithmically determined" autocorrects are neutral—that they inevitably distill the uncorrupted truth of a given subject—conceals the fact that they merely index user biases and corporate limitations (which admittedly have their own evidentiary value). It also, of course, obscures just how misleading these autocorrects can be—just how powerfully they can misrepresent particular search terms. If, as numerous studies have indicated, dominant search engines are capable of dramatically altering perceptions of candidates for public office, then they are at least as likely to shape popular understandings of queer cinema, tendentiously suggesting that the category is largely if not exclusively by, about, and for gay men.[78]

The Work of "Gay" in the Age of Internet Distribution

The goals of this book are twofold: to explore how the internet makes gay sense of contemporary queer cinema, and to advocate on behalf of what might be considered perverse archives in a media archaeological approach to that filmic category.[79] By "perverse archives," I mean to evoke those sources that aren't simply unconventional, understudied, or even completely unacknowledged, but that are also unauthorized, openly fetishistic, libelous, and downright pornographic—that require "surfing the distant shores of the internet," to quote Wendy Robinson.[80] A perverse archive is thus a counterarchive—a term that, for Tim Dean, "refers less to a determinate place or archival content than to a strategic practice or a particular style of constituting the archive's legibility. Less an entity than a relation, the counterarchive works to unsettle those orders of knowledge established in and through official archives."[81] The disruptive potential of perverse archives is evident in the way that they critique received knowledge about cinema and human sexuality, exploding homonormative constructions for the sake of liberating queer desire. Blogs that boldly position queer films in terms of unknown, unnamed, or underrepresented sexual fetishes—that allege that Lee Daniels's *The Paperboy* (2012) is actually and profitably about Zac Efron's bare "boyfeet," or that the erotic appeal of Oliver Parker's *Dorian Gray* (2009) lies in the way that Ben Barnes crushes a live maggot beneath his boot—potentially reconstitute these films as radically queer objects. After all, as Kara Keeling claims, queerness "offers a way of making perceptible presently uncommon senses," and digital networked technologies are never queerer—never more challenging and inspiring—than when they enable users to read queer films through, say, foot and crush fetishism, shifting erogenous zones away from hegemonic hard cocks and splayed anuses, and understanding desire as a mode of transgression that critiques homonormativity as forcefully as heteronormativity.[82] "Common sense" may dictate that gay men are drawn to *Dorian Gray* on the basis simply of its star's sheer handsomeness—of his normatively bodied, well-dressed, cis-male splendor. When, however, the queer-identified YouTube channel The Curious Watcher (2007–) remaps *Dorian Gray* according to those for whom feet constitute sexual organs—and for whom the crushing of insects constitutes the epicenter of erotic pleasure—it demonstrates the power of "uncommon senses" to recast queer cinema, and reposition its online reception, as genuinely pathbreaking, pushing past homonormative cartographies of the body.[83] As Lacan asks in his critique of normativity, "what has this absurd hymn to the harmony of the genital got to do with the real?"[84] What, in other words, does an emphasis on genital relations, and an associated commitment to the imaginary and the symbolic—to, as Tim Dean puts it, "the images and discourses that construct sex, sexuality, and desirability in our culture"—distort, discredit, and occlude?[85] The algorithms of Netflix and IMDb might situate *Dorian Gray* along a stale and utterly unconvincing "Gay & Lesbian" axis, but The Curious Watcher, operating within the often-oppressive, corporate and copyright-driven boundaries of YouTube, manages to further queer the film, providing textual and graphical accounts of what Ben Barnes does—for the possible delectation of crush fetishists—to an unsuspecting little insect.[86]

Standard scholarly approaches would likely downplay the significance of The Curious Watcher and of its erotic interventions in queer cinema reception, subsuming the channel under the sheer restiveness and indeterminacy of the broader digital landscape. "Key features of digital technology exceed the intentions of any user," argues Dean. By this logic, there is no reason to assume that a challengingly queer cultural production—one premised on a personal, libidinal resistance to homonormativity—won't automatically lose its oppositional identity upon entering circulation on the internet, becoming assimilated into the very paradigms that it purports to dismantle. For Dean, "the ungovernability of the digital image represents an essential part of its structure," and it is precisely this allegedly intrinsic unruliness that would seem to render digital artifacts at least as susceptible to conservative co-optation as conducive to queer world making.[87] Dean, however, indulges an essentialist approach that tacitly revives the techno-utopianism of the 1990s, suggesting that digital creations are necessarily nomadic, even necessarily fugitive—always impossible to pin down. In reality, however, corporate constraints—including copyright protections and planned obsolescence—are often all too effective in ensuring that digital productions, far from becoming vagabond artifacts, remain in preordained place. It is plainly naïve to assume that a digital file is inevitably "free" or inherently "hackable." Indeed, Brad Epps's critique of what he calls "the fetish of fluidity"—queer theory's often ahistorical admiration for "movement against, beyond, or away from rules and regulations, norms and conventions, borders and limits"—seems especially urgent amid scholarly celebrations of an ill-defined "hacktivist" approach to digital networked technologies, which similarly tend to ignore precisely those factors of race, class, nationality, gender, sexuality, and mental and physical health that make "hacktivism" possible (or, more to the point, survivable) in the first place.[88] Reflexive valorizations of "hacktivism" are rarely alert to what it costs some of its practitioners, particularly when the state defines such individuals as unacceptably queer. Diagnosed with "gender identity disorder" by the Army, Chelsea Manning now languishes in prison, and hers is only one of many examples—perhaps the most famous reminder that digitally skilled opposition to the state is multiply punishable when aligned with pathologizing constructions of "deviance." Recognizing the callowness of much "hacktivist" rhetoric, Alexander R. Galloway has gone so far as to question any "creative misuse of technology, the idea that the limits of a tool can be transgressed by hacking, breaking, or otherwise misusing it for some other purpose":

> Creative misuse is certainly one of the most essential aspects of how people interface with technologies. But such transgressions must be understood as a kind of motile window, wherein the framework of determination moves from one context to another. Furthermore, hacking and creative disruption are today so intimately integrated into the technological infrastructure as to be considered technologies in themselves (not anti-technologies, as they are still romantically construed), and thus worthy of their own scrutiny as determining systems.[89]

Certain stereotypes of male homosexuality are among the determining systems that shape the online reception of contemporary queer cinema, threatening to limit this reception to particular sites of activity, modes of distribution, and spheres of influence. What is perhaps most deterministic about technologies that read "queerly" is their tendency to ignore or devalue anything that isn't interpretable as firmly and trendily "gay." Thus bots are designed to read "gay" where "queer" might seem more convincing; social networking services need to deliver gay men to advertisers, often at the expense of those who identify differently (and who are thus deemed "waste"—unworthy of intensive targeting); gay male internet celebrities must learn how to "organically" articulate the "gay appeal" of a range of films if they are to receive corporate sponsorship; and so on.[90] As Alice E. Marwick argues in *Status Update*, "[T]hose deemed successful at social media usually fit into a narrow mold," while "those who don't are criticized."[91] Such evaluative partitioning is powerfully evident in the increasing disaggregation of "white gay male" from other identity categories, even as the internet is said to offer a welcome and egalitarian home for all sexual and gender minorities. Despite these inauspicious conditions, there is something startlingly queer at work when internet users flout both the copyright claims of cultural producers and the guidelines of particular websites in order to guard against the domineering effects of homonormativity. The Curious Watcher, for instance, functions in express opposition to other, more popular YouTube channels, on which vidding serves only to consolidate the conventionally defined sex appeal of performers like Barnes and Efron, showcasing clips of the actors' shirtless beauty and setting those clips to cheerful pop songs that often, via their very lyrics, further normalize square jaws and "twelve-pack" abs as objects of gay male desire.[92]

As these examples suggest, copyright and terms-of-use violations are not, in themselves, sufficiently queer. They need to be coupled with practices that position sexuality "as something more than sex," and that understand queerness as pleasurably disruptive of familiar representational schemas—including those that, in venerable slash fashion, centralize male same-sex eroticism as a function of two dudes hugging, kissing, or engaging in "tasteful" anal intercourse. Taking inspiration from Tara McPherson's analysis of the early operating system Unix, Kara Keeling's imagined queer OS "seeks to make queer into the logic of 'an operating system of a larger order' that unsettles the common senses that secure those presently hegemonic social relations that can be characterized by domination, exploitation, oppression, and other violences."[93] Crucially, these characteristics describe homonormativity as accurately as any heterotopia, and it is important to peer beyond the popular, Facebook-friendly practices that may seem "queer enough." Tim Dean, writing about porn pedagogy, champions what he calls "the process of making visible a range of options" that "remain irreducible to mere consumer choices." These options force us to think in terms of "psychical mobility," moving us beyond not merely the limitations of normative embodiments but also the formulae of particular digital platforms. Dean suggests that it is precisely the type of cultural production that is screened out of sites like YouTube, Facebook, and Twitter—a production such as, in Dean's example, same-sex amputee porn—that effectively "extends the horizon of possibility by furnishing conditions for sexual mobility."[94] I agree, but I also acknowledge that social media behemoths occasionally—and almost certainly unknowingly—host content that is daringly, compellingly, even esoterically queer, as The Curious Watcher so ably demonstrates within the boundaries of YouTube.

Blogs—whether tied to Tumblr, Blogger, or WordPress—are additional sources not simply of generally gay-identified, libidinous online practices but also of the very films that these practices attempt to uphold, deconstruct, and even sell. When I parse foot-fetish websites in chapter 2, or Nollywood-focused, Nigerian-authored

Tumblr pages in chapter 5, my suggestion is not that these sites represent the only or even the most illuminating sources of online archaeologies of contemporary queer cinema. They are, instead, case studies: examples selected through my attention to specifically erotic digital productions—to the types of paratexts that themselves parse, for gay-identified purposes, a series of queer films, and that, in a vast number of cases, represent reliable sources of those films (from mere clips to entire pirated features). Gay-identified eroticism is thus the central thread tying all of my case studies together, but this thread is itself multivalent, committed as much to detailing the "daring" same-sex eroticism of Nollywood films (the subject of chapter 5) as to manufacturing it in the online reception of the sexless Allen Ginsberg biopic *Howl* (the subject of chapter 3). That queer films, like other types of cinematic texts, increasingly exist online is by now practically axiomatic. But it doesn't answer persistent questions about specific archives or about particular fan and corporate practices. Where, exactly, do contemporary queer films go after being screened at exclusive festivals, or following their ephemeral commercial appearances in a few art house theaters in downtown Manhattan (such as the IFC Center, Cinema Village, and Film Forum, to name three relatively reliable sites for the exhibition of queer cinema)? What, indeed, do they do—to what purposes are they put—online? This book attempts to answer those questions by embracing an array of erotic, gay-identified archives—from the American to the African to the biographical and beyond. Taken together, these understudied archives comprise—and can profitably enable—a range of media archaeological practices, some of which surely limit queer cinema to a series of gay male identifications, but all of which prove the importance of turning to the internet for evidence of queer cinema's multidirectional survival, its relationship to ever-evolving gay male fantasies and desires.

In the following pages, I embrace the style of topos analysis so central to Erkki Huhtamo's influential work, in which Huhtamo describes the topos as "a stereotypical formula evoked over and over again in different guises and for varying purposes."[95] If this book focuses on one particular topos in its media archaeological approach to the gay-identified online reception of contemporary queer cinema, it is the use of digital technologies to extract, enhance, and share filmic depictions of male-male erotic encounters in such a way as to exceed homonormative constraints. Indeed, the vast majority of the paratexts that I examine in this book are attempts to condense and queerly extend the sexual representations of such films as *Brokeback Mountain, Men in Love* (Moses Ebere, 2010), and *Interior. Leather Bar.* (James Franco and Travis Mathews, 2013), among many others. The diverse methods and discrepant justifications of these paratexts shed light not simply upon gay fandom but also upon internet spectatorship more generally, and they serve the additional purpose of pointing toward various stages in the authorized and illicit online availability of contemporary queer cinema. "Identifying topoi, analyzing their trajectories and transformations, and explaining the cultural logics that condition their 'wanderings' across time and space is one possible goal for media archaeology," argues Huhtamo. This book uses the libidinous, gay-identified online reception of contemporary queer cinema in order to illuminate some of the ways that the internet both feeds and functions as media archaeology—what Huhtamo describes as "a critical practice that excavates media-cultural evidence for clues about neglected, misrepresented, and/or suppressed aspects of both media's past(s) and their present and tries to bring these into a conversation with each other." For Huhtamo, media archaeology "purports to unearth traces of lost media-cultural phenomena and agendas and to illuminate ideological mechanisms behind them."[96] This book embraces such methods in attempting to make sense of the online circulation of a series of queer films and of their gay-identified, largely user-generated, occasionally corporate-influenced construction. The subcultural sharing of queer audiovisual creations—everything from stag films to Jean Genet's *Un Chant d'amour* (1950), Jack Smith's *Flaming Creatures* (1963), Kenneth Anger's *Scorpio Rising* (1964), and Todd Haynes's *Superstar: The Karen Carpenter Story* (1987)—represents one of the illicit, material traditions out of which the online dissemination of unauthorized queer-themed films and paratexts has emerged. Such "underground" circuits have contributed to a truly transmedial topos—the construction of queer cinema as a corpus to be articulated, circulated, and dissected through syncretic methods, whether VHS bootlegging in the case of *Superstar* or the GIF as applied to *Brokeback*'s tent scene. Acknowledging these and other histories, Helen Hok-Sze Leung reminds queer theorists to "turn away from the argumentative and towards the archival and affective aspects" of queer production and reception practices—aspects that I centralize in *Pink 2.0*.[97] I argue that media archaeology can reveal gay fandom in its more obscure, anti-homonormative dimensions, and that media archaeologies of and on the internet can clarify various aspects of the production, distribution, and especially reception of contemporary queer cinema.

Queer Cinema and Database Culture

> We no longer watch films or TV; we watch databases.
> —Geert Lovink

To explore queer cinema on the internet is to encounter an abundance of efforts—whether personal and libidinal or corporate and cynical—to circumscribe the category according to a range of gay male identifications. *Pink 2.0* considers that encounter as a precondition for accessing queer cinema in the digital age. Indeed, it is increasingly difficult to address queer films without acknowledging their online presence, a presence that isn't simply a matter of streaming video—of the digital distribution of entire features—but that should also be understood as a proliferation of short, extractive media such as GIFs, Vines, photomontages, tweets, Facebook uploads, Instagram renderings, Tumblr productions, and various other forms of digital encoding. This book offers a close examination of their often-erotic permutations: how they address a perceived post-gay vogue while becoming caught up, in many cases, in corporate efforts to monetize movie-minded gay male desires (chapter 1); how they blur the line between online pornography and a certain sexually explicit strain of contemporary queer cinema (chapter 2); how they complicate the historiographic operations of so-called gay biopics, especially those that focus on the Beat Generation (chapter 3); how they highlight and actively combat the homophobic, heterosexist circuits that have suppressed the anti-establishment comedy *I Love You Phillip Morris* (Glenn Ficarra and John Requa, 2008, 2009, 2010), starring Jim Carrey and Ewan McGregor (chapter 4); and, finally, how they confront the disjuncture between global anti-gay laws, especially those in sub-Saharan Africa that outline the "alien" qualities of homosexuality, and the efforts of new regional film industries to depict the existence, as well as the specific sexual and cultural practices, of gay African men (chapter 5).

That the above examples all define gayness as a cultural as much as a sexual identity is telling, pointing toward the potentially manifold meanings of "gay" in the digital age—and not just in Europe and the United States but also, as chapter 5 suggests, in sub-Saharan Africa (specifically, Nigeria). We can justifiably expect a sexually explicit, gay-receptive cinematic representation to end up as a digital image file—a still or a GIF—on a "dirty," gay-identified Tumblr, but we can equally imagine its online reconfiguration in any number of other ways, thus recalling Parker Tyler's emphasis, in *Screening the Sexes*, on "an idea of sexual behavior that achieves magnitude through variety of form, hence variety of sensation and emotion."[98] Parker's theorization of "the homosexes"—his notion that gay masculinity gains in erotic interest through its atomization across a range of representational styles and sites of production, exhibition, and reception—is powerfully prescient of digital paratexts that parse the "hot gay" aspects of contemporary queer cinema. As publicly circulated products, such online incarnations often precede the official releases of the films from which they've been so carefully, even lovingly extracted, thus rendering a "virgin" viewing all but impossible for anyone with an internet connection, but also ensuring that we cannot convincingly discuss the one—the GIF or the theatrical film—without discussing the other. Would it be remotely acceptable to analyze the reception of, say, *Stranger by the Lake* (Alain Guiraudie, 2014) without addressing the explosion of digital productions that showcase the film's money shots? Whatever its erotic specialization—whether fisting or foot fetishism—a sexually explicit, gay-identified blog was likely, in early 2014, to feature various versions of those money shots, what with their gorgeous, enormous cocks and torrents of cum. Not only titillating (although titillation remains an inescapably important component of the public life of a sexual minority), such online productions tend also to categorize *Stranger by the Lake* as the kind of queer film whose gayness needn't be inferred.

Pink 2.0 considers some of the global conditions for and consequences of queer cinema's online reception, attending to both corporate constraints and user-driven possibilities. Simply put, it isn't enough to denounce the capacity of digital networked technologies to reproduce seemingly limited and limiting gay formations. It is also necessary to interrogate those formations on their own terms—particularly when they arise on the Deep Web, beyond the reach of standard search engines and without the aid of industrial, scholarly, or popular classification.[99] The point is not to fetishize, and automatically uphold as liberatingly queer, any practice that seems remotely illicit, but rather to take seriously the products and strategies that queer scholarship, like the broader field of film and media studies, often excludes. This book is my contribution to a queer theoretical project that isn't utopian—that identifies and inveighs against constraints (corporate and otherwise) while simultaneously respecting some of the practices that take place within those constraints, and holding out a modicum of hope for the future. What I consider to be beyond the pale is not a digital construction of gay film fandom but rather the kind of online commentary that carefully and disingenuously evacuates queerness of anything that cannot be defined in, say, Neil Patrick Harris's image. I remain committed both to exposing the consistent valorization of gay men as "majority queers" and to probing the notion that "some queers are better than others," with the goal of defamiliarizing the commercial internet as a space of cultural and sexual expression.[100]

1 Digitizing Gay Fandom

Corporate Encounters with
Queer Cinema on the Internet

> To simply *charge* visibility politics with a restrictive sexual conformity or complicity with consumerism has its own limits. First, it cannot explain how it is or what it means, for example, that commercial representations have acquired political functions. And second, it cannot progress very far beyond a simplistic calculus of ideological purity and contamination: the mistaken idea, for example, that one can simply choose to be outside capital. Reducing analysis in this way to a game of paintball—once you're stained, the game is over—can only bemoan, rather than fully understand, the conditions it evokes.

> Eric O. Clarke, *Virtuous Vice*

> Digital media do not refer. They communicate.

> Sean Cubitt, *The Cinema Effect*

THERE IS A moment in Darren Stein's 2013 film *G.B.F.*, a high school comedy about three straight girls who compete to claim a token "gay best friend," when everything hinges on an iPhone app. Dubbed GuyDar, the app is a satirically unsubtle facsimile of Grindr, the wildly popular mechanism through which millions of male-identified users may "find gay, bi, curious guys nearby, for free."[1] In *G.B.F.*, the Grindr so commonly associated with "sleaze"—with easy sex made easier through advanced geolocation technology—is transformed into something a bit less salacious, though no less likely to link gay men to a limited, libidinous conception of networked activity.[2] (One character, self-consciously mimicking the language of advertising, describes GuyDar as "the new app that lets gay guys find other gay guys through state-of-the-art globally positioned technology"; another simply calls it "a slutty gay hook-up app.") When the three female competitors—all aspirants to the throne of prom queen—catch wind of GuyDar, their immediate impulse is to use its geolocation capabilities to "out" one of its active subscribers, who happens to be a high school student still struggling to define his sexuality. One girl even inspires the president of the school's Gay-Straight Alliance, which is being dissolved due to the conspicuous absence of a single out gay student, to set up a fake GuyDar account—using images of allegedly gay-friendly male media stars, of course—in order to "locate a gay." All of these app-savvy girls seem distinctly ignorant of the fact that GuyDar, like Grindr, openly invites and even cultivates "curious" users—men who may not self-identify as gay or even as bisexual—and they fail to understand that a technologically facilitated tracking of sexual minorities smacks of the most punitive of pursuits, the type of "witch hunt" that is well documented in David K. Johnson's *The Lavender Scare* (and to which a concerned teacher, played by Natasha Lyonne, alludes). In their zealous quest for a cachet-conferring "gay best friend," the girls take GuyDar to be a diagnostic tool of the highest caliber: a digital, mobile means of making clear who's queer—and, moreover, of shaping such queerness into an exclusive and thus "manageable" homosexuality.

Free to operate, the actual app on which GuyDar is based—Grindr—relies on advertising revenue, thus raising key questions about the kinds of ads that it carries, and about their capacity to complicate conventional sexual taxonomies. In April 2014, ads for the Christian group GodLife began appearing on Grindr—much to the dismay of users familiar with the group's stance against pornography and "sexual immorality."[3] Widely believed to offer "conversion therapy"—a process intended to transform a person's sexual orientation from gay to straight—GodLife in fact refuses mention of homosexuality in its Grindr ads, all of which employ vague language, obligatory references to Jesus Christ, and images of Mt. Sinai. Inveighing against "sex perversions" without identifying homosexuality by name, the ads are symptomatic of the way that gayness is both everywhere and nowhere on Grindr—and both everywhere and nowhere on digital platforms more generally. Despite the assumptions of the vapid girls of *G.B.F.*, an app like Grindr cannot "prove" that its users are all gay men. Indeed, Grindr guards against such limitations in a familiar capitalist manner: by invoking a sexual inclusiveness that rejects "restrictive" labels, Grindr cultivates a relatively broad base of users—"from gay to bi to curious." At the same time, however, cultural commentators consistently position the app as an emphatically and exclusively gay one, even as, in other contexts, they uphold the dubious notion that the United States has at last earned its "post-gay" as well as "post-racial" credentials, preferring in social, cultural, and juridical terms to see Americans as "just people," rather than as racialized and sexualized citizens.[4] However, as Jasbir Puar points out, institutionalized racism and queerphobia persist, intertwine, and diverge in startling ways, even amid the accretion of "inclusive" legislative measures: "Don't Ask, Don't Tell, Don't Pursue" (1994), which notoriously banned all manner of "gay identifications" within the United States military, was repealed on the very same day that Congress defeated the DREAM Act, which was designed to offer a "path to citizenship" for those who had immigrated to the United States as children.[5] In *Terrorist Assemblages,* Puar suggests that what is widely understood as a landmark gay-rights victory—the 2003 Supreme Court decision that struck down longstanding anti-sodomy laws—has in fact enabled new forms of discrimination and surveillance. More recently, the 2015 Supreme Court ruling that made same-sex marriage a nationwide right guaranteed by the Constitution—and that has been hailed as yet another, universally beneficial gay-rights landmark—has similarly upstaged some sobering, newly strengthened discriminatory measures, particularly those that target transgender immigrants of color. Instructively, President Barack Obama's much-praised declaration that the 2015 Supreme Court decision represented a "victory for America" was preceded, by just two days, by his public—and also widely praised—shaming of a transgender "heckler," Jennicet Gutiérrez, concerned about the abusive detainment and deportation of transgender immigrants. "You're in my house," Obama told Gutiérrez, adding ominously (and all too tellingly), "you can either stay and be quiet or we'll have to take you out."[6] That Obama spoke those words at a White House event celebrating Pride Month only underscores the painful reality that gay-rights gains often coincide with—even arrive at the expense of—manifold losses for queers of color. Unsurprisingly, a number of prominent, gay-identified blogs, including Queerty, responded to Gutiérrez's "disruptive" remarks by producing a "rude houseguest" meme, positioning Gutiérrez's "heckling" as "no way to celebrate Pride" and offering hyperlinks to "the right way": urban consumerism as sanctioned and structured by GayCities, a website tied to an American gay and lesbian tourism industry with its own, overtly homonationalist agendas to uphold.[7] This classist presentation of Pride as a profoundly exclusionary, even gentrifying tradition was, around this time, codified in a new iPhone app—Atari's Pridefest, an interactive social-simulation game that exhorts its player to demolish "old and decrepit" buildings in order to make way for "fun and rainbows" (in the form of big, "gay-friendly" businesses, of course). The App Store's official description of Pridefest may highlight the game's "customizable avatar" ("Personalize with different body types, skin tones, clothes and accessories!"), but the player (required to simulate the activities of a big-city mayor) will encounter no transgender characters while literally pinkwashing the metropolis. As Zachary Small points out, Pridefest, despite its claims to queer inclusivity, is clearly aimed at gay men: its chat function (complete with geolocation technology) appears to have been patterned on Grindr, and erecting a state-of-the-art gym (and thereby activating representations of heavily muscled men) enables the player to access a special Pride float.[8]

More than simply "locked in" by monotonous software, corporate constructions of gay masculinity are also key components of what A. Aneesh calls "algocratic governance," or "the rule of code"—a condition of bureaucratic control in which programming languages determine the limits of inclusion and the contours of interaction, preempting dissent whenever and wherever possible.[9] Monitoring, reflecting, and rewarding what is "best" about the gay male consumer, software applications also confirm and reproduce the exclusion of such "unfamiliar," "suspicious," or otherwise "disruptive" subjects as the "undocumented" Gutiérrez, ensuring their censure. On the internet, optimization and surveillance thus routinely function at the expense of queer subjects who experience similar forms of discrimination in other aspects of their daily lives. Indeed, as Aneesh's concept of the algocratic suggests, the lines between "user-friendliness" and governmentality—between online encounters and offline realities—blur as the rule of code reigns supreme. Predictably, Gutiérrez's White House "outburst" was captured by multiple cameras—not merely the fixed, official cameras of the presidential event but also those of various smartphones wielded by the event's participants. Disseminated online, clips of Gutiérrez were invariably ported through celebrations of Pride that proffered white, normatively bodied gay men as upstanding neoliberal subjects, eminently capable of embracing free market principles as reflections of their agency within new state formations. But they also tended to confirm Sherry Turkle's reflections on the way that information and communication technologies inhibit empathy, cultivating suspicion of spontaneity and difference.[10] "Surprisingly," even "unnaturally" critical of Obama, Gutiérrez threatened to "ruin" Pride. Negative, downright viral responses to her ordeal evoke what Eric Herhuth refers to as the "general diminution of negotiability" characteristic of the algocratic turn, a decline in the capacity of digital systems and their users to accommodate debate, ambivalence, and ambiguity.[11]

Individual Facebook users may have posted their support for Gutiérrez—or at least for her broad, anti-transphobic, anti-racist, and anti-imperialist message—but Facebook is itself responsible, through its pronounced surveillance capabilities and drone-assisted, neocolonialist incursions into the global South, for some of the very conditions of inequality to which Gutiérrez was responding.[12] As Queerty so vividly demonstrated, even purportedly queer-friendly websites were unable to extricate their accounts of Gutiérrez from the manufacturing of support for the particular forms of discrimination and imperialism that "gay pride" is so often used to conceal. When Gutiérrez took to the website Washington Blade (tellingly dubbed "America's Leading Gay News Source") in order to recount her experiences and elaborate her political position, the sponsor-supported site surrounded her words with advertisements for Roland Emmerich's notoriously racist, transphobic, gay-focused film *Stonewall* (2015), the men's clothing store Universal Gear (featuring heavily muscled white men modeling underwear), and the website's own "Best of Gay DC" section, which regularly sustains the very homology—between white male power brokers and homonormative political formations—that Gutiérrez, in her remarks at the White House, was critiquing in the first place.[13] That most of these advertisements were designed by various ad agencies and delivered by diverse intermediaries hardly mitigates the harsh irony at work here: a website like Washington Blade prides itself on publishing exclusive, "alternative" queer content like Gutiérrez's essay while simultaneously hosting ads that contradict Gutiérrez's point. Gutiérrez may argue that considerations of "equality" must encompass more than just the white gay man, but her words are necessarily surrounded by images that restrict queerness to that very figure, and that, given the crudeness of certain digital surveillance strategies, are supplied to all users suspected of being "non-straight," regardless of their actual practices. Low-income, transgender women of color like Gutiérrez may be deemed "waste" and thus ignored by advertising firms and other agencies that engage in online surveillance, but that does not mean that they will be spared, say, Dustin Lance Black's Tylenol commercial, which features two white, well-dressed gay men enjoying fatherhood in their impossibly plush suburban home.[14] In some cases, the demonstrably "non-straight" associations of such queer users as Gutiérrez will simply be read as "gay," and publishers, advertisers, and content farms will respond to these users accordingly. My point is not to suggest that they *should* be targeted as specifically transgender and given their own trans-identified ads, as if digital surveillance were somehow in need of expansion and improvement; it is simply to question the logic of inclusion that characterizes those queer websites that must rely on advertising revenue, and to highlight how a hegemonic gayness colonizes all manner of online territories. In other words, Jennicet Gutiérrez is produced as abject even—perhaps especially—when she articulates her political position on the internet. Despite her authorship of an online op-ed, Gutiérrez does not, in Judith Butler's terms, "enjoy the *status* of subject," and her "living under the sign of 'unlivable'" would seem a necessary condition of production of a "queer" internet.[15] Far from "unrepresentable" online, Gutiérrez becomes the abject figure against which the gay consumer is defined, as on Queerty and other websites where native advertising aligns male homosexuality not simply with purchase power but also with political clout and an uncritical support for a "queer-friendly" American president.

Even as it cooperates with targeted advertising strategies, joining other websites that pursue what David J. Phillips calls "a top-down, panoptic structure of visibility and classification," Washington Blade features almost no alternatives to white, normatively bodied gay men in its prominently placed ads, reflecting the continued impoverishment of "queer" as a marketing concept—and perhaps sustaining, in its own way, the alterity of the transgender user of color.[16] Using "cookies" to differentiate its visitors and, via targeted ads, interpellate them accordingly, Washington Blade nevertheless relies on sponsors whose understanding of "queer" is extremely limited. Viewed through the prism of queer theory, targeted advertising thus suggests both a confirmation and an extension of a Foucauldian conception of panopticism, in which "the observer, the operator and coordinator of the panoptic system, is invisible to the observed."[17] What happens, then, when the non-white, non-male, non-gay queer subject remains equally invisible even amid widespread strategies of surveillance and differentiation, whereby "different advertisements are served to members of different classes"?[18] Washington Blade—the one queer commercial publication to provide a platform for Gutiérrez during the widespread social-media campaign to shame her—offers a useful example of the persistence, the normalization, of Pink 2.0, which, whatever the discrepant revelations of "cookies," here divides visitors into a series of indistinguishable "queer" (i.e., gay male) categories. The visitor with a "verifiable" interest in cinema gets an ad for a major studio production like *Stonewall,* a film with a "marketable" gay male protagonist and its own semiotic contributions to U.S. nationalism and transphobia; the visitor with "political interests" gets a reminder of the "Best of Gay DC" (and thus images of cute, white, "baby-gay" clerks in expensive suits); and everyone, it seems, gets an underwear ad featuring a white man's eight-pack abs. These, apparently, are the only options, and they remain semiotically significant—not to mention cruelly ironic counterpoints to Gutiérrez's specific concerns. To read her words on Washington Blade is, in a sense—and through no fault of her own—to support some of the objects of her critique, including the ongoing production, commodification, and politicized celebration of a certain queer constituency capable of crowding out alternative subjects and political formations. The sponsor-supported interface of Washington Blade, like that of countless other "queer" websites, provides a striking reminder of some of the operations of homonationalism, even as it seeks to accommodate the concerns of a transgender immigrant of color—someone openly, even "rudely" critical of Obama. That is because, in Jasbir Puar's terms, homonationalism is an assemblage—of global capitalism, information and communication technologies, political systems, and cultural practices—that, in conditioning access to the internet, is impossible to completely avoid online (or, for that matter, offline), no matter where or how one lives and works.[19]

The notion that there is a "right way" to recognize Pride Month is strikingly central to such websites as Queerty, where it nevertheless competes with a range of potentially countervailing premises about sexual and gender minorities. Fittingly, then, tensions between constriction and expansiveness tend to characterize those contemporary queer films whose characters engage directly with digital networked technologies. It is instructive that, in *G.B.F.,* the gay boy who valorizes GuyDar, and who seems so proudly, even defiantly queeny, in fact refuses to discuss his emergent sexuality with all but his closest (and equally closeted) male friend, thus embodying a gay identity that is both readable and under erasure—both "obvious" and unavailable. His mother, who is eager for her son to come out, decides to introduce him to *Brokeback Mountain* (Ang Lee, 2005), a film whose own capacity to confuse conventional homo-hetero binaries is often subsumed under its clichéd reputation as a "gay Western." However, the specificity of the same-sex erotic practice depicted in a key scene in Lee's film—the famous tent scene, in which two cowboys engage in anal intercourse—is sufficient to stimulate the gay spectator's own libidinal desires, as *G.B.F.* suggests in a moment of high comedy, in which mother and son squirm in mutual recognition of the "relevance" of Jack and Ennis's lovemaking. With its emphasis on a stereotypically gay-specific sexual practice, *Brokeback Mountain* remains a major point of identification for gay spectators, whatever their methods of public self-definition—at least according to the *G.B.F.* that links *Brokeback* fandom with internet use. For *G.B.F.*'s closeted gay boy, *Brokeback* is embarrassing only when he watches it with his mother, via their living room's DVD player and huge, immobile television set; stuck with her on the sofa, he's unable to make *Brokeback* his own, even as he clearly "relates" to its representations. At the same time, he's searching for gay fellowship online, linking film and internet spectatorship within the rubric of his emergent gay subjectivity. Seated beside his mother while watching *Brokeback* on a big TV screen, he can't help but squirm. Turning to GuyDar, however, he's likely to find more "private," personalized ways of engaging with the film. After all, as he himself avers, "small media"—mobile, handheld, web-enabled devices—are potentially ideal vessels through which questioning kids can begin to engage with queer peers as well as with queer cinema. The problem, as *G.B.F.* makes clear, is that the internet may also—and in contrast to its utopian rendering in some forms of digital media theory—limit the expressive possibilities for emergent sexual subjects, upholding the homo-hetero binary and sublimating an expansive queerness to a gay male specificity.[20]

An American film set in the moneyed suburbs, *G.B.F.* presupposes an internet that is thoroughly accessible yet annoyingly inadequate, suggesting that complaints about a hegemonic online gayness are among the exclusive luxuries of Western democracies. If simplistic, corporate constructions of male homosexuality seem inevitable, even oppressive aspects of the internet in the United States, they are allegedly less likely to emerge as powerful cultural forces—or even at all—in other parts of the world. Matthew Tinkcom reports that the Qatari government has prevented internet users—including Tinkcom himself—from accessing information about global movements for marriage equality, even as the news network Al Jazeera, which is based in Qatar, has maintained a website where bloggers may critique Arab political regimes. In Qatar, as in other parts of the Arab world, online intimations of homosexuality become "prohibited materials"—content that, Tinkcom claims, simply cannot be accessed.[21] In his work on Sufi homoeroticism, Usman Shaukat implicates the internet in the suppression of all queer content in Pakistan, stressing how Sufism has become thoroughly heterosexualized online, in tandem with the attempts of the Pakistan Telecommunication Authority to ban the term "gay pride" from the language of digital networked technologies.[22] My own extensive experiences of the internet in sub-Saharan Africa, where numerous countries continue to criminalize homosexuality, have been substantially different, however, suggesting that no definition of the so-called "digital divide" can neatly separate the global North from the global South. As I argue in this book's final chapter, internet users in African countries are increasingly responsible for inscribing gay male subjectivities online—even when such inscriptions are obvious violations of government policy, as they are in Nigeria. While it may seem politically promising to enjoy uninterrupted access to online queer content in sub-Saharan Africa—and downright thrilling to stream gay porn in Senegal—it is always possible to perceive, and always necessary to critique, the internet's queer shortcomings, even in parts of the world where it may be tempting to celebrate the smallest of victories for queer visibility. If, as a number of scholars have suggested, agents of neoliberalism are learning to embrace social media services for their coercive, consensus-building potential, then what are the chances that an abundance of queer identifications will emerge within the "algorithmic architectures" of the internet?[23] What, moreover, are the chances that insurgent forms of gay representation on Nigerian websites will open the floodgates to even queerer local constructions, rather than calcify into an example of what Puar calls "homonationalism"—perhaps as a means of consolidating ideological resistance to Boko Haram and thus boosting Nigeria's global image?[24]

If "achieving the utopian promise of a queer symbolic" must surely involve more than simply "sewing the scraps of a pink triangle onto the American flag," as Lauren Berlant and Elizabeth Freeman so powerfully suggest, then it must also demand an awareness of the many limitations of a medium such as the internet—and of information and communication technologies more generally.[25] "The internet is not the gift that keeps on giving," cautions Nguyen Tan Hoang, describing the experiences of a friend who visited the purportedly exhaustive porn aggregator XTube, searched for "Asian top" and "Latino bottom"—and found nothing.[26] As Nguyen's anecdote suggests, the internet is prone to omission and outright failure in ways that often seem disturbingly at odds with queer theory and practice, despite the intriguing suspicion that there may well be a "queer art of failure," to quote Jack Halberstam.[27] *G.B.F.* seems especially alert to these limitations, how they threaten to shape queer youth and "allies" alike, and how the promises of the so-called "infinite scroll"—an endless supply of web content—can in fact seem far less liberating than face-to-face interaction. If Google, in implementing infinite scrolling for its image search results, furnishes not a dazzling diversity of graphics but rather a monotonous roster of duplicates and "related" icons, then two queer boys, in meeting offline to discuss their dreams and desires, do so without the forbidding influence of any kind of algorithm.

The Hazards of Tagging

> Technology, as a mode of production, as the totality of instruments, devices,
> and contrivances which characterize the machine age is thus at the same time
> a mode of organizing and perpetuating (or changing) social relationships, a
> manifestation of prevalent thought and behavior patterns, an instrument for
> control and domination.
>
> —Herbert Marcuse, "Some Social Implications of Modern Technology."
>
> Every production of "identity" creates exclusions that reappear on the
> margins like ghosts to haunt identity-based politics.
>
> —Lisa Duggan, "Queering the State."

In his book *The Black Box Society,* Frank Pasquale suggests just how endemic gay-identified biases are to the broader landscape of digital networked technologies. Pasquale reports that, in the early 2000s, digital video recorders (DVRs) began "inferring" male homosexuality from the recording of queer films—even those films that do not depict gay men and that instead elect to explore less determinate sexual orientation identities. One DVR "took it upon itself to save a number of gay-themed shows for its owner after he recorded a film with a bisexual character in it," further demonstrating that, algorithmically speaking, "gay" is often the default designation not simply for queer films but also for those who watch them.[28] How—under what historical conditions—have such powerful gay algorithms emerged, and how have these algorithms come to structure the online reception of contemporary queer cinema? I mean, in this instance, to evoke William Uricchio's description of "algorithmic interventions"—processes and programs "with clearly defined limits" that not only determine our engagements with digital media but that also, and in increasingly confining terms, tell us who we are, often by way of telling corporations and policymakers how to "handle" us.[29]

Presently indispensable, a queer suspicion of algorithms is also a well-established strategy. It can, in fact, be traced back to Eve Kosofsky Sedgwick's *Epistemology of the Closet,* which Sedgwick describes as "resolutely non-algorithmic"—the product of her desire "*not to know* how far [the book's] insights and projects are generalizable."[30] However, in an indication of the sheer difficulty of escaping algorithmic interpellation, Sedgwick couches her "resolutely non-algorithmic" analysis in the language and logics of mathematics, as Lee Edelman has pointed out. Edelman notes that the opening sections of *Epistemology* "abound in striking instances of mathematical enumeration; they offer the reader charts or graphs and return obsessively to figures of mapping, calculus, and logical declensions. What, we might ask, does it mean that Sedgwick's 'non-algorithmic book'—a book that wants to avoid the fatality of knowing its generalizability—opens with a chapter that bears, of all things, the title 'Axiomatic'?"[31] A similar predicament characterizes studies of the internet that must necessarily rely upon the medium's most manipulative, ethically compromised elements—including the algorithms that lend it "functionality." An algorithm, in the words of Virginia Eubanks, "is a set of instructions designed to produce an output" and is thus "a recipe for decision-making, for finding solutions" to perceived social problems and corporate conundrums.[32] In Uricchio's view, the algorithmic turn "does not preclude human agency, nor the stubborn fixities of the world viewed" but, rather, "resituates them, defining their parameters and enabling their interactions."[33] Eubanks provides some vital reminders about the material effects of algorithmic decision making—from the racism and classism of predictive policing to the equally alarming biases of remote, automated welfare-eligibility programs, in which algorithms "act less like data sifters" (as with Google's PageRank algorithm) "and more like gatekeepers, mediating access to public resources, assessing risks, and sorting groups of people into 'deserving' and 'undeserving' and 'suspicious' and 'unsuspicious' categories."[34] When Netflix sorts Todd Haynes's queerly unclassifiable film *Safe* into its "Gay & Lesbian" category, it not only upholds identity politics and the authority of single authorship, reading a polysemous queer film through the fixed lens of its gay director's allegedly stable social position.[35] It also affects the way that queer cinema becomes accessible and intelligible online.

That Netflix applies its "Gay & Lesbian" tag to such films as *Boys Don't Cry* (Kimberly Peirce, 1999) and *Transamerica* (Duncan Tucker, 2005) suggests some of the specific hazards of tagging, which, contrary to Tim O'Reilly's rather utopian claim that the practice rejects "rigid categories," can in fact concretize and perpetuate transphobia.[36] (*G.B.F.* includes a knowing reference to Netflix: satirized as "Webflix," the rental service stupefies one character by including *Boys Don't Cry*—along with *Brokeback Mountain* and *Milk*—in its "Gay & Lesbian" section.) Through its descriptive inadequacies, Netflix vividly recalls earlier efforts to define Brandon Teena as a woman and a lesbian—efforts that, confined to "old" media, prompted considerable scorn. Netflix, however, appears to get a pass, routinely misidentifying films, filmmakers, film characters, and even national sites and sources of production in ways that often seem strikingly racist and transphobic. When in 1994 Donna Minkowitz blithely called Brandon Teena a butch lesbian on the pages of *The Village Voice*, there was an instant and consequential outcry.[37] When Netflix repeats Minkowitz's infamous faux pas, reproducing the writer's own (apparently unwitting) style of discursive violence, silence ensues.[38] Nothing happens. Netflix gains more subscribers and more power over the broader media landscape, and trans characters continue to be classified under the heading "Gay & Lesbian"—even when, in the films in which they appear, they eloquently argue against such a classification. Anticipating criticism, Netflix often falls back upon the allegedly inevitable distortions of database culture. When confronted, the company will either ignore complaints or issue a boilerplate defense that rests on the nonhuman (and thus presumably non-nuanced) agency of algorithms, as I discovered firsthand when attempting to alert Netflix to its alarming misidentification of a film by Ossie Davis as a film by Ousmane Sembene, and its related misidentification of one woman of color (the actress Peggy Pettitt) as another (the actress Mbissine Thérèse Diop). The aw-shucks, machines-do-the-darnedest-things alibi that Netflix regularly offers for its own mistakes—and that subscribers seem only too happy to accept—reliably obscures the fact that someone had to impose the label "Gay & Lesbian" (and reject the term "queer") in the first place, just as someone ignorant of African and African American film histories had to find a way of visually identifying an already distorted version of Sembene's *La Noire De . . .* (1966), and just as webmasters in the employ of NBCUniversal had to decide what interpretations of *Brokeback* were bad for the brand.

Despite the protest cultures that thrive on social networking services, opprobrium would seem to be reserved for the queerphobic infractions of "old media," as if a newspaper article from the pre-internet period were somehow singular in its cultural power and thus eminently disputable. By contrast, the mistakes of database culture appear to be accepted, even indulged—appropriated and recontextualized—or else ignored. Netflix, inadvertently generative of a new shorthand for celebrating casual genital eroticism ("Netflix and Chill"), persists in applying the "Gay & Lesbian" label to films about transgender characters who identify as straight. Why, then, do protests appear to avoid the compromises and outright cruelties of online platforms, as if discursive violence were limited to a few overtly queerphobic tweets rather than endemic to the commercial internet? Why does the digital get a pass? Why are we so forgiving of our algorithms, as if they were unruly, alarming, yet charismatic and, ultimately, irresistible children? This strangely tolerant approach may have something to do with the way that, as in the examples cited above, statistics are supplied as guarantors of authenticity—or, at the very least, as ways of precluding conversation, of preempting dissent. By this apparently prevailing statistical logic, if Netflix algorithms are rooted in majoritarian conceptions of what constitutes a cinematic genre, then maybe most people really do think that Hilary Swank plays a butch lesbian in *Boys Don't Cry*, and, well, we'll just have to accept that—we'll just have to accede to the classification of *Boys Don't Cry* as a lesbian drama.[39] (Incidentally, Peirce's film enacts its own erasure, eliminating all references to Philip DeVine, a man of color who was executed alongside Brandon Teena and Lisa Lambert.) In this sense, the internet, in its current commercial configurations, would seem merely to preserve and extend the biases of structural linguistics, presenting them strictly in terms of functionality—of what "works" online—as if certain complex power relations do not apply. Rather than apolitical inscriptions of an allegedly universal lexical logic, "user-friendly" functions reflect, reward, and sustain the ideal speaker so beloved of linguistic theory—the "highly educated North American" whose mastery of normative English inevitably produces the marginalization and pathologization of nonstandard or otherwise queer dialects and speakers.[40] Despite their professed investment in cutting-edge technologies and practices, prominent theorists of digital media are scarcely enamored of the notion that new or long-minoritized languages might queerly assume center stage online, disturbing research paradigms premised on the authority of dominant—and allegedly autonomous—linguistic structures. For instance, in *Uncreative Writing: Managing Language in the Digital Age*, Kenneth Goldsmith proposes that "an appropriate response to a new condition in writing today" is to refuse the introduction of new languages and texts and to focus only on those that already exist—that are already in circulation online. While such an argument would seem to appreciate the queer potential of remix culture, its insistence on the abundance and diversity of what is "already here" fails to acknowledge the power dynamics that, through processes of standardization and exclusion, produce the extant as an ideologically limited category (to say the least). In the cases of Netflix, iTunes, YouTube, Hulu, Nintendo Wii, Amazon, and other influential platforms, the careless and altogether offensive application of the label "Gay & Lesbian" to films about transgender characters is especially alarming when its recurrence is guaranteed through collaborative tagging—a system of meaning-making that Thomas Vander Wal terms a "folksonomy," and that strives to enhance a topic's searchability through the use of shared (i.e., demonstrably popular) vocabularies.[41]

That the tag "gay" enjoys a far greater online incidence than the tag "trans"— and specifically within contexts of queer cinema reception—can be visualized through a range of search engine tools. DeeperWeb and TagCrowd, which generate tag and word clouds—visual representations of data frequency—indicate just how popular the term "gay" remains on websites ostensibly devoted to broad questions of queer or LGBT cinema. Rendering the most popular tag or word in the largest font, and thus creating a weighted list, TagCrowd uncovers the terminological hierarchies in which "gay" clearly crowds out alternative labels in the online reception of contemporary queer cinema. Consider, for instance, a 2014 feature on Advocate.com, in which the website's editors identify and describe "The Top 175 Essential Films of All Time for LGBT Viewers"—beginning with *Brokeback Mountain*. Stressing that they arrived at this list collaboratively, through a voting process that smacks of democratic ideals, the editors present themselves as diverse stand-ins for a broad base of internet users, and while they challenge such users to offer alternative film lists, they also couch their top 175 as queerly inclusive. Entering the webpage's URL into TagCrowd, however, reveals that, apart from "film," "gay" is by far the most frequently occurring label in this enumeration of nearly two hundred queer-themed features—just as, equally tellingly, the term "man" enjoys a far greater incidence than the term "women," which additionally suggests the persistence, both in cinematic texts and in their online reception, of certain ideals of masculine individualism over and against constructions of femininity. (The word "woman" does not appear at all, although "boys" does. "Girl" and "girls" are similarly absent.) Such results are not uncommon, spanning the highest-ranked websites in Google searches for "queer cinema," and while they may well reflect the biases of individual queer films—as is unquestionably the case with Gary Morris's popular essay "A Brief History of Queer Cinema," from the blog of defunct online DVD rental service GreenCine— they also indicate the popularity of particular rhetorical strategies, some of which seem strikingly retrograde. A 2012 feature on the *Guardian*'s website, tellingly titled "New-Wave Queer Cinema: 'Gay Experience In All Its Complexity,'" yields a word cloud in which "gay" is plainly dominant and "queer" absent altogether, having lost out to such terms as "business," "tech," "travel," and "fashion." That the *Guardian* feature doubles as a promotion for the DVD and Blu-ray releases of Andrew Haigh's *Weekend* (2011) suggests one reason for its privileging of gay male subjectivity—and a further reflection of the influential intermingling of certain commercial and taxonomic imperatives, which rarely cease to shrink queer cinema down to a manageable gay male consumerism.

To be fair, a number of other webpages produce dramatically different results when confronted with DeeperWeb and TagCrowd. The relatively high-ranking Global Queer Cinema—a collaborative research project that is part of REFRAME, an international, open-access academic digital platform—is the source of word clouds in which "queer" predominates, edging out "gay" in every instance. Such results are perhaps unsurprising, given the website's academic bent and the credentials of its contributors (including Rosalind Galt and Karl Schoonover), who are decidedly unlikely to ever employ "gay" as a queer catchall. Other sites— especially commercial ones—are not so lucky, however, and their prominence contributes to, and is a direct result of, what Elizabeth Van Couvering calls "search engine bias." A process involving both "systematic bias towards classes of websites and specific exclusion or censorship of particular websites," search engine bias helps to explain why—despite the persistent utopianism of certain strains of digital media theory—it is often exceedingly difficult to use the authorized tools of the commercial internet in order to uncover or produce an expansive, diversely defined queerness.[42] Search engine censorship is plainly incompatible with radical queer politics (as distinct from homonormative gay-rights discourse), especially if we understand this censorship's purview as being far broader than representations of genital eroticism—as bleeding into arenas where "unauthorized," anti-Western, and generally non-normative cultural productions abound, dramatically limiting their accessibility to internet users. Human agents repeatedly intervene in order to ensure the lasting prominence of discursively constrained, Western commercial sites in search engine results.[43] These include search engine producers (who operate, as Van Couvering argues, within an internet culture that conflates economic achievement and the public good) and search engine marketers or optimizers (who employ so-called white hat and, more notoriously, black hat techniques in order to increase a website's exposure).[44] Conceivably, anyone can optimize a website, given some basic digital skills or the resources to hire a professional optimizer. But the need to provide the most popular keywords—"gay" and "men" over "queer" and "transmasculine," for instance—combined with, say, Google's title-tag restrictions and the requirement that one receive legitimation (in the form of links) from "reputable" websites, suggests the sheer difficulty of honestly optimizing iconoclastic queer content on the commercial internet. Such discursive honesty—the availability of digital platforms and processes capable of distinguishing "trans" from "gay," for instance—would not, of course, automatically redress certain power imbalances, online or off. Corporate constructions of gay masculinity may be "locked in," colonizing and redefining an array of digital spaces, but "transgender," too, can produce certain erasures, as David Valentine has demonstrated. Arguing that the institutionalization of the term was achieved at the expense of poor, gender-variant people of color, and as a direct contradiction of its earlier deployment as a sign of "inclusivity and radical transformative potential," Valentine's research reveals some of the risks involved in dogmatically disarticulating gender from sexuality.[45] Such risks are plainly worth the rewards for white, middle-class gay men of an accommodationist bent, for whom, Valentine suggests, "transgender" helps to produce male homosexuality as both privately sexual and properly masculine, in express contrast to its historical stereotyping as gender inversion. The "inclusion" of "transgender" in various institutional and activist contexts has already initiated a policing of categories—as well as the ongoing production of firm, ontological distinctions between gender and sexuality—that the internet will only streamline.[46]

Queerness and the Corporate Limitations of Fandom

No critique of the internet's homonormative tendencies would be complete—or remotely convincing—without a consideration of fandom. In 1992, Henry Jenkins was already cautioning against the valorization of slash—fan fiction that trades in male same-sex eroticism—as admirably "resistant" and counterhegemonic, noting that such an approach "runs the risk of celebrating gay male experience (and more traditional forms of male bonding) at the expense of developing alternative[s]."[47] A survey of some of the most prominent fan archives and wikis—from Fanlore to the Archive of Our Own—indicates the lasting dominance of slash among fan engagements with queer cinema. Nearly all of the explicitly queer-themed groups, conventions, products, and practices that Fanlore archives are examples of slash, with the most common centering on such pairings as Starsky and Hutch, Kirk and Spock, and Clark Kent and Lex Luthor. Searching Fanlore for "queer cinema" yields much of the same—that is, slash that (further) eroticizes the white, normatively bodied (indeed, mostly muscle-bound) male characters of *Brokeback Mountain,* James Ivory's *Maurice* (1987), Jonah Markowitz's *Shelter* (2007), and Zach Snyder's *300* (2006). Surprisingly, searching for "queer cinema" on the Archive of Our Own yields even less—a single thread of slash centering on the relationship between Tony Stark/Iron Man (Robert Downey, Jr.) and Steve Rogers/Captain America (Chris Evans) in Joss Whedon's 2012 film *The Avengers.* Lest these results seem painfully tame and altogether limiting, it is important to acknowledge the capacity of slash—and of fan fiction more generally—to accommodate broad practices and interpretations. Examining fan fiction as an archive of women's culture, Abigail De Kosnik describes its expansive potential, arguing that it "gives women readers the chance to imaginatively engage with a [fictional] relationship repeatedly, through diverse reworkings, and experience the relationship through lenses that alternately reinforce, ameliorate, or transform dominant narratives of gender and sexuality."[48] In a similar vein, Alexis Lothian argues that "the mockable, uncritical, reproductive-of-capital facets of fandom coexist with its radical transformative capacities," suggesting that fan labor as a mode of world making is always at least *potentially* queer.[49]

When fandom becomes monetized, however, corporate sites often act as agents of censorship, excluding erotic content and, in the process, further obscuring the presence of radical cultural productions online. Kindle Worlds, Fanfiction.net, Scribd, and Wattpad are all examples of sites whose terms of use place considerable constraints upon expression, banning "explicit content" in ways that often seem indistinguishable from specifically queerphobic tactics.[50] When Kindle Worlds emerged in 2013, it partnered with Amazon and Warner Bros., whose properties provided the authorized points of departure for derivative fan creations. By this particular logic, if the licensed productions of major film studios tend to peddle impoverished notions of what it means to be a sexual minority, then such notions provide the only frameworks for fans functioning within the hard boundaries of Kindle Worlds and other corporate sites. According to Karen Hellekson, such sites "set the tone" for fan labor, often justifying their censorial practices by invoking vulnerable youth, and always endeavoring to "maintain the integrity of the commercial property" around which any given fandom revolves.[51] Fans are thus constrained not simply by censorship policies that police their creative productions but also by strict regulations regarding the type of proprietary content they can access, and how.[52]

At a time when gay men continue to be the main (and, in many cases, the only) targets of queer-conscious films and advertising campaigns, the study of gay-identified digital paratexts can shed considerable light upon the logics of narrative and marketing, which often function to uphold gay formations, even as the post-gay movement mixes with the "metrosexual," "lumbersexual," "spornosexual," and "stromo" phenomena to produce peculiarly contradictory masculinities.[53] And while they may reflect many of the biases of the broader media landscape, gay-identified paratexts habitually provide frameworks for resisting homonormativity. They do so precisely by injecting eroticism into a range of digital platforms—both with and without permission—and in ways that occasionally reveal the kernels of a more radical queerness. As Jack Halberstam suggests, "desire remains as interface running across a binary technologic"; desire may violate the boundaries of digital networks even as it throws them into sharp relief.[54] The point, then, is not to reduce queerness to the dimensions of genital eroticism, or to endorse the essentialist conflation of gay men with promiscuity, but rather to locate a politics of resistance within a number of digital strategies—including and especially those that exceed and explode the censorial constraints of certain corporate sites.[55]

I am fundamentally concerned not merely with how and why gayness customarily trumps a broader queerness online, but also with how and why the internet has become so conducive to gay-identified fan practices—particularly those that parse the male same-sex eroticism of contemporary queer cinema in ways that make the parsing seem indistinguishable from the digital practices and online platforms that enable it. Which came first—the gay-identified impulse to create a "dirty GIF" of Ennis fucking Jack in *Brokeback,* or the social networking sites that serve to share such creations? *Brokeback* is especially relevant to my argument here: its production, and the immediate, web-enabled pirating of it, coincided with the emergence of YouTube. The earliest, gay-identified, viral, and piracy-driven practices of parsing *Brokeback* were thus coterminous with the popularization of the site, suggesting a certain, unexamined synergy between queer cinema reception and a series of fabled social media platforms. The internet, it seems, cannot have one without the other. *Brokeback*'s gay-identified fandom was born along with a website whose motto is "Broadcast Yourself"—and that self has subsequently been positioned, via various corporate and user-generated efforts, as gay when not straight, and as male when not female. YouTube has, in its own way, helped to reproduce this dubious consensus, brokering methods for monitoring and monetizing the practices of self-identified gay men even while restricting their citations of contemporary queer cinema. In its infancy—years before mawkish coming-out videos and gay-identified, sponsor-supported "lifestyle" channels became mainstays on the site—YouTube was perfecting techniques for particularizing queerness according to age, race, income, and "taste." Following the explosion of piracy-driven *Brokeback* paratexts in late 2005 and early 2006, YouTube joined forces with Disney and Time Warner in order to develop content-identification software—dubbed Content ID—that could help copyright holders (including NBCUniversal, which owns *Brokeback*'s distributor, Focus Features) ferret out unauthorized fan productions and "protect" their assets. Content ID—a mode of machine reading—not only automated the detection of copyright-infringing videos but also allowed for the extensive surveillance of YouTube users, furnishing statistics based on their tags, comments, likes, and other digital inscriptions. Simply put, Content ID has helped NBCUniversal to dramatically limit the pirating of *Brokeback Mountain* while simultaneously teaching the corporation about the consumption habits of the film's fans—and perhaps even reinforcing the bifurcating marketing strategies by which that film has been sold to straight women and gay men.[56]

The Commodification of Gay Reception Practices

Despite the prevalence of certain post-gay protestations, the gay man remains a necessary construction both for corporate profit and social conservatism. Indeed, one of the high costs of incorporating gay-identified productions into various digital domains is not only the suppression of alternative queer figurations but also the strengthening of a corporate stranglehold on gay representation, which often, as so many controversial gay-conscious ads make clear, leads to a striking conservative backlash. Consider, for instance, the coincidence of Honey Maid's "This Is Wholesome" campaign and the passage of Senate Bill 2681, which Mississippi governor Phil Bryant signed into law on April 3, 2014. Honey Maid's campaign kicked off with a thirty-second ad featuring, among other adoringly "wholesome" parents, a pair of gay dads who push a stroller down a sun-dappled suburban sidewalk, and who later pose, holding boxes of graham crackers, in front of an elegant house. Fitted with a conspicuous American flag, and flanked by a well-manicured lawn and lush shrubbery, the house evokes a certain suburban ideal that seals the viewer's sense of the men's privilege and that points up their whiteness, fashion-forward fastidiousness, and conformist resemblance to one another. Looking very much like twins—and in accordance with a persistent view of gay sexuality as conflating identification and desire, ego-ideal and object-choice, "being" and "having"—the men breezily embody a privilege and purchase power that obviously far exceeds the acquisition of Honey Maid graham crackers, extending into the realms of suburban home ownership, adoption and/or technologically assisted reproduction, and sartorial investment. Somewhat disturbingly, these clones evoke Lauren Berlant's reading of an untitled poem by John Ashbery, which Berlant interprets as a "sendup of suburban pleasures," but which also exhibits a certain complacency regarding the privilege of white gay men in contemporary suburbia—a place where "the comforting sound and slightly dull rhythm of cliché performs exactly how much life one can bear to have there, and

Figure 1.1. Homonationalism in the cereal aisle: Honey Maid's "This is Wholesome" campaign (2013).

what it means to desire to move freely within the municipality, a manicured zone of what had been a fantasy."[57] The gay men of Honey Maid's "This Is Wholesome," hired to "play themselves" and thus to act as documentary evidence of a "wholesome" homosexuality, appear as the very indices of homonationalist conformity.

Perhaps predictably, the controversy surrounding "This Is Wholesome" failed to highlight the racial, class, or nationalist dimensions of the commercial's gay representation. Instead, as Andrew Solomon argues, the extensive anti-gay backlash had everything to do with the commercial's unfamiliar, even traumatizing equation between gay subjectivity and "wholesomeness."[58] In response to the backlash, the media-savvy Honey Maid brand fought back, enlisting the help of the ad agency Droga 5, which hired two young multimedia artists, Linsey Burritt and Crystal Grover, to "take the negative comments"—culled from social networking services and printed on paper—and "turn them into something else," in this case a cluster of rolled-up sheets that spells out "love." A video detailing their labor, released on social media shortly after the debut of the first commercial in Honey Maid's "This Is Wholesome" campaign, made clear that, for every anti-gay tweet the company received, it "earned" ten positive, gay-identified messages—a statistic that Honey Maid uncovered through data mining technologies, thus reinforcing the notion that it is easy, and inarguably affirmative, to locate gay subjectivities via corporate surveillance and data profiling.

On the day that Droga 5's "Honey Maid: Love" premiered on social media, S.B. 2681 was signed into law in Mississippi, "allowing those with religious rationales to act out their [anti-gay] bigotry, and enjoining government from interfering when they do so."[59] It would be difficult to prove that there is a causal connection between a "gay-positive" Honey Maid commercial and a piece of anti-gay legislation. Indeed, I am less interested in positing such a connection than in exploring the implications of Honey Maid's efforts to locate gay consumers through new technologies of surveillance—not only because those efforts evoke the startling Grindr parody in *G.B.F.*, which critiques the chilling epistemological confidence of gay-centered geolocation apps (and of those who use them), but also because they promote a "gay participation" understood to be "inevitably" affirmative and enabling. Kim Hester-Williams has stressed the need to "examine the price that is exacted for participating in corporate-mediated cyberspaces that take advantage of our search for 'beloved community' on the net by reifying and subjecting our identities to the law of the market."[60] By a familiar consumerist logic, it is not enough simply to denounce the anti-gay responses to Honey Maid's "This is Wholesome" campaign; one must also—if one is truly committed to equality, to "gay representation"—purchase a product whose brand identity is inescapably "pro-gay." Though the company has preferred to present itself as "naturally," reflexively "progressive," Honey Maid in fact used data profiling to determine the viability of gay men as demographic targets. When the resultant ad campaign received the expected anti-gay complaints, Honey Maid simply revived the strategy, re-deploying the tools of data profiling in order to "prove" the pro-gay, "equality-minded" stance of the majority of its customers. "Honey Maid: Love"—the YouTube video that spells out this stance—is thus a paratext. It refers to a source text—an original work (in this case a commercial) whose meanings and impact it annotates. In transforming anti-gay tweets into the word "love," the video enacts a process that Thomas Elsaesser has described, in which multitudes—whether of objects or of humans—are made to form "a recognizable likeness," thereby underscoring "the coercive, normative power of such software as operates the Internet at the level of the algorithms, of the codes and protocols" that are "mostly hidden from view and in any case incomprehensible to the ordinary user."[61] In this sense, "Honey Maid: Love" both relies upon and materializes data profiling, in the process naturalizing the links between Twitter and various gay affirmations. If we ask ourselves what, beyond a graham cracker, the video actually promotes, then we confront the corporate stakes of gay visibility online, and of gay-identified digital visual culture, which includes the kinds of "positive" Twitter hashtags that "Honey Maid: Love" upholds as common among the brand's consumers. At the same time that it presents itself as "inclusive" through the representation of gay men, Honey Maid precludes a nonwhite, non-nationalist queer expansiveness—and rests upon the "incontestable results," the "statistical certainties," of data profiling in order to excuse this omission, this structured sidestepping of multiple queer modalities. Gay men, in other words, *are* the queer internet; the "proof" is in the data profiling.

Figure 1.2. Droga 5's viral YouTube video "Honey Maid: Love" (2013) turns anti-gay tweets into a material tapestry of "love."

As the Honey Maid case makes clear, the line between promotion and suppression is frequently as fine, in the digital age, as that between producers and consumers. In order to demonstrate the profitability of the gay male demographic, more and more companies are relying upon online identifications of "productive" gay men—the kinds of target consumers who can bring their own digital skills (their perceived facility with social media and penchant for producing paratexts) to bear upon a "brand," be it gastronomic or cinematic. A stereotype is thus at stake—is, in fact, at the center of a relatively new epistemology of male homosexuality: when a user downloads, provides a link to, or embeds a video, we "know" that he's gay if that video extracts the male same-sex eroticism of a queer feature film. After all, who else would be so "invested" in such eroticism as to produce a readily sharable video version of it? Never mind that Henry Jenkins, in his 1992 book *Textual Poachers,* had cautioned against conflating gay-receptive fan practices with actual gay consumers, arguing that, in fact, self-identified straight women have frequently been the sources of such practices, communicating their experiences of "the pleasure of reading male-male erotica."[62] If, according to marketing executives, gay men are the most likely consumers to see contemporary queer films, then they are also the most likely to make fan videos that rely upon or otherwise refer to those films. Such an assumption says as much about contemporary queer cinema as about the "gay associations" of certain practices of online reception: as a broad, potentially permeable category, queer cinema continues to overwhelmingly privilege the "G" in the acronym "LGBT," the result being that the vast majority of queer-conscious marketing campaigns and even individual, user-generated productions are focused on gay formations—on generating, strengthening, or resisting them.

Today's cultures of surveillance, with their roots in online "tracking" and metadata collection, reliably extend to film promotion and distribution, as anyone who has received a cinema-specific email alert, or who subscribes to the suggestion-dispensing, algorithmic Netflix, can attest. Despite clichéd celebrations of the resistant potential of internet users, which tend to suggest that "amateur content" is diverse and multidirectional—intensely and idiosyncratically "personal" rather than generic—corporations are, in fact, increasingly telling such users how to shape their online fan practices, and these users are often all too eager to comply. The cultural cachet of a user-generated production is tied to its perceived honesty, spontaneity, and uniqueness, and yet corporations continue to see this cachet as being rooted in a distinct formal structure—the video mashup, say—that offers only the semblance of the "amateur," and that is thus eminently reproducible. When Warner Bros. reedits its own, original *Magic Mike* trailer for You-Tube, it seeks to acquire this cachet—this sense of spontaneity, of "resistance" to fixity. When it outsources the practice of visual reinterpretation to gay-identified fans, however, it seeks to acquire even more: the "authenticity" of subcultural production, the sense of "mattering" to minority groups whose presence on the internet is often taken to be commercially significant and extremely influential.

Viral Paratexts before Facebook and YouTube

Consonant with the reading strategies that Stuart Hall famously identified as "resistant" and "oppositional," the cultural practices examined in this section are additionally distinguished by their digital trappings—by the production of online paratexts intended to comment on gay identities, at once collective and individual, public and private.[63] Two such paratexts proved remarkably popular in the early 2000s, a period just prior to the emergence of Facebook, YouTube, and other sites and services so crucial to the operations of Pink 2.0. One of these paratexts was a user-generated video that stitched together "vintage" clips of an animated public service announcement (first televised in the late 1980s in conjunction with the children's series *G.I. Joe*), adding an original, "gay-themed" audio track. Dubbed to express his desire for the cute skater boys surrounding him, the PSA's brawny, mustachioed star, who certainly resembled a gay stereotype (what with his visible Village People trappings, his unbuttoned denim vest and patrol cap), suddenly got to sound like one, too. Titled "Mr. LaFitte," the video, which began circulating in 2003 on such pre-YouTube video-sharing sites as eBaum's World and Albino Blacksheep, thus managed to distill, into a cheeky, lispy audio track, the gay-specific (albeit stereotypical) essence of the PSA's iconography. For those

Figure 1.3. "Mr. LaFitte" (2003) turns a 1980s PSA into a "gay statement"—with more than a little help from the PSA's original animation.

who, like me, had been raised on the animated, 1980s *G.I. Joe,* the show's episodes, and their associated PSAs, had always *seemed* gay; now they seemed even gayer, thanks to the tech-savvy, parodic contributions of Chicago-based filmmaker Eric Fensler, whose company, Fensler Films, produced a total of twenty-five such parodies—all of them disseminated online as embedded QuickTime videos—before facing charges of copyright infringement. Removed from eBaum's World, the videos later resurfaced on YouTube, having been uploaded by numerous users and under a whole host of new titles, indicating just how much had changed since the days when a simple cease-and-desist letter could effectively preempt or interrupt the site-specific, MPEG-4 playback of unauthorized media.

Another influential user-generated text—one that proliferated in the pre-YouTube era—was little more than a compilation of clips from the film *The Rules of Attraction* (Roger Avary, 2002). Titled "The Gay Rules of Attraction," the video first appeared on eBaum's World in early October 2002, mere days before the formal release of the film from which its content had been culled (or, as copyright law would have it, stolen).[64] Roughly six minutes long and with a relatively low audiovisual quality reflecting its illicit modes of production and distribution, "The Gay Rules of Attraction" distilled those scenes that feature, as the video's official description put it, "the pure gayness" of Ian Somerhalder's character, Paul Denton, a self-identified bisexual student at the fictional Camden College (a shameless stand-in for Dartmouth, down to its New Hampshire setting and extremely prominent Greek scene). Usefully fusing the surprisingly numerous moments during which Denton attempts to seduce young men, or that feature his fearsome blue-eyed gaze fixed lasciviously on limber male athletes and burly, beer-guzzling frat boys, "The Gay Rules of Attraction" functioned not merely to titillate the gay-identified user but also to confirm the "lie" of Denton's bisexuality—or at least of the film's occasional, dialogue-based endorsement of his "flexible" self-identification.

Using *The Rules of Attraction* as its sole audiovisual source, "The Gay Rules of Attraction" evinces its difference from the later, superficially transformative "Mr. LaFitte." "The Gay Rules of Attraction" doesn't dub Paul Denton; it simply lets him speak for himself in his pursuit of same-sex erotic contact. Clearly coded as gay, the *G.I. Joe* PSA, as recycled by Fensler Films in 2003, wasn't recontextualized, exactly; rather, its gay codes became a bit clearer, even to the point of seeming redundant. As Sean Griffin argues, the queer appeal of animation, its amenability to "alternative" readings, is rooted in its adaptable impersonation, through drawings, of popular understandings of gender and sexuality: the normative Snow White might look like Linda Darnell, but the deviant Ursula the Sea Witch, from *The Little Mermaid* (Ron Clements and John Musker, 1989), is a deliberate dead ringer for Divine.[65] Furthermore, the iconographic, narrative, and thematic centrality of metamorphosis to animation has rendered it ripe for the sort of sexual maturation that "Mr. LaFitte" represents—the transformation, through added audio, of a chaste children's program into a sexy guide to gay cruising. Viewed from this perspective, the 2003 video appears less to impose an erotic "update" on the original *G.I. Joe* PSA than to allow it to "grow into itself"—to express audibly what it had already expressed visually, through the physical and sartorial codes of a stereotyped gayness.

Fensler Films' "revision" of the PSA raises crucial questions about the program's origins—about the cultural contexts that created it—thus ensuring its discursively productive online "afterlives." The 2003 video sheds light upon the value of excavating an "old" media product, of digitally annotating it, and of circulating it online—a process that, I argue, constitutes a crucial form of queer historiography, one with a particular relevance for gay men whose representations have, since the 1970s, seemingly been both everywhere and nowhere, both pervasive to the point of appearing inescapable and so amorphous, so inarticulate, as to seem entirely inaccessible, subsumed under trendy "post-gay" celebrations of sexual fluidity or, worse still, rejected altogether under a reactionary, heterosexist rubric. Through parody, "Mr. LaFitte" succeeds in telling a particular truth: that global constructions of gay male sexuality and culture have shaped a variety of moving-image forms, and that such constructions have equally influenced a cultural interface that, through new and dynamic digital technologies, functions to archive, annotate, and adjust audiovisual instances of gay specificity for polemical and libidinal purposes.[66] In an influential 1997 essay, Lev Manovich outlines the multiple permutations of the term "interface" for the development of digital media theory, moving from the basic human-computer interface (or HCI), which entails the user's myriad interactions with a material computer, to more complicated, culturally contingent contexts. Acknowledging that "we are no longer interfacing to a computer but to culture encoded in digital form," Manovich introduces the term "cultural interface" in order to express the evolution and variegation of HCI according to a wide range of cultural constructs and subject-positions.[67] Examined through this lens, then, the viral "Mr. LaFitte" becomes a key component of Pink 2.0—of, that is, a cultural interface that encodes the "gayness" of audiovisual media, disseminating it through multiple technologies of playback in order to express particular, gay-identified reading practices, and to promote those reading practices through the mechanisms of file sharing.

When, in 2003, "Mr. LaFitte" first arrived in my email inbox in the form of a URL, it came with the following claim from a longtime friend and fellow faggot: "This vid does what we did when we were kids." Indeed, we had always attempted to clarify the contours of our gay fandom by "queering" a wide range of media texts, often "talking over" those texts in order to contribute our own, exaggeratedly fey commentary on their (always shaky) heterosexist pretentions. Whether working to "drown out" the dialogue of the television series *Home Improvement* (1991–1999) with our own eroticized exchanges (often in such a way as to transform the Zachary Ty Bryan and Jonathan Taylor Thomas characters into teen lovers), or highlighting the hotness of the American *Queer as Folk* (2000–2005) with hoots of appreciation, we were always doing, in the real time of embodied spectatorship, what "Mr. LaFitte" would do through digital revision: we were making "gay" media even gayer, drawing out and augmenting those elements that to us made sexual and cultural sense. Since the advent of Web 2.0, reception techniques like ours have become infinitely easier, and thus prominent to the point of online pervasiveness, suggesting an important yet largely unacknowledged bond between the diversification, the enhanced interactivity, of the internet and the manifold ways of "being gay" through digitally enabled practices of media production and reception. In addressing gay male subjectivity, David Halperin asks how "male homosexual desire connects with specific cultural forms, styles, modes of feeling, and kinds of discourse." Concluding that there is, inarguably, a "sexual politics of cultural form," Halperin suggests ways of rethinking gay male subjectivity beyond familiar psychological models, and outside of the identity-questioning, dogmatically anti-essentialist postmodernism of much of queer theory—a post-modernism that digital media theory has tended, in its own way, to embrace.[68] Manovich, for one, has even gone so far as to suggest that computer software "made postmodernism possible," purely by privileging "selection from ready-made media elements over creating them from scratch."[69]

On the one hand, a viral video like "Mr. LaFitte" might seem an example of postmodernism par excellence: it turns to a "ready-made media element," one ripe for an explicitly gay narration, and implicitly argues that it has in fact contributed, through its shimmering bears-and-twinks iconography, to the social construction of male homosexuality—a construction that "Mr. LaFitte" reinforces through its knowing commentary on the commercial detritus of the not-so-distant past. On the other hand, however, this "gay reading" of a superficially straight-identified *G.I. Joe* PSA is clearly at odds with postmodernist queer thought: it upholds—indeed, depends upon—a binary model of sociosexual organization, by which its source text, the original PSA, represents the (unconvincing) application of a heteronormative identity to the muscle-bearing subject who, in the 2003 "remake," gets to emerge as exclusively, vocally gay. For the makers of "Mr. LaFitte," that subject's appearance bespoke an obvious, and therefore hilarious, gayness, as did his voyeuristic fixation on a group of skater boys; he signaled, in short, a "negative"—a limiting and laughable—stereotype of male homosexuality, one that post-Stonewall developments in visibility politics have struggled to disavow. For Halperin, such a disavowal, with its principled opposition to essentialism—to "the merest acknowledgment or recognition of any cultural patterns or practices that might be distinctive to homosexuals"—has succeeded in "screening out the question of how, for a large segment of homosexual American men during the past century or so, being gay has been experienced through highly patterned forms of embodied sensibility," some of which might seem painfully stereotypical.[70] Halperin goes on to suggest that the "general denial of any and all homosexual specificity, especially cultural specificity, is an eloquent symptom of our current predicament"—of a moment of crisis occasioned by a climate of renewed political conservatism that can seem indistinguishable, at times, from that of ostensibly progressive post-gay protestations, the kinds that seek to suppress articulations of gayness.[71]

Following a series of legislative "victories" for sexual minorities, the gay label might itself suggest a relic of the binary-minded, segregationist past—a symbol of "difference," of distance from the mainstream. Equalitarian rhetoric rests upon efforts to subsume disparate identity formations under the banner of political fairness, just as the postmodernist proclivities of queer theory have often led to the rejection of "regulatory" categories of subjectivity. However, as Barry Adam once argued, "queer theory will never be able to account for why so many [homosexuals] defy the odds to affirm identity again and again," and neither will

Figure 1.4. User-generated descendants of "The Gay Rules of Attraction" (2002) abound on YouTube, all of them identifying Paul Denton as "gay."

digital media theory, with its axiomatic allegiance to the allegedly boundary-blurring experiences of interactivity, be able on its own to account for the recent explosion of emphatically gay-identified digital practices (such as, for starters, the promotional, polemical, and prurient distillation of *The Rules of Attraction* into "The Gay Rules of Attraction").[72] If there is a gay ontology, then surely it has acquired new dimensions through computing, while still remaining recognizably gay; similarly, if there is such a thing as queer cinema, then surely some of its gay-receptive entries have lately enjoyed novel lives online, entering into complex digital matrices of identification and desire. *The Rules of Attraction* may be queer, but "The Gay Rules of Attraction" is—well, as gay as it sounds. How did it get that way, and why? What is at stake—politically, creatively, and erotically—in the use of digital manipulation to say something "gay" about contemporary queer cinema? "Gayness" is not the ghost in the new media machine but, rather, a central, increasingly clear component of computational culture, one that draws its force from the way in which it appropriates moving-image media (especially cinema) in order to enact, as Halperin would put it, "how to be gay."

Such phenomena as the online production and dissemination of "porny" paratexts are, perhaps, only superficially new, distinguished more by their digital trappings and networked itineraries than by any artistic criteria or editorializing inclinations. "There is nothing like that old party pooper 'historical consciousness' to dull the gleeful celebrations of progress and the new," writes Charles R. Acland in *Residual Media*.[73] Indeed, in several crucial respects, paratexts do now what they have always done. Whether uploaded to YouTube or to Tumblr, paratexts still comment on their sources either directly or obliquely; they still evince an obsessive interest in "legitimate" cultural artifacts and how to defamiliarize them; they still generate charges of plagiarism and parasitism—charges that are no less conservative now than when Richard Carpenter and A&M Records denounced (and successfully suppressed) Todd Haynes's *Superstar: The Karen Carpenter Story* in the late 1980s. It is well worth resisting the familiar binary opposition between "new" and "old" media, particularly as accounts of the former threaten, through their frequently hyperbolized dimensions, to limit knowledge of the latter, even as the internet is said to make all histories abundantly available, whether via Wikipedia or some other manifestation of a hive mind. As I argue throughout this book, personal loss, corporate lacunae, and various modes of suppression continue to structure the cultural landscape of queer cinema, the internet, and associated technologies, doing little to alleviate—and much to exacerbate—the tendency toward gay-identified streamlining that the concept of Pink 2.0 describes. Those hoping, for instance, to find any of the major films of Andy Warhol on YouTube, or even to access reliable information about them on Wikipedia, are in for a rude awakening. Such films are perhaps *less* accessible now than when they were first exhibited, owing to a complex yet not uncommon confluence of authorial design and the mechanisms of the museum-industrial complex. Database culture is an ineffective engine of recovery of the queer past, and individual networked actors are hardly capable of altering certain conditions of scarcity, whatever their flair for coding. "Hacktivists," for instance, are no more likely to turn Warhol's films into online staples than techno-utopians are to convincingly suggest that digital paratexts are without precedent—that the alleged ease of of use of new technologies, coupled with their saturation, has suddenly enabled individuals to creatively comment on all manner of cultural texts. Even "Mr. LaFitte" has its own, decidedly analog antecedents, including Dick Fontaine's physique films of the 1950s and 1960s, some of which (like 1965's *Hot Harem*) Fontaine "updated" with the fey, recontextualizing voice-over commentary of Glory Holden.

It would be more persuasive to aver that digital paratexts are merely extensions—or, to borrow a techno-utopian buzzword, "remediations"—of earlier practices.

That is precisely what legendary gay avant-garde filmmaker James Bidgood calls them in Ira Sachs's queer film *Keep the Lights On* (2012), in which Bidgood claims that "that stuff that's on the internet now is exactly what Avery Willard was and we all were" during the mid-twentieth-century explosion of experimental media-making. Indeed, the invitations to creative accretion that a paratext inevitably offers on social media are, ultimately, little different from, say, those issued by Manhattan's Charles Theater in 1962. As J. Hoberman and Jonathan Rosenbaum point out in *Midnight Movies*, it was at the behest of Jonas Mekas, one of the deans of experimental cinema during this period, that the Charles began hosting open screenings—opportunities for filmmakers of all stripes (who routinely "lined up around the block") to share their work, much of which was plainly paratextual.[74] These open screenings both reflected and precipitated some of the equally extractive, exegetical techniques of such underground films as Jack Smith's *Flaming Creatures* (1963), a paratextual meditation on Maria Montez and the cinema of Josef von Sternberg, and Warhol's *Tarzan and Jane Regained . . . Sort Of* (1963), in which Taylor Mead and Naomi Levine portray the titular couple. To assume that digital paratexts are somehow easier to produce than the celluloid creations that patrons brought to the open screenings at the Charles is, however, to presuppose not simply mastery of various software but also access to computers and the internet—access that of course implies a whole host of other privileges, from the national to the bodily and beyond. Digitization is hardly a "natural," inevitable, or even indiscriminate process; time-, labor-, and capital-intensive, it is enacted according to certain expectations regarding cultural value—a process that Wolfgang Ernst calls "digitization on demand."[75] Just as Google would claim that its overwhelmingly gay-identified search results merely reflect (rather than reward) the gayness of queer content on the internet, and just as Netflix justifies its conflation of gender and sexuality (or of African and African American) as a reproduction of majority logic and an algorithmic envoy of "ease of use," technolibertarians might argue that, if the queer texts of yesteryear are not presently available in digital form, it is because no one has demanded them. What happens, then, when we *do* demand alternatives to digital platforms as they are presently configured? What queer uses might we make of what we currently have?

Fucking with the Interface, Or: How to Queer the Gay Internet

There is no single theoretical, historiographic, or affective lens through which to view the preponderance of online practices that construct gay subjectivities, just as there is no one way of defining fans and fan culture. By examining an array of gay-identified digital visual cultures, I suggest new ways of understanding contemporary queer cinema's dazzling online presence. At the same time, I consider the price of gay participation in queer cinema's online reception—the gay essentialism necessary for corporate targeting and the selling of individual products, as well as the "readable" discursive strategies that tend to limit the meanings of individual queer films, distorting fictional characters and living artists for the sake of "spreadability."[76] If, however, the internet makes it hard to parse a profoundly disruptive queerness, then perhaps that's a good thing—it means that queerness, imagined as a limitless process, hasn't yet been monetized, that its promises and particularities remain too powerful and too plentiful for extant interfaces and algorithms to assimilate them. "If we consider queerness simply in terms of sexual preference or as an alternative formation within an established set of desiring modes, then describing any form of computing as 'queer' may seem absurd," writes Jacob Gaboury. "If instead we understand queerness as a process of self-shattering rather than self-fashioning, then we begin to align it with . . . exceptional objects and practices that exist beyond the limits of a system such as computation."[77] Queerness, thus understood, is irreducible to technological structures, even if it appears, in a number of divergent dimensions, to have underwritten a series of specific cultural technologies, from Alan Turing's "imitation game" (1950), with its investment in questions of gender performance and "passing," to Christopher Strachey's campy love-letter generator (1952), which Gaboury describes as "a kind of joke, a critique of 'real' epistolary writing and 'real' love by means of automation through digitization."[78] From a queer theoretical perspective, however, the artifice of automation may be insufficient to sustain a personal or collective politics of transgression—may, as Gaboury suggests, codify and reproduce a relatively limited condition of queerness, immunizing itself against the indeterminacy and variability of strategies far more radical than the gender essentialism of the Turing Test (which is premised on the existence of a distinct, imitable femininity) or the code-bound, anti-Victorian irony of Strachey's love-letter generator.[79] The paradigm-shifting praise so prematurely showered upon digital networked technologies in the field of new media theory isn't simply offensive, given its general utopianism and blindness to a range of embodied realities; it is also motivating—a reminder that we must search for evidence of past and present alternative practices and for the promise of a future expansiveness.

By examining the online distribution and reception of a broad yet perpetually stymied cinematic category, I suggest that this orientation toward the future need not consist of what Kate Thomas calls "forever deferred political aims," or correspond to Lauren Berlant's understanding of "cruel optimism" as "a relation of attachment to compromised conditions of possibility whose realization is discovered either to be *im*possible, sheer fantasy, or *too* possible, and toxic."[80] The point, then, is not to deliquesce into a state of permanent yearning, hoping beyond hope that digital networked technologies will better reflect and more easily enable a wider range of engagements with contemporary queer cinema. Acknowledging that the internet is not yet queer in several crucial respects means requiring, in the short term, certain practical changes, including the abolishment of "Gay & Lesbian" as a queer catchall on Netflix, Hulu, YouTube, and other influential sites and services, and the shift in queer consciousness that various strategies of dataveillance demand. Through its semiotic dominance in the digital domain, and especially with respect to a standard corpus of queer cinema that invariably includes *Boys Don't Cry* (which, whatever its much-debated relationship to a so-called "lesbian gaze," is still a biographical account of an individual who chose to identify as a straight man), the term "Gay & Lesbian" almost always encodes transphobia (much like the iPhone application on which I am currently relying, which insists on the unacceptability of the term, autosuggesting "trams phobia"—the fear of a particular form of public transit?—instead).[81] As a fraught entrée into the worlds of digital media, "Gay & Lesbian" encodes transphobia whether users know it or not—and, indeed, in emphasizing the affective dimensions of this encoding process, I hope to suggest how transphobia may be assimilated unconsciously, as a consequence of the "convenience" and concision of digital networked technologies. This is, after all, what affect theory "does," or aims to "do": it enables us to work toward recognizing the disturbances that may occur beneath, beyond, or despite cognition. We may "know" that "Gay & Lesbian" is "just shorthand"—that it "means well" (or is, ultimately, "meaningless")—while still responding (with shame, disgust, delight, pride, fear, or cruelty) to its displacing potential, to the violence that it enacts in the name of visibility politics.

The online inclusion of transgender-identified individuals and categories does not, however, necessarily signal resistance to homonormativity; often, it suggests the opposite, as when a social networking service caters to gay men partly by embracing the term "transgender," thus illustrating a politically correct commitment to the strict separation of gender and sexuality that mirrors accommodationist gay male strategies. As David Valentine argues, invocations of transgender identity are central to the contemporary consolidation of gayness as white, middle-class, and normatively gendered. It is precisely by honoring the legitimacy of "transgender," then, that many gay men manage to distance themselves not only from stereotyped conceptions of homosexuality as gender inversion but also from certain categories of race, class, and culture. Still, transphobia persists online in ways that determine the intelligibility of contemporary queer cinema, just as the reflexive valorization of gay masculinity is often the dominant condition of access to representations of sexual and gender minorities. If, of all contemporary queer films, *Brokeback Mountain* came closest to inspiring a popular reevaluation of "gay" as a term of colonization—one that has, since the 1970s, so often succeeded in seizing, shrinking, and commodifying various queer landscapes—then its monotonous recurrence on various digital platforms would seem to guarantee that the film will forever be known as "the gay cowboy movie." And yet desire may well complicate any such confining tag—even a desire conditioned by digital networked technologies. Indeed, Gilles Deleuze's conception of desire as "not a natural given" is deeply relevant here: "Desire is wholly a part of the functioning heterogeneous assemblage. It is a process, as opposed to a structure or a genesis. It is an affect, as opposed to a feeling."[82] Desire, for Deleuze, is decidedly not what Foucault theorizes as "pleasure": the latter term, in Deleuze's reading, appears to foreclose possibilities, to set boundaries and consolidate power.[83] Pink 2.0, as a confining cultural interface, is all about pleasure—primarily the pleasure of knowing oneself, and of knowing one's objects, as "gay." The alternative practices that function despite or in direct opposition to this interface are more aptly understood in terms of desire—and perhaps even as Deleuzian "lines of flight," as that which "leaks out on all sides" of Pink 2.0.[84] From this perspective, simply knowing that your self-fashioned, web-enabled queer identity is subject to corporate misrecognition and thus inevitably contributes to the consolidation of what José Muñoz calls "a crypto-universal white gay subject that is weirdly atemporal"—simply recognizing the effects of this consolidation on the online intelligibility and accessibility of contemporary queer cinema—is one way of queering the internet.[85] "We must vacate the here and now for a then and there," writes Muñoz in *Cruising Utopia*. "What we need to know is that queerness is not yet here but it approaches like a crashing wave of potentiality . . . Willingly we let ourselves feel queerness's pull, knowing it as something else that we can feel, that we must feel. We must take ecstasy."[86] In tracing the online reception of contemporary queer cinema, I hope to suggest that the internet has only just begun to engage the category's possibilities.

2 Epistemology of the Blogosphere
Queer Cinema on Gay Porn Sites

One may think of the Web as a "great records machine" but it also accelerates the ephemeral logic of the commodity fetish that weeds out and deletes those parts of the past no longer adjudicated as having sufficient display and exchange value.

Ken Hillis, *Online a Lot of the Time*

The Internet is not a porn shop in the bedroom but rather a library or mall with secret exits to porn shops that one accidentally finds by looking too far afield (much like the video store with its pornography section visually cordoned off).

Wendy Hui Kyong Chun, *Control and Freedom*

W<small>HEN</small> *NEW YORK TIMES* critic Stephen Holden proposed that Travis Mathews's 2012 film *I Want Your Love* "blurs the line between narrative storytelling and pornography," he offered a fairly familiar characterization of the taxonomic indeterminacy of certain sexual representations—those that, in Linda Williams's words, blend "the real and the performed," creating a mélange of erotic artifacts.[1] However, when Holden suggested that *I Want Your Love* "seems a conscious effort to take back gay sex on film," he appeared to mobilize a model of authorship that elevates the gay-identified, art-conscious Mathews above the fray of porn producers who privilege Viagra-assisted pricks over "honest" cocks, and easy profit over hard-won pleasure.[2] When Holden situates Mathews in explicit, principled opposition to "typical" pornographic practice, he evokes the stereotyped specter of certain gay-for-pay schemes, from those that artificially induce erection to, somewhat less salaciously, those that see straight Hollywood stars "going gay" for Oscar's sake, as in films as varied as *Kiss of the Spider Woman* (Héctor Babenco, 1985), *Brokeback Mountain* (Ang Lee, 2005), and *Milk* (Gus Van Sant, 2008).

Mathews's *I Want Your Love*, based on his 2010 short film of the same name, follows the experiences of Jesse (Jesse Metzger), a young gay man who, unable to sustain a life of perpetual underemployment in "freewheeling" San Francisco, prepares to return to a more modest existence in the Midwest. As Daniel Robichaud points out in a review for the *Vancouver Weekly*, Jesse's storyline intersects with "a plethora of penises," and the film features sex that is "raw, uncut," and thus ostensibly deserving of categorization as pornography—"material presented with the intention of titillating an audience."[3] When Robichaud stresses the "accuracy" of the pornographic label as applied to *I Want Your Love*—when he maintains that he is, without a hint of homophobia or moral dudgeon, "simply calling [the film] what it is"—his defiant tone suggests that he is arguing against the sort of approach that Holden takes in the *Times*. To suggest, as Holden does, that Mathews's film represents the artsy transcendence of smut is to ignore the productive—indeed, as Robichaud has it, the "hot" and "titillating"—intersections between *I Want Your Love* and some of the most popular gay-porn websites. If, in terms both of formal elements and of narrative structure, *I Want Your Love* looks a lot like the widely viewed online features *Boyfriends* (2012) and especially *Golden Gate* (2012), then that is perhaps because all three films share the same production and distribution company, Naked Sword, whose flagship website ("Where the World Watches Gay") boasts "the largest collection of gay porn on the net," as well as the most paying subscribers of any such site. That Naked Sword is not opposed to porn stars of the gay-for-pay variety—that the studio makes no claims about its films' "gay authenticity," even as it aggressively targets a gay-identified market—must have rankled the Stephen Holden who prefers to see *I Want Your Love* as being resolutely separate from, and perceptibly better than, the artless products of "the porn industry." The unquestioned assumptions at the heart of Holden's take on *I Want Your Love* are plainly symptomatic of Pink 2.0, particularly in the way that they construct a kind of imperiled gay purity—one constantly under threat of erasure at the hands of "fake" gays, inchoate queers, and anti-identitarian discourses.

In its online version, Holden's *Times* review is even more strikingly reflective of the corporatized terms and conditions of Pink 2.0, incorporating an eroticized image of the gay musician Jobriath, as well as a "gay-inclusive" Kindle ad whose inclusivity consists of showing two white, wealthy gay men making purchases at a tropical resort.[4] The notion that *I Want Your Love*, with its own iconographic reliance on white gay men, needs to "take back gay sex" is simply absurd, raising some pressing and far from palatable questions: Take it back from *whom*, exactly? From queers of color who have "sullied" it? From "inauthentic" capitalists craving the commodification of queer desire? Indications of the extreme similarities between the emphatically gay-identified, commercially available *I Want Your Love* and typical online representations of gay subjectivities abound on the *Times* website. Indeed, it would be difficult to argue that Mathews's film, whatever its political and aesthetic merits, represents anything new in the way of gay representation: Frank Ripploh explored similar themes, albeit with far more style and humor, in his explicit, autobiographical *Taxi zum Klo* (1980); strictly as a showcase for "real sex," *I Want Your Love* closely resembles both Ripploh's film and

Michael Winterbottom's straight-identified *9 Songs* (2004), which boasts scene after scene of unsimulated penetration and even includes a cum shot. Equally dubious is a point that Holden so tendentiously makes: that *I Want Your Love*, however much it may "blur distinctions" between simulated sex and hard-core fucking, is safely removed from the commercialized distortions of "the pornography industry." Look online, one wants to say to Holden—look, in fact, at the sponsor-supported interface of the *Times* website—and you will see just how easily *I Want Your Love* has been enveloped into various gay-specific pornographic networks, not all of which are commercial, or even legal.

This chapter examines those networks and the way they function to reduce contemporary queer films to meat and money shots, in the process appearing to promote confining conceptions of gay subjectivities and internet spectatorship. Whatever Mathews's artistic and commercial ambitions, and however much Holden may believe them to be "safe" from inauthentic co-optation, *I Want Your Love* has enjoyed an unauthorized online prominence that not only limits its commercial prospects but that also positions it as gay porn—a piece of audiovisual smut like any other. Indeed, a certain equalitarian rhetoric abounds on porn aggregators, which promise "endless free videos from around the internet," "hot clips from across the web," and "the widest selection of real sex movies." On XVideos.com, one of the most popular online porn aggregators, "hard-core clips" from feature-length art films coexist with cum shots selected—that is, pirated—from a variety of porn studios, which also, of course, provide authorized content for free, in the hope of boosting that content's visibility.[5] In the site's so-called "Gay Section," a clip of *I Want Your Love* is available alongside videos whose titles include *Camp-Site Outdoor Anal Fucking, Austin and Ryan Get Dirty,* and *Two Twinks Go Crazy for Each Other.* No attempt is made to distinguish qualitatively, or even taxonomically, between the *I Want Your Love* clip and the various videos produced by traditional porn studios. Whether the latter defile the former—drag an art film down to the dirt of the earth, as it were—is an open question. Perhaps, rather than being "tainted"—cheapened—through its proximity to "pure porn," *I Want Your Love* confers upon its discredited brethren the cultural capital of what Holden calls "authentic" representation. In any case, rather than "taking back gay sex" from the allegedly aesthetically and morally impoverished porn studios, *I Want Your Love* has effectively joined them— whether its director and critical champions have wanted it to or not. Through its prominent, often-pirated online circulation, Mathews's film has revealed its iconographic, acoustical, narrative, and affective parallels with gay porn, making it impossible to track its reception without considering the kinds of sites that are often beyond the boundaries of conventional critical research.

If XVideos, Free Gay Porn, Only Dudes, Man Hub, and GayTube are among the partly piracy-driven online porn aggregators where *I Want Your Love* has been illicitly accessible, and if they should be studied as such, then they aren't the only "deviant" sites where one can discover both contemporary queer cinema and evidence of its gay-coded reception. In the second half of this chapter, I turn to—and endorse—archives that might seem particularly perverse, and that are indisputably pornographic: gay-identified fetish websites—those that are non-commercial, user-generated, and, like the above examples, reliant upon pirated images whose sources run the gamut from mainstream Hollywood cinema to subscription-based gay porn sites. My use of "archive," in this instance, might appear to contradict standard definitions of the term, which plainly privilege qualitative over quantitative distinctions, and which centralize careful deliberation in contrast to a putatively mindless acquisition of objects. However, I am deploying it in the spirit of recent historiographic interventions, which, as Tim Dean suggests, understand archives in a far broader, Benjaminian sense: as "counterarchives, migrant archives, and queer archives," and in terms of "a multipronged, cross-disciplinary project of identifying, collecting, and preserving the traces of that which otherwise remains obscure, ephemeral, itinerant, and precarious."[6] A foot-fetish Tumblr, or a crush-fetish YouTube channel, clearly involves not the thoughtless amalgamation of audiovisual materials that critics of Web 2.0 view as one of the ills of interactivity and database culture, but the careful identification, collection, and preservation of fetish objects: bare male feet, bug-crushing boots, and so on. Far from impossible in an age of accelerated media convergence, and far from peripheral to the database-driven operations of computer culture, preservation emerges as an achievable ideal within explicitly archival fetish websites—one that is vulnerable not to interactivity per se but to the anti-piracy crusades of Content ID (on YouTube) and various other instantiations of copyright protection.[7]

With Content ID a constant threat not simply to individual YouTube channels but also to the independent bloggers who embed videos from those channels, piracy and its permutations remain crucial to an understanding of the erotic blogosphere, particularly as it intersects with both commercial gay porn and contemporary queer cinema. Lest my use of "piracy" suggest a strictly institutional conception of the term—one that fails to problematize a corporation's proprietary right to content—it is necessary to point to recent scholarly efforts to queerly redefine piracy beyond considerations of ownership, legality, and compensation (however significant these factors may be, particularly in the case of Mathews's *I Want Your Love,* a feature film whose commercial viability has almost certainly suffered as a consequence of piracy). As Shujen Wang suggests, piracy, typically a "maligned term," has been critically "recuperated and revalidated" in ways that enable new interpretive approaches to the circulation of media, including those that address the politics of resistance immanent in various forms of unauthorized content acquisition (from the digitization of analog sources to the "mere" reblogging of embedded video). I use the term "piracy" not in any moralizing or corporatist capacity, and not as a synonym for sampling and remixing, but as a means of signaling what Wang describes as piracy's power as an analytic—a term that, extricated from exclusive considerations of compensation and copyright, legality and illegality, opens up manifold "possibilities for engagement and critique."[8] I intend the term to serve at least two queer purposes: to resist the logic by which piracy becomes a "problem" for Hollywood insofar as it threatens the latter's "admirable" and belated embrace of queer subjects (as in the American Film Institute's simultaneous valorization of *Queer Eye for the Straight Guy* and denunciation of the "crime" of film piracy in 2003); and to respect the manner in which the term is deployed by self-identified pirates themselves—users who *do* see themselves as stealing content, and who seize upon precisely those audiovisual elements that, ripe as they are for fetishistic recuperation, copyright holders are unlikely to ever isolate and sell, let alone acknowledge.[9] Centering my analysis on a case study of foot-fetish websites, I suggest that such sites, and their niche-oriented pornographic counterparts, provide some of the most useful points of access to the gay-identified online reception of contemporary queer cinema. Fetish websites, which extract and disseminate evidence of a film's "relevance" to particular erotic fixations, are often the first sites to celebrate the gay-specific appeal of certain popular cultural products. At the same time, many of them filch from commercial, subscription-based fetish websites like My Friends' Feet and Jock Foot Fantasy, further blurring distinctions between art and pornography in an attempt to make gay sense of contemporary queer cinema.

When screenshots of Jude Law's bare feet, taken from the queer film *The Talented Mr. Ripley* (Anthony Minghella, 1999), show up on a foot-fetish Tumblr alongside images taken from a gay porn site, they not only position *Ripley* as an emphatically gay-receptive rather than queerly unclassifiable film, but also suggest that it is as pornographic—as erotically satisfying—as media that would seem strictly, even egregiously salacious. If, given the conditioning power of Pink 2.0, it is increasingly difficult to guard a limitless queerness against gay-specific online appropriations, then it is perhaps equally difficult to, as Holden puts it, "take back gay sex . . . from the pornography industry"—and not because that industry is commercially committed to cribbing from contemporary queer cinema. Holden's conception of pornography as an industrial practice appears to be severely restricted; it begins and ends with for-profit fucking, the kind whose contours are hyper-familiar, widely practicable, and therefore—allegedly—void of gay verisimilitude. Such verisimilitude isn't exclusively a matter of the kind of "comfortable, non-performance-oriented lovemaking" that Holden so appreciates in *I Want Your Love;* it may well encompass precise physical gestures that resonate with fetishists—the on-screen flexing of bare male feet, perhaps, or the gleeful, gratuitous crushing of a bug by a burly "bro." Within Web 2.0, pornography has become more expansive and accessible than ever before, as countless studies have suggested.[10] Within Pink 2.0, however, the complex, even contradictory permutations of pornography have consistently called into question standard accounts of queer cinema and gay spectatorships. Indeed, if the acquisition practices that are at the center of this chapter demand an expanded definition of pornography, then they equally demand an updated, radically reconceived notion of what it means, in terms of gay spectatorships, to engage with queer cinema on the internet.

User-generated fetish websites, like online porn aggregators, reveal the sexual resemblance—the erotic equality—between queer art films and pornography, demonstrating the ease with which cinematic images can be parsed for "porny" purposes online, as well as the frequency with which such images can be made to reflect, reproduce, and satisfy gay subjectivities. Fetish websites provide especially illuminating online cartographies of gay desire. Perhaps more importantly, however—especially from a media archaeological standpoint—their archival richness tends, if often accidentally, to exceed the reach of copyright and other legislative restrictions. While it may no longer be true that, as Chuck Kleinhans once so sweepingly suggested in a discussion of pornography's evolution across competing formats, "streaming video downloads escape all local government attempts at control," it is clear that there remain—even in today's climate of increased internet surveillance—certain pockets of the blogosphere where even the kinkiest of queers might fear to tread, but where studies of cinema spectatorship must travel if they are to begin to understand a broader collection of online reception practices than those currently central to scholarship on the subject.[11] Indeed, user-generated, gay-identified fetish websites conceivably cultivate resistance to the prescriptions both of narrative cinema—which so rarely represents sexual fetishes at all, let alone as common sources of erotic enjoyment—and of conventional fan blogs, which, as David Bordwell and Kristin Thompson suggest in *Minding Movies,* often function as deliberate tributes to (or shameless imitations of) mainstream print criticism. Indeed, the persistent, almost dogmatic orientation of film-focused blogs toward Hollywood itself—an aspirational orientation that sees individual bloggers bucking to "matter" critically and commercially—precludes the kind of engagement with seemingly minor but sexually seismic textual details that fetish websites so openly value.

I Want Your Love has routinely appeared on such sites, often alongside videos whose fetishistic appeal would seem to have been consciously structured rather than "accidentally" produced. Mathews's film was not, by all accounts, intended to target, let alone erotically satisfy, foot fetishists—and yet, in its representation of a male nudity that extends from cock to toes, it manages to set itself up for a wide range of fetishistic recuperations. When *I Want Your Love* turns up, anonymously, on piracy-driven online porn aggregators, it is often described in terms of a "bear fetish"—a sexual predilection for hairy, heavily built men—and consigned to corresponding archives. When, however, images of the bare soles of its male stars show up on user-generated foot-fetish websites, *I Want Your Love* joins an even wider range of media representations, from "paparazzi shots" of "hot male celebrity feet" (on Best Gay Feet, Famous Male Feet, and other aggregators) to stills pirated from commercial fetish websites like My Friends' Feet and Jock Foot Fantasy. If *I Want Your Love* deliberately blurs the line between art and pornography, then it intersects with fetish-driven representations in ways that might seem accidental but that are, in fact, abundantly archived across the blogosphere. In her groundbreaking book *Hard Core*, Linda Williams advanced the notion that, in the 1980s, moving-image pornography became legitimized—even, in her words, "normalized"—as a narrative component of "the entertainment mainstream." This was due not merely to legal changes and technological innovation, but also—and perhaps most importantly—to the fact that entries in a hard-core corpus were, in commercial outlets, increasingly situated alongside examples of other, older, "cleaner" genres. Williams points to "the many videocassette rental outlets that offered X-rated adult videos on the same shelves as or adjacent to the latest horror film or teen comedy."[12] This chapter explores what such adjacency has come to mean on the internet—what it "does" both to boundary-blurring films like *I Want Your Love* and to voracious, gay-identified modes of online spectatorship.

I argue that one of the best ways to gauge the distribution and reception of contemporary queer cinema is to consider the category's intersections with the gay-identified, erotic blogosphere—with websites that run the gamut from porn aggregators to foot-fetish Tumblrs. Relatively low-budget, barely publicized films like *I Want Your Love* and *Stranger by the Lake* (Alain Guiraudie, 2013) might seem so "small"—so little seen, so "insignificant"—as to exist beyond the boundaries of online productions, to be profoundly peripheral to the interests of those who, with decidedly viral aspirations, create and circulate paratexts. The films' explicit sexual content, however—the meat and money shots so strikingly central to their formal fabric—make them quite at home on an abundance of sites that trade in "gay sex." They offer a queer corollary to Wendy Chun's claim that the internet is "fundamentally indeterminate and pornographic"—that erotic productions, whatever their industrial origins and cultural aspirations, represent the subtly enforced rule rather than the illicit exception in online life.[13] Chun indirectly suggests, in fact, how and why Pink 2.0 is possible in the first place, stressing the way internet users become habituated both to seeing as well as to reproducing pornographic images—particularly those that, under a banner of boundary-shattering flexibility, funnel expansive desires and subject-positions through preordained, even gender-normative and erotically homogenous categories. Chun's emphasis on "the tension between freedom and control that underlies the internet as a new mass medium"—her argument that online pornography persists and pervades both through the promise of liberation and through portals that privilege seemingly limited and limiting keywords like "boy" and "gay" and "penis" and "feet"—helps to explain why and how contemporary queer cinema can so quickly and so convincingly intersect with gay porn. Indeed, one may deliberately search for and easily find a wealth of erotically stimulating online images of gay movie characters, but one may just as easily come across those images simply by typing the seemingly innocuous search terms "male youth" and "top athletes." All of which is to suggest that the portals through which internet users discover queer cinema are often pornographic—whether one is actually seeking an erotic experience or not. Studies of the online availability of gay-identified film reception therefore need to incorporate these pornographic portals, rather than rely exclusively upon more conventional, clearly demarcated, "chaste" research pathways such as the Internet Movie Database, Yahoo! Movies, and Flixster.[14]

In this chapter, I suggest some of the unavoidable limitations of any study of queer cinema reception that would stop short of evaluating instances of what I am calling mutually anonymous online display—the shared namelessness, on certain erotic websites, of user-producers and of pirated clips of queer cinema. *Stranger by the Lake* may well remain as anonymous—as unidentified—as the user who uploads clips of the film to Gay Foot Blog, but that does not mean that its disassembled presence on the site should be ignored or discredited. Indeed, it is only by paying close attention to pirated productions—those whose cinematic sources, often by necessity, go without explicit identification, and circulate promiscuously—that we may better understand the critical, affective, and libidinal relations between gay-identified internet users and the queer films that they "pornographically" condense. All the examples of eroticized online zones that I explore in the following pages—all the user-generated, gay-identified spaces for experiencing representations of male-male sexuality—exhibit a refusal to distinguish qualitatively, politically, or libidinously between equally pirated versions of hardcore porn and the latest crop of queer films, between sexually stimulating "smut" and intellectually challenging cinema.

"Where the World Watches Gay"

Queer histories of cyberporn have shifted, since the start of the twenty-first century, from the utopianism of the earliest digital media theorists to a more sobering acceptance of the way that pornographic interfaces work increasingly to divide human sexuality into easily manageable, mutually exclusive categories. Any quantitative investigation of queer dating and hookup websites would surely expose the predominance of gay male identifications—the majority status of gay subjectivities in an online landscape where lesbian desire is downplayed, bisexual behaviors "debunked," and trans and intersex recognition all but unavailable (because plainly "uncomputable"). As Rich Cante and Angelo Restivo put it, "pornography remains the one genre where, in numerical terms, gayness is unquestionably *much, much* more commonly represented than in any other category of U.S. moving-image product."[15] Furthermore, if the geosocial networking application Grindr is now, in many ways, a popular metonym for gay male sexuality, then it tends also to stand in for all non-straight, erotically inflected engagements with the internet, as the film *G.B.F.* makes so amusingly clear. Grindr's acceptance of "nude pics" notwithstanding, the app operates in a networked, peer-to-peer capacity that is distinct from the majority of porn sites, whose managers select clips for potentially "open" spectatorship—for, that is, virtually anyone who wanders online (and, in the case of subscription sites, pays to access content). If Grindr's administrators claim that, in order to use the app, one needs not only an iPhone, Android, or BlackBerry, but also to self-identify as "a man interested in other men," then one needn't self-identify at all when accessing an online porn aggregator; there is a vast difference between constructing a Grindr profile that effectively produces an identity, however fictive, and simply visiting a site like GayTube, interacting with its interface, and coming away with a sense of how it manages audiovisual representations of "gay" eroticism.

That does not mean, however, that the free play of identity is sanctioned on websites that cater to gay male sexuality—a point that theorists of cyberporn have

Figure 2.1. "GuyDar" use in *G.B.F.* (2013).

been making for several years, attempting to reconcile what seems an endless supply of multidirectional "smut" with the simplifying, circumscribing devices of websites where, as Cante and Restivo suggest, gay subjectivities are very much in the majority, in terms of both representation and address. "In theory," writes Zabet Patterson, "this wealth of [pornographic] images would seem to offer a truly emancipatory scenario allowing subjects to project their virtual selves into a seemingly endless variety of scenarios and environments, and to embody an infinite variety of freely chosen subject positions, roles, and desires." Such, of course, was the promise that proved so central to the earliest intersections between queer and digital media theory—the promise of boundlessness, of a decisive break from binary thinking. "Yet, in reality," Patterson continues, "what cyberporn tends to offer—especially with a rapidly consolidating market—is an environment in which desire and subject position are produced as 'truths' of the self through a discourse of categorization and classification."[16] In other words, you may not self-identify as a gay man, but if you click on a particular "tag"—on hypertext that reads, say, "gay interest"—you run the risk of endorsing, and of perpetuating, the privileged online position of cisgender, male-identified homosexuality, which any one of an abundance of "non-straight," "all-male" websites do indeed produce as a "'truth' of the self." "Part of the captivation of cyberporn," Patterson argues, "is that it allows images to be managed and categorized so readily, allowing the subject to assimilate and emulate a particular subject position while retaining the hallucinatory promise of fluidity. The 'contract' and financial exchange entailed by 'clicking through' to a Web site, or in signing up for a particular site, then, forces this schema of classification to become fixed through acceptance and repetition."[17]

It also functions to normalize a film like Mathews's *I Want Your Love* as an example of gay porn. Indeed, the emphatic and repetitious way in which *I Want Your Love* has been catalogued online—as, that is, a series of porn clips of "gay interest"—greatly exceeds the exegetical claims of the mainstream press, and certainly of Mathews himself. This is partly a function of availability: it is simply far easier to access Mathews's film on a porn site than through any other platform, provided one has reliable, relatively open access to the internet. The links between access and taxonomy thus demand reappraisal in the digital age, particularly with respect to queer films whose lives—beyond an already circumscribed, even elitist festival circuit—consist exclusively, or almost exclusively, of uncredited, pirated appearances on pornographic websites. If, like YouTube, such sites routinely record and display the number of times a particular video has been watched—elevating the most demonstrably popular to a special section, as happened to an unnamed, condensed *I Want Your Love* on the website Free Gay Porn in 2012—then it is often difficult, if not impossible, to infer the extent of user knowledge of the videos' sources, whether porn studios or independent production companies specializing in queer art films. Of the hundreds of thousands of users who watched the version of *I Want Your Love* that appeared on Free Gay Porn, how many understood the video's source to be a Travis Mathews project—a seventy-one-minute film intended first for theatrical release and later for commercial home-video distribution? Comment sections are scarce on many porn aggregators, precluding any direct, sustained engagement with the textual responses of individual users—responses that, in any case, would carry a dubious evidentiary value, however much they might illuminate particular conventions of reception.

The question of whether the source of a pirated online video is a porn studio or an art film is unusually complicated in the case of *I Want Your Love*. In contrast to Holden's conviction that the film is far removed from what he calls "the porn industry," *I Want Your Love* was in fact produced with extensive support from prominent representatives of that industry. These included Naked Sword, a licensed, subscription-based online porn aggregator (its official tagline is "Where the World Watches Gay") and Jack Shamama, the editor of the website Gay Porn Blog and a prolific writer and producer of what he proudly calls "smut."[18] Further complicating a media archaeological approach to the distribution and reception of *I Want Your Love* is the fact that the film exists in two director-approved versions: a short and a feature that evince an extreme iconographic as well as narrative resemblance to one another, making it particularly difficult to distinguish between the two on porn-aggregating sites whose practices of piracy preclude clear identifications of source material. Producing the fourteen-minute short as a kind of calling card in 2010, Mathews sent it to Naked Sword in 2011, pitching his plan to adapt it into a feature-length film—one that would duplicate and extend the short film's use of explicit sex, and also "dare to capture the uncensored zeitgeist of modern-day San Francisco unlike any film before it."[19]

While Mathews's stated intention to "blend real people with real sex" suggests precisely the kind of hybrid style that Holden champions—the combination of a patient, documentary-style approach to human subjects and a prototypically pornographic reliance on penetration and sexual climax—the fact that he sought production support from a successful porn website is telling. It suggests that, in the context of what Williams calls "the hard-core art film"—defined as a genre that interweaves graphic, unsimulated sex and various narrative scenarios whose principal purpose is not to titillate, but rather to educate and even ennoble—the "hard-core" exceeds and subsumes the "art." One wonders what would have happened if, say, Mathews had sought the support of a celebrated documentary filmmaker instead of a website that describes itself as "the largest gay [video-on-demand] brand in the world, reaching over 90 percent of the market."[20] Holden's notion that *I Want Your Love* is equal parts sex and sociological investigation—that its documentary value lifts it above the level of a "typical" porn film—seems spurious when considering its production history (not to mention the sheer documentary value of pornography). The participation of Naked Sword certainly doesn't invalidate Mathews's attempts at providing a realist take on a particular place (San Francisco) at a particular time (the dawn of the twenty-first century); in fact, it confirms and even compliments them. Naked Sword has long been engaged in producing Web content that aspires to a certain "*vérité* quality" in the narrative sequences that surround meat and money shots, and that includes the ambitious porn series *Golden Gate,* which, like Mathews's film, tracks the experiences of "men in everyday situations in San Francisco." Indeed, even beyond Naked Sword, the abiding documentary value of pornography, whether as an index of popular sexual fantasies or of various material conditions for fucking, is well known, and almost axiomatic in film studies. However, it is precisely through the repetitious, monolithic categorizations that Patterson describes—the hyper-specific "schemas of classification" so central to cyberporn—that *I Want Your Love* becomes recuperated not merely as exclusively gay (rather than broadly queer, in keeping with Mathews's panoramic ambitions), but also as purely pornographic.

In her conclusion to *Screening Sex,* Linda Williams suggests that new platforms—particularly online platforms so closely associated with the search for sexual stimulation—will continue to complicate critical, taxonomic conceptions of on-screen sex. While Stephen Holden maintains that *I Want Your Love* bears no resemblance to "the pornography industry," the film's own website (www .iwantyourlovethemovie.com), isomorphic as it is with so many aspects of Naked Sword, tells a strikingly different story. Not only are references to Naked Sword omnipresent on the site; so are images that appear to promise on-screen sexual contact—images of naked men in bed, their arms and thighs and faces and feet touching in tableaux of sheer erotic intimacy. Instructively, *I Want Your Love* is not "watchable" on its own website. The user who wishes to access the film as a moving-image feature is either instructed to order a DVD through Naked Sword or ported, via hypertext, to the company's website, where Mathews's film, as a "playable" audiovisual production, co-exists with—is inescapably adjacent to—a variety of videos apparently produced without Mathews's auteurist aspirations, and that are not, to say the least, the official selections of a series of prestigious queer film festivals. Sandwiched between the porn productions *The Mix* and *Frat House Cream*—and with *Fuck & Cum* close by—*I Want Your Love* is available for high-definition playback on Naked Sword, the only website for which it is currently licensed (but hardly the only one on which it appears). Indeed, if *I Want Your Love* has a vibrant life across a wide range of piracy-driven online porn aggregators, that is partly due to its prominence on Naked Sword—itself an aggregator as well as a producer of pornography, a company that generates "original content" while maintaining a "curated" collection of other companies' pornographic productions. Naked Sword, in other words, enjoys licensing arrangements with major porn studios (most notably Corbin Fisher)—a set-up that lends the site a diversity (in terms of production) that is duplicated on illegal aggregators.

If, as Patterson suggests, cyberporn tends to interpellate the user as someone operating within, and in emphatic approval of, a binary sexual system (wherein "non-straight" equates to "gay male"), then gay-identified porn aggregators similarly hail the media products that they pirate, positioning them as the only legitimate alternatives to heterosexual representations. They do this, in some cases, without identifying those products in much detail—by categorizing them only in terms of their alleged "gay content." While *I Want Your Love* is listed under its actual title, and also as a Travis Mathews film, on Naked Sword (where it appears alongside *Frat House Cream* and *Fuck & Cum* in a way that suggests a distinct equivalence among the three), it appears anonymously—without identifying information of any kind—on a variety of piracy-driven porn aggregators, from those that specialize in "hipster" images (such as Hipster Gay Porn, Gay. Pop.Nerd, and Gay Hipster Porn Blog) to those that claim a wider range of representations (such as Only Gay Porn Vids, Damn Hot Gay Porn, and Gettin' It Up and Gettin' Off). Enveloped by such emphatically "porn-only" websites, *I Want Your Love* vividly demonstrates its extreme iconographic and narrative resemblance to what Stephen Holden terms its antithesis—the typical, gay-identified products of the porn industry. Consider, for instance, the film's anonymous presence on Only Dudes, a website whose tagline is "quality gay porn only," and whose logo is an erect pink penis: positioned between content culled from the websites Alpha Male Fuckers and Dirty Boy Video, Mathews's unnamed *I Want Your Love* seems neither more nor less "artistic," neither more nor less "cinematic"—and certainly neither more nor less *pornographic*—than *Hot Hairy Men: Dean and Duke* (2012) or *Fuck Him Deep* (2013). This is not to suggest that Mathews's film should be excluded from analysis as queer cinema. Rather, the point is that the internet in general—and the gay-identified, erotic blogosphere in particular—presents challenges to conventional theorizations of the relationships among queer cinema, its distribution streams and exhibition venues, and its audiences. Indeed, even the vast majority of scholarship on online spectatorship suggests that individual internet users are, without exception, consciously accessing queer films, contributing to the maintenance of fan cultures that centralize specific, well-defined titles. What happens, however, when a user encounters *I Want Your Love*—a little-known work whose commercial availability is relatively limited—only through its anonymous, pirated online appearances? This is precisely the kind of question that studies of queer cinema reception will need to address if they are to move beyond conventional critical models.[21]

While it remains difficult to gauge users' knowledge of media products that circulate illicitly and anonymously, it is indisputably the case that Mathews's *I Want Your Love* is more readily accessible as a pirated online video than as a

DVD. This is due not simply to the general conditions of access that make free online spectatorship far more "convenient" than authorized material playback (with its commercial underpinnings and multiple component parts). It is also because acquiring the *I Want Your Love* DVD requires knowledge of Naked Sword's participation in its production: the disc must be ordered through the company's website, a process that might further stymie those whose reluctance to be interpellated as porn consumers precludes their providing credit card information to porn websites. More than most contemporary queer films, *I Want Your Love*, which hasn't even had a life on Netflix, exists most prominently on the erotic blogosphere, and in ways that complicate its relationship to less "porny" cinematic products, as well as to familiar modes of film spectatorship.

In February 2013, perhaps motivated not simply by the film's graphic sexual representations but by their imbrication with online pornography, the Australian Classification Board banned *I Want Your Love* from the country's film-festival circuit—a decision that inspired a wide range of online protests, from James Franco's impassioned YouTube advocacy to a Change.org petition.[22] In Franco's YouTube video, which Mathews uploaded to the site in March 2013, the actor suggests that *I Want Your Love* is a film for "adults" perfectly capable of consenting to the public screening of sexual representations. Despite his reliance on language that has long governed public advocacy on behalf of pornographic films, Franco claims that *I Want Your Love* is "not pornography"—that it "uses sex not for titillation but to talk about being human." In the course of another contradictory argument, Franco suggests that sex should be honored, particularly through its on-screen representation, because it is "how we create children"—thus undermining his stated intention to uphold a non-procreative same-sex eroticism, a certain "queer" and anti-normative sexuality, as deserving of cultural esteem. If Franco failed in his bid to overturn the ban—the Australian Classification Board was notably unmoved by his advocacy—then he also failed to prevent the user-generated alignment of Mathews's film with online pornography. As of this writing—nearly three years after Mathews first uploaded it—Franco's YouTube video has received only 129,008 views; *I Want Your Love* has received almost five times as many in its pirated version on the website Porn MD (where it goes by its own name, but without information about Travis Mathews or queer cinema), and almost nine times as many on GayTube (where it is known only as "Hairy Hipsters Fucking"). Clearly, even an aggressively art-conscious celebrity intervention like Franco's cannot possibly prevent a film like *I Want Your Love*—or any audiovisual text, for that matter—from being enfolded into various, emphatically pornographic pockets of the internet, or from appealing to any one of a number of so-called "fetish communities." In the next section, I turn to those communities, and to their gay-identified online productions, as a way of further exploring the eroticized circulation of contemporary queer cinema. The fate of *I Want Your Love*—a film whose global festival run was curtailed through its associations with pornography, and that has been available online in a variety of pirated, explicitly porn-identified versions—is instructive. Mathews's aspirations may well have been, as Holden claims, "to take back gay sex" from the porn industry, but the erotic blogosphere has ensured that *I Want Your Love,* with its origins in that industry, will be returned to it, at least discursively, ad infinitum—money shots and all.

Fetishizing Queer Cinema

If *I Want Your Love* indeed satisfies a certain "hipster fetish," then the film's illicit availability on sites that cater to the so-called "hipster community" is far from surprising. However, the film's appearance on a number of more focused fetish sites—from those that trade in images of bare male feet to those whose icono-graphic contours consist of pirated shots of hairy male armpits—suggests impor-tant and unheralded pathways for a media archaeology of queer cinema. From a digital feature screened at North American film festivals to a pirated GayTube video to a series of still images of erect cocks compiled for a "dirty" Tumblr, *I Want Your Love* has enjoyed a multitude of online lives. In each case, however, it has represented not a cinematic incursion into certain well-defined spaces of reception but, rather, a text whose sexually explicit imagery has aided its trans-formation from a discrete film into a range of other, distinctly digital media prod-ucts. *I Want Your Love* didn't simply find a "home" on such websites as XVideos, Free Gay Porn, Only Dudes, Man Hub, and GayTube; it also helps to define—and has in the process *become*—those sites. Media archaeology can thus uncover not merely the discursive locations at which a film has been situated but also what, in generic and material terms, it has been. *I Want Your Love* has "been" GayTube inasmuch as its onetime appearance on the site was barely contextualized. Dubbed "Hairy Hipsters Fucking," and archived with the tags "anal," "bear fetish," and "amateur," *I Want Your Love* lost its identity as an art film—lost its auteur, Travis Mathews (whose name is not available on the site), and lost as well its non-erotic narrative "interludes." In order to identify it as a Travis Mathews film, a GayTube user must bring "outside" knowledge to the site—must recognize *I Want Your Love,* in excerpted form, as something available elsewhere, something "more" than just an audiovisual instantiation of the pleasures of anal sex. Had the film's "fuck scenes" been presented on GayTube as the hot parts of a plot-driven whole—as the erotically explicit nodes of a narrative feature film—then it would be considerably harder to say that *I Want Your Love* has "become" the site. The epistemological question that I posed at the beginning of this book—the ques-tion of how to determine the presence of a paratext in an age of constant digital distribution and "manic visual reinterpretation"—intensifies in urgency within the purviews of online pornography. Just as the digital age has dramatically destabilized the standard relationship between text and paratext, so too has it confounded efforts to locate a default site for gay spectatorships. What and where is *I Want Your Love*'s most "legitimate" edition? The feature-length film-festival version would seem, according to scholarly convention, to exceed all others, both generically and discursively—to be the "real" or "original" text against which all other versions are judged. And yet that site-specific form—the feature film scaled for festival inclusion—is no less ephemeral, no more "substantial," than pirated versions circulating online, and it is a near certainty that more people have seen *I Want Your Love* through illicit websites than at Outfest, Frameline36, and Inside Out combined. The question of what a queer film "is"—of what it represents taxonomically—is too complex for familiar film-studies approaches that would

The Gay Hipster Art Porn Flick That the Whole Internet Is Talking About

*Posted by **Brian O'Brien** in Uncategorized | **4 comments***

It seems that just about every blog has written something about "I Want Your Love," the verité porn project by director Travis Matthews. Now it's our turn because what we've seen so far is frankly amazing.

Figure 2.2. Calling it "the gay hipster art porn flick that the whole internet is talking about," the porn aggregator Fleshbot highlights the "hipster appeal" of Travis Mathews's *I Want Your Love* (2012), providing a link to Gay Hipster Porn Blog. April 2012.

privilege festival screenings over piracy-driven websites, and audiovisual "purity" over what Lucas Hilderbrand has so productively called "bootleg aesthetics."[23]

The argument with which I began this book—that web-enabled digital platforms and user-generated paratexts increasingly represent the inaugural rather than the eventual sites both for queer films and for their reception—is especially applicable to the frenzied operations of the erotic blogosphere. Within that sphere, fetish-oriented sites seem particularly attuned to the erotics of media representations—and particularly prone to uploading stills and clips of films well in advance of their release, and even ahead of their completion. On those (increasingly rare) occasions when a fetish-driven excerpt of queer cinema does *not* precede its source's theatrical release, it may still appear to supersede that source—to offer the only accessible version of a queer feature film. This is of course partly due to queer cinema's dramatically diminishing prospects for theatrical distribution, which B. Ruby Rich has so well documented: whatever one's predilections—even if one is like the Linda Williams who, in *Screening Sex,* confesses a preference for occupying a position "in a public place before [a] big screen" to sitting alone before a laptop—one cannot, if one is reliably connected to the internet, avoid encountering queer cinema online before finding it anywhere else.[24] Gay-identified fetish websites seem to ensure that queer films survive—particularly as erotic artifacts—in an age of few commercial opportunities for such works as Andrew Haigh's *Weekend* (2011), Haim Tabakman's *Eyes Wide Open* (2009), and Jean-Marc Vallée's *C.R.A.Z.Y.* (2005). All three of these films offer ample "eye candy" for gay fetishists—the first with its close-ups of bare male feet emerging from beneath bed sheets and becoming lovingly entwined, the second with its eroticized images of Orthodox Jews (part and parcel of all-male "Hasidic porn"), and the third with its gay protagonist's wide-eyed perspective on his sexy, polyester-clad, platform-shoe-wearing older brothers. Indeed, fetish-friendly images from these three films proliferate online—specifically on the gay-identified erotic blogosphere, on such sites as Best Gay Feet, Hipster Jew, and 70s Gay Porn Whore, respectively—to an extent that dramatically discredits the notion that, on the basis of their negligible box-office returns, low DVD sales, and scant viewership via various Video On Demand services, they are culturally inconspicuous.

Clearly, it is not so much that *Weekend* was widely seen in theaters (since its release was extremely limited, even by queer-cinema standards) or a "hit" on Netflix (where it has been streaming, off and on, since 2012), but that its visual attention to bare male feet makes it an ideal agent for enlivening user-generated, gay-identified foot-fetish websites, of which there are (at least) hundreds. Unlike the pirated versions of *I Want Your Love* that fail to identify the film—that rely on a generalized "pornographic" rubric, aggregating anything and everything that offers images of unsimulated male-male sex—gay-identified fetish websites tend to function in a more overtly archival capacity, offering new and clearly defined pathways for the analysis of queer cinema reception, erotically inflecting the scholarly model of "active audiences," proponents of which have only recently (and only tepidly and tentatively) begun to consider online platforms. Fetish websites tend to demonstrate the use-value of contemporary queer cinema in ways that should not be discounted, and that stand to contribute to our understanding of the structuring of spectatorial desire. Instead of "stealing a film's thunder"—and perhaps erasing its prestige—by pirating and "rebranding" it, as in the examples cited in the previous section, gay-identified foot-fetish websites tend to annotate the appropriated images on which they rely, conceivably promoting queer cinema by highlighting its pleasurable visual contours. In fact, a vast number of the creators of these websites self-identify in precisely this fashion—as "bona fide film fans" who "find what's worth sharing" about contemporary queer cinema, including and especially its fetish-friendly images. Such practices don't simply spell out the libidinal appeal of queer cinema through the use of digital tools and online sharing; they also shed considerable light upon the intertextuality of eroticism and the formal structuring of desire. "Erotic response," argues Peter Lehman, "is shaped by form, and we should pay careful attention to the manner in which any single film or video scene or even moment within a scene is represented in regards to lighting, camera position, cutting patterns, and so forth." Writing in the wake of the publication of Linda Williams's seminal *Hard Core,* Lehman's intention was to advocate for a careful, sustained formal analysis of the structuring of desire. There is to my mind no better way of understanding this structuring, and how it operates within the boundaries of queer cinema reception, than by examining gay-identified fetish websites. I am not attempting an exhaustive account of these sites or of their characteristic practices; instead, I am using foot fetishism as a case study in my effort to uncover fresh media archaeological approaches to queer cinema on the internet.[25]

Consider, for instance, the case of the queer film *The Paperboy* (Lee Daniels, 2012), in which the actor Zac Efron frequently flexes his bare feet for the camera, in shots that have been libidinously excerpted across the blogosphere—and perhaps most memorably on BuzzFeed, where gay writer Louis Peitzman provided a cheeky feature entitled "The 25 Hottest Zac Efron GIFs From 'The Paperboy,'" promising the user that these short, extractive media "will save you the energy of fast-forwarding. And now you don't have to watch *The Paperboy*."[26] An undisputed icon of the gay-identified foot-fetish community—a conventionally handsome young man who once insisted on wearing flip-flops to film premieres, and whose bare feet played a prominent part in the *High School Musical* franchise (2006–2008)—Efron further endeared himself to that community by parodying his own, pronounced fetishistic appeal on *Saturday Night Live*. As the host of an episode that aired on April 11, 2009, Efron appeared in a foot-fetish sketch in which *SNL* cast member Jason Sudeikis (playing Efron's "weird" brother) rubbed and oiled Efron's feet, and proceeded to suck the young man's toes. Galvanizing the gay-identified blogosphere, the sketch was immediately pirated and uploaded to YouTube, embedded on a range of user-generated sites, and swiftly suppressed by NBCUniversal, which claimed that the video's online presence violated copyright. While the disciplinary removal of a pirated YouTube video is plainly par for the course, particularly when *Saturday Night Live* is involved, what happened next was less predictable: NBC eliminated the sketch from the full *SNL* episode's downloadable iTunes version, raising the distinct and unpalatable possibility that homophobia—in this instance, a fear of fetishistic same-sex eroticism—had precipitated the decision.[27] Banned from NBC.com, the sketch has since appeared in places where corporate powers, anti-porn crusaders, and media scholars are perhaps equally unlikely to look: user-generated foot-fetish websites, where the sketch now enjoys a prominence that both archives an officially suppressed media product and serves to illustrate—and quite possibly produce—a particular gay-identified fetish.

More than just a fixation on feet propels this "pornographic" pirating of a suppressed *SNL* sketch. Since NBC's decision to excise it from all commercially available versions of the Efron episode (the twentieth episode of the series' thirty-fourth season), considerable debate has swirled throughout the gay-identified blogosphere, culminating in powerfully articulated complaints about the network's apparent "double standards"—the way in which it labors to retain and promote straight-oriented erotic jokes while inhibiting their gay-identified counterparts. The first publication to put forth an explanation for the sketch's sudden disappearance, and to link that disappearance to corporate homophobia, was the *New York Daily News,* which wasted no space in suggesting that NBC was suddenly "in hot water over Zac Efron's *Saturday Night Live* appearance," having apparently capitulated to internal objections. For the *Daily News,* the obvious explanation for the sketch's suppression was that it represented "a kinky foot-fetish scene in which cast member Jason Sudeikis seductively sucked Efron's toes."[28] Taking a similar approach, a variety of gay-identified blogs—from Queerty to Just Jared—suggested that something unseemly was behind NBC's decision to conceal evidence of having aired a sketch in which "Jason Sudeikis eats Zac Efron's foot." In a post entitled "Why Did NBC Yank Zac Efron's Foot Fetish Video From the Entire Internet?" Queerty wryly observed, "Looks like anyone out there with a fetish for Zac Efron's feet will have to go digging through a media vault somewhere." Instructively, Queerty often advocates precisely this tactic, deploying the language of media archaeology in order to exhort visitors to "excavate the internet for clips"—and, moreover, to search vast mediascapes in order to locate content that can be digitized and thus uploaded to various websites (like Queerty

The 25 Hottest Zac Efron GIFs From "The Paperboy"

This will save you the energy of fast-forwarding. And now you don't have to watch *The Paperboy*.

posted on Jan. 10, 2013, at 6:53 p.m.

Louis Peitzman
BuzzFeed Staff

Follow 2.3k   **Follow**

f   y   ✉   ⓟ   g+

1.

ohnopurple.tumblr.com

Figure 2.3. Upholding the GIF as a superior lens through which to engage with contemporary queer cinema, BuzzFeed argues that its own Efron archive "will save you the energy of fast-forwarding"—thus presupposing gay-identified Efron fetishism as the sole reason for seeing *The Paperboy* (Lee Daniels, 2012).

itself). Queerty's exhortations to users to "scour the internet" for evidence of gay desire—and of suppressed or forgotten representations thereof—is key to understanding the archival significance of fetish websites. Instructively, Queerty consistently refuses multiple forms of inhibition, from the "moral" to the juridical—from, that is, those that would avoid reviving "objectionable" media to those that would assiduously honor copyright claims. In the name of queer desire—a desire most often reduced to an admittedly "vanilla" gay male eroticism—Queerty advocates the excavation, digital preservation, and online dissemination of "yesterday's representations," particularly those that that can "prove" the persistent cultural presence of heterosexism and homophobia, but also of libidinous resistance to various straight constructions. When John Cameron Mitchell, promoting the Broadway revival of his play *Hedwig and the Angry Inch* in early

2014, claimed that David Letterman once refused to shake his hand during a taping of *The Late Show* in 1998, Queerty immediately tasked its gay-identified visitors with finding visual evidence of such an apparently homophobic refusal. Under the banner of interactivity—of an avowed "give and take" between producers and consumers of Web content—Queerty thus outsourced the media archaeological labors that it identifies as so vitally necessary to the online maintenance of gay subjectivities.[29]

Tellingly, after issuing its instructions to visitors, the website typically offers its own, preferred media archaeological methods—methods that conceivably shape the efforts of users, thus serving a determinative function. Having failed to discover a clip or a single still image of Mitchell's appearance on *The Late Show,* Queerty—after asking visitors to perform the labors of media archaeology in the service of the site, and with the implicit promise that their findings might end up prominently and appreciatively displayed there—simply, as usual, archived erotic images of male stars as a means of "celebrating queerness." While ostensibly waiting for gay-identified media archaeologists to "do their thing"—to, that is, locate and revive "dead media"—Queerty seemed content to perform an archaeology of its own, curating Instagram images of reality TV star Dan Osborne "getting naked," as well as older pics of "sexy vintage men in skimpy swimsuits." Describing a series of digitized images from a period spanning the 1920s to the 1980s, Queerty wrote, "We thought we'd take a trip back in time and dig up old photos of hot guys from decades past sporting skimpy swimwear." This particular mode of eroticized media archaeology—a mode that Queerty appears to prefer as a means of generating "original," "exclusive" content—would seem to have structured user responses to the website's various archaeological requests, such as the one that centralizes the political significance of "digging up" evidence of David Letterman's alleged "snub" of John Cameron Mitchell. If no such evidence has materialized as of this writing, then that is perhaps because, following Queerty's lead, users of the site have been generating content that the site seems to favor, despite its occasionally more radical exhortations—content not dissimilar from the examples of "beefcake" cited above. This includes numerous images of gay actor Neil Patrick Harris (star of the 2014 Broadway revival of Mitchell's *Hedwig and the Angry Inch*) vacationing with his husband David Burtka—images that expose the men's bare chests, bare legs, and especially bare feet.

Erotic archaeologies of queer cinema, such as those displayed on foot-fetish websites, may seem indistinguishable from the images of Harris and Burtka that appear on Queerty, but they tend to reveal more than just the beauty of men's bare soles. They also revive queer media that may not be widely available, in the process archiving the formal devices that feed gay fetishes. When, for instance, Zac Efron Barefoot Photos, a "spinoff" of the website Male Star Feet, provided a

MEDIA MYSTERIES

Why Did NBC Yank Zac Efron's Foot Fetish Video From the Entire Internet?

🐦 Share on Twitter   **f** Share on Facebook   ✉ Email   💬 Comments (7)

Figure 2.4. Promoting queer media archaeology: Queerty encourages visitors to "go digging through a media vault somewhere" in order to archive the commercially unavailable "Foot Rub" (2009).

photomontage that included images from the *High School Musical* franchise as well as "Foot Rub"—that, in fact, placed those images side by side—it suggested more than just their general iconographic similarities. It also illustrated the way those similarities were formally structured—through, in this case, the frontal shooting of Efron's feet from a slightly low angle, and with a lighting pattern that throws the soles into stark relief. When the website began incorporating shots of Efron's feet as framed by *The Paperboy*, it brought all three sources together under a rubric of gay-identified foot fetishism, suggesting not simply a definite, star-driven representational trend, but also its culmination in queer cinema. After all, *The Paperboy* is perhaps prototypically queer, from its openly gay auteur to its narrative's kinky same-sex erotic encounters, and the way in which it frames Efron's bare feet seems especially gratuitous—pleasurably so, as many a foot fetishist could attest.

A vast number of archived, digital *Paperboy* paratexts are thus part of the fabric of online, user-generated, gay-identified foot fetishism. To Google the search terms "Paperboy" and "gay" is, as of this writing, to uncover two general modes of gay-identified reception: those that centralize, and condemn, the fact that Matthew McConaughey plays an allegedly "self-loathing," semi-closeted, bondage-obsessed gay man in Daniels's film, and those that uphold Efron's bare feet—so unusually prominent in *The Paperboy*—as meeting some of the scopic needs of gay foot fetishists, satisfying their desire to see, as one popular Tumblr puts it, "tasty boy soles."[30] That the latter mode of reception far outnumbers the former, at least in terms of archived instances of user-generated production, signals the importance of turning to unusual online repositories—in this case, the kinds of websites that might easily be dismissed as frivolous, meaningless, or merely in the minority, but that (evoking Nick Davis's productive approach in *The Desiring-Image*) privilege the formal patterning of gay desire rather than the concern with "good versus bad" representations so typical of visibility politics. To put it another way, and to cite specific examples, when writer Eddie Scarry complained, on the blog Fishbowl DC, that McConaughey's character is a "self-loathing gay man"—the latest in a long line of "bad" and "embarrassing" cinematic ambassadors of male homosexuality—he did little to shed light on the aesthetic properties of *The Paperboy*; by contrast, when the gay-identified foot-fetish websites Heavenly Soles, Gay Foot Blog, Best Gay Feet, and Foot Slave 17 (among many, many more) archived screenshots of Daniels's film, they managed to shed considerable light on the formal and narrative logics by which Efron's character could emerge as so ripe for fetishistic appreciation.[31] In other words, such sites, through their tendency to assimilate clips and screenshots, serve a distinct pedagogical purpose: rather than suggesting that their creators have somehow managed to *produce* fetishistic appeal by excerpting, freezing, and uploading "throwaway" moments from major motion pictures, they in fact demonstrate how desire—even a doubly "niche" desire like gay foot fetishism—is formally structured in contemporary queer cinema. Whenever openly gay director Lee Daniels was asked to address his film's alleged objectification of Efron—and he was asked to address it in virtually every professional interview during the course of promotion—he answered by invoking the subconscious processes by which erotic desire frequently finds visual expression. By isolating and disseminating such expressions, gay-identified foot-fetish websites respect their underlying psychic mechanisms—the patterns that produce what Thomas Waugh has called "the iconographies of desires."[32] Indeed, if we are to take cinematic eroticism remotely seriously, then we must also acknowledge, investigate, and contextualize websites where users can extract, expand, and expound upon that eroticism—however "niche" or fetishistic it may be. The material and conceptual conditions of Pink 2.0, which tend to promote the production of paratexts for libidinal pleasure, transform fetish websites into key sources of imagery that would otherwise go unnoticed, and that, as the case of Efron's *SNL* appearance attests, is often suppressed through "official" circuits.

Digital Equivalences

In a discussion of the 1995 film version of Vito Russo's seminal *The Celluloid Closet,* directed by Rob Epstein and Jeffrey Friedman, Heather Love draws attention to the potentially traumatizing way in which the film assimilates clips from a wide variety of queer-themed productions, the vast majority of which offer alarmingly offensive figurations of queer life and desire. Love suggests that the only way for such aggregated film clips to counteract rather than enforce "a trauma of queer spectatorship"—a trauma centered on painfully stereotyped or otherwise misguided representations—is to provide "layered historical and personal contexts," a multidirectional and deeply resistant commentary.[33] The interviews that Epstein and Friedman conduct, and that for Love evince the significance of those "knowing subjects [who] speak over and against" outrageously retrograde images, offer crucial counterbalances to what otherwise would serve merely to browbeat—to regulate queer identities through exclusively pathologizing patterns. What happens, however, when queer images proliferate beyond the boundaries of resistant interventions, and seem to lose all cultural and historical context—when, that is, they turn up online, and without explicit identification or any remotely exegetical clues?

In turning to the piracy-driven contexts of online pornography, I mean to suggest some of the avenues through which film stills and clips—both attributed and unattributed—appear to be reduced to a gay male eroticism, and thereby aligned with multiple modes of gay porn. This is not to say that images lifted from feature films, and subsequently uploaded to pornographic video-sharing sites, necessarily "become" pornography—as if proximity to hardcore clips were sufficient for generic transformation. But proximity plainly matters, particularly when websites juxtapose cinema and cyberporn, implicitly positioning the former as part of the fabric of the latter, and thus producing a new, if hardly obvious or authorized, point of entry for the study of queer cinema reception on the internet. My intention is not to suggest that this is a one-way process of "contamination"—as if *only* cyberporn could possibly "pollute" queer cinema, or as if "art" were by definition unable to "infect" and thus profoundly influence one's thoughts about pornography. I also, as those scare quotes should make clear, want to move away from the binarism of basic qualitative distinctions, which tends to militate against respect for (or even recognition of) the complex intermixing of licensed and pirated, commercial and amateur, and cinema and pornography that I take to be characteristic of the gay-identified erotic blogosphere.

Roland Barthes's theory of the "third meaning" is especially useful here, in that it describes the effect of the "ultimate layer" of signification of an image—that which intellect "cannot quite absorb," nor conventional classification master. Barthes's theory would seem to inform, or at least resonate with, Linda

Williams's take on the complex interplay between Hollywood cinema and hardcore porn—the "sublime" and thus difficult-to-describe points at which the two modes of moviemaking intersect. Writing of the extent to which, in narrative pornography produced in the wake of *Deep Throat* (Jerry Gerard/Gerard Damiano, 1972), spectacular scenes of penetration evoke the equally spectacular "explosions" of song and dance in classical Hollywood musicals, Williams encourages a reading of spectacle that resists yet acknowledges the surrounding logics of narrative, that respects what Barthes sees as the tendency of the "third meaning" to "structure the film *differently* without . . . subverting the story."[34] Indeed, while his focus is on stills of Eisenstein's films, and not on Hollywood musical or hardcore "numbers," Barthes seems to anticipate Williams when he writes that the third meaning "is the epitome of a counternarrative"—that which resists conventional or even conscious interpretation, functioning as a disguise in plain view. Like the decidedly fantastical (but not entirely "unmotivated") musical number, and like the "sublime" fuck scenes that punctuate the perfunctory plots of post-1960s narrative pornography, the "third meaning," for Barthes, "transcends psychology, anecdote, function."[35] Furthermore, and in a way that helps to describe the powerful online presence of largely unattributed, constantly intersecting forms of cinema and cyberporn, the "third meaning" is "both persistent and fugitive, apparent and evasive." Indeed, the relative ease of producing and circulating digital clips of feature films makes such clips seem, like the operations of Pink 2.0 more generally, both everywhere and nowhere—both "obvious" and all but indecipherable. Indeed, as the internet makes all too evident, omnipresence does not guarantee transparency; in fact, it may preempt it, particularly when practices of piracy render attribution—the relationship between text and paratext, producer and consumer—difficult indeed.

In addressing the relative seamlessness of digital fan productions—those that rely upon new, user-friendly technologies and that, as a result, frequently blur distinctions between original and copy—it is important to reflect upon previous forms of fan production, particularly those that sought to "queer" conventional cinema through "imperfect," analog means. If the commercially motivated, culturally embraced "perfection" of digital technologies makes it remarkably difficult to perceive the differences between, say, a film's official and fan trailers, or between an authorized montage sequence and its illicit reinterpretation, then the inevitable degradations of now-defunct analog formats often, during their heyday, telegraphed the amateur or simply bootleg dimensions of user-generated productions. Indeed, their very materiality tended to vividly distinguish paratext from text, copy from original—or, for that matter, copy from copy. In Cecilia Barriga's justly celebrated compilation tape *Meeting of Two Queens* (1991), the visible distortions of VHS duplication make it especially easy to see the differences not simply between original and copy but also between the component parts—in this case, the "pirated" Hollywood scenes—of a paratextual whole. Barriga famously interweaves the screen performances of legendary "dykons" Marlene Dietrich and Greta Garbo, fusing, at one point, Dietrich's *Dishonored* (Josef von Sternberg, 1931) and Garbo's *Queen Christina* (Rouben Mamoulian, 1933) into a shot/reverse-shot set-up that suggests that the stars are about to fuck. Yet Barriga first recorded *Dishonored* and *Queen Christina* onto two separate VHS tapes—tapes that experienced inevitably differential material lives and that, when brought together for Barriga's compilation, couldn't help but expose their separateness, even after they were both transferred to a single "master" cassette.[36] Lucas Hilderbrand has examined the "authoring" potential of analog degradation—what he calls a determinative "bootleg aesthetics"—and it seems clear both from his analysis and from Barriga's videotape that the materiality of "old" media tends to resist the kind of iconographic homogeneity that we so often see (or, at least, *think* we see) online— and especially on piracy-driven websites that rely upon equally digital productions, both in cinema and cyberporn.[37]

Indeed, if the showpiece sex scene from *I Want Your Love* looks astonishingly like a similar scene from the porn website Randy Blue, then that is because both were shot using equivalent digital equipment. The "visible grain" that so many hipster filmmakers fetishize in celluloid cinema, protesting what they perceive to be the iconographic homogeneity of the "digital turn," is as unavailable on the majority of online porn aggregators as the tape-based distortions of Barriga's *Meeting of Two Queens,* further complicating efforts to distinguish between cinema and cyberporn. The popular Gay Hipster Porn Blog, which purports to offer "a (usually nude) view into the world of real queer men," is as committed as Travis Mathews to privileging an exclusive homosexuality among mostly white males, and its pirated compilations consistently evoke the filmmaker's own images, in terms both of their human subjects (young, urban hipsters) and formal features (high-quality digital renderings of hairy chests and circumcised cocks bathed in natural light and set against the backdrop of beige bed sheets). It was thus unsurprising when the website furnished unattributed images of *I Want Your Love,* placing them alongside the kinds of Instagram selfies whose filters mimic Mathews's visual style (or is it the other way around?). Stills of Mathews's film (typically user-generated screenshots, but sometimes actual production stills lifted from the film's official website) are no less likely than moving-image clips to "fit" with the original (i.e., non-pirated) content of Gay Hipster Porn Blog and other such popular sites. That is precisely because these sites prominently feature moving-image entries that seem, in many ways, indistinguishable. After all, there are only so many ways of shooting two hairy, muscular, sexually unadventurous white men who roll across queen-sized beds while bounded by stacks of vinyl records—even, I would add, when relying, like Mathews, on advanced digital equipment. The conventionalized hipster aesthetic (even among gay men) often militates against the central promises of digital technologies—their inherent and increasingly irreverent manipulability—precisely by being so self-consciously, dogmatically beholden to a retro minimalism, to the very nostalgia symbolized by vinyl and other antiquated material objects. Paradoxically, however, the modern hipster fetishizes the "old" while frequently announcing such fetishism through the "new"—by, say, blogging about cassette tapes, or simply by using digital technologies, such as Instagram filters, to produce an approximation of Autochrome photography, a simulacrum of the analog past.

At the same time that this hipster minimalism coexists anachronistically with its digital representation, the hegemony of advanced technologies makes it ever more difficult to find, on the internet, evidence of certain media archaeological practices—the kinds typified, in fact, by the very hipsters who seek to "keep vinyl alive." Digitization doesn't exactly eliminate analog distortions; rather, it tends to preserve them, as anyone who has seen a particularly grainy, bootlegged YouTube version of Barriga's *Meeting of Two Queens,* or of Todd Haynes's suppressed *Superstar: The Karen Carpenter Story* (1987), can attest. But presupposing the visibility of analog origins, and interpreting such visibility as evidence of the "pastness" or "authenticity" of a particular digitized object, doesn't help us to distinguish between those practices of media archaeology that seek to revive official film trailers for online circulation and the illicit fan productions that represent purely user-generated (yet still often generic) audiovisual entrées into contemporary feature films. As of this writing, to type "Brokeback Mountain trailer" into YouTube's search engine is to discover a series of videos of roughly the same length, each evincing a professional editing style as well as "clean" sound and crisp visuals—videos whose formal and generic contours seem, therefore, equally reflective of a typical film-trailer style. So which one is the "real thing"—which, in other words, is the *original* theatrical trailer of *Brokeback Mountain*? Only a few such videos are helpfully, textually identified as "alternative" or "re-cut" versions of the film's official trailer (the one that screened in mainstream movie theaters across the United States in the fall of 2005). By contrast, those that go without much identification—that are tagged only with the search terms "Brokeback" and "trailer," and that include audiovisual elements that seem reasonably trailer-like—do not immediately announce themselves as strictly user-generated productions, and thus could easily be confused for that often-elusive "real thing." When dealing with pristine digital images whose professionalism seems indisputable, how might one tell the authorized from the pirated—the original from the imitation, the official from the amateur?

That such questions are often difficult to answer does not mean that we should ignore those archives that consistently blur distinctions, challenge assumptions, and thwart traditional analytic tools. In fact, we should work ever harder to trace the trajectories of media objects in the digital age, understanding that in many cases we may well be examining the online dissemination not of a digitization of, say, a celluloid original, but of a completely reedited, radically recontextualized copy of a copy of a copy—one that is several technological generations removed from a "foundational" text, but that may, given its formal coherence, hardly seem thus. I myself learned this lesson the hard way: preparing an essay on the exhibition history of *Brokeback Mountain*—a history that I thought I knew so well, given the time and labor that I had devoted to tracking it—I decided to provide a brief analysis of the film's original theatrical trailer. Believing that I clearly remembered that trailer, having seen it play in theaters prior to the screening of seemingly countless films from *Jarhead* (Sam Mendes, 2005) to *Rent* (Chris Columbus, 2005), I resolved to confirm my recollections by watching it on YouTube. What I searched for was the original theatrical trailer for *Brokeback Mountain*; what I got, and what I watched, was something entirely different—though close enough in tone and in style that I naïvely took it to be the real thing. It was only after watching the original theatrical trailer on my official *Brokeback Mountain* DVD that I realized the mistake that I had made: the YouTube version that I had watched was purely user-generated—a fan creation lovingly and seamlessly stitched together from pristine digital clips of the film, beginning with Ennis anxiously awaiting Jack's arrival after years of separation (a scene that, in fact, appears toward the end of the official trailer) and proceeding to showcase moments that the user in question ("David Moya") took to be the most important.[38] I had been duped—usefully so, since the experience reinforced for me the dangers of accepting digital, audiovisual search results at face value, as if their sophisticated trappings are necessarily evidence of any authorized or "official" status. Indeed, fan production in the digital age forces us to reconsider longstanding assumptions about the aura of the amateur—about the allegedly perceptible residues of illicit or resistant creations, those material traces of "negotiation" so beloved of cultural studies. The point is not that YouTube represents an unacceptable source of research materials—a "bad," quasi-archival object to be avoided at all costs—but that the practices that it accommodates are far more diverse than conventional assumption might allow, marking the site as a place where "original" artifacts are profoundly if imperceptibly alterable, and where text and paratext are potentially indistinguishable.

A similar epistemological conundrum inevitably structures the user's experience of porn aggregators and fetish websites, where textual identification is rarely so explicit or so reliable as to provide clear delineations between pirated content and original productions—between images of bare male feet that come from *I Want Your Love* and those whose provenance is the cluttered bedroom of a real-life, iPhone-wielding, narcissistic hipster. The gay-identified foot fetishist may well want to know more about the source of a particularly stimulating image or clip—may well want to find out for himself if it has any close commercial kin, any surrounding stills or scenes that are aesthetically and erotically similar. Since registered users can comment on—and thus "interact with"—any Tumblr whose manager allows the function (and most do across the gay-identified, foot-fetish blogosphere), such users can also ask questions about the sources of the still images and clips that appear on sites like Cute Guy Feet and Foot Slave 17. In many cases, these questions represent attempts to ascertain identifying information about an image that is much liked and widely circulated within the fetish community—not for the purpose of "proving" or of policing piracy but instead as part of an explicit effort to extend and sustain erotic pleasure. When, in March 2014, the blog Best Gay Feet uploaded a screenshot of a barefoot Marc Blucas, it identified the image only by the actor's name, prompting users to pose pressing questions: Was the image derived from a film or a television show? If so, what film or television show? Is this the only such image of Blucas's bare feet, or are there other media scenes in which he shows off his "hot soles" while spread, shirtless and seductive, across an unmade bed? In this case, clarifying information was supplied not by the administrator of Best Gay Feet but by dozens of other self-identified fetishists who re-blogged the image on their own respective sites, demonstrating their media archaeological prowess in excavating not simply the title and year of release of the image's cinematic source—John Sayles's 2002 film *Sunshine State*—but also material copies that they promptly pirated and uploaded to the internet, proving that the answer to the oft-asked question "Does the source contain other images of Blucas's feet?" is a resounding and libidinous "Yes."

It may be overly simplistic to suggest that narrative—what Williams describes in terms of a "classical" unfolding of events, of a typical temporality of linear progression and clear causal relations—has given way to brief clips devoid of context, thus returning "the frenzy of the visible" to its pre-narrative origins, to the short "story-free" bursts of optical content made possible by the earliest technologies of moving-image production. Within such a reading, the presently popular (indeed, practically omnipresent) GIF would work like Muybridge's zoopraxiscope, making visible the mechanics of movement by isolating a circumscribed set of optical "data," such as that which presents a horse at full gallop—or a cock achieving full erection.[39] It is instructive that the zoopraxiscope has itself received the GIF treatment—virally so, as evidenced by the popularity of particular digital versions of Muybridge's original spinning discs, such as those archived on Giphy and various Tumblrs. (In a further indication of the way the GIF functions anachronistically as a metonym for Muybridge's zoopraxiscope, Wikipedia's definition of the latter includes an example of the former—a digital simulation of a spinning disc that it presents as a pedagogic entrée into Muybridge's work.) "[I]f Muybridge's first audiences came simply to learn the new truths of bodily motion," writes Williams, "they stayed to see more because this new knowledge was also infused with an unsuspected visual pleasure"—with, that is, "the appeal of seeing . . . nearly naked [human] bodies." For Williams, the case study of the "typical" zoopraxiscope spectator, who exhibited such a keen fascination with the human form, offers "an illustration of Foucault's point that the power exerted over bodies *in* technology is rendered pleasurable *through* technology."[40] Similarly, what I refer to throughout this book as a "dirty GIF"—having borrowed the term from the gay-identified blog His Dirty Little Secret—is in fact a major yet understudied means through which contemporary digital media both satisfy libidinal desire and promote what Foucault calls "the knowledge of pleasure." The seemingly simple but actually immensely complex dirty GIF, even more than the hardcore film and video pornography that so interests Williams, represents a form of what she, following Foucault, describes as "the 'knowledge-pleasure' of sexuality"—a form that inflames both desire and a conscious awareness thereof, that tempts both libido and cognition.[41]

It is in this sense that the GIF, like the Vine, functions as a sexual script. Introduced at the height of the gay liberation movement by the sociologists John H. Gagnon and William Simon, and further developed by the psychiatrist Robert Stoller, the concept of the sexual script refers, in Chris Straayer's words, to "a condensed story representing an individual's sexual desire."[42] The sexual script is thus a "microdot": "a highly compressed and encoded system of information out of which can be read—by one who knows how to read it—the history of a person's psychic life."[43] This emphasis on readability is crucial to the function of GIFs, Vines, and other extractive media online: for those inclined to read them as erotic, these media operate as powerful agents of community building, inspiring and sustaining networks of users who define as fetishists (whether of the cinematic image as such or of the bodily techniques, behavioral practices, and inanimate objects depicted therein). At the same time, however, these erotic dimensions may be unreadable to others—unavailable to the "semiotically incompetent"—and thus unlikely to attract the kind of censorial attention that might lead to a moralizing, copyright-driven crackdown.[44] Such is the case, for instance, with GIFs, Vines, and brief YouTube clips in which the actor Paul Bettany, clad in the trappings of rough trade for his role as "white trash" in the family film *The Secret Life of Bees* (Gina Prince-Bythewood, 2008), cruelly crushes a cockroach with one of his filthy cowboy boots as the culmination of a scene of fatherly sadism. Barely readable to some users—except, perhaps, as an example of the altogether disagreeable capacity of digital networks to "unthinkingly" upload and circulate anything and everything, including representations of seemingly mundane actions like bug crushing—such media are immensely meaningful to others. As illustrations of their sexual fetishes, they are also useful tools for the satisfaction of erotic desires—masturbation aids far easier to access, perhaps, than previous, now-archaic sources that required the use of, say, TV, VCR, VHS cassette, and remote control.

By cyclically presenting a particular motion—by offering what is known as a "simple animation," or a low-resolution digital video clip that plays on a loop—the GIF can provide a gesture whose constant recurrence lends itself to comedy (as in so-called reaction GIFs that condense quirky visual jokes, replaying them over and over again) as well as to pornography (as in dirty GIFs whose sources run the gamut from porn websites to "hot" Hollywood dramas). "The slow frame-per-second rate of these animated GIFs," argues Lisa Nakamura, "produces a slow, deliberate quality in the user's gaze that draws attention to the use of slides to represent a whole body."[45] By slowing down discrete physical gestures and then replaying them ad infinitum, GIFs atomize erotic representations within the idiom of the moving image. The unique, unmistakable form of the GIF lends itself particularly well to visual imaging practices that attempt to outline certain equivalences—especially erotic ones—between ostensibly discrepant media productions. The blog Get Gay GIFs is exemplary in the way that it parses both pornography and "clean," mainstream, straight-identified productions, combining simple (re)animations of "hot men" (culled from sites like Sean Cody and Corbin Fisher) and similarly "GIF-ified" clips from television commercials, like one for Kraft's Zesty Italian salad dressing, which features a conventionally handsome, heavily muscled male model who literally loses his shirt while preparing vegetables. GIF versions of, say, blow jobs are simultaneously pleasurable and pedagogic in ways that may seem rather obvious: restricting the act of fellatio to a single, persistent physical gesture—the movement of a mouth as it envelopes an erect penis—GIFs of *Jeffrey Blowing Brock* (whose source is Sean Cody) replay the visual pleasures of oral sex and, in so doing, become effectively instructional through repetition. For someone hoping to extend the visual appeal of a pornographic commonplace, what could be hotter than a GIF that sustains a close-up of cock sucking—of, specifically, lips that part in order to "devour" a penis? For someone hoping to learn how to give just such a blowjob, what could be better than a GIF that, because "simple" and cyclical, can serve as a moving-image manual, one whose steps are clear (albeit limited by the format's palate of 256 colors) and recurrent? What is perhaps most valuable about Get Gay GIFs is that the site—like a whole host of similarly gay-identified, GIF-driven blogs—places porn GIFs alongside productions whose pleasurable and pedagogic potential may seem less obvious.

Consider, for instance, the aforementioned Kraft commercial, which Get Gay GIFs explicitly recasts as "gay porn"—even though, as an advertisement intended for network television broadcasting, it of course contains no nudity whatsoever. The original version of the commercial begins with a male model removing his suit coat and addressing the camera by saying, in a low, seductive voice, "Ladies, let's make a salad." A parody of cooking shows that lean on beefcake, the commercial reproduces the typical terms of address of those shows, positing a straight female viewer eager to combine her culinary and erotic interests. On Get Gay GIFs, however, the commercial loses its aural elements, becoming a strictly visual representation—and one that, because entirely silent, and thus detached from its original heterocentric narration, can easily be recuperated as soft-core "gay porn" (much in the manner in which, back in 2003, a *G.I. Joe* PSA could be transformed into "Mr. LaFitte"). Without the spoken address to "ladies," and in transfigured, easily embeddable GIF form, the commercial can seem clearly oriented to gay male desires. By giving him "the GIF treatment," Get Gay GIFs turns "The Zesty Guy" (as model Anderson Davis has come to be known) into a form of gay-identified "knowledge-pleasure."[46] It does this partly by placing his GIF version next to those produced through the pirating of gay porn, thus illuminating the pronounced physical resemblance between Davis and various "adult" stars, as well as the equally striking congruence between the Kraft commercial's objectifying formal elements (including close-ups of glistening pectoral and abdominal muscles) and those of, say, *Randy & Ryder: Bareback* (as pirated from the porn website Sean Cody).

If a GIF can vividly align something as seemingly innocuous as a Kraft commercial with hardcore gay porn, then it can also suggest iconographic and discursive connections between art films and such sites as Lads Next Door, Hot Older Male, and Spank Buddy. In the early months of 2014, the gay-identified erotic blogosphere—typified by sites like Get Gay GIFs, Bacon Bits, and Another Blog That Nobody Reads—embraced numerous ways of graphically engaging with the French film *Stranger by the Lake,* which famously (perhaps even infamously) contains multiple meat and money shots. At a time when *another* French film, *Blue Is the Warmest Color* (Abdellatif Kechiche, 2013), was inspiring widespread debate about its use of prosthetic vaginas during a much-publicized "lesbian" sex scene, *Stranger by the Lake* galvanized viewers to evaluate its use of "real penises"—its images of unsimulated same-sex erotic contact. As was widely reported in the mainstream press in Europe and the United States, *Stranger by the Lake* employs body doubles to "bear the burden" of unsimulated sexual representation, sparing its actors not simply the discomfort of pornographically enacting various scenarios, but also the awkwardness of operating the kind of prosthetic penis that one cast member dismissed as akin to "a [gear] stick in a car." Indeed, the actor Christophe Paou, who plays a murderous, muscled-and-mustachioed object of collective obsession in this film about the goings-on at a gay cruising spot (southern France's Lac de Sainte-Croix), complained to *Empire* magazine about the "false ejaculations and false phallus" that first characterized the shoot, and that were later discarded in favor of "porn doubles."

By digitally interweaving the embodied performances of art-film actors with those of porn stars, *Stranger by the Lake* concretizes the kind of confluence that is at the center of this chapter. That does not mean, however, that the film has managed to preempt online attempts to further align it with "pure pornography." In fact, the meat and money shots that embellish the image track of *Stranger by the Lake,* and that would appear to vividly confirm the film's connections to hardcore pornography, are perhaps more likely than "chaste" representations to inspire the kind of online labor that attempts, through piracy and other practices, to "prove" the imbrication of contemporary queer cinema and porn websites. Rather than doing the "dirty-minded" fan's work for him—incorporating "porn shots" so that he won't have to—*Stranger by the Lake* astutely sets itself up for eroticized online analysis. It does this partly by adopting erotic tropes and formal devices honed across countless gay-porn websites, thus inviting considerable curiosity about its multiple online counterparts. If *Stranger by the Lake* embraces the erotic trajectory that famously typifies the wildly popular European gay-porn site Bel Ami—a trajectory in which a medium two-shot of shirtless, shoeless, side-by-side lounging gives way to close-ups of anal penetration, culminating in a penultimate glimpse of one man's face as he asks another for a kiss, and closing with a money shot in which cum rains upon rippled abs—then it seems reasonable to ask whether it duplicates other pornographic devices. Confronting the challenge that *Stranger by the Lake* extends through its iconographic and narrative evocations of Bel Ami, countless gay-identified fan sites have taken the film's "porn parts" as invitations to locate their *other* online correlates— those shots from, say, Sean Cody and Monstercockland that share the film's formal elements and erotic contours. Crucially, the producers of *Stranger by the Lake* have actively encouraged such reception tactics, writing on the film's official Facebook page, "We're really enjoying finding gifs [sic], fan art, and alternate posters on the internet! Feel free to share what you find here!"[47] Such statements plainly function like the Queerty exhortations quoted above—as friendly challenges to gay fans that, at the same time, suggest fresh ways of theorizing media archaeologies of and on the internet.

Depicting Internet Cultures in Queer "Sex Films"

If *Stranger by the Lake* has galvanized the gay-identified erotic blogosphere not by omitting sex but by prominently featuring it, in all its hardcore glory, then it is scarcely alone among contemporary, digitally hybridized queer films. Several others—most notably James Franco and Travis Mathews's *Interior. Leather Bar.* (2013) and Lars von Trier's *Nymphomaniac* (2013)—have similarly managed to incorporate "actual porn" while carefully maintaining their art-film credentials, in the process inspiring, rather than disabling or eclipsing, user-generated visual imaging practices on the internet. Obsessively documenting the equivalences between contemporary queer cinema and such sites as Sean Cody, Corbin Fisher, and Bel Ami, these practices provide a wealth of media archaeological findings, articulating just how limited—just how dependent upon meat and money shots—representations of same-sex eroticism can be. If *Stranger by the Lake* looks a lot like any number of gay porn sites, its images mimicking their interfaces and embedded videos, then so do the cinematic examples to which I turn in this section—albeit for different reasons. Mathews, for his part, has increasingly engaged the very online communities that have illicitly co-opted his film *I Want Your Love*, using it as a source of erotic enjoyment and also as the object of efforts to demonstrate that the differences between "art" and "pornography" are nonexistent—an argument that is familiar from scholarly accounts like Linda Williams's (especially in her book *Screening Sex*), but that has not been applied to the piracy-driven contexts of the erotic blogosphere, let alone to its gay-identified clusters of user-generated production. Mathews must be well aware of the extent to which his film, for all its merits, has become trapped in a morass of online eroticism—lost, that is, in a sea of gay-identified representations of male-male sex, most of which hail from the world of "pure porn" rather than the more rarefied realm of avant-garde cinematic production. Indeed, it seems possible to deduce Mathews's awareness of the cannibalizing, boundary-blurring tendencies of the erotic blogosphere—to infer a certain cognizance of those porn aggregators that eliminate distinctions between media texts—from his own work, particularly the projects that he has produced since *I Want Your Love* in 2012.

Interior. Leather Bar., the 2013 film that Mathews co-directed with James Franco, addresses the overlapping iconography, narrative elements, and "erotic invitations" of three categories of media: mainstream Hollywood cinema (exemplified, in this instance, by William Friedkin's 1980 film *Cruising,* starring Al Pacino), social documentary (understood as a mode of "representing reality" and a means of "giving a voice" to gay men), and online pornography (typified here by hardcore productions). For Mathews and Franco, Friedkin's *Cruising* represents a key text in queer epistemology, a film whose alleged "documentary value" raises urgent questions about the relations between fiction and fact, and between simulated sex and "actual fucking." Friedkin's cast and crew famously "infiltrated" a series of gay-identified bars and S&M clubs in New York City—clubs in which Pacino's character goes "cruising for a killer," to quote the film's infamous tagline—thus mixing Hollywood stars and unknown "fag extras" to create a complex erotic tapestry. Not only is a beefed-up Pacino on objectifying display as a straight man who passes as gay (and perhaps succumbs to his own "inner homo") while in pursuit of a serial killer, but dozens of equally muscular men can also be seen in various states of undress. Who among these men are "actually gay," and who are (presumably like Pacino himself) "completely straight"? Who are "actually fucking" in the background of certain crowded shots, and who are deriving erotic satisfaction from the sexual acts that they are "merely" simulating? Perhaps more pressing, at least for Mathews and Franco, is a question that centers on the ap-

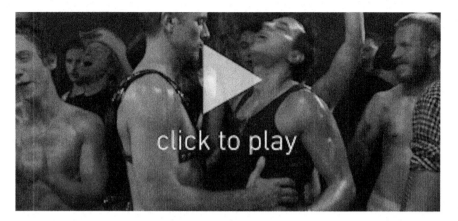

Figure 2.5. Back to the source: *Interior. Leather Bar* online.

proximately forty minutes of *Cruising* alleged to have been cut (or ordered cut) by the Motion Picture Association of America, which threatened the film with an X rating: of what, exactly, did this footage consist? Building on this question, Mathews and Franco posit another: Would it be palatable, or even possible, to "re-create" this footage, which the filmmakers insist was destroyed—completely eradicated rather than simply deleted from *Cruising*'s final cut? An opening title card tells us that, in 2012, "James Franco and Travis Mathews collaborated to imagine their own lost footage"—to make a film about what it might mean to make a film about Friedkin's tantalizingly "incomplete" *Cruising*. The result, *Interior. Leather Bar.,* is as close to a filmic approximation of fan fiction as we are ever likely to get—a film that synthesizes this chapter's concerns with the internet-enabled intersections between queer art films and pornography, and between gay-identified film fandom and "deviant" fetishes.

At the same time, however, the film reinforces this book's broader argument about the frequency with which the word "queer" operates online not as an inclusive catchall but as the hip insignia of a sexual identity understood to be exclusively gay, emphatically male, and undoubtedly white and wealthy. *Interior. Leather Bar.* may flaunt its superficially queer credentials, giving its documentary subjects ample opportunities to voice their support for "queer theory," but it also, in so doing, proves the structuring influence of Pink 2.0. Gathered to discuss the prospect of appearing in what they call a queer James Franco film, several young men proclaim that the gay blogosphere will be abuzz over the project—that gay-identified internet users will effectively categorize it in advance of its completion, guaranteeing its association with a gay exclusivity rather than an expansive queerness. Once again, it is the promise of erotic enjoyment that is assumed to undergird this perceived co-optation of a queer film by "dirty-minded" gay men.

Several of the documentary subjects of *Interior. Leather Bar.* refer to Franco's sex appeal—particularly as experienced by gay men—as militating against broadly queer or remotely political spectatorial interpretations of the project. "The gays will be excited—titillated," says one young man. "[They're] gonna wanna see [Franco] naked!" Another suggests that *Interior. Leather Bar.*, in whole or in part, will take root on some "shady" website—an especially evocative way of referring to those aggregating pockets of the internet that I have described in terms of their simultaneous reliance on piracy, orientation toward eroticism, and refusal of explicit identifications of their cinematic or pornographic sources (and that are sometimes hard to find). Such online spaces are, in other words, "shady" in just about every sense—legally suspect and shrouded in networks that manage to uphold gay male desires even as they blur all manner of discursive lines.

 Interior. Leather Bar. doesn't simply describe this paradoxical process; it also enacts it. The film opens with Franco discussing a book he read "at Yale"—Michael Warner's *The Trouble with Normal*, whose critical project Franco characterizes in terms of a principled resistance to the kinds of conventional, heretofore completely straight-identified social practices (like marriage) that, when extended to queers, threaten to dilute their complex identities and dampen their transgressive desires. Franco passionately concurs with what he takes to be Warner's central argument, announcing his own resistance to methods of "normalizing a queer lifestyle that actually is incredibly valuable"—a "lifestyle" (an altogether infelicitous word choice, to say the least) that Franco defines as multivalent and anti-capitalist. The establishing shot that precedes this quasi-Marxist speech, however, is of the Chateau Marmont, the famous luxury hotel on Sunset Boulevard in West Hollywood—a place to which the impossibly privileged James Franco repairs in order to discuss his Ivy League education with Travis Mathews, advocating an expansive queerness even while identifying as exclusively straight, and "honoring" the Mathews who appears to identify as exclusively gay. When the time comes for him to speak, Mathews can only concur with Franco's interpretation of queerness, voicing his concern that "assimilation into straight culture is erasing all the radicalness and the queerness of . . . that sort of world"—one in which, presumably, anything might happen, boundlessness having been promised to all of its denizens. Once again, however, as the remainder of *Interior. Leather Bar.* will make so disturbingly clear, "queer" is here just a synonym for "white gay male."

 The film enacts this reduction in multiple ways. When the actor Val Lauren, one of Franco's friends and the star of his Sal Mineo biopic (2011's *Sal*), shows up to participate in this ill-defined "imaginative recreation" of *Cruising*'s "destroyed scenes," he plays an angry, admonitory voicemail message from a man (his agent or manager?) who dismissively refers to *Interior. Leather Bar.* as "the Franco faggot project." However, instead of correcting this limited (if delightfully alliterative) description, and offering a few words about the project's capacity to "queer" the filmic remake, and thus to call into question the very labels (like "faggot project") with which *Cruising* itself has been met, Lauren is content simply to suggest that "freedom of expression" should embrace "gay representation"—an orientation toward the experiences of "men who like men." Addressing the potential diversity of this in-progress film's future spectators, one young man, on hand to play a gay bar patron, proclaims that the shared nature of the project's authorship— the fact that *Interior. Leather Bar.* is being "co-directed"—will "confuse" and even "upset" some people. He outlines his vision of a divided community of queer spectators, describing this division in terms of the separation of those gay men who will want to see a "naked James Franco" and those for whom gay authorship is everything, and who will thus put faith in Mathews's capacity to "get things right." Queer spectatorship is thus reducible, for this prominent participant in *Interior. Leather Bar.,* to "two camps" of gay men—those whose spectatorship is strictly libidinous (identity categories be damned!), and those who "aggressively" centralize identity politics. Predicting "angry" blog posts declaiming the straight Franco's involvement in telling a "gay story," this unidentified participant raises thorny questions about the purpose of *Interior. Leather Bar.* itself. Does the film purport to tell a "gay story," or is it instead an imaginative account of a straight-authored film—of, that is, the *Cruising* that was multiply marked by the kind of "straight intervention" that protective gay bloggers are apparently bound to denounce?

Unsurprisingly, confusion is endemic on the set of Franco and Mathews's "imaginative recreation" of *Cruising*'s "missing material," leading Lauren to complain that he lacks a script where Pacino in fact had one (penned by Friedkin himself, no less). "Fuck scripts," says Franco, who then announces that he wants his actors to "reach inside"—to delve into their collective subconscious in order to get at something "queer." What comes out, however—what emerges through this strict neo-Stanislavskian process—is a series of gay stereotypes. For Franco, this is a testament to "brainwashing"—to the fact that heteronormativity, as a conditioning process, has effectively produced reactionary clichés of homosexual identity, rather than simply ensuring a straight consensus. Franco complains, "I've been brought up to think a certain way. I don't like . . . realizing that my mind has been twisted by the way that the world has been set up around me." The world of *Interior. Leather Bar.,* with its all-male participants (save the occasional female assistant or "makeup girl" who becomes a fleeting, indirect documentary subject), has been set up largely through the internet: several men describe "an email that went around," traveling along a listserv whose membership was limited to actors of a certain age, the vast majority of whom identify as male and as gay. The occasional straight cast member, announcing his heterosexuality while waiting for a directorial cue from Franco or Mathews, becomes an object of pedagogic intervention for the gay men who surround him. One self-described

Figure 2.6. Self-identified gay men discuss libidinous online piracy as a "gay practice" in *Interior. Leather Bar.* (James Franco and Travis Mathews, 2013).

homosexual attempts to "teach" a straight-identified guy about *Cruising,* implying that Friedkin's film is known only among "the gays." In the process, he offers a hackneyed, pop-Freudian explanation for audience resistance to *Cruising,* which "bombed" at the box office while being panned by critics: those who were most likely to shame and shun the film in fact, he claims, "had the most kink in them." This particular interpretation, voiced by a documentary subject during the "backstage" sequences of *Interior. Leather Bar.,* complicates surrounding references to those online productions that combine film fandom with a "pornographic" interest in gay male eroticism, suggesting a certain valorization of a present historical moment in which the internet facilitates the expansion of sexual consciousness. The insinuation is that the men who, back in 1980, fled Friedkin's *Cruising*—who feared identifying with the film's "kink" while in a public arena of collective spectatorship—are, in the second decade of the twenty-first century, suddenly likely to use the film (and others like it) as a springboard for eroticized self-confession on the internet, a global platform that is simultaneously public and private, collective and individualized, subject to intense surveillance and "safely" anonymous. Throughout *Interior. Leather Bar.,* the internet is upheld as an agent of gay epistemology—a source of certainty about the (homo)sexual and gender identities of those who use it to distill and eroticize their cinema spectatorship, to encode their particular reception practices: if an image of a "naked James Franco"—pirated from whatever cinematic source—ends up online, then it was plainly put there by a "randy" gay man.

It would be difficult to overstate the naïve confidence and the obsessive, almost incantatory frequency with which gay identifications are made in *Interior. Leather Bar.* Asked if he has ever "played a gay guy," Val Lauren responds immediately—almost programmatically—by saying, "Yes, Sal Mineo," making no attempt to acknowledge the complicated circuits of closeting, outing, artistic experimentation, and rumor that have produced this reading of the late actor, or merely to allow for its anachronistic qualities. Whether or not the historical Sal Mineo was "really gay," that label had only just emerged (as what David Halperin describes as a "piece of political jargon") at the time of Mineo's death in the liberationist 1970s, making it highly unlikely that the actor—whatever his sexual practices and patterns of self-identification—would have used it.[48] By means of verifying its claim that Mineo was "openly gay," Wikipedia's entry on the actor provides citational hypertext that takes the user to a questionable "Sal Mineo Website" whose bland, antiquated interface betrays its amateur authorship—its distance from the impregnable officialdom that it prominently and persistently claims for itself. Indeed, this website is exemplary of the way that an exclusive male homosexuality emerges as a certainty—as an intractable mark of identification—through various online interfaces. A textual reliance on terms like "gay" and "homosexual" coexists with graphical evocations of "beefcake," as well as with hypertext that's ported to sources (like Boze Hadleigh's *Hollywood Gays*) whose truth claims have long been in dispute.[49]

The keenly internet-conscious *Interior. Leather Bar.* takes a similarly tendentious approach to positioning male homosexuality, even as it asserts an expansive and multiply accommodating queer theory as its driving force. When Mathews, invoking queer theory's persistent interest in a "liberating" promiscuity, directs participants to enact "whatever would be realistic within a gay S&M bar," he cites examples both from *Cruising*—a straight-authored narrative fiction film—and "pure pornography," thus positing the imbrication of the two. That this imbrication is especially evident on the internet is not lost on Mathews, as when he identifies the persistent pornographic trope—so beloved of sites like GayTube and Man Hub—of boot worship, instructing an actor to lick the leather shoes of a fellow gay-identified performer. Addressing the question of whether Mathews and Franco want their actors to "actually fuck," several performers offer contradictory conceptions not simply of their own participation in *Interior. Leather Bar.* but also of the film's ostensible cinematic source. Lauren, for his part, maintains that *Cruising*'s deleted scenes consisted of men "actually having sex"—this despite the fact that he himself has not viewed these scenes, suggesting a double distance from epistemological persuasiveness. For even if he *had* viewed these deleted scenes (assuming they ever existed), Lauren would need to demonstrate how, exactly, he knows that their visible subjects are "actually having sex." As Linda Williams points out, the epistemology of hardcore pornography is dauntingly, multiply contingent: in order to identify a screen representation of unsimulated sex, one must remain alert not simply to bodily parts, transformations, and gestures (vaginal expansion and secretion, the swelling of the penis, the apparent penetration of an orifice), but also to aspects of film form such as framing, focal length, and perhaps especially editing.[50] Added to this list of considerations is a topic upon which Williams, writing in 2008, only briefly touches: digital manipulation—particularly of the sort that supplies erect penises "pirated" from pornography and grafted onto images of male movie stars. Indeed, this fan-driven, paratextual trend is by now so pronounced that entire feature films have managed to enact, by their own hybrid image tracks, the imbrication of art films and "pure porn." Such an imbrication is surprisingly common, extending even to the Oscar-winning *The King's Speech* (Tom Hooper, 2010), whose central scenes utilize the very same background—reflect, in fact, the very same art direction and set design—as that of the porn producer UK Naked Men.

Other, considerably queerer films extend the visual strategies of *The King's Speech* into strikingly phallocentric territory. Consider, for instance, Lars von Trier's *Nymphomaniac* (2013), which singlehandedly provides the kind of adjacency—between, specifically, Hollywood stars and "porn pricks"—that has long been the stock-in-trade of the piracy-driven online aggregators explored in this chapter. *Nymphomaniac,* true to its title, tracks the boundless, decades-spanning sexual experimentation of a woman named Joe (played by Stacy Martin and Charlotte Gainsbourg). Shia LaBeouf shows up as Joe's first love, Jerôme, whose swaggering sexual confidence is both a challenge and a turn-on—for Joe as much as for the film's hypothetical gay spectator, whom *Nymphomaniac* addresses through tropes familiar from gay pornography (particularly in scenes featuring Jamie Bell as a brutal, BDSM-peddling young "mystery man" whose erotic toys—and anally oriented techniques—seem lifted from such sites as Straight Hell, Bad Master Boys, Extreme Boyz, and Master Cameron's Dungeon of Despair). Once again, as in *Stranger by the Lake,* a contemporary art film registers some of the more seismic effects of gay pornography. Any attempt to interrogate *Nymphomaniac*'s erotic representations needs to be alert to the film's remarkable intertextuality, which draws upon the cultural presence—even the ubiquity—of gay-porn websites while simultaneously referencing the hallowed status of certain European art films.

When, at the end of *Nymphomaniac,* Joe shoots the elderly aesthete (Stellan Skarsgård's Seligman) with whom she has been occupying a seedy, scarcely furnished room, she recalls the Jeanne of Bernardo Bertolucci's celebrated, seminal *Last Tango in Paris* (1972), who, as played by Maria Schneider, casually fires a gun at Marlon Brando's pathetic Paul, ending his abject life. At the same time, Trier deliberately evokes—even painstakingly approximates—the iconography of certain styles of gay porn, particularly those confined to "quick clips" on various popular websites. That Trier had gay pornography partly in mind when making *Nymphomaniac* is clear from his statements in interviews, and even if we weren't inclined to take him at his word (and, indeed, Trier the unrepentant provocateur is perhaps the least trustworthy of living filmmakers), we would still have the evidence of the film itself—evidence that has made *Nymphomaniac* particularly ripe for co-optation across the gay-identified erotic blogosphere. As far back as 2004, gay-identified websites from The Advocate to Madonna Nation claimed that Trier was engaged in efforts to "revolutionize gay porn," partly by recasting the practice within "Dogma philosophy"—derived from Dogme 95, the avant-garde filmmaking manifesto that Trier co-authored, and whose "Vows of Chastity" reject simulation, including and especially of sex.[51] While a "Dogma approach to gay porn," as The Advocate put it, would seem to suggest a redundancy, it was Dogme 95's orientation toward inveterate artistry and "emotional authenticity," rather than its support for unsimulated sex, that prompted the comment. A "non-Dogma" gay pornographic production was thus characterized, in this reading, by a patently "inauthentic," gay-for-pay approach, as well as by a coldly clinical distance, on the part of the director, from the erotics of the profilmic event. Trier would, according to his champions in the gay press and on the blogosphere, help to transform gay porn into a media product that might "mean something more" to gay men—more, that is, than a rote collection of erotic acrobatics, and more than a mere masturbation aid. In the process, perhaps, he himself would "discover" his own homosexuality—a prediction that persists online, as on a fake Twitter account maintained in Trier's name (@LarsVonNympho), which attributes to Trier the following observation: "Been watching a lot of gay porn 4 #Nymphomaniac, and I must say: @ColbyKeller"—a prominent gay porn star, known partly for his ManHunt.net series *In Bed with Colby Keller*—"makes me question my sexuality. What a man."[52]

If Trier is widely believed—at least on the gay-identified erotic blogosphere—to be conspicuously conversant in gay pornographic practices, then that is only partly due to the iconographic and narrative evidence of his film *Nymphomaniac*. It is also attributable to fan knowledge of the fact that Zentropa—the Danish production company that Trier cofounded and currently co-owns, and that backed *Nymphomaniac*—has also generated its share of gay pornographic films, most notably Knud Vesterskov's *HotMen CoolBoyz* (2000). In December 2013, the blog Indiewire published a "*Nymphomaniac* Cheat Sheet" that included a close account of the Zentropa-sanctioned connections between Trier's film and gay pornography, pointing to particular scenes and suggesting Trier's abiding commitment to blurring cultural distinctions and transgressing generic boundaries.[53] The precise formal elements of *Nymphomaniac* are perhaps more interesting than any ill-defined directorial philosophy, however—even if they may well derive from it. When Trier first announced the project, he touted *Nymphomaniac* as a film that would require its stars to "actually have sex" on set—and thus on screen. However, the realities of shooting—as well as of star performance—were hardly conducive to these aspirations, forcing Trier to take another page out of the repertoire of gay pornography (particularly online pornography). Like the website Corbin Fisher, which has digitally superimposed erect cocks over the flaccid penises of its "straight jock" performers, and like the Falcon Studios that, famously, digitally removes condoms to create a corpus of "barebacking" videos, *Nymphomaniac* provides the (literally) hard evidence of pornographic penetration where it otherwise would have relied upon shadows, simulation, and other forms of star-sanctioned cinematic trickery.[54] When Shia LaBeouf, as the aforementioned sexual prodigy—a Lawrentian brute who climaxes quickly—penetrates Joe at the close of the film's first part, it is with a borrowed erection, not LaBeouf's own. Digitally grafted onto the actor's groin, this hard and thrusting "porn prick" provides the penetrative aspects of his character's erotic labor, lending the film the imprimatur of a phallocentric hardcore pornography, even as its digital precision blurs the lines between erotic websites and contemporary, post-celluloid art cinema. *Nymphomaniac*, like *Stranger by the Lake* and *Interior. Leather Bar.*, thus suggests what Chris Straayer calls "meta-porn," inasmuch as it represents a particularly "self-aware form"—one that invites "knowing viewers [to] find pleasure via both their familiarity with and perceived superiority to more conventional pornography."[55] In this reading, the art film benefits from the immediately recognizable aspects of gay porn—those that legitimate "artsy" eroticism even while seeming aesthetically inferior to it.

The piracy-driven adjacency, and digitally enabled intermixing, of queer cinema and pornography—phenomena that this chapter has traced across the erotic blogosphere, from "dirty GIFs" to YouTube channels to foot-fetish websites—are now, increasingly, part of the fabric of art films themselves, as *Nymphomaniac* demonstrates. It is unclear whether Lars von Trier in fact pirated (rather than paid for) the "porn prick" upon which his film relies, and the director has—true to his puckish public image—refused to clarify the erotic contours of *Nymphomaniac*. When the project was first announced, it was as a film that would require unsimulated, penetrative sexual performances of its actors, whether household names or newcomers. Following its theatrical release, *Nymphomaniac* is now known as something else—though *what*, exactly, is as yet undetermined (and perhaps indeterminable). The film's website offers no help in this regard—no illumination whatsoever on the subject of the fusion of Trier's own images and those "borrowed" from pornography, no way of further understanding how the lower quarters of Shia LaBeouf came to offer the swelled penis of someone else. The film's closing credits suggest precisely the sort of indirection—the calculated vagueness—that, I have argued, is central to piracy-driven porn aggregators, a way of prompting an epistemological crisis about where appropriation begins and where, precisely, it ends. Rather than acknowledging the legal processes by which it acquired images from elsewhere—a typical, and typically mandatory, closing-credit device familiar from filmic citations of various archival sources—*Nymphomaniac* relies upon a vague description that serves only to assure the spectator that she did not, in fact, see Shia LaBeouf's own penis. Exactly whose erect member is grafted onto LaBeouf's groin, from where (industrially speaking) it comes, and whether it was pirated or its "owners" properly compensated—in short, the hard questions of contemporary, digitally hybridized pornographic practice—are unanswerable on the basis of Trier's film text alone.

Within the expansive corpus of contemporary queer cinema, visual imaging practices are increasingly dependent upon the internet not simply for inspiration but also for the hard material of real erections, as exemplified by the case of *Nymphomaniac*. For its part, *Interior. Leather Bar.* participates in this process less directly: working with gay men willing to "actually fuck" before their cameras, Franco and Mathews do not need to produce images composited with borrowed graphics, but their shared awareness of—and avowed interest in—online pornography lends the film an erotic authority, an authenticity that the two directors consistently tout as prototypically queer. However, the "mystery" of Friedkin's "butchered" *Cruising* seems little more than a pretext for the gay phantasmagoria that is *Interior. Leather Bar.*—a phantasmagoria that, instructively, depends upon the participation of gay porn stars who fuck, engage in fetish-friendly "foot play," and afterward express their confusion about what Franco and Mathews are trying to "do" or to "prove." As more and more participants confess their complete lack of knowledge of *Cruising* (most haven't even heard of it, much less of its connections to queer cinema history), and as Mathews's authorial interventions increasingly evince a lack of interest in Friedkin's film, it seems clear that *Interior. Leather Bar.* is not going to address the industrial and aesthetic history that it takes as its "basis." Surprisingly, not one of the film's participants (including Franco and Mathews) notes that *Cruising,* in at least two scenes, intercuts clips from gay pornographic films—a fact that would seem distinctly relevant, even indispensable, to the proceedings. The "old" *Cruising* itself enacts the process of boundary blurring—of blending "art" and "pornography"—that is at the center both of *Interior. Leather Bar.* and of the erotic blogosphere, as when Friedkin, for a conspicuously "artsy" murder scene, relies on "subliminal" imagery that turns out to be of actual anal penetration. Indeed, while watching *Cruising,* it is difficult if not impossible to tell the difference between these "shock cuts"—these brief, associative glimpses of gay porn—and the graphic sadomasochistic imagery for which the Oscar-winning Friedkin was himself responsible. Where, exactly, does a "borrowed" clip of gay porn end and Friedkin's own representations begin? These are questions that *Interior. Leather Bar.* can only address indirectly, through its own shattering of distinctions between producers and consumers, pornographers and "queer theory enthusiasts"—as well as through its own aware-ness of the internet's role in establishing new epistemological quandaries.

"Cinema," writes Patricia White, "is public fantasy that engages spectators' particular, private scripts of desire and identification."[56] This is perhaps the best way of characterizing *Interior. Leather Bar.*—a very public cultural prod-uct (streaming on Netflix at the time of this writing) that seems to say more about Travis Mathews's "private desires" than about William Friedkin's *Cruising*, which Mathews first watched as a young man (or so he says). Mathews's desiring relationship to *Cruising* cannot, however, be reduced to his own apparent sexual predilections; indeed, as his film makes clear, it is inextricably linked to gay-identified fan practices that span the internet, and that seek to revive "old" me-dia for the purposes of erotic reevaluation.[57] "Equally at stake in spectatorship," White reminds us, "are the way organized images and sounds psychically im-print us and the way they mediate social identities and histories."[58] Complicating conventional understandings of fan production, the erotic blogosphere has ef-fectively imprinted such films as *Stranger by the Lake* and *Interior. Leather Bar.* Rather than being the "victims" of a domineering representational system, and fighting back according to the "active-audience" model that John Fiske so famously formulated in relation to what he termed "television culture," gay-identified inter-net users have so influenced contemporary queer cinema that it is now necessary to start with their visually rich online creations—to use them as the basis for understanding not simply the circulation but also the *production* of sexually ex-plicit films.[59]

To look at *Stranger by the Lake*, for instance, is to see a hybridized image track that takes two generic elements—pornography's seemingly simple money shot and queer cinema's contrastingly complex, anti-heteronormative arrange-ments of human and nonhuman subjects within the film frame—and puts them together in a way that has long characterized the porn-aggregating, fetish-friendly websites that I have explored in this chapter, and that plainly (and sometimes not-so-plainly) rests upon pastiche. When Sasha Weiss, writing in the *New Yorker* in 2013, referred to such a web-enabled practice as "manic visual reinterpretation," she managed to evoke, if not exactly to endorse, the pathologizing way in which fan production is often positioned in dominant discourse.[60] In light of the opera-tions of the gay-identified, erotic blogosphere, however, contemporary queer cinema seems, in many senses, to be "manically" committed to self-remediation—whether out of a pronounced respect for the perceived sexual tastes of gay men (as gleaned through gay porn sites) in the case of *Stranger by the Lake*, or out of a more cynical acknowledgment of the inevitability of online co-optations (includ-ing and especially piracy) in the case of *Interior. Leather Bar.* Lars von Trier's *Nymphomaniac*, for its part, proves that the digitally enabled fusion of queer cin-ema and online pornography isn't exclusive to the erotic blogosphere.

I began this chapter by asking what the adjacency between equally gay-identified pornographic and non-pornographic audiovisual productions actually looks like—and also what this adjacency might mean—online, particularly within those piracy-driven pockets of the blogosphere where aggregating systems seem, in a word, indiscriminate, beholden only to a generalized gay algorithm. *Interior. Leather Bar.*, *Nymphomaniac*, and *Stranger by the Lake* make clear that, for a certain, sexually explicit subset of queer cinema, such adjacency means everything, forming the basis not simply of a broad iconographic style—a consistently "porny" aesthetic—but also of narrative itself, of the "hot" reflexivity with which a story might unfold. In *Stranger by the Lake*, the protagonist is torn between—and equally turned on by—the seemingly truth-telling, semen-spraying cocks that surround him (and that bespeak the importance of sexual pleasure), and the more mysterious, even completely unreadable physical stances, emotional poses, and politicized gestures that he witnesses from a distinctly spectatorial, downright voyeuristic vantage point. Lounging on the rocks by a lake, and looking at the indecipherable men who pass by—none of them incontestably gay, and all of them, fat or thin, "hot" or homely, reminiscent of the aura of the film star, the on-screen subject who seems both thrillingly close and impossibly distant—he begins to resemble nothing so much as the gay-identified spectator of queer cinema, the man who, confronted with the genre's resistance to normative disciplines and conventional epistemologies, must consistently question the images before his hungry eyes.

Like many of the online practices that I explore in this chapter, *Stranger by the Lake* is light on exposition. We don't know much about the characters—can only, in most cases, make vague inferences—and so, amid this epistemological crisis, the money shots explode as moments of irrefutable truth, inviting the spectator to say, at the very least, and even while remaining aware of the compromised claims to indexicality of digital media, "Yes, that *is* a cock—and, yes, it *is* ejaculating." If such shots seem distinctly recognizable as formally central to gay porn websites (as well as to moving-image pornography more generally), then so do the cock shots that show up in *Nymphomaniac* (a film with its own connections to the industrial production of gay porn). For its part, *Interior. Leather Bar.* simply wouldn't exist without the internet: in order to acquire participants in their "imaginative recreation" of *Cruising*'s deleted scenes, Franco and Mathews sent a series of emails, employed multiple social networking services, and generally relied upon the very fan communities that have made queer cinema reception a plainly pornographic pursuit. Some of these fans, pulled into the production of *Interior. Leather Bar.*, hailed from the world of online, gay-identified pornography—and, for Franco and Mathews, chose to reenact their "adult" skills on a makeshift soundstage, all for the sake of "extending" the experience of *Cruising*. What happens, however, when such erotically adventurous, emphatically gay-identified fans find a queer James Franco film to be unacceptably chaste? How have they used digital technologies and online dissemination to introduce same-sex eroticism into the ongoing reception of *Howl* (Rob Epstein and Jeffrey Friedman, 2010) and *The Broken Tower* (James Franco, 2011)—two biopics about the gay past? It is to these questions that I turn in the next, partly Franco-focused chapter—an exploration of some of the online consequences of the actor's queer, consistently gay-baiting stardom.

3 Franco, Ginsberg, Kerouac & Co.

Constructing a Beat Topos with Digital Networked Technologies

In the principal texts, the beat generation is never an empowered brotherhood but always an embattled one, disobedient and in struggle against demands that they conform to the wishes of an older generation's authority. The beat generation is not yet a democracy of brothers, that is, but rather a *democratic revolution in progress*.

Leerom Medovoi, *Rebels*

[I]n deciding to actively construct his own image, and by situating himself as his own biggest fan through his forays into celebrity art, [James] Franco productively reflects the queer fandom that circulates at the margins of Hollywood culture. In this way, James Franco, as actor, writer, director, and celebrity artist, has become his own "queer" text.

Adrian Jones, "Playing With Himself"

WHEN ASKED TO expound upon their preference for celluloid film over digital technologies, the directors Rob Epstein and Jeffrey Friedman often uphold the "imperfect," even archaic qualities of analog media. "We shot in Super 16mm" for its "documentary feel," Epstein said of the process of making the quasi-biopic *Lovelace* (2013), which he co-directed with Friedman. Arguing that digital manipulation "never looks authentic," Epstein proclaimed that celluloid's power far exceeds the perceptible stoking of nostalgia.[1] His way of understanding—and also of selling—16mm thus hinges on celluloid's capacity to circumscribe meaning by making visible a film's historicity, its rootedness in the facts and practices of its period setting, which prominently include the limitations of now-outmoded technologies. But Epstein and Friedman, in so celebrating 16mm, do not account for the inevitable—for the computational manipulation that is now the fate of all films, even nostalgic, celluloid-dependent, documentary-style ones, like *Lovelace* and its directors' previous effort, the equally biographical *Howl* (2010). If, recalling a classic cultural studies model of media reception, textual manipulation creates meaning—"negotiates" with extant narratives, drawing out their thematic possibilities—then digital technologies, which, with their bitmaps, are manipulable by definition, deserve analysis in relation to the historicist conservatism of the documentary-style biopic genre. This is especially so since they threaten to disturb or efface the model of the cinematic image that Epstein and Friedman exalt. Shot on film for the sake of its "celluloid-friendly" subject (the gay Allen Ginsberg), *Howl* is hardly gay enough, as numerous print critics and online commentators have made clear.[2] With its largely sexless image track, the film exhibits an obvious reluctance to illuminate some of the embodied experiences of gay male eroticism that Ginsberg's most famous poem evokes. Enter digital networked technologies, and, in particular, those gay-identified fans willing to tweak a gay biopic so that it becomes something a bit more brazen—and, in this case, something far more in tune with the daring digital projects of an especially gay-friendly Hollywood star, the prolific James Franco. In the process, such users prove that efforts to transform what B. Ruby Rich has called "one of the most conservative genres in cinema"—the dramatic biopic—can result in a radical reimagining of what it means to be a gay man.[3]

This chapter traces the gay-identified fan practices surrounding the surprisingly withholding *Howl,* its comparably audacious star, James Franco, and a series of films about the Beat Generation. Spanning the social media landscape, these practices emerge from two distinct reading strategies. For those willing to uncover and extend the often radical, gay-specific cultural and erotic subtexts of otherwise conventional, even conservative biographical and documentary-style films, various forms of file-sharing and "derivative" content creation can come in handy. Digitized while still in production, *Howl* formally entered the matrix of online manipulation in 2011, and it has since been mined for gay-identified Vines, GIFs, photomontages, and YouTube clips that render it relevant to a wider range of queer concerns than its historical subject could possibly have imagined. Such gay-identified online practices powerfully recall Stuart Hall's definition of negotiation—of "encoding" and "decoding," reception strategies that obliterate the linearity of the simplistic sender-receiver model by blurring distinctions between production and consumption.[4] "Negotiated" readings, in the sense that Hall intends, are hardly the only reception practices open to gay-identified Franco fans, many of whom have used digital technologies to confirm and celebrate, rather than uncover and "create," the abundant gay content—the explicit gay sex and equally explicit gay themes—of Franco's directorial efforts, including and especially his own queer biopic *The Broken Tower,* which explores the life of the poet Hart Crane. Like Franco's similarly gay-literate projects *Sal* (a semibiographical account of the life and death of actor Sal Mineo) and *Interior. Leather Bar.* (a treatise on the transhistorical gay S&M scene that is also an account of the making of William Friedkin's controversial gay-themed film *Cruising*), *The Broken Tower* is both an example of and fodder for the gay-identified fan practices at the heart of this book, those that use digital technologies to locate, extend, celebrate, and recontextualize gay specificity in a range of gay-themed films. If gay-identified fans are mining *Interior. Leather Bar.* for images that illuminate gay desire, then Franco's film itself uses *Cruising* as a launching pad for a particularly gay cultural commentary. Furthermore, if users look to *Sal* for a visual evocation of the historical Sal Mineo's gayness (via the dreamy, often-shirtless substitute Val Lauren), then this strange and unsettling biopic itself turns to Mineo's performance in *Rebel Without a Cause* (1955)—as do, instructively, several of Franco's online efforts, such as a Funny Or Die video that he produced with his brother Dave (in which Mineo is identified as exclusively gay) and Franco's own contribution to the omnibus experimental film *Rebel,* which explores the lasting cultural impact of Nicholas Ray's iconic film.[5]

Franco's own digital films and fan practices aren't simply gay-identified; they don't merely use digital technologies and new online conventions to "draw out" the gay cultural and erotic specificities so central to various cinematic and literary landmarks. They are also, because "uncommercial" by conventional standards, and thus untethered to powerful, studio-sanctioned forms of copyright protection, tailor-made for recuperative or confirmatory online fan practices. With their extremely limited theatrical releases—their partial and fleeting commercial availability—Franco's directorial efforts would seem to belong almost exclusively to the realm of YouTube, Dailymotion, Vimeo, and other free video-sharing sites, as well as to the world of GIFs, Instagrams, and Vines, where, condensed into a potentially infinite number of brief combinations, their "gay content" is rendered instantly consumable, becoming in the process all but indisputable. Whether in the form of "dirty GIFs" on the online aggregator Giphy, which show Franco, as Crane, going down on a male co-star in *The Broken Tower,* or of "vile Vines" on the search engine Vine Viewer, which expose the film's infamous prosthetic penis in conjunction with cut-aways to Franco's appreciative, libidinous face, or of an even more "porny" Fleshbot compilation entitled "Here's That Video of James Franco Sucking a Dick," Franco's own films existed as condensed indices of gay sexualities almost as soon as they emerged as completed projects. Their promiscuous appearance via new digital formats and platforms—in editions created through iPhone apps and other networked vehicles—offers a gay-specific and highly erotic exemplification of Web liveness and simultaneity, of what can happen when a film deemed undeserving of a commercial theatrical run begins its life as a YouTube upload (as did, in 2011, Franco's *The Broken Tower*). However, given the retrospective approaches of Franco's queer films—their obvious historicist pretensions—it is all the more important to link their online recasting to the fan practices that deconstruct, after a considerable time lag, a more conventional product like *Howl.* A film that enjoyed a relatively protracted theatrical release (in contrast to the few days that *The Broken Tower* would eventually receive at the IFC Center in Manhattan's West Village), *Howl*—shot on film and distributed by Oscilloscope Laboratories—formally reached the internet via Netflix in 2011. It has since become emblematic of the kind of queer film that seems distinctly less than the sum of its parts—and that is therefore ripe for online excavation. Since those parts include a number of sexy, gay-friendly, even uniquely gay-literate actors, from Franco to Jon Hamm, Jon Prescott, and Aaron Tveit, countless fans have worked to highlight those human participants who, whether through their signature tics or through specific star vehicles (the gay romantic comedy *The One* in Prescott's case, or, in Tveit's, the musical *Les Misérables*), "make sense" to gay men (as one Tumblr poet put it in presenting visual evidence of *Howl*'s "hotness"). Alternately receptive and resistant, unquestioningly celebratory and hypercritical, these gay-identified fan practices together demonstrate (despite the entreaties of Epstein and Friedman) that a film's gay "veracity" often lies in its user-generated digital manipulations, not in its quaint and "grainy" style of analog production. Even the smallest of online homes matter, and it is to those homes that *Howl* has repaired—with frequently provocative results.

"Look at Daddy's Bulge!": Eroticizing the Gay Biopic

An imaginative account of Allen Ginsberg's life and work that is intercut with re-enactments of the obscenity trial of his publisher, Lawrence Ferlinghetti, *Howl* is a hybrid affair: the Hollywood superstar James Franco portrays Ginsberg in sequences that require him to read entire passages from the poem that gives the film its name, furnishing an air of documentary legitimacy.[6] Franco is joined by a whole host of Hollywood luminaries who lend their idiosyncratic talents to the courtroom showdown between "pure expression" and homophobic prudery, presented here as a staging of the historical trial's actual transcripts. In *Howl*, star power competes with the historical record, but the specific star persona of James Franco, with its persistent implication in efforts to illuminate gay-specific cultural and sexual experiences, competes with the film. It would seem that, for many gay-identified fans, Franco's participation was crucial to *Howl*'s identity as a "gay project": "This movie just got gay; James Franco was cast," proclaimed a user on Logo's NewNowNext blog (as if Ginsberg were not a guarantor of gayness), while Oh My GAHH, conceding that Franco is only "possibly gay," nevertheless identified an early *Howl* still as evidence of Franco's capacity to "make everything gay."[7] It would be wrong, I think, to couch this Franco-centered reception tactic as a product of pure ignorance—whether of Ginsberg's life, work, or gay iconicity—and it would be silly to dismiss it as a mere function of a wish-fulfilling fandom. In the context of *Howl,* such commentaries seem not benighted or misguided but, instead, prophetic: although written and directed by self-identified gay men, both of whom are towering figures in the field of queer documentary, *Howl* is sexually tame—more *Night and Day* (the 1946 Michael Curtiz film that, notoriously, could not directly depict Cole Porter's gay appetites) than Franco's own *The Broken Tower*, with its copious, GIF-friendly cock shots.

Howl, like the later *Lovelace*, isn't simply a celluloid project, rich in the visible evidence of analog distortions; it is also, in a sense, a "closed" (if not quite closeted) text that focuses on the complex semiotic registers of Ginsberg's groundbreaking poem and on the pervasive cultural consequences of his publisher's courtroom victory, here depicted as a blow against the generally repressive forces of the early Cold War period. But the film itself is, perhaps, equally repressive, confined by its reliance on the least steamy components of the archival record— but not by the practices of file-sharing, clip-taking, and GIF-making that digitization enables, and that can strike their own collective blow against circumspect representations and authorized reading strategies. The biographical films of Epstein and Friedman, of which *Howl* is perhaps the most notable example, may reflect the observable distortions of "old" analog technologies—to better generate a "subliminal" effect, and to secure a certain spectatorial trust in historiographic operations—but their inevitable introduction to the online realm, to the digitization to which their makers claim to be aesthetically as well as ideologically allergic, renders them eminently vulnerable to gay critique, revision, and recontextualization. In December 2012, a YouTube user whose channel is devoted to extracting images of "gay romance" from mainstream media took a sequence from *Howl*, titled it "allen & neal (gay romantic scene)," and cut it to suggest something far sexier than what actually appears in the film—precisely by cutting out the self-censorship and societal condemnation that Ginsberg experienced during his youth, and that the film, with its period-specific purview, privileges.[8] In *Howl*, Franco's Ginsberg begins to go down on Jon Prescott's Neal Cassady, but he's cruelly interrupted, in one of the film's most shamelessly melodramatic moments, by Cassady's heterosexist female companion, thus ending what had promised to be, both for the character and for the biopic that commemorates his life, a flowering of gay erotic expression.[9] As a revisionist paratext, "allen & neal" ends the scene with the image of Franco's Ginsberg falling to his knees and facing Cassady's crotch, thus rendering it a gay romantic scene (befitting the parenthetical part of the paratext's title), rather than a missed erotic opportunity. In other words, "allen & neal" ends the scene with the promise of erotic pleasure, and not on a melodramatic note of withheld plenitude. Ginsberg, perhaps, would have approved.

New, digitally enabled strategies of seeing and sharing—of cropping and condensing—do not necessarily make for a postmodern proliferation of contradictory meanings, as per some popularized strains of digital media theory. In fact, obsessive content creation and circulation is, conceivably, just as often the product of a principled commitment to uncovering coherence. The streaming of digital

You‍Tube ≡ ·

▶ ▶▶ 🔊 1:00 / 1:06   ⓘ ⚙ ▭ ⌞⌝

allen & neal (gay romantic scene)

isla mari

▶ Subscribe 4,833   310,681

╋ Add to   ◀ Share   ••• More   👍 734 👎 53

Figure 3.1. The fan video "allen & neal (gay romantic scene)" (2012) excerpts only those *Howl* shots that seem to promise gay romantic as well as sexual fulfillment, carefully excluding the film's "tragic," withholding follow-ups.

feature films, particularly via Netflix, has afforded gay-identified and gay-allied users the opportunity to draw out the hidden or undercooked gay specificities of certain gay-themed films. Simply put, streaming—along with uploading to You-Tube and other video-sharing sites—makes possible the siphoning of still images (rendered through screen-capture technologies) and even entire scenes for exportation to various social media outlets, where they may then be mined for latent or hyper-legible gay meanings. Emblematic of the work of "prosumers" in general, such efforts acquire a certain urgency and even legitimacy when engaged with the work of James Franco. That is because, in addition to professing a commitment to depicting gay men in American media, Franco maintains an inescapable online presence—as both author and subject, both content creator and "victim" of copyright infringement. Digital piracy is not the sole focus of this chapter, but it undergirds the public lives of Franco's gay films (even *Howl*) as much as it informs the productions of Franco's gay fans. Such practices of piracy, broadly defined, are not new to gay-identified fan communities. Bootleg videotapes, particularly of

Wakefield Poole's pornographic *Boys in the Sand* (which constitutes the subject and provides much of the audiovisual content of Ivan Lozano's 2009 digital short *Signal Noise*), have long been vital to gay-identified fan subcultures. Perhaps more famous still are those fans whose unauthorized slash fiction is at the center of Henry Jenkins's *Textual Poachers*—fiction that, in many cases, transforms *Star Trek* into a gay(er) treatise. The fans who "steal" scenes from *Howl*—like those who illicitly upload *The Broken Tower* in its entirety—are different, however. As "poachers," they have been transformed by—and have themselves transformed— the latest digital revolution, in a way that has further promoted the now-heretical (or at least unfashionable) concept of a universal gay culture. When those gay fans of Allen Ginsberg who were hoping for a bit more from *Howl*—more same-sex eroticism, at the very least—take from that film what most entices them, they often repurpose it to demonstrate its powerful pan-gay appeal. This is particularly the case in those digital creations that recast Jon Hamm's role in the film as a function—almost a manifestation—of an allegedly common gay desire: to be "dominated" by a tall, dark, and handsome he-man, the Hamm whose hyper-masculine trappings place him at the center of a certain erotic imaginary. If such a desire, so articulated, is spurious at best—utterly unbelievable as an index of the erotic appetites of all gay men—then it still speaks to and for a singular, self-identified "type." Frequently couched in essentializing hyperbole (though perhaps facetiously so), such uses of *Howl*'s largely prim-and-proper, documentary-style, live-action images are part and parcel of the process of producing a specifically gay visibility online.

For its part, *Howl* is hardly monolithic at a formal level; it is clearly an aesthetically hybridized film, but to call it a hybrid of fiction and documentary would be disingenuous. The film is scarcely dramatized in any conventional sense, and so those elements that seem fictional—whether because they feature famous actors or because of the formal precision that attends to them—belong to the realm of reenactment, which is documentary-friendly terrain, to say the least. Even the film's courtroom sequences, in which the title poem is on trial for obscenity, and which build up some basic juridical tensions, are tentative and truncated: a sketch involving a bespectacled Mary-Louise Parker, as a prudish academic of dubious credentials, ends with Jon Hamm, in period-appropriate Don Draper dress as publisher Lawrence Ferlinghetti's defense attorney, coldly commanding the woman to "step down" from the stand. She, initially, is as dubious as we: can this man really have rejected the cordial, or at least formalized and stylized, protocol of the courtroom, whereby words like "may" and "please" provide a semblance of agreeability amid the smoke of legal battle? But he presses on, with precisely the sort of curt command that has endeared Draper to gay male masochists the world over. When he says, "Step down," and then says it again, and again, one can be certain that he does not, necessarily, relish having to do so; one senses instead that the disgust behind the command has kept itself from coalescing into something more sadistic, something that would derive pleasure from rude repetition. Nevertheless, Hamm's casting in *Howl* galvanized the gay-identified blogosphere by suggesting just how cruel—just how much of a cold and domineering Draper type—the actor had made his real-life character. After Elton called Hamm's lawyer a "daddy," while hashtags referring to the figure as a "dom top" began proliferating on social media, where they served to further confirm *Howl*'s gay credentials—its capacity to express, even through a straight actor in a straight role, some familiar, gay-specific erotic practices, and to call to mind many of the colloquialisms associated with those practices.

Perhaps most notably, Hamm's pokerfaced performance as Ferlinghetti's sexy "dom top" of an attorney, with his starched mid-twentieth-century suits and clipped manner of speaking, seemed for some gay-identified fans to signal the character's resemblance to Clark Kent, causing those fans to queer Zack Snyder's then-gestating *Superman* reboot with stills of Hamm in *Howl* stitched to cartoon images of the iconic superhero. The website ComicBookMovie, which depends for its content upon diverse "volunteer contributors," offered an especially telling juxtaposition of Hamm's "brutal-top" dominance in *Howl*'s courtroom scenes and Superman's "superiority" over both villains and romantic "victims." On the basis of *Mad Men* but also, explicitly, of *Howl,* Hamm represented numerous gay fans' first choice for the role of a more "mature," confident, aggressive Superman, who, as Clark Kent, could "kill" in a suit and tie. Finally, a pair of digital videos extended the eroticized gay meanings of Hamm's *Howl* character, contributing to widespread online efforts to extract the most sexual and cultural gayness from Epstein and Friedman's film—even from its nominally straight protagonists and self-identified straight actors. The first was a much-viewed video (promoted on various sites including The Huffington Post and YouTube) of Hamm and James Franco comparing the historical trial depicted in *Howl* to the cultural, political, and juridical controversies surrounding California's Proposition 8, the initiated constitutional amendment eliminating the rights of same-sex couples to marry. "Hotties Franco and Hamm Fired Up Over Prop 8!" screamed a headline on E! Online, above an article describing Hamm's physical appearance in the video as "delicious"; for its part, the gay-authored Tumblr page Homobrute positioned Hamm, who is bearded in the video, as a "hairy daddy bear"—but also, significantly, as a man capable of exuding sex appeal when clean-shaven, as evidenced by his iconographically identical roles in *Mad Men* and *Howl*.[10] The second much-discussed video to centralize this "hot" Hamm-*Howl* connection was a digital short that premiered on a May 2011 episode of *Saturday Night Live,* and that represented the live-action debut of Robert Smigel and J. J. Sedelmaier's Ambiguously Gay Duo, played in this instance by Hamm and Jimmy Fallon. Fittingly, given gay fans' frequent online translations of Hamm into the prototypical gay top, here the actor is portrayed as occupying the "dominant," insertive sexual position, with Fallon assuming the receptive role of the "bottom," albeit through a series of visual puns. ("The Ambiguously Gay Duo," whose broadcast history had traced a transition from traditional cell to computer animation prior to the introduction of Hamm and Fallon's live-action digital sketch, is well known for centralizing the sight gag of two tights-wearing superheroes engaged in world-saving activities that closely resemble a certain kind of gay sex.) This *SNL*-approved use of the actor as the embodiment of confident-top dominance seems scarcely different from the gay fan practices described above. Both bespeak a willingness to queer a straight actor (as well as that actor's willingness to queer himself) not simply by destabilizing a general sense of heteronormativity but also by introducing a considerable degree of gay erotic specificity: a dom's drill-sergeant instructions (so familiar from gay porn and gay practice), or the range of positions available for anal intercourse—not to mention the various colloquialisms and slang terms ("bear daddy," "yard boy," "total top") that together belong to an especially sexy, and perhaps prototypically gay, vernacular toolbox.

That such specificity is almost entirely visually absent from *Howl* does not mean that the film ignores the complex erotic currents that can connect gay men. Even Hamm's "ruthless" courtroom scene, in which he is so cruel—so curt—to Parker's pesky witness for the prosecution offers its own evocation of erotic role-playing. The Vines that have relied on this scene haven't recast it, exactly; they have merely removed the silences—the dead spots—between Hamm's thrice of-fered command to "step down," thus condensing the scene into a series of orders barked in quick succession, so that it suggests Hamm's facility for dominating in "true-top" fashion, without tolerance for even the smallest hint of dissent. But *Howl* itself suggests this facility; what the Vines remove are Parker's reaction shots, which slightly prolong the sequence by showing her disbelief at being so contemptuously addressed. Of course, the quick contempt of curtness, rather than the performed enjoyment of the sadist trained in offering ever more florid complaints, may be far more satisfying to a practiced masochist—a possibility that *Howl* makes reasonably apparent in a sequence involving Beat pinup Neil Cassady's sexual rejection of Franco's Allen Ginsberg. Cassady, having willfully broken the bounds of constipated propriety that so often separate straight and gay male bodies (he holds Ginsberg in the bed that they are forced, by circumstance, to share), later sends his friend a breakup letter explaining why he "can't," or won't, be the poet's queer companion. The actor John Prescott, who plays Cassady, reads the letter in voice-over. It is his speech that we hear while watching a dejected Ginsberg pore over the pages of the letter. As Ginsberg finishes reading, and Prescott ceases to speak, the "point" of the scene becomes clear: it is to prove not merely that Cassady doth protest too much, but also to indicate that his repetitious rejection—rendered in the sort of rambling prose that would inspire

Truman Capote to say of Beat king Jack Kerouac's novel *On the Road,* "That's not writing; it's typing"—tells of a man incapable of maintaining power over a besotted subordinate.[11] Franco's Ginsberg has, by this point in the film, already made clear his craving for the approval not merely of his distant poet father but also of the equally distant and far more "dreamy" Neil Cassady. As soon as Cassady expresses his true motivations through polite and overly explicit prose, the magic dies; the masochist must now search for something that will truly, compellingly perplex him—something not unlike the unaccountably cold, cruel curtness of a statement like Hamm's "step down."

Hearing the attorney's words for the third time, Parker's witness must finally capitulate to their command. Like the mesmerizing Vines, the casting here conspires to render intensely erotic something that was, in fact, probably just a simple breach of decorum back in 1957, worth little more than an eyebrow lifted in pique. But because the actor who plays Jake Ehrlich is Jon Hamm, the character's erotic significance can scarcely be overstated. Indeed, Hamm's erotic popularity among gay men is no more difficult to determine than his appeal for straight women: rare in 2010, the year of *Howl's* release, was the gay-authored blog that didn't mention the fourth season of *Mad Men,* or that its star's "bulge"—allegedly indicative of a generous manhood—could so often be seen through his pants. The gay-identified blog Just Jared, for instance, made much of the complex conjunction of cock, Hamm, *Howl,* and *Mad Men,* creating photomontages that worked to draw all of these "gay-friendly" elements together, highlighting an erotic visibility said to be of specific relevance to gay men. In *Howl,* Hamm's pleasurably deep voice—a rare feature among modern movie actors, each of whom sounds more boyish than his generic, Gyllenhaalian predecessor—is on hand to put Mary-Louise Parker, as Gail Potter, "in her place." But Parker, as expected, heads there with a wobble—tottering as if on the brink of full-fledged insanity. One of the great eccentrics of contemporary stage and screen, the Second Coming of Sandy Dennis, Parker is the perfect, lascivious recipient of Hamm's command. She plays a woman tasked with testifying for the prosecution that the poem "Howl" is a piece of irredeemable smut, and if the combination of actress and role seems incongruous—after all, the queer Parker of *Longtime Companion* (Norman René, 1990), *Boys on the Side* (Herbert Ross, 1995), and *Angels in America* (Mike Nichols, 2003) is a gay favorite of many years' standing—then it is worth lingering on the eroticized exchange between lawyer and witness, which brings an end to the scene as well as to Parker's function in the film. (Her role is little more than a fleeting cameo.) The Parker who, as Tony Kushner's Harper, attempts to enjoy sex with a semi-closeted and altogether inept Joe Pitt (played by Patrick Wilson), provides in *Howl* yet another master class in masochism, lingering on the stand long after a hot, scolding lawyer has told her to leave it.

If such eccentricity, coupled with Hamm's lack of lawyerly politeness, helps to define and redeem the scene (which would otherwise seem a simple transcript reading), then it can't quite distract from the fact that *Howl* has, through its courtroom sequences especially, established certain techniques for belittling those who belong to the anti-Ginsberg team, thereby corroding the ethos of documentary objectivity to which it elsewhere adheres. That is not to say that didactic denunciation is incompatible with the documentary form—far from it. It is, instead, to suggest that a heavy-handed approach to Ginsberg's plight, which requires Hamm to scoff sexily in reaction shots whenever someone is testifying to the deleterious social effects of the poet's work, is at odds with the scarcely narrativized—dare I say Brechtian?—devices that the film otherwise favors. For instance, Franco is regularly required to step out of character in order to deliver readings of Ginsberg's most famous poem, in a voice-over whose inflections are distinctly different from those of the embodied Allen. Lest we begin to suspect that such moments—in which Franco's modern-stoner voice joins Carter Burwell's commemorative music as acoustical accompaniment to animated images—are the product of Ginsberg the biopic subject, the film hastens to provide the doubling, but not redundant, device of the visible Ginsberg reading the very same passages from "Howl," in black-and-white sequences reenacting the poem's public unveiling at San Francisco's Six Gallery. The film, in other words, consistently reminds us to consider the poem as a text that has to be read, and in the process reconceived—a text whose recitation requires a range of vocal choices on Franco's part. In *Howl,* the title poem is never presented as an autonomous semantic mass amenable to the traditional biopic's resuscitative intentions. It is, then, all the more ironic that the film itself has been co-opted to emphasize a gay relevance and specificity that exceeds the outlines of Ginsberg's life and of his poem—that spans social media to make even Jon Hamm's lawyer a gay-literate object of libidinal desire.

Howl is not, of course, a traditional biopic. Nevertheless, Epstein and Friedman take pains to uphold the film's self-legitimating, ostensibly documentary-friendly devices, identifying them most clearly through the text that closes the opening credit sequence, whereby we learn just how beholden *Howl* is to "the facts"; as A. O. Scott points out in his positive *New York Times* review, "every word spoken in [*Howl*] is part of the historical record."[12] The history of the docudrama—the cinematic form that, in Derek Paget's words, "openly proclaims both a documentary and a dramatic provenance"—helps to illuminate *Howl*'s general taxonomic location, which mainstream critics have questioned before concluding, with nary an exception, that the film's generic status is indeterminate ("Not quite a biopic, not really a documentary and only loosely an adaptation" is how Scott describes it).[13] If *Howl* is a docudrama, then it is perhaps misguided to complain that the emotionally manipulative reaction shots, which reveal the all-too-readable responses of the many witnesses to Ginsberg's social effects, degrade the film's documentary legitimacy, although the quantity of such shots is another matter entirely. (As J. Hoberman asks in his rightfully exasperated review, "Is it really necessary to affirm [Ginsberg's] ecstatic footnote ["Holy! Holy! Holy!"] with a montage of smiling reaction shots?")[14] Perhaps most egregious is the invented response of a cheering, almost ecstatic black woman to the not-guilty verdict in Ferlinghetti's trial—a shot that alternates with that of the pinched face of an irate old white woman, who clearly doesn't approve of what the court has wrought. Taken together, these are the most offensive of the numerous, crude courtroom cutaways, which include a remarkably undemanding shot of a rosy-cheeked young woman who sits, expressionless, and listens to the legal combatants discuss "vulnerable" readers of contemporary poetry. It's like a rhyming device out of *Sesame Street*: the vulnerable-seeming girl is a readily recognizable visual match for the substance of juridical speech.

Most objectionable, according to the vast majority of professional critics tasked with evaluating *Howl,* is the film's reliance on animation. Hoberman, for instance, describes graphic artist Eric Drooker's approach to these sequences as "literal-minded" and "a distraction"; A. O. Scott, for his part, calls them "nearly disastrous." Indeed, they seem, despite their reliance on cocks and cum, to suggest yet another *Sesame Street* device—one more effort to make the film effective pedagogically. However, if we take *Howl* to be a kind of documentary—or at least read it in relation to documentary history and theory—then it is worth pointing out what none of the film's mainstream critics have noted: the remarkable, if only superficial, resemblance between its animated sequences and those of Ari Folman's 2008 documentary *Waltz with Bashir,* which helps to situate *Howl* amid a historically specific set of documentary techniques. But if *Waltz with Bashir* uses a combination of Adobe Flash cutouts and traditional cell animation to recreate the 1982 Israeli invasion of Lebanon, then for what purposes does *Howl* achieve a similar aesthetic? Surely a key creative difference between the two films lies in the latter's application of animation to strictly imaginative sequences—its use of a cartoon format in order to anthropomorphize penises and plants, gusts of wind and various ghostly formations. However much it might iconographically resemble *Bashir, Howl* contrasts strikingly with the techniques of Folman's film, in which animation—in a process that recalls but most definitely is not rotoscoping—is used to expand the expressive contours of traditional interview setups. But if, for Folman, animation can represent actual interviews, then that is perhaps because the filmmaker's interviewees seem so traumatized, their view of the world so distorted.

In *Howl,* it is the presumed difficulty, or unabashed dynamism, of the title poem that seems to demand animation. Either way, the cartoon sequences are, at the very least, curious. If they're meant, in the style of *Sesame Street,* to outline the key themes of Ginsberg's work, then they're woefully shortsighted, suggesting only a few superficial dialectics (stasis and flight, repression and sex) instead of some far less heralded tropes (such as Ginsberg's use of agricultural metaphors to evoke both the receptive and insertive experiences of anal sex). If, on the other hand, the animated sequences are meant as metaphors for the general tone of the title poem, then they're inadequate to the task. "You can't translate poetry into prose," says one of *Howl*'s witnesses for the defense. By this very same logic, animation cannot be made to approximate the experience of reading a poem so beholden to embodied realities—to the sensations of a cock in one's ass, or of one's own ass in another person's face. It could be argued, of course, that words themselves—even Ginsberg's own—constitute distortions or dilutions, and that even these tools are, by definition, inadequate to lived experience. If we accept this poststructuralist axiom, then we might think it foolish to object to the film's animated sequences. It might seem antiquated, if not downright ignorant, to complain of animation's deficiency as an adjunct to poetry reading. My point, however, is not to echo, say, Stanley Cavell's notorious dismissal of animation as "not cinema," but instead to suggest that *Howl* uses the form to demonstrate that the experience of which Ginsberg writes—what he in his poem calls "the charm of reality"—deserves multiple expressive modes, just as it seems to substantiate the longstanding critical belief in documentary's unique capacity to assimilate a variety of representational styles.[15] Viewed from this perspective, then, the digital, gay-identified fan practices that have proliferated around *Howl* represent still more styles—still more forms—for the figuring of Ginsberg's gayness.

"That's Racist!": Online Activism and *Howl*'s Offensive Analogies

For a number of online commentators, *Howl*'s animation seems far "gayer" than the live-action sequences with which it alternates, offering cocks where Franco and company show none. In a somewhat less salacious mode, however, one might simply point out that the live-action sequences depict no moments of same-sex erotic contact, and that they barely even suggest the possibility of such contact in basic iconographic terms. "No one even kisses!" cried one of my students after a screening of the film, and he was right: there is no same-sex kiss to be seen— except, perhaps, in the animated sequences, which offer apparitional figures that appear androgynous, but that at least get to frolic among phalluses, each drawn as if it were a stiff blade of thick grass on a storyboard for the bucolic *Doctor Zhivago* (David Lean, 1965). The relative tameness of *Howl*'s live-action sequences—the absence of eroticism that characterizes them—should not, however, be seen as a function of the film's ethos of documentary fidelity to the archival record. After all, historical documents—whether transcripts of Ferlinghetti's obscenity trial or published press accounts thereof—do not indicate that courtroom spectators were seen to cheer and rue the verdict, as do the two women who occupy the aforementioned didactic reaction shots. Such moments are the all-too-obvious products of creative license, but they are no less objectionable than a dramatized moment of same-sex erotic contact could possibly be. Is the cheering black woman so happy because she's a lesbian, because she's black, or because she's both? Just why is she so happy to see the legal establishment strike a blow against homophobic prudery? One cannot help but suspect that, in the hyper-familiar tradition of Hollywood liberalism to which *Howl* regrettably belongs, she is cheering only because she is black—and essentialized as such. Viewed from this perspective, the scene can be said to offer yet another false equivalence between black and gay experiences—the sort of sentimental linkage that recurs in Crayton Robey's 2011 documentary *Making the Boys* (about Mart Crowley's groundbreaking play *The Boys in the Band*), in which the civil rights movement is presented as strictly homologous with gay liberation. Indeed, such an approach is rooted in the first gay-identified films of the post-Stonewall period, including Christopher Larkin's *A Very Natural Thing* (1974), in which documentary footage of the 1973 Gay Pride Parade is used to advance the thesis that white gay men can well understand—and do, in fact, share—the struggles of black Americans, with one interviewee going so far as to proclaim an equivalence between racist and homophobic slurs.

By this very same strategy, *Howl* is free to present an anonymous old white woman as an enemy of First Amendment protection in general and of queer expression in particular, her angry face alternating with the beatific openness of the only woman of color present in the sequence. Such analogies between race and sexuality, wherein black women act as the silent, undifferentiated champions of white gay men while starched old white women stew contemptuously in the corner, are perfectly capable of offending gay-identified fans, as evidenced by certain *Howl*-themed digital creations. Offering a vital reminder that corrective, gay-identified online fan practices often center on representations of race, the production in question began by adopting a much-cherished meme: a two-second, animated reaction GIF, sourced from a 2005 episode of the MTV2 sketch comedy series *Wonder Showzen,* in which a young black boy screams, "That's racist!" The website Know Your Meme archives several viral uses of this GIF, which include its superimposition over the upper-right-hand corner of an image of racist "lolspeak" (a deliberately, deliriously grammatically incorrect statement, in this case claiming that Mexicans are gluttonous and inclined to cheat at games). Other uses, however, involve the linking of the "That's racist!" meme to a variety of examples of white gay racism. One such instance—a compilation of GIFs—brings together the shared "mammy" iconography of recent gay-themed media, from the NBC sitcom *The New Normal* (with its reliance on a "sassy" black woman of size to provide comfort as well as "household help" to a pair of wealthy, white gay men) and *Howl*. The *Wonder Showzen* boy, with his powerfully succinct allegation of racism, is thus made to denounce the way that contemporary gay-themed films and television shows often exploit mammy figures.

If this type of *Howl* tie-in suggests a disgusted response to the film's apparent racial politics, then still other tie-ins seem only to reproduce those politics. Ruth Du's *Six '55* (2011), a digital short about Ginsberg that distinctly suggests a corrective or at least supplemental response to *Howl*, also places an appreciative black woman among the crowds gathered to hear Ginsberg read his poem, but a clear contrast to this rather clichéd rendering of transracial solidarity can be seen in the film's depiction of a young Asian man who both lusts after and hopes to "become" the famous poet. *Six '55* thus offers a young person of color who struggles to reconcile his embryonic artistic aspirations with a general curiosity about same-sex erotic contact. Distracted by a straight couple having sex in a back room, he asks the woman to describe how the man's cock feels as it enters her body, and then reemerges to "witness history": Ginsberg's public unveiling of his poem at the swank San Francisco gallery.

Six '55 might profitably be read as a reaction to the limitations of Epstein and Friedman's *Howl*—as, that is, a corrective digital text, first uploaded for free viewing on Vimeo. This exciting short film retains, however, *Howl*'s emblem of "analogous" strife—the silent, supportive black woman who nods appreciatively from the periphery, her gaze fixed on the white man who occupies center stage. According to an odious "post-racial" approach, American citizens have jumped ahead to some utopian point at which the prosthetic memory of oppression (the images of suffering that they have inherited but not directly experienced), coupled with some inchoate, broadly affective "connection," justifies the amalgamation of black women and white gay men in a vast array of cultural productions. The defense against racist essentialism that "post-racial" purports to provide—the alibi that allegedly guards against the suggestion that a black woman, because black, is bonded to the white gay man who, because gay, adores her—is one that American popular culture persistently mobilizes. It is thus important to underscore the significance of those seemingly casual moments of transracial solidarity that show up in *Howl*, and that the film shares with several other contemporary queer productions, including Cam Archer's 2006 drama *Wild Tigers I Have Known*. Set in the twenty-first century, *Wild Tigers* tracks the middle-school experiences of Logan (Malcolm Stumpf), a boy whose delicate androgyny endears him to a slightly older, studly student named Rodeo (Patrick White), but whose growing sexual desire for Rodeo drives the two boys apart. Realizing that his "girlish" features are conducive to cross-dressing, and that Rodeo may not be so straight as to refuse the advances of a boy in drag, Logan begins to wear women's clothes, a blond wig, and even ruby-red lipstick. Along the way, he stops to watch a Nina Simone television special, which is presented (perhaps anachronistically) as part of a broadcast on Logan's 12-inch television set, rather than as a digital video viewed on, say, his computer screen (via YouTube, which, precisely at the time of the film's production, was just beginning to showcase such rotoscoped old television programs). In any case, Logan's engagement with this 1961 televised performance of Simone's "When I Was in My Prime" is shot in such a way as to suggest a deep connection between white gay child and black female artist. The sequence begins, in fact, with Simone the sole occupant of the film frame. Seated next to an unseen guitarist who provides her voice's sole instrumental accompaniment, Simone begins to sing, in her sparest, harshest style—the slow and mournful style that characterizes some of her earliest recordings.

From this point forward, the sequence crosscuts between Simone's televised image and shots of Logan, who, from his bed, stares at that image, narcissistically transfixed. At first, Simone's relevance seems strictly a matter of her lyrics, which include bitter references to the "false young man" who stole her heart, and whose falseness—whose willingness to seduce irresponsibly, to inspire sentiments without requiting them—is clearly akin to that of Logan's elusive love object, Rodeo. But as the film continues to cut back and forth between Logan and Simone, and especially as it begins to zoom in on a Simone who stares directly at the camera, the significance of this performance of "When I Was in My Prime" appears to encompass more that just lyrical resonance. It becomes yet another means through which a contemporary queer film can establish its rather dubious "transracial" credentials—or at least offer up the clichéd assumption that black women share with white gay men (and with white gay boys) both a general experience of oppression and a "soulful" artistic response to such oppression. However, by this rubric, black women are doubly subjugated—something that Simone's song, with its references to racism and sexism, makes all too clear, but that *Wild Tigers I Have Known*, with its all-white cast, declines to acknowledge, falling back on an all too familiar analogizing of race and sexuality.

An even more disturbing deployment of this analogy between black straight female and white gay male occurs at the very beginning of the queer film *C.O.G.* (Kyle Patrick Alvarez, 2013). Based on an autobiographical short story by gay humorist David Sedaris, *C.O.G.* opens with the disembodied voice of a self-identified black woman complaining in increasingly florid terms about the father of her unborn child. Before revealing the source of this voice, the film slowly fades in on the face of David (Jonathan Groff), a blue-eyed, shaggy-haired white boy whose ivory sweater is emblazoned with a big red "Y"—for Yale University, his alma mater—and who gazes in agony through the window of a bus, presumably distraught at having to hear his black seatmate tell of her troubles. For about the first minute of the film, David's white face is all we see, while the black woman's voice is all we hear. The visage of the white gay man is thus the screen on which the pain of an unnamed, as-yet-unseen black woman is projected, and it is no coincidence that this woman, in articulating her history of heterosexual woe, peppers it with plenty of gay-baiting remarks. Describing her partner's "faggoty-ass, worm-sized dick," she recalls having instructed him to "suck the cream out of my old granddaddy's cum-stained *cock*," thereby demonstrating her conversance in the sexualized lingo that, as the film will later make all too clear, is so beloved of certain young gay men. The black straight woman thus "knows" her audience—understands that her rhetorical choices will resonate with the white gay man who is her reluctant interlocutor. That the scene is played as farce—that the black woman is meant to be mentally ill, a mere bus-bound crazy—does not mitigate its racism, especially since the woman's kookiness is only fodder for the writerly aspirations of the white gay protagonist. In familiar Sedaris fashion, he will use her story to write and sell his own, and become acclaimed as a great American humorist—or so the film, with its focus on David's edifying exposure to various pathologized racial and sexual formations, implies.

Unchallenged—unavailable for even the crudest comedic recuperation—is David's racism, rendered most explicit in a scene in which he accuses migrant Mexican laborers of having stolen his money. "You didn't succeed in your own country," he tells them. "What makes you think you can make it here, huh?" Having outperformed these laborers in the task of apple-picking, David graduates to a job with "fat dykes"—each of whom he describes as dumb and intimidated by his intelligence—in an apple-processing plant, from which he later flees to join up with a "Jesus freak" named Jon (Denis O'Hare, once again playing a raging homophobe, not entirely dissimilar from his John Briggs in *Milk*). After affirming that a precise description of his physicality could be a description of "anyone," and thus demonstrating his privileged blindness to (at the very least) race and gender, David finds Jesus, becoming a true "Child of God" (or C.O.G.)—though only, at first, because he thinks religion will save him from being raped by Curly (Corey Stoll), a butch gay man who resents David for being "better" than him. The film ends with Jon, David's mentor, angrily complaining both about the "towel-heads" he encountered during the Gulf War and the "faggots" who, like David, don't deserve Christ. David agrees, claiming that he's "as sick as they come," and walks tearfully away, trailing yet another analogy between race and sexuality—this one a means of linking the gayness of the white David to the Arab otherness of the turbaned non-Christian. A film that begins by presenting David as a magnet for a black woman ends, after many a racist remark, with the suggestion that, in his gay rejection of Christianity, David is in solidarity with the racial other of the Arab world.

If there remains a rather extreme disjunction between certain post-gay protestations and the emphatically gay-specific techniques of many contemporary queer films, then so too is there a separation between queer theory, on the one hand, and those films that conflate race and sexuality, on the other. For years, queer critics have been suggesting the inextricability of race and sexuality without synonymizing the two terms. Siobhan Somerville, in her 2000 book *Queering the Color Line,* affirms the importance of "resisting any attempt to see race and sexuality as metaphoric substitutes."[16] Kobena Mercer, in his essay "Skin Head Sex Thing," writes, "Although analogies facilitate cognitive connections with important cultural and political implications, there is also the risk that they repress and flatten out the messy spaces in between." For Mercer, "analogies between race and gender in representation reveal similar ideological patterns of objectification, exclusion, and 'othering.'"[17] Equally offensive are the queer films that feature no characters of color and those that insist upon a liberal equation between black Americans (especially black women) and white gay men. The persistence of the latter approach may well be attributable to the legacy of the Oscar-winning gay-themed films of the early 1990s—the "big," mostly straight-directed films released as mainstream counterbalances to the New Queer Cinema, and whose formal techniques and ideological tasks have, sadly, served as obvious templates for many of today's gay filmmakers. This is precisely the point that B. Ruby Rich makes in complaining that Gus Van Sant's 2008 biopic *Milk* feels, on its own terms, "constrained" and "conventional"—a far cry from many of Van Sant's earlier, experimental, iconoclastic works.[18] But if *Milk,* so perversely true to its title, eliminates blackness altogether, then at least it does not offer a false and condescending equivalence between white and black experiences of sociopolitical oppression. By contrast, another major gay-themed film, Jonathan Demme's 1993 melodrama *Philadelphia,* from which *Milk* otherwise borrows so much (including an iconography of martyrdom as well as a portentous opera fandom), is nothing if not a paean to the "shared" (and implicitly equated) civil rights struggles of black and gay Americans. (This connection becomes explicit in the film's courtroom sequences, but also in the appearance of Joanne Woodward's character, who makes casual references to Rosa Parks, enjoining her AIDS-stricken son against sitting "in the back of the bus.") If, however, gay-identified fan practices can make a sexless biopic like *Howl* "much hotter" (to quote a YouTube user comment on "allen & neal"), they can also question such a film's approach to blackness, using the "That's racist!" meme to critique a troubling yet tenacious conflation of race and sexuality.

"Watch This, Not That": *Pull My Daisy* and *Six '55* as *Howl*'s Online Alternatives

A fan video such as "allen & neal (gay romantic scene)," which relies upon *Howl* but recuts it, points to the prominence of YouTube as a site for fan-driven revisions of popular media—a place where the user can take pleasure in a mere film clip made "gayer" through digital manipulation. YouTube is also, however, a site where a different form of protest may occur—the kind of protest that derives from the intense dissatisfaction so often surrounding media availability issues. The abiding, downright maddening lack of purchasable versions of certain gay-themed media products, including and especially avant-garde short films, has long mobilized gay-identified fan communities, either by awakening them to the possibilities of illicit, underground videotape duplication and circulation, or by prompting public challenges to the kind of queerphobic corporate myopia that often declares gay-themed works unfit for commercial release. Like Shirley Clarke's long-commercially-unavailable *Portrait of Jason* (1967), *Pull My Daisy,* the 1959 short film that Robert Frank and Alfred Leslie directed from a script by Jack Kerouac, has had a severely, notoriously limited exhibition history. Not available on DVD at the time of *Howl's* release, *Pull My Daisy* was uploaded to YouTube—and also to Vimeo, MySpace, and Dailymotion—by users who had managed to acquire digital versions of the film through various online circuits, many of them explicitly identified as gay or gay friendly. In the film, Allen Ginsberg appears with his partner, Peter Orlovsky; as in *Howl,* here the two men form a somewhat sexless pair, occupying frequently distanced positions (background and foreground, far left and far right) within the short film's stylized mise-en-scène; thus separated, the two men fail to suggest an eroticized intimacy, just as a familiar still from *Howl,* which depicts Franco's Ginsberg with his back to that of Tveit's Orlovsky, is more apt to connote a brotherly bond than, say, a "top-bottom" one. Identifying *Pull My Daisy* as one of *Howl's* forerunners, as so many MySpace and YouTube users have done in uploading the film for free viewing, suggests not that *Pull My Daisy* provides a vaunted eroticism in contrast to the circumspection of its documentary-style descendant; instead, it indicates the possibility of placing *Howl* on a less-than-sexy continuum whose point of origin can be traced back to the 1950s. Illicitly uploading *Pull My Daisy* as a kind of prologue to *Howl* serves the obvious purpose of introducing online users to the image of Ginsberg himself—the historical Ginsberg, not Franco's impersonation of the poet; it also works, as one YouTube description suggests, to "unearth" the rhetorical style of the Beat Generation (represented in *Pull My Daisy* by Kerouac's own compositions) that Ginsberg helped to develop. But uploading *Pull My Daisy* also, of course, grants users an entrée into precisely the kinds of "outsider" politics and gay-specific struggles that *Howl* so fitfully, and perhaps unsatisfyingly, addresses. That is because the 1959 film presents Ginsberg as both "himself" (which is to say, a poet by the name of Allen Ginsberg whose boyfriend is Peter Orlovsky) and as an exemplar of the type of urban artist whose disgust encompasses such bêtes noires as the nuclear family, formal education, and "clean living."

From the perspective of digital media theory (and, of course, of numerous digital media users), another bête noire may well be copyright, the formal means through which a film is circumscribed for the sake of its "protection"—and, in this case, kept from gay viewers who may want or even need it, and who have turned to YouTube and other video-sharing sites in order to get it. A copyright-imposed scarcity is frequently the object of considerable online scorn. The many gay-identified or avowedly gay-friendly users who upload *Pull My Daisy,* and in so doing identify it as *Howl*'s clear correlate, suggest a central thematic connection between the two films, one that exceeds the boundaries of biography and whose confirmation requires the interventions of an "unauthorized" online fandom. Illicit uploading thus acts as a mode of resistance—a principled, and ultimately pedagogically effective, reaction to the often constricting vagaries of commerce and copyright, and a practice through which, in the words of Lucas Hilderbrand, "binary code can . . . be sent virtually to innumerable, anonymous" users.[19]

Simply put, those hoping to contextualize *Howl*—and to see more of Ginsberg himself—have often had to rely on video-sharing sites in order to do so, and with some immediately available benefits. If the digital fan practices associated with queer cinema and with gay men are often efforts to confirm or extend gay cultural and sexual specificity, then simple (albeit illicit) uploading can serve a similar purpose, particularly when tied to the comparison-making frameworks of YouTube, a site that routinely provides lists of purportedly similar videos, making such lists available as scrollable sets of recommendations—of, that is, instantly viewable, textually identified "options." In early 2013, I was hardly surprised, for instance, to find that YouTube was touting "allen & neal (gay romantic scene)" as a top recommendation in relation to an illicit upload of *Pull My Daisy,* in the process demonstrating the website's occasional inability—despite the persistent efforts of Content ID—to instantly detect and police "improper" uses of moving images. From the perspective of copyright law, "allen & neal" and the YouTube version of *Pull My Daisy* are equally illicit—homologous examples of media piracy that yet managed to evade Content ID, sailing beyond YouTube's generally restrictive radar. That they both centralize gay subjects and themes makes their unexpected prominence on the site even sweeter.

Gay fans of queer films curate their own festivals on YouTube, sometimes with clips created through the double digital manipulation of a cinematic source (as when "allen & neal" was taken directly from *Howl*'s authorized streaming version and then further altered through YouTube-friendly video editing software), and sometimes by uploading a film in its entirety. *Pull My Daisy,* as a complete and "untouched" (albeit digitized) film, has been uploaded and shared so many times that it would be virtually impossible to track down the original celluloid or VHS source of its countless online lives. Instructively, *Pull My Daisy* was not, at the time of *Howl*'s release, available for purchase as a Region 1 DVD. Uploading some illicitly acquired digital file of the film, and disseminating it via Vimeo,

YouTube, and other such video-sharing sites, suggests, then, an activist response to the way that access often coalesces around precise geographic, economic, and cultural factors. For the gay fan who cannot, for whatever reason, repair to Manhattan's Anthology Film Archives (where 16mm prints of *Pull My Daisy* regularly screen for free as part of the repertory house's Essential Cinema series), file-sharing sites represent an excellent—even preferable—alternative, particularly given their imbrication with editing and image-creation software, an imbrication that signals their sheer amenability to fan-driven expansion. *Pull My Daisy* has thus become a digitized product as well as a digital tool, in the process transforming antiquated (or simply corporate) ideals of access and pursuit. In describing cinema's multidirectional loss of materiality—its digitization at the levels of production, distribution, and exhibition—D. N. Rodowick describes, in admittedly nostalgic terms, the extent to which film history, for the members of Rodowick's generation, "was a pursuit founded on scarcity, for any film not still in its commercial run was difficult to see, and the only way to see a film was to see it projected." Rodowick's concern is primarily philosophical: he questions what is at stake for the art of cinema in its digitization, often casting backward glances at a time, not terribly long ago, when "it was still possible to believe in film as an autonomous aesthetic object because the physical print itself had to be chased down."[20] The love of such a chase may constitute a kind of Benjaminian connoisseurship, but largely, I would argue, for those committed to the commercial mainstream, whose products, however scarce and dispersed, could nevertheless be located, whether as tattered 16mm or pristine 35mm prints. For queer avant-garde films, this history has been considerably different—marked more by the affective registers of loss and frustration, as Juan Antonio Suárez suggests, than by a confident zest for detective work.[21] In uploading *Pull My Daisy* in its entirety, YouTube users confirm the film's outlier status; a relatively little-known, little-seen film for which there is allegedly no "legitimate" commercial market (and which therefore demands the hyperbolic, coercive label of "Essential Cinema" at Anthology Film Archives) is far more likely to remain an accessible presence on video-sharing sites. The same, of course, can be said of YouTube uploads of James Franco's *The Broken Tower*, whose biographical subject (the gay poet Hart Crane) is as allegedly "uncommercial" as the film's avant-garde approach. If *Howl*, with its slightly more mainstream trappings and associated copyright protections, cannot be found, in its entirety, as a YouTube upload, then it can clearly be seen as the film that informs, and even explicitly frames, illicit (and seemingly necessary) YouTube uploads of *Pull My Daisy*. A version of the latter film, uploaded to YouTube in late 2012, described it as "the ORIGINAL *Howl* (James Franco)," while a Vimeo version, uploaded in February 2011 but removed two weeks later when the associated account was suspended (apparently for terms-of-use violations that had nothing to do with *Pull My Daisy*), rather cheekily positioned it as the "Beat film that beats *Howl*."

The significance of *Pull My Daisy* as a record of the Beats—and also of certain mid-twentieth-century modes of experimental filmmaking—cannot be overstated. But the film assumes the form not of direct cinema—not of a proto-vérité engagement with urban reality—but rather of a prose reading with visual accompaniment. It is this formal approach, in particular, that makes the film seem so snug a fit for Vimeo and YouTube, as well as for transgressive memes that promiscuously and ironically combine unrelated (or tangentially related) sounds and images—that employ vocal recordings as the sole acoustical accompaniment to photomontage. (I am thinking of such famous examples as "christian bale rant" [2009], in which an audio recording of the actor Christian Bale's "breakdown" on the set of his 2009 film *Terminator Salvation* is tied to an image of his disturbed *American Psycho* character Patrick Bateman, and "Christian Bale & Mel Gibson Phone Fight" [2010], in which a kind of obscene poetry emerges from interspersed audio clips of Bale's comments and Mel Gibson's equally notorious 2010 voice-mail recordings.) In *Pull My Daisy*, it is Jack Kerouac who, in voice-over, ventriloquizes through Allen Ginsberg, with words that Kerouac wrote. When considered as a commentary on this particular history, *Howl* can thus seem a rebuke not simply to the biographical distortions of *Pull My Daisy,* in which Ginsberg literally lacks a voice of his own and appears to be little more than Kerouac's puppet, but also to the culturally powerful (yet limited and often stereotyped) Ginsberg-Kerouac connection itself. To view the two writers as forever bonded beneath a Beat rubric is, of course, to downplay the individual achievements of each. But it is also to suggest that the connection between them contained an eroticized dimension, given the presumptive sexual freedom of the Beats but also the specific career intersections of Ginsberg and Kerouac (career competition offering, arguably, one of the most common lenses through which American culture has historically depicted homoeroticism). It is precisely this dimension that *Howl* introduces, and then almost immediately discards: Franco's Ginsberg develops a crush on Todd Rotondi's Kerouac, but a crush that the film presents as little more than an innocuous schoolboy fascination, rather than the intense and unrequited longing of one artist for another, which other representations of the Beats have favored.

Pull My Daisy is set in a New York apartment whose doors remain open to various poets, musicians, aestheticians, and religious gurus, but which, at the beginning of the film, is the domain of no more than a mother and her son. Suddenly, Allen Ginsberg enters the space, trailing poet Gregory Corso and carrying cases of beer and wine. According to Kerouac's voice-over, Ginsberg is "all bursting with poetry," but we have to take his word for it, because Ginsberg remains silent throughout the sequence—simply a camera subject whom Kerouac's narration identifies and psychologizes. As the mother is dressing her son for school, fitting him with a "respectable" uniform, a loitering Ginsberg remains cloaked in a hooded parka. His refusal to remove the hood in the presence of mother and son is the first suggestion of what Kerouac will later call Ginsberg's aversion to "order"—both to the timely structuring of a day and to the subtle and stringent oppressions of family life. It is Ginsberg who drinks "inappropriately" in the early hours of the morning, while the mother readies her son for school. And it is Ginsberg who later looks out the window and soliloquizes about what he sees—although it is, of course, Kerouac's soliloquy that we hear, Kerouac's opinions that the film ascribes to the poet who happens to occupy the shot. According to Kerouac, Ginsberg is fixated on "all those cars out there"—on the automobiles that pass slowly by, carrying men and women bound for work, all of them slaves to "order." The ventriloquizing bent of Kerouac's narration suddenly asserts itself, as Kerouac speaks for a Ginsberg whose lips barely even move. (No attempt at believable dubbing is made in this unceasingly avant-garde work, another formal feature that it shares with the viral YouTube creations described above.) Kerouac's Ginsberg continues to point at the traffic outside the apartment window, and cries that there's "nothing out there but a million screaming ninety-year-old men being run over by gasoline trucks!"—a cry that sounds so unmistakably like a complaint that Ginsberg's companion, Greg Corso, commands his friend to "throw a match" on the madness below, if it really bothers him so much. But Ginsberg, presented through Kerouac's patronizing prose as the gentle poet, the implicitly gay peacemaker, says simply, "No, that's all right."

Viewed today, *Pull My Daisy* seems remarkably condescending to Ginsberg, tied as it is to Kerouac's own words and voice. *Howl* could thus profitably be seen as the cinematic project that gives Ginsberg a chance to finally reverse these terms, albeit through James Franco's surrogate. In *Howl*, Ginsberg is indeed speaking for himself, describing his experiences and reciting his poetry, but he is also, in an inversion of the interpersonal hierarchy of *Pull My Daisy*, speaking through—and for—a Kerouac who remains as mute as the earlier film's version of Ginsberg. Ironically, it is through this revisionist presentation of Ginsberg as being far more committed to locating what could be called a gay community than to ruing his unrequited affections for Kerouac and Cassady—it is in this corrective portrayal of the poet as something other than a masochist—that the film fails to offer the sort of open, visible eroticism that so many gay-identified online fans expected, and perhaps even longed for (irrespective of Franco's specific sex appeal). Again, there is no same-sex kiss to be seen in the film, and Ginsberg himself stops short of sucking Cassady's cock after assiduously preparing to do so. In an especially melodramatic moment, Cassady's female companion bursts through the door just as Ginsberg is falling to his knees, thus ending the poet's plan to fellate his friend. It is precisely this aborted blow job that "allen & neal (gay romantic scene)," with its expert editing, "corrects," so that it culminates not in a melodramatic, heterosexist interruption, but instead in Ginsberg's bending to tend to Cassady's cock. Cutting there, "allen & neal" not only removes the disgusted woman who walks in, it also ends on the promise of completion, of mutual sexual pleasure and plenitude. It is thus a powerful reminder of how remediation works—not simply as a technological improvement upon past formats (digital technologies here shortening a conventionally paced scene into something characterized by a staccato, perhaps even Vine-ready sexiness), but also as a principled mending of a past aesthetic and (anti-)erotic "mistake." Isla mari, the gay-identified YouTube user responsible for "allen & neal," appears to have hated *Howl*'s melodramatic techniques; rejecting them, he used digital technologies not to eradicate a cinematic source but to distill and redefine some of its sexiest, most erotically promising elements.

Still other digital fan creations suggest the difficulty of discerning the line between appreciation and critique. If, as uploaded to contexts that question the contributions of *Howl* to queer history, *Pull My Daisy* suggests both an antidote to the later film's pretensions to documentary "truth" (precisely by showing Ginsberg himself) as well as an equivalent victim of cinematic chastity (a comparably "sexless" account of the Beats), then certain, similarly experimental short films themselves suggest a precipitous combination of *Howl*'s best and worst elements. The influence of Epstein and Friedman's film—or at least of the historiographic impulse behind it—can be seen in Ruth Du's digital short *Six '55* (2011), which re-enacts Ginsberg's first reading of his most famous poem at San Francisco's Six Gallery in the fall of 1955. Suggesting the lasting power of the Ginsberg-Kerouac connection, *Six '55* begins with a confrontation between the contrasting personal styles of the two writers. The first voice we hear, in fact, is Kerouac's: he's soliciting donations for Ginsberg's reading, and in a soothing, sexy, and altogether successful way. We see his hands held out in supplication, we hear his voice with its mixture of masculine bombast and boyish neediness, and we see the women who all too eagerly dispense dimes, nickels, quarters. Du then cuts to the smug face of a male patron—a mustachioed man who also serves as the event's emcee—as he goads Ginsberg by praising Kerouac, whom he calls "such a charmer." A visibly distressed Ginsberg, nervously puffing on a cigarette, concedes begrudgingly, "He has a way with people. All kinds of people."

Du continues to crosscut between Kerouac's antics and Ginsberg's unconcealed discomfort, offering the psychologized dialectic common to virtually all popular accounts of the Beats: the battle between the sort of easy charm that threatens to self-extinguish and the special brand of meekness that must compete with dreams of artistic success—between, that is, the crazy-sexy Kerouac and the more publicly circumspect Ginsberg, who must learn to toss caution to the wind. But what seems, in *Six '55*, to be a mere recreation of Ginsberg's public unveiling of "Howl" turns suddenly into something else entirely, before coursing

Figure 3.2. Ruth Du's *Six '55* (2011) places a gay Asian man in the audience for Ginsberg's first public reading of his poem *Howl*.

just as quickly back to its biographical, documentary-style beginnings. As a still-anxious Ginsberg asks the emcee if he has seen Ginsberg's boyfriend, Peter Orlovsky, Du suddenly inserts a shot of a young Asian man who stares at the poet, carefully mimicking the man's smoking technique. The emcee reassures Ginsberg that Peter will show up, and the young man keeps on staring—curiously, even longingly—at the star of the hour. He pretends to take out a tape recorder, holding the invisible object in front of his face, and finally begins to speak. "It is this man that I want to become," he says, still staring at Ginsberg. "It is this man that I want to come inside me."

From this point forward, *Six '55* follows the young man, who introduces himself as Arden, as he makes his way through the gallery, past anachronistic club kids and women wearing equally anachronistic hot-pink wigs and glitter; he gets involved in heated debates about "art"; he watches a man and a woman having sex, and asks the woman how, precisely, it feels to ride a cock. At the end of this array of hazy, hedonistic moments, which together recall the psychedelic "Superstar" sequence of *Midnight Cowboy* (John Schlesinger, 1969), *Six '55* returns to Ginsberg, still clad in period-appropriate attire, and still visibly distressed in preparation for taking the stage. Finally at the microphone, and ready to recite his poem, Ginsberg becomes emboldened, crushing his crutch of a cigarette underfoot as if it were an odious little insect. When he speaks, Arden listens. No longer distracted by his fellow revelers, he stops to stare once again at the poet whom he wants both to be and to have.

As Ginsberg reads "Howl," *Six '55* begins to risk seeming a mere retread of the gallery-set sequences of Epstein and Friedman's film, wherein adoring young people nod approvingly at the poet's sentiments. Here, Du captures such reverence, but she also reiterates Kerouac's insufferable charisma, in the process permitting it to morph into something even more upsetting. As Ginsberg reads, Kerouac shouts, at the top of his lungs, "Woo-woo! This is the renaissance, my friends!"— an utterance that he will repeat more than once. In so shouting it, he ends up sounding like a violently drunk and altogether off-putting frat boy—the bane of this hipster ball. That Jack Kerouac is, in *Six '55*, the most disruptive member of Ginsberg's San Francisco audience is telling. It reflects the recent popular turn toward representing Kerouac as a kind of heel who lacked the artistic talents of the gay men who (like Ginsberg) momentarily succumbed to his masculine charms—a turn that queer revisionism has inarguably occasioned, but that the 2012 Walter Salles adaptation of *On the Road* goes some way in reversing. Salles's film presents Sal Paradise (Kerouac's clone) as a sensitive soul beholden to a brutish but charming fellow named Dean Moriarty (the Neal Cassady figure, who happens to fuck men as well as women, and who is played in the film by the ravishing young Garrett Hedlund). That there is no Ginsberg surrogate to be found in *On the Road* is possibly a reason for the film's funneling the bulk of Beat sensitivity into the vessel of Jack/Sal. In *Six '55*, however, Ginsberg sheds his reticence, while Kerouac, never tactful to begin with, becomes increasingly insufferable.

Ultimately, the queer achievement of *Six '55* has less to do with its iconoclastic approach to Kerouac, and still less to do with its rehabilitation of Ginsberg (a rehabilitation that Franco's forceful, butch portrayal certainly shares), than with its presenting the poet as the principal object both of desire and of identification for a young man of color. This Ginsberg may be "taken," may already have found his true love, but that only makes him more of a behavioral model for the aptly named Arden. "Holy Peter," Ginsberg reads from his poem, at the very point at which the actual, flesh-and-blood Peter—Peter Orlovsky, Ginsberg's boyfriend—finally enters the gallery, smiling at his beloved in a way that Arden can well understand. Hearing Ginsberg's voice crack with emotion as he utters his mate's name, and only seconds later hearing that voice rise and roar for the line "I'm with you in Rockland," Arden becomes emboldened, straightens his back, lifts his chin. *Six '55* has carefully, intelligently prepared for this representation of the appreciative reaction of a person of color to white-authored art. After all, and in striking contrast to the beatific but anonymous black woman who turns up in *Howl*, the young, Asian Arden is Du's protagonist—not some nameless, exotic outlier. It is through Arden's eyes that we see Ginsberg. Here, after the woman of color who in *Howl* cheers the poet's victory for no reason other than that she is lazily made to signify solidarity-amid-oppression, is a gay Asian boy who is obsessed with sex, who is more than a bit eccentric (with his invisible tape recorder and almost constant soliloquizing), and who seems secure in his erotic identity. Here is a boy who both appreciates Ginsberg and wishes to use his experience of the poet's landmark public performance as a platform—a jumping-off point—for his own art.

From Ginsberg to Crane: Franco's Digital, Biographical *Broken Tower*

It is notoriously difficult to depict a poet in mainstream cinema, which is probably why the experimental *Six '55* succeeds so thrillingly in capturing both Ginsberg's capsule biography as well as his artistic impact. Somehow, despite or perhaps because of its anachronisms, the film offers stronger stand-ins for Ginsberg's flights of poetic fancy than does the far more literal-minded *Howl*. (Indeed, such obviousness struck even straight reviewers, including A. O. Scott, whose words of praise for *Howl* are peppered with more than a few disparaging remarks about the film's animated sequences: "It is as if an earnest, literal-minded undergraduate had set out to illustrate 'Howl' without understanding the essential difference between poetic and pictorial imagery.")[22] In *Six '55*, it seems especially fitting that Du uses a wildly bewigged and sequined woman (who looks as if she's auditioning for the Milla Jovovich role in *The Fifth Element* [Luc Besson, 1997]) as a visual equivalent of Ginsberg's "angel-headed hipsters," instead of the kind of correlate that *Howl* offers through animation: a gentle, alabaster apparition that glides through the night.

Six '55 is not the only film to gain force through its pointed deviations from Epstein and Friedman's biopic. Whether deliberately or inadvertently, Du's work benefits, quite simply, from not being *Howl*, but it also benefits—perhaps intentionally—from its own digital form and function, as an eminently "uploadable" work whose online sharing can conceivably re-create the communal, gay-specific meaning-making characteristic of Ginsberg's first public readings (at least as described by Ginsberg himself in his journals). So does James Franco's Hart Crane biopic, *The Broken Tower* (2011), perhaps a more obvious descendant of *Howl* that, like its predecessor, features uninterrupted poetry readings, documentary-style testimonials, and polemics about the importance of queer art. However, unlike *Howl*, it also offers an abundance of explicit eroticism—an exultant same-sex eroticism that, while not necessarily reflective of Crane's poetry, can seem a retroactive contribution to the Ginsberg biopic that so badly needs it. Franco's own film is thus a form of fan practice: it plainly exhibits the influence of several of the queer auteurs with whom the actor has worked, especially Gus Van Sant. In fact, with *The Broken Tower*, Franco appears to be recreating the sensuous surface aesthetic of Van Sant's breakthrough black-and-white film *Mala Noche* (1986), the principal difference being that the graininess of Van Sant's 16mm film stock is here replaced by the pristine homogeneity of consumer-grade digital recording. Prior to its brief commercial run at Manhattan's IFC Center, and even prior to its licensing to Netflix, *The Broken Tower* was available in multiple versions on YouTube, Vimeo, and Dailymotion. Its most persistent, unauthorized online presence, however, has not been in the form of a feature film to

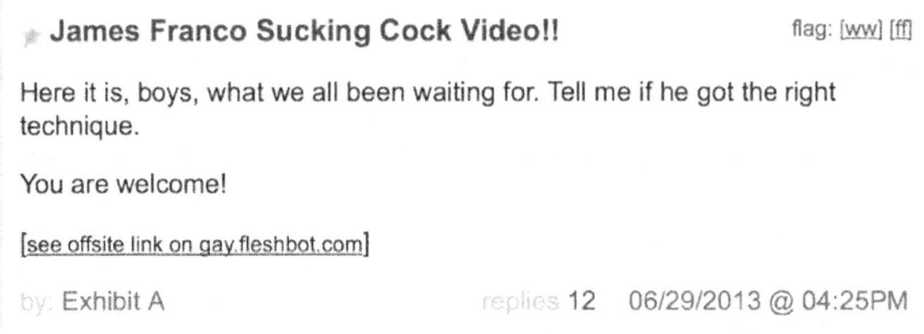

⚡ James Franco Sucking Cock Video!!   flag: [ww] [ff]

Here it is, boys, what we all been waiting for. Tell me if he got the right technique.

You are welcome!

[see offsite link on gay.fleshbot.com]

by: Exhibit A   replies 12   06/29/2013 @ 04:25PM

Figure 3.3. On The Data Lounge, an internet forum for "gay gossip, news and pointless bitchery," a threaded discussion addresses James Franco's *The Broken Tower* to gay men, condensing the film into a clip of "Franco sucking cock." June 2013. datalounge.com.

be watched in its entirety on YouTube (à la *Pull My Daisy*); it has, instead, assumed the forms of GIFs, Vines, Instagrams, and photomontages all created from a single source: a scene in the film depicting the expert fellatio techniques of Franco's Crane.

What makes *The Broken Tower* such a fascinating case study is the film's sexually explicit content, which can now be widely accessed online and condensed into a series of digital forms, from GIFs to Vines. More than just a matter of the abovementioned cock-sucking scene (a screenshot of which went viral in 2012, being tweeted and retweeted, blogged and reblogged, often with the accompanying information that Franco's mouth surrounds, in fact, a prosthetic penis), the erotic content of *The Broken Tower* comes to encompass a series of gay-specific sexual practices. "THE TRUTH IS INDECENT," screams the film's official poster, in stark all-caps font, above which sits the smaller and considerably more specious claim "Based on the True Life Story of the Poet Hart Crane." If these two uses of the word "true" seem especially tendentious (or, at the very least, redundant), it is clear that they have set a certain tone for fan-authored online uses of Franco's film, which tend to insist upon the gay-specific veracity of its erotic depictions. "James Franco Has No Gag Reflex, Wishes He Sucked Real Dicks," proclaimed Logo's NewNowNext blog, which addressed its account of Franco's "true desire" to the "gays of the world" who could properly appreciate it, and who, if made aware of Franco's "indisputable" fellatio skills, would surely buy tickets to see *The Broken Tower* in its entirety. Championing the film's commercial prospects was thus, in this instance, a matter of making it "speak" to gay men, primarily through references both to allegedly gay-specific techniques of oral sex and to Franco's capacity to accurately capture them on screen. "James Franco is sucking cock . . . and, yes, it's him," promises the gay-identified Tumblr ALEKZ, describing a clip of Franco in which his mouth is wrapped desirously around a dildo; at issue for ALEKZ is not whether said dildo is a "real dick" but, rather, whether Franco is "truly" and "accurately" performing "gay fellatio." Apparently, according to ALEKZ, the clip in question, taken from *The Broken Tower* but (like "allen & neal") digitally condensed to accentuate its "sexiness"—and, importantly, to eliminate the depictions of sheer heterosexism that surround it—"proves" that Franco can suck cock "like a gay man"; the cock's prosthetic status is thus embarrassingly beside the point.

Still other sites, in seeking to suggest that *The Broken Tower* is "true" to gay men's erotic experiences, seized not upon the famous fellatio sequence but instead upon a scene depicting anal intercourse. For its part, with an entry entitled "James Franco Gets Topped," The Male Star Blog, which is designed to align mainstream film and online porn actors as equally evocative of "hot gay" culture, offered a clip of one of *The Broken Tower*'s sex scenes that had been recorded illicitly by a gay fan who attended one of the film's rare commercial screenings at the IFC Center, and who wanted to extract and share what to him was the film's "hottest" and most "adult" sequence. Calling the result a "badly taped video," The Male Star Blog later offered its own "supplements"—still images taken not from a shaky camrip but, rather, from a pristine YouTube upload that suddenly and conveniently appeared. Condensing the sex scene into three still images, The Male Star Blog created an especially titillating triptych: one image was of Franco and Michael Shannon kissing in medium shot, another was of them kissing in close-up, and a third and final image showed Shannon and Franco forming the "fag missionary" position (with Shannon on top). Notable about this triptych was that none of its constituent images represented an unedited screen shot; each tweaked the film beyond simply freezing its frames. For instance, the second shot in the series—the close-up—was created through cropping; it was hardly a telling indication of what can actually be seen through a conventional viewing of Franco's film, even as the blog on which it appeared insisted that it was an example of how "true" *The Broken Tower* is to gay men's experiences of anal sex. Another gay-identified blog, My New Plaid Pants, borrowed this triptych but provided its own self-identified "supplement"—a GIF labeled "NSFW" (or "Not Safe for Work") that purportedly reveals how "expertly" Franco fellates even a fake cock. My New Plaid Pants thus used the source of a more widely circulated meme—a scene that allegedly "exposes" Franco's awareness of the "true" techniques of oral sex—to suggest that *The Broken Tower* offers an equally "accurate" depiction of anal intercourse. That the latter scene did not receive the GIF treatment does not indicate that the administrator of My New Plaid Pants considered it undeserving of such treatment; rather, this gay-identified fan simply seemed more interested in providing digitally manipulated "evidence" to support his endorsement of what he called "Jimbo's *Broken BJ*."

James Franco Has No Gag Reflex, Wishes He Sucked Real Dicks

February 13, 2013 • by Chris Spargo

Figure 3.4. "James Franco Has No Gag Reflex, Wishes He Sucked Real Dicks," proclaims Logo's NewNowNext blog in a video-driven entry on Franco's "gay biopic" *The Broken Tower*. February 2013. newnownext.com

Of course, the comment sections of these sites suggest just how flippantly some fans respond to the possibility that James Franco might himself "really be" gay, even as they attempt to address those digital fan creations that claim for Franco only an "academic knowledge" of gay erotic and cultural specificities. While Franco does not publicly identify as gay, the actor's distinctly queer internet presence offers copious indications of—as well as obvious resources for—his ostensible queer commitments. Consider, for instance, his celebrated contributions to the comedy website Funny Or Die, one of which—part of a tongue-in-cheek series entitled "Acting with James Franco"—offers a recreation of a scene from *Rebel Without a Cause* that culminates in arguments about that film's queerness. In this sketch, Franco plays himself playing the James Dean role, while Franco's own brother, Dave, plays himself playing the Sal Mineo role. What begins as a standard reading of a film script eventually devolves into an argument between the two brothers, with one—the elder, more famous Franco—insisting that Mineo's character is gay and in love with Dean's eponymous rebel, while the other—the insecure Dave—expresses both his skepticism and his inability to concede that Mineo's was, in fact, a great role (and one for which the actor received an Oscar nomination, a fact that Dave conveniently forgets). When Dave refuses to sniff the James Dean jacket that his brother has handed him—when, in a parody of youthful, queerphobic masculinity, he scoffs at the implications of such sniffing—James shames him with a brief, hilarious lecture on the history of gay male eroticism, of the gay-specific use of such fetish objects as black leather boots and jackets, citing Dean and Mineo as well as Marlon Brando in an effort to erase Dave's insecurities.

Facetious as it is, the Funny Or Die video nevertheless manages to suggest the legitimacy of gay-specific reception practices; the joke is not on some monolithic gayness but instead on the faux-homophobic Dave, on his willful blindness to gay codes and representational conventions. Fittingly, the elder Franco, with his wealth of queer historical knowledge, is on hand to teach Dave a lesson or two. Without overstating his significance to queer pedagogy, I would like to suggest that the many gay-specific permutations of James Franco's star image—including those over which he has no apparent control, such as the ones that emerge from pirated or otherwise unauthorized fan creations—have made "James Franco" a key discursive point around which popular discussions of queer cinema often pivot. Given its star's heartthrob status—but also his persona's longstanding association with erotic play—it is perhaps understandable to approach a virgin viewing of *Howl* with the expectation that the film will offer glimpses of the gay sex that Ginsberg experienced, and about which he wrote. But what does such an assumption—as well as the disappointment that its obliteration may engender— tell us about the directions into which contemporary queer films have lately been moving? In other words, is *Howl*'s lack of "hot sex" simply a perverse gesture, a way of cruelly withholding a desired plenitude—a way of making the film seem, for instance, as sadistic as one of its key characters, the force of whose repetitive courtroom command is that it stops short of even rote politeness? If so, then does such abstemiousness seem especially productive or pedagogic? It may be possible to convincingly defend, in some odd inversion of Jake Ehrlich's 1957 courtroom summation, a queer film's right to sidestep visible sexuality. But to venture such a defense would, of course, be to enter a trap. Because what, exactly, is visible sexuality? An erect cock as captured by a camera? If we claim instead that male homosexuality can be visualized through the subtleties of gesture and of facial expression, or that it can come fully to life through dialogue, then we risk seeming "square" at best and regressive at worst—willing to search for the sort of behavioral stereotypes that Richard Dyer claims are so central to "closeted" representations of gay men.[23] Moreover, we risk apologizing for a film that denies us both the simple pleasure of seeing two men kissing and the heady charge of watching James Franco, in particular, fuck another man—perhaps an inescapable craving at a time when the actor's iconoclasm has culminated in memes explicitly linking him to gay sex, to erotic practices that go well beyond topping and bottoming.

Franco's connections to the visibility of gay sexuality are more than just discursive. His prominent role as codirector, coproducer, and costar of the experimental docudrama *Interior. Leather Bar.*, which "reimagines" the production of William Friedkin's controversial gay-themed film *Cruising,* has played an inescapable role in further linking Franco to the explicit and experientially "real" particularities of gay sex, especially since his directorial partner on the project, Travis Mathews, is openly gay. Itself an example of a gay-identified (and at least partly gay-authored) digital production designed to highlight, extend, and re-contextualize the gay content of a mainstream feature film, *Interior. Leather Bar.* has also served, in turn, as a primary source for its own fans' imaginative recastings. Still and moving images showing Franco's iconic centrality to *Cruising*'s deleted, imagined S&M scenes—as both diegetic and offscreen (co)director—combine with efforts to locate equivalences between his directorial "style" and that of the gay Travis Mathews, thus creating a compendium of digital investigations into the epistemology of gay authorship. On a somewhat less complex level, Franco's general association with gay-identified S&M is now so pronounced—so iconographically and biographically "available"—as to render his role in *Howl* a disappointingly chaste one (especially considering Ginsberg's own, daring descriptions of gay male sexuality). To note that Franco's Ginsberg goes only so far as to place his head of cherubic curls on the muscled chest of another man—Jon Prescott's Neal Cassady—is to acknowledge that the film's almost perverse timidity stands in stark contrast both to the once-actionable eroticism of an old poem and to the self-conscious "risk-taking" of an unusually gay-literate Hollywood star. Fortunately for many libidinous gay fans, that star gave himself a chance to depict some of the extremities of same-sex eroticism within a biopic context, turning his film *The Broken Tower* into a sexy go-to source for appreciative, confirmatory fan creations.

In the case of *Kill Your Darlings,* John Krokidas's 2013 Allen Ginsberg biopic, which dramatically ups the erotic ante on *Howl* and *Pull My Daisy,* similarly complex star personae emerge to mediate the gay-specific claims so central to the film. Widely circulated statements that the film's star, Daniel Radcliffe, has made about the "beauty" and legitimacy of gay male desire have themselves become textual adjuncts to countless gay-identified digital fan projects, appearing as captions for GIFs that show Radcliffe's Allen Ginsberg in poses of intimacy with Dane DeHaan's Lucien Carr and with Jack Huston's Jack Kerouac. In other cases, the Radcliffe quotes—particularly those that refer to gay sex as "natural" and "not shocking"—are made to accompany GIF, Vine, and various other online versions of the central gay sex scene in *Kill Your Darlings,* thus recalling efforts to use Franco's frequently articulated offscreen politics to frame fan-authored online renderings of *The Broken Tower*'s most erotic moments. Gay-identified fans of Radcliffe and of *Kill Your Darlings* have thus managed to turn what, despite its sexual heat, is yet another dispiriting presentation of gay pathology into something far more encouraging, centralizing the gay-friendly persona of its marquee name. In the process of recontextualizing—of "updating"—this historical film about a queer murder (Carr's killing of David Kammerer), fans have rather openly relied upon Radcliffe's "modern," gay-friendly stance, thus recalling similar online appropriations of Jon Hamm, and of Hamm's publicly articulated conviction that the historical *Howl* in fact speaks to contemporary gay concerns. However, in the absence of memes that imagine Hamm's straight lawyer as a gay and ruthless "dom top," or that self-consciously "return" James Franco to the realm of the sexually explicit *Sal, The Broken Tower,* and *Interior. Leather Bar.,* would *Howl* be remotely enjoyable—anything other than a quaint, docudramatic depiction of the queer past? It is arguably in relation to online paratexts—to fan-produced digital tie-ins, which have as much to do with extending the film's gay subject matter as with participating in its star's on-going, avowedly gay-friendly cultural project—that *Howl* can justifiably take its place as a key queer film in the contemporary media landscape. It is, in the sense intended by Umberto Eco—and in express contrast to its makers' self-described, documentary-specific, historicist "commitments"—an eminently open text, one that benefits tremendously from a wide range of gay-identified digital fan practices. Whatever the intentions of Epstein and Friedman, their film has become a protean part of Franco's creative compendium of queer interventions. As such, it doesn't simply benefit from the close, fetishistic attention than fandom affords. That is because, in this case, such fandom tends to be as tech-savvy as its hyper-productive, omnipresent object—as open to gay-themed online remediation as Franco himself. *Howl*—a gay-themed James Franco film—is thus, despite its sexual circumspection (or perhaps because of it), central to the efforts of digital media-makers to emphasize Franco's connections to gay-specific online activism and artistry. If Franco himself can mine *Cruising* for more explicit, imaginative, empowering sex than is actually visible in Friedkin's finished film—if, with the help of the openly gay Travis Mathews, he can turn his interpretive techniques into a digital product that draws from a variety of exploitable sources—then so can his fans make of *Howl* something far more than the staid biopic that it appears to be.

In illicitly uploading full versions of Franco's *The Broken Tower* well before the film was given its extremely limited commercial theatrical run, gay-identified prosumers exhibited an impatience that isn't just part and parcel of a frenzied fandom, and that didn't simply seek to supplant, for the sake of free access, Netflix and various Video On Demand options. As I have argued, a gay-authored ethos of file sharing can combat the kind of elitism that centralizes New York and Los Angeles—and, by extension, such venues as the IFC Center and Anthology Film Archives—as the only viable locations in which to legally watch gay-themed films, both old (*Pull My Daisy*) and new (*The Broken Tower, Sal, Interior. Leather Bar.*). Furthermore, online file sharing, especially as activated through such sites

Figure 3.5. Embodying gay reception strategies: James and Dave Franco (2008) discuss Sal Mineo's "actual" homosexuality as they attempt to reenact an especially "gay scene" from *Rebel Without a Cause* (Nicholas Ray, 1955).

as Vimeo and YouTube—sites that work especially well with a wide range of image-creation and editing software—facilitates boldly extractive fan practices. These include the kinds of projects that consistently manipulate gay-themed films for the sake of pointing up their gay-specific sexual and cultural contours—the "hot" elements that can be condensed into a six-second "porn Vine" (as with *The Broken Tower*'s sex scenes on various gay-identified sites), or the erotic and political appeal that needs to be "teased out" of a film, often through captioned GIFs and video mashups (such as those combining *Howl,* Jon Hamm, and gay superheroes). "Stealing" gay-themed media is therefore more than just a means of gaining free access; it is also, and often, the first step in digital fan creation—as well as a form of fan creation in itself. While it is unclear whether James Franco, who has consistently claimed a cultural rather than commercial objective in producing so many gay-themed films, would approve of this practice, it is unlikely that *The Broken Tower, Sal,* or *Interior. Leather Bar.* would ever have made much money in commercial theatrical release, due not necessarily to their explicit gay content but rather to their formally experimental extremes. They are, one and all, avant-garde films, by any definition of the term, and as such they differ from a recent feature that was withheld for a period of years despite its seemingly obvious mainstream appeal: the Jim Carrey-Ewan McGregor vehicle *I Love You Phillip Morris,* whose much-publicized, high-concept combination of *Catch Me If*

You Can, Steven Spielberg's 2002 blockbuster, and *Brokeback Mountain,* Ang Lee's queer megahit, couldn't quite rescue it from the distribution doldrums. Following a period of intensive re-editing (reportedly in response to "concerns" surrounding its explicit gay sex scenes), a brief legal battle, and a transferring of rights from one small distributor to another (and then to another), *I Love You Phillip Morris* was finally released in the United States in December 2010, nearly four years after the project was first announced in the trade press.

As if to make up for this longer-than-usual time lag, with its undeniably homophobic dimensions, gay-identified fans have taken to the blogosphere in untold numbers to ensure that *Phillip Morris* enjoys plentiful, legible, gay-friendly lives. The following chapter returns to the topic of illicit or unauthorized fan creations—those that seek to sidestep heterosexist circuits of commercial theatrical distribution, and that in this case seize upon streaming editions of a long-withheld film in order to pay it a range of libidinous digital compliments. Mining the sex-fueled *Phillip Morris* for various GIF and Vine versions of its most erotic moments, gay-identified fans don't just uphold those moments as "hot." They also use them to differentiate the film from its unofficial spinoffs—the television programs and web series that turn its real-life subject, the gay con artist Steven Jay Russell, into a sexless example of pure criminal pathology. If *Howl,* the filmic focus of the present chapter, exhibits a chasteness that digital fan creations, drawing from a variety of eroticized star texts, transform into something far more sexually and politically pleasurable, then *Phillip Morris,* the cinematic center of the next chapter, gives its fans something different: a chance to celebrate the uninhibited gayness of a contemporary, star-driven narrative film, in the process combatting not merely post-gay theory but also the popular, almost axiomatic upholding of television (allegedly experiencing a "golden age") over cinema. Perhaps surprisingly, digital television, in a range of network and cable incarnations, has generated a consistently chaste, post-gay Russell, while *I Love You Phillip Morris,* which was shot on 35mm and intended for theatrical exhibition, furnishes big, beautiful movie stars who enact a delirious array of gay erotic practices. In appreciating *Phillip Morris,* gay-identified fans rely upon its digitization, only to demonstrate that a mastery of digital manipulation can make a gay film even gayer, extending its "hotness" across the ever-shifting landscape of contemporary visual culture, and affirming the art of cinema even amid reports of its demise.

4 Liberating Gayness

Selling the Sexual Candor of I Love You Phillip Morris

[T]he historical illegality of gender trespassing and of queerness have taught
many trans/queer folks that their lives will be intimately bound with the legal
system.

> Eric A. Stanley, "Fugitive Flesh"

Say what? They held the pickle and it's still too much for America to take?
Would they have preferred a pig bottom rather than a bear bottom? Or
maybe if at least one of them had done a *Brokeback* and tragically died? In
any case, this film's DVD release will certainly give *me* a release.

> Michael Musto on the long-withheld *I Love You Phillip Morris*

IN PRECEDING THE theatrical release of a contemporary queer film, a fan-
produced online tie-in needn't reach for interpretive extremes. It needn't
challenge the film's thematic focus, offering its own powerfully articulated
alternative—a tremendous sexual success replacing, say, the literally show-
stopping specter of homophobia. As Michael DeAngelis suggests, a reverse process of replacement is just as likely to occur, with a "chaste," culturally gay (or
even assimilationist) paratext attempting to eclipse an erotically explicit, user-
generated representation—as was the case, for example, with the production of
video responses to "Wicked Mountain," a 2006 club remix of Chris Isaak's song
"Wicked Game" that samples Gustavo Santaolalla's Oscar-winning *Brokeback
Mountain* score. Produced by the Swedish rock band Midnight Cowboys, "Wicked
Mountain" suggests not simply a queering of Chris Isaak (by way of Santaolalla's
score) but also a discursive fusion (secured through an allusive band name) of
Brokeback Mountain and John Schlesinger's 1969 film *Midnight Cowboy*, both of
which tackle the topic of "rugged" same-sex couplings, albeit through different
erotic registers. (In *Brokeback*, Jack and Ennis actually fuck, while, in *Cowboy*,
Joe and Ratso do not—however much they may want to.) One of the most viewed
of the fan-created music videos for "Wicked Mountain," uploaded to YouTube in
2008, featured *Brokeback*'s lone representation of penetrative gay sex—the famous tent scene—and extended it through the use of slow-motion software,

suggesting a visual metaphor for the languorous strains of the song (as well as recalling Herb Ritts's use of slow-motion in his iconic black-and-white video for Isaak's "Wicked Game," in which Isaak frolics in the surf with supermodel Helena Christensen).[1] Linking "Wicked Mountain" to *Brokeback*'s sex scene, the video also linked Ang Lee's film to *Midnight Cowboy*, via a reference to Harry Nilsson's "Everybody's Talkin'"—the song that is virtually synonymous with Schlesinger's film. For its part, a 2012 video response (also uploaded to YouTube) claims that the only "real" connection between *Brokeback* and *Cowboy* is that the two films are equally "sad"—that they're not about sex but about solitude, loneliness. As if to emphasize this point, the video features a single elderly man who, gripping a guitar and gazing into the camera, plays a portion of Santaolalla's score, extricating that score from the Swedish mashup and restoring as well the "real," allegedly sexless connection between a pair of major American films.

Despite the presence of de-eroticized online recuperations of queer cinema, YouTube has become a key site for celebrations of male same-sex desire, particularly as that desire is rendered in a cinema whose surrounding circuits—of culture and commerce—place considerable constraints upon libidinous images, limiting their general profitability as well as their capacity to reach gay fans. When a theatre chain refuses to exhibit a gay-themed film—or when an entire state, such as Utah or Idaho, opts out of booking *Brokeback Mountain* or *Blue Is the Warmest Color*—a clear call to arms tends to galvanize gay fans, inspiring them to acquire and to upload those scenes that seem the most obvious objects of homophobic condemnation.[2] In late 2005 and early 2006, YouTube's newly hired content regulators were compelled to work overtime in response to the concerns of Focus Features (and of its parent company, NBCUniversal) regarding the explosion of video versions of *Brokeback*'s showpiece sex scene. That several illicit uploads were identified as specific responses to the film's Utah theatre cancellations—and as ways of permitting that state's gay residents to see what those in the rest of the country could legally pay to behold—appeared to be lost on Focus Features, which assumed no responsibility for failing to overturn the decision of powerful multimillionaire Larry H. Miller, the owner of a Utah multiplex chain, to ignore his contract with the distributor. (Miller, owner of the NBA's Utah Jazz, imposed an embargo on *Brokeback* shortly before its scheduled premiere; Focus threatened to sue Miller but settled for temporarily refusing to conduct business with him.)[3] As efforts to expand access to a queer and therefore relatively rare and potentially illuminating film, YouTube uploads of *Brokeback*'s tent scene collectively represented one of the first major test cases of the website's fair use policies.[4] Because *Brokeback* was deemed deeply commercial by a distributor with vast ambitions for the film (which was already turning an astonishing profit by the end of 2005), YouTube's site managers were compelled to aggressively guard against the "leaking" of its scenes, despite protests from gay-identified

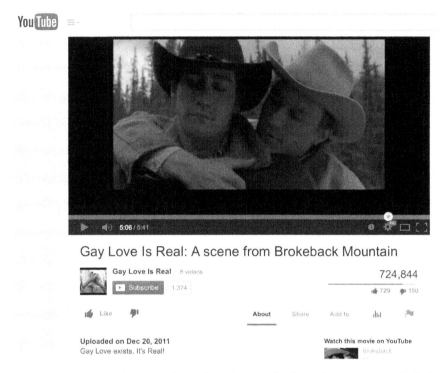

Figure 4.1. Gay media archaeology online: the YouTube channel Gay Love Is Real, which excavates "realistic" gay scenes from contemporary queer cinema, affirms, "Gay Love exists, It's Real!" using a clip from *Brokeback Mountain* (Ang Lee, 2005).

users who asserted the pedagogic (and not just libidinous) significance of shots that were censored elsewhere—and that would, in fact, be excised for *Brokeback*'s heavily publicized premiere on cable television network Bravo (also owned by NBCUniversal) in 2008.[5] During the film's original theatrical run, NBCUniversal was intensifying its vigilance over the illegal dissemination of all its copyrighted media, particularly video segments of *Saturday Night Live* (such as the digital shorts *Lazy Sunday* and *Natalie's Rap*).[6] Above and beyond broad claims about the commercial damage that illicit uploads can cause is, of course, the frequently erotic content of those uploads: when *Brokeback*'s tent scene first started showing up on YouTube, stereotyped assumptions about gay men's quest for titillation almost certainly complicated claims of fair use, which, as Lucas Hilderbrand suggests, tend to centralize a pedagogic "value" that is carefully extricated from any and all pornographic trappings.[7]

In the post-*Brokeback* period, distribution problems for queer films have continued to inspire gay-identified fans to upload entire scenes for free online viewing. This particular practice becomes especially complicated and contentious, however, when the film in question is not an avant-garde James Franco short but, instead, a relatively big-budget, star-studded film with mainstream aspirations, such as Glenn Ficarra and John Requa's *I Love You Phillip Morris* (2008, 2009, 2010), which features Jim Carrey and Ewan McGregor. The film offers an account of the life and crimes of the notorious con artist Steven Jay Russell, a self-identified gay man who, in the 1990s, escaped from no fewer than five Texas prisons (including a pair of maximum-security facilities), impersonating a CEO, a judge, an FBI agent, and an AIDS patient along the way. Following its completion, *I Love You Phillip Morris* suffered at the hands of a number of cautious, seemingly censorial film distributors, inspiring a remarkably persistent mode of gay-identified reception. Animated less by an interest in a queer star persona (such as Franco's) or by a desire to intervene historiographically (for instance, by eroticizing a chaste Allen Ginsberg biopic) than by a concern about the boundaries governing the commercial distribution of an especially "sexy" gay-themed film, gay-identified fans of *Phillip Morris* have tended to highlight its long-suppressed content, uncovering its "sincere" eroticism by uploading entire sex scenes to YouTube and other video-sharing sites. This particular fan-driven use of *Phillip Morris* is not, however, reducible to strictly celebratory dimensions, nor is it always a reflection of a desire to circumvent certain structures of commerce—to avoid having to actually pay for media. *Phillip Morris* sex scenes first appeared online as part of an apparent effort to ensure that the film would in fact enjoy a commercial life despite the much-publicized suspicion that it was considerably less than salable due to its erotic "gay content."[8] Languishing in limbo—in the distribution doldrums—*Phillip Morris* appeared, for several years, to need more than a little help from its fans, as well as from those simply hoping to see it on the big screen one day.

Amid the earliest, user-generated efforts to attract attention to the film, an obvious question emerged—that of how best to "sell" softcore, gay-themed media. On the one hand, numerous gay-identified fans took to the internet to reveal the extent to which *Phillip Morris* is "sexually gay," uploading (and rarely reconfiguring, except through the relatively slow-motion graphics of a GIF) those moments from the film that simulate the vagaries of anal and oral sex using two major movie stars as models. On the other hand, albeit in rare instances, similarly gay-identified fans elected to downplay the film's eroticism, generating chaste and poetic images in an effort to promote its alleged resemblance to a European art object. As exercises in understanding gay-themed media at the crossroads of personal (homo)sexual experience (and appetite) and the harsh realities of commerce and of homophobia, gay-identified online uses of *Phillip Morris* have enjoyed remarkable lives both prior to and following the film's belated theatrical release. As a film whose commercial life in many ways depended upon the internet's powers of promotion, *Phillip Morris* marks a major case study in the way that an emphatically gay-themed film can mobilize equally gay-identified online fans, particularly as those fans blur the lines between promotion and piracy, pedagogy and libidinousness.

It is perhaps surprising that *Phillip Morris,* which was directed by men who do not identify as gay, and which stars famously straight actors, has been met with such obvious appreciation from gay-identified fans, whose efforts to confirm and to celebrate the verisimilitude of the film's numerous gay sex scenes are at the center of this chapter. In 2009, with a withheld *Phillip Morris* failing to inspire distributor confidence in its commercial prospects, those hoping to "sell" it by drawing attention to its eroticism were, whether consciously or not, placing themselves in direct competition with other kinds of paratexts, particularly those that sought to reconfigure the film as "straight friendly." The latter productions, which include GIFs that accentuate Jim Carrey's chameleonic qualities (the way that, for instance, his rubbery face contorts into a wide variety of expressions within a single shot), are sometimes quite campy, since they collectively suggest a queer, digital Trojan horse whose visible exterior is indistinguishable from what one GIF creator called "a typical Carrey comedy," but whose invisible insides, writhing in anticipation of an eventual theatrical release, consisted of scenes in which two beloved actors simulate blowing each other. While some fan productions are undeniably bad according even to the most relaxed of aesthetic standards, and while the occasionally painful, embarrassing sincerity of others suggests Susan Sontag's familiar definition of camp as "failed seriousness," qualitative considerations are not necessarily productive when analyzing promotional paratexts, particularly those that seek to "prove" a film's salability by attracting all manner of attention to it.[9] What Matthew Tinckom and Steven Cohan have both understood to be the dialectical perspective at the heart of multiple historical modes of gay fandom—the ironic stance toward mainstream texts, the complex double consciousness of a product's "official," straight-identified function and of its unauthorized, "underground" meanings—may operate as much through an understanding of gay sexuality as through the conscious application of a camp sensibility.[10] Manipulating a digitized image of James Franco to suggest sexual completion, rather than an aborted blowjob, is not, per se, part and parcel of camp practice, if camp is understood, in Cohan's persuasive formulation, as applying a queer interpretation to a "confining straight context."[11] It is, however, just as dialectical—just as simultaneously attuned to high and low, chaste and erotic, "clean" and "dirty."

It is instructive, for instance, that in offering online renderings of *I Love You Phillip Morris,* gay-identified fans have seemingly been divided between de-eroticizing this deeply erotic film (ostensibly for the purpose of "promoting" it to the straight mainstream) and exposing, with as few digital alterations as possible, its remarkably varied gay sex scenes. Such a split recalls Michael DeAngelis's suggestion that the operations of fantasy often comprise, for gay fans, complex and contradictory public negotiations of "homosexual personae"—the production of paratexts that express the apparently binary alternatives of gay social acceptability and gay erotic fulfillment.[12] DeAngelis, in investigating gay fandom and crossover stardom, sees a constant shift between the sort of "wishful thinking" that positions, say, Keanu Reeves as being culturally gay (and thus, in his mainstream success and "cooperative" cultural presence, an admirably assimilationist role model) and the sort that forcefully inserts him into sexually explicit scenarios, extending the gossipy terms of Kenneth Anger's *Hollywood Babylon* beyond the confines of the written word and exploring the possibilities of moving-image fantasy—possibilities that have, with the advent of Web 2.0, expanded exponentially. DeAngelis, in a discussion of Mel Gibson, cites *The Advocate's* famous 1992 fusion of a still of Gibson's *Mad Max* (from *The Road Warrior* [George Miller, 1982]) and a remarkably similar image of leather-clad gay porn star Jeff Stryker—the sort of imaginative melding that has become even more common with the digital manipulation of images.[13]

What for a print publication in 1992 was a way of highlighting the iconic homology between a homophobic actor and a queer porn performer would become, for countless blog sites beginning in 2009, a way of visualizing a different kind of connection: the believable affinity between a gay-friendly actor (Jim Carrey) and a series of gay-specific cultural and sexual identities (as expressed in but scarcely limited to *I Love You Phillip Morris*). In June 2010, the popular, fan-driven discussion forum Survivor Sucks, which is a prominent part of the social networking service Yuku, introduced a lolspeak-inspired thread entitled "Jim Carrey: I can haz buttsecks?"[14] Within hours of its debut, the thread had generated a series of still images of Carrey, culled from a key scene in *Phillip Morris,* performing the penetrative role in anal sex. At the time, the film had not yet been released theatrically, and so the obviously pirated images of Carrey's character enjoying "buttsecks" were contextualized not in relation to the film's plot (which, as part of an unseen film, remained largely unknown) but instead in relation to allegedly "authentic" gay sexual experiences, particularly those attuned to the question of whether to "cum" in a partner's ass. In addressing the incidence of such a demand within "real-life" scenarios of barebacking, "Jim Carrey: I can haz buttsecks?" would go on to centralize some of the iconic and thematic connections among *Phillip Morris,* gay pornography, and gay "reality," ultimately pressing for the release of a film that appeared to promise considerable clarification in this regard. However, would the finished film, as a whole, speak to as well as for gay men? Would its other scenes seem as "porny" as the one featuring Carrey as an especially avid top? Apparently, only a commercial release of the full feature, as opposed to a piecemeal leaking of its most provocative shots, could offer illumination.

Other efforts to make preliminary sense of *Phillip Morris* on the basis of bootlegged "bits" tended to similarly suggest an interest in the complex nexus among the film, gay pornography, and gay experiential realities. Queerty, for instance, in recognizing the lack of availability of the full feature film, itself pursued pirated versions in a quest to confirm the "graphicness"—and also the verisimilitude—of its showpiece "gay sex scene." Explaining that the website had had an opportunity, earlier in the film's complicated prerelease history, to read about the barebacking scene, Queerty sought to defy "old" ways of accessing information, offering up a defiant explanation of its methods for making sense of the still-suppressed *Phillip Morris:* "This is the Internet, after all, and Morris has already premiered in other countries."[15] Acknowledging that the gay blog LA Rag Mag had first "tipped us off" about the wide online availability of pirated versions of Carrey's sex scene, Queerty complained about the blog's failure to provide an embedded clip. "So we went out and got one," the website announced, before describing the scene not with the language of cinema studies (or even of traditional film criticism) but instead with webspeak: "It's not as graphic as we thought it'd be, but it's still NSFW, and will shock staid American audiences." The description of the scene as "NSFW"—that is, not safe for work—underscores its status as an internet clip extracted from its narrative surroundings. Long denied a theatrical release, *Phillip Morris* was initially, in the United States, reduced to a series of clips that could, for instance, be watched on a workplace computer screen—a far cry from the relative privacy and shadowed eroticism typical of the traditional exhibition experience. Working to redefine the inadequately distributed *Phillip Morris* as an exciting source of NSFW clips, Queerty gave implicit thanks to the internet for its capacity to keep illicit media alive and readily available, remarking that, while EuropaCorp (the film's French distributor) requested that all *Phillip Morris* clips be removed from the site, Carrey's sex scene in particular remained "online all over the place"—seemingly impossible to expunge. Fittingly, the last four words in this Queerty quote ("all over the place") appeared in hyperlink form; when clicked, they ported the user to a page on TinyPic, a free photo and video-sharing service where countless versions of the scene could be accessed.[16]

If, as paratexts, these versions differ from, say, those *Howl*-inspired videos that seek to "correct" that film, they nevertheless exhibit a striking similarity to illicit uploads of James Franco's many gay sex scenes, which function primarily to make available a suppressed or poorly distributed work (like *The Broken Tower*). What distinguished the earliest online efforts to "expose" the eroticism of *Phillip Morris,* however, was the film's widely acknowledged status as a star-driven conversation starter (in contrast to, say, *Sal,* whose mere existence has rarely received mention in mainstream media, and whose champions have tended to see themselves as lonely voices, estranged from certain corporate-fueled operations of fandom and wholly committed to the film's multidirectional queering of the biopic genre). Perhaps the most galvanizing source for early debates about *Phillip Morris* was a 2009 post on the *Village Voice*'s blog. Written by Michael Musto, the post compiled the author's thoughts on the finished film (including his contention that it "might not get a theatrical release in the US because people are too squeamish about a gay sex scene in it"). Not having seen *Phillip Morris,* which in this account amounts to an urban legend of sorts, a cinematic myth demanding rare empirical clarification, Musto was forced to rely upon the firsthand knowledge of a friend, Lewis Tice, a marketing executive for famously queer-friendly U.S. distributor TLA Releasing. Asked to describe "what he got from" the suddenly legendary, little-seen *Phillip Morris* sex scene—a question that itself suggests the film's relationship to gay pedagogy, its capacity to "speak to" gay fans—Tice replied by noting that no penis is even remotely visible at any point in its duration, but that its sexiest, most surprising, and most encouraging accomplishment is that it reveals a gay bottom to be a muscle-bound "bearish type," masculine and demanding, in contrast to stereotyped renderings of sissified weaklings. What's more, the "bearish" bottom, who in the scene is posed "on all fours," receives "a really hard pounding by Carrey." Proceeding to point out that Carrey, in his long and prolific career, has rarely been sexualized on the big screen, Tice adds the actor's relatively chaste star persona to the list of mainstream strikes against *Phillip Morris.* In other words, it is not just that the film defies gay male stereotypes—and in the process confirms gay male "realities"—by representing a bottom who is considerably more masculine than his top; it is that the top is fucking hungrily, that he's "really pounding," and that he's played by Jim Carrey. For gay fans reading Musto's blog, it would have been hard to find a more compelling or more readily debatable set of assertions regarding the film's "difficulty" for the straight mainstream.[17]

As shrill as it is repetitive, *I Love You Phillip Morris* suggests some of the perils—but also many of the politically productive consequences—of high-concept moviemaking in the twenty-first century, particularly given the film's telegraphic amalgamation of two wildly different but equally successful projects. An obvious filmic model for a tale of con artistry—and a relatively recent, critically and commercially successful one—is, of course, *Catch Me if You Can,* Steven Spielberg's 2002 tale of Frank Abagnale, Russell's straight 1960s antecedent. The other model for *Phillip Morris,* or so the filmmakers claimed throughout the film's production—and even intermittently after its long-delayed release—was *Brokeback Mountain.*[18] How two so seemingly disparate films could possibly be profitably joined was anybody's guess, but hopes were sufficiently high among queer-conscious commentators that some started concluding simply that the scheme would "work"—and thereby ended up sounding not unlike the film's con-artist subject, desperate to drum up some distracting fervor. The prerelease attention that *Phillip Morris* received suggests that a certain cynicism regarding high-concept filmmaking subsides in the face of a gay-identified effort; whether this in itself suggests a hollow, opportunistic liberalism—a self-consciously socially conscious stance—or a more sincere adherence to the importance of queer visibility is an open question. In any case, it is worth remembering that the making of *Phillip Morris* occasioned considerable enthusiasm in the mainstream press, and that it was precisely by citing this high-concept project's apparent templates that many critics managed to defuse potential detractors.[19] After all, *Brokeback* had been a big hit; why, then, was *Phillip Morris* barely and belatedly distributed?

The Paratext as Prison Break: Freeing *Phillip Morris*

One of the hallmarks of Pink 2.0 is that principled political responses— particularly to heterosexism and homophobia—so often seem to require diverse digital productions. When the gay blog Towleroad responded to Lewis Tice's remarks about *Phillip Morris* being perhaps "too gay" for straight American moviegoers, it didn't settle for a simple prose-based rebuttal; it also cited a variety of digital fan productions, including trailers (most of them relying upon footage from films other than the withheld *Phillip Morris,* such as Jim Carrey's romantic 2004 drama *Eternal Sunshine of the Spotless Mind* and Ewan McGregor's queer 1998 fantasia *Velvet Goldmine,* in which McGregor simulates fucking Christian Bale). In this way, Towleroad offered extensions of its own earlier strategies, such as its use in 2008 of a still from *Phillip Morris,* in which the film's stars share a kiss under the caption "This is what a Jim Carrey–Ewan McGregor Kiss Looks Like."[20] Elsewhere in the gay blogosphere, that image would be made to move; animated as a GIF, it would offer a perpetual locking of lips—a star-centered same-sex plenitude that, beginning a full two years before the film's U.S. theatrical release, implicitly critiqued the "official" suppression of *Phillip Morris.* If several circuits of distribution had placed a moratorium on the film, freezing it from licit public consumption, then what better vehicle than a ceaselessly repeating GIF to suggest the defiantly lasting life of a libidinous gay product? In centralizing the explicit same-sex eroticism of *I Love You Phillip Morris,* online excerpts of that film are perhaps more vulnerable to censorship than more idiosyncratically fetishized materials—those that focus on bare feet rather than star faces. And yet, in many cases, the very online presence of these excerpts attests to the official suppression of *I Love You Phillip Morris*; they are circulated partly in order to "prove" that the film's depictions of homosexuality still have the power to frighten and offend.[21]

The urgency of such fan productions seems to intensify in relation to gay biography—in, for instance, the use of a gay biopic to make convincing claims about gay cultural and sexual specificities. The mode of wishful thinking behind revisionary *Howl* paratexts appears to combine a familiar form of fan-focused

Figure 4.2. "Gay GIFs" of *I Love You Phillip Morris* (Glenn Ficarra and John Requa, 2008, 2009, 2010) rely on the film's suggestive images and dialogue in a libidinous archaeology. From the blog Binary Frog.

fantasy (a desire to see James Franco enact gay eroticism on screen) and a more challenging historiographic commitment to "uncovering" Allen Ginsberg's gayness through the tools of new media—through software that includes Corel VideoStudio Pro, which permits stop-motion animation and time-lapse effects, and Roxio Video Lab HD, which some Franco fans have used to convert *Howl* clips into 3D images whose haptic qualities suggest that the responsibility for sexually "gaying" Ginsberg literally lies in the hands of the viewer, who here encounters a "touchable" image of the poet (as played by Franco). In the case of "allen & neal (gay romantic scene)," a fan's intention to digitally manipulate an especially unsatisfying *Howl* sequence resulted in a video clip showing an "ideal" erotic scenario—but a clip whose capacity to mislead its viewers about the "true content" of the film generated more than a few admonitory comments (along with far more plentiful words of excitement and appreciation) on its YouTube page, thus raising further questions about the relationship between a theatrically released feature and the digital forms that feed its exegesis. What does an unauthorized, online fan creation have to do with marketing? How, why, and with what verifiable level of success have gay-identified fans sought to establish ways of promoting contemporary queer cinema?

This chapter addresses those questions through the prism of *I Love You Phillip Morris,* a long-delayed, apparently reluctantly released biographical film whose fans have embraced its explicit depictions of gay male eroticism, funneling them through various digital paratexts in order both to celebrate the film's gay-specific sexual verisimilitude and to promote it as deserving of the gay dollar. In this instance, the line between promotion and suppression—between commercial success and free file-sharing—can seem extraordinarily indistinct. In upholding the "hot" yet long-withheld *Phillip Morris* as being worthy of wide commercial distribution, gay-identified fans have systematically "stolen" its content, creating GIFs, Vines, and video mashups that, in assimilating the film's various sex scenes, would appear to satisfy a libidinous interest, and thus to preclude, or at least to limit, the film's profitability among those hoping only to see Ewan McGregor simulate sucking Jim Carrey's cock. In other words, one of the salient questions about the digital forms that active gay fans appear to favor ultimately concerns the ongoing obsolescence of the discrete feature film—its apparent failure to attract attention on its own terms, as a continuous narrative, whether in theaters or via home viewing (and whether shot on 35mm, as was *Phillip Morris*, or with the exclusive aid of digital technologies). Whatever their evaluative thoughts on the film as a whole, gay-identified fans of *Phillip Morris* have so promoted its many sex scenes that their collective contention, conveyed through the combined power of seemingly omnipresent GIFs, Vines, and video mashups, is that non-erotic narrative elements—chaste interstitials—simply don't matter, that *Phillip Morris* is indeed reducible to its "accurate" depictions of oral and anal intercourse. Why bother with plot when all that ass-pounding is so prominent, so pleasurable, and so easily extractable? Why bother with the full film when its fuck scenes are so ripe for Vining, so widely available as GIFs and YouTube videos?

Here, I hope to complicate the celebratory, sex-obsessed online fan practices that promote yet partition *Phillip Morris,* and I hope to do so primarily by advocating analysis of the original film's integrated textual details—its deliriously nonlinear narrative, complex star performances, and critical take on a range of discursive constructions, from "post-gay" prison rape to "post-gay" biography and beyond. Simply put, the preponderance of user-generated productions positing the accuracy—and attesting to the "hotness"—of the many *Phillip Morris* sex scenes suggests a principled, collective commitment to locating and upholding gay specificity in contemporary media, and it is to my mind laudable for that reason, but it cannot illuminate the film's broad interventions in queer politics and history. In considering *Phillip Morris* and the multiple forms of gay-identified fan production surrounding it, I argue that the film has been instrumental in online efforts to understand prison sex as potentially consensual, and as the result of explicit, gay-specific erotic desire rather than of rape (the construction of "post-gay" rape being prevalent in a multiplicity of current, popular and even scholarly renderings of gender segregation, which tend to position "men among men" as inevitably and "unthinkingly" engaging in sexual acts—as fucking without the aid of labels or even of complete consciousness). I hope to suggest, however, some of the dangers of wholeheartedly embracing those fan practices that "verify" the gay sexual and cultural specificity of a feature film, often at the expense of engaging with that film's finer points, its broader narrative and thematic resonance. Simply put, the remarkable *Phillip Morris* is far more than the sum of its sexy paratexts.

If my description of the film evokes a conventional, perhaps even nostalgic approach to cinema criticism, that is because, as D. N. Rodowick so persuasively suggests, the evaluative and contextualizing tools of traditional analysis of the cinematic object have persisted even within the practices of so-called "new media"—even when, for instance, advanced digital forms appear to "supersede" the representational function of cinema while openly relying upon individual films for their content and cultural relevance. Writing at the dawn of YouTube, Rodowick rightly notes that "most so-called new media are inevitably imagined from a cinematic metaphor"—even, I would argue, the YouTube that has so famously relied upon a televisual model, from its name and corporate iconography all the way down to the particulars of its interface, but that has come increasingly to be seen as a site for "cinematic" experiences, as with the unbridled uploading and wide viewing of otherwise unavailable James Franco films in 2010 and after.[22] However much they may have shared the disgust of Franco fans over the homophobic and philistinic circuits of commerce that prevent such films as *Sal* and *The Broken Tower* from attaining mainstream exposure, those hoping to see the long-suppressed *Phillip Morris* did not take the extreme step of uploading the entire film to YouTube, arguably owing to a whole host of factors, from the film's relatively high-profile, much-monitored status (as a star-driven "gay film" and post-*Brokeback* cause célèbre) to the lack even of "underground," bootleg copies of the film. Unlike, say, *Sal,* whose only prerelease controversy centered on the question of whether the ever-productive Franco could possibly make a "watchable" film, *I Love You Phillip Morris* was ensnared in much-publicized legal disputes involving its distributors, their seemingly homophobic cold feet, and widespread concern regarding its commercial viability.[23] It was, in other words, truly tied up—entangled in the type of trap that effectively prevented its complete "leaking" online. Little by little, however, it began to see the light of day; gay-identified fans caught wind of its erotic content; and entire sex scenes ended up on YouTube, even as the full, hour-and-forty-minute feature languished in litigious limbo, lacking a commercial release date.

That *Phillip Morris* enjoyed considerable early success at film festivals (in 2009, it was a widely covered, applause-generating hit at both Sundance and Cannes) would seem to suggest that homophobia was behind its later suppression.[24] The film's verifiable impact at the abovementioned festivals should, of course, have inspired a bidding war. Instead, it portended a complex and dispiriting period of adjustment, during which the film's directors, Glenn Ficarra and John Requa, were compelled to recut the film, despite or perhaps because of its initial success at Sundance, where the dominant question was whether its explicit sex scenes were the objects of a prurient "gay interest" that couldn't possibly translate into mainstream (i.e., straight) appeal.[25] In any case, no major company pursued the film's distribution rights; the editing suite seemed the only recourse for a film whose high-concept "hook" (Jim Carrey pursues Ewan McGregor against considerable odds, in a *Catch-Me-If-You-Can-meets-Brokeback-Mountain* kind of way) had encountered an entrenched heterosexism mixed with an equally familiar homophobia. It remains unclear just how much of *Phillip Morris* was cut following its Sundance premiere; if memory preserves an erotically daring first version, present circumstances provide a similarly sexy final cut. In March 2009, two months after Sundance, the British *Sunday Times* reported that this "gay film" had seemed, to its potential distributors, "too risqué for cinemas."[26] In the weeks leading up to Cannes, the film's running time was shortened to 102 minutes, and in May 2009, Consolidated Pictures Group, a small, California-based company, acquired its U.S. distribution rights, promising that a limited release would soon follow its fêting at the French festival.

In contrast to the Queerty examples quoted above, some of the earliest online paratexts presented the film not as an especially sexy experience but instead as an exceedingly "respectable" product—a much-admired work of art. That these efforts often involved fabrication—or, at the very least, the slight stretching of the truth—suggests a certain fan-specific desire to override official circuits of suppression, and by any means necessary (including mendacity). In May 2009, IMP Awards, a website devoted to movie posters, acquired—in the form of a JPEG file—an allegedly official poster advertising the Cannes "triumph" of *I Love You Phillip Morris*.[27] Featuring a grinning Jim Carrey (wearing a tie and toting a briefcase), the poster appeared to belie the film's title—to turn the project into something chaste and perhaps even "straight"—by omitting an image of Ewan McGregor. What's more, it indicated, through the familiar iconography of a laurel wreath, that the film had won a prize at Cannes when, in fact, it had not. Apparently unaware of this error, the website Movie Poster Addict reblogged the image, identifying it as an "official poster" for *I Love You Phillip Morris* and noting that it is both similar to and different from "typical Carrey fare"—similar in its use of Carrey's familiar "goofy face," and different in its use of a "Cannes logo." One of the website's registered users, Matt Riviera, noticed several red flags, however, and wrote in the comment section, "I'm pretty sure this poster is a fake. For one thing this film did not win the Camera d'Or in Cannes. For another, the photoshopping is terrible."[28] In suggesting that, with a friend like this particular poster, *Phillip Morris* didn't need enemies, Riviera attempted to promote honesty as the mode most appropriate to advocating on behalf of the film. His truth-telling approach to publicizing the suppressed *Phillip Morris* is thus crucial to contextualizing subsequent, gay-authored efforts to uphold the film as an "accurate" representation of gay cultural and sexual specificities—efforts that openly promoted the film's "gay status" as well as its erotic content, and that avoided false suggestions of the film's award-decorated "legitimacy."

Just how "correct," however, can an out-of-context YouTube clip really be? That the earliest YouTube versions of the *Phillip Morris* sex scenes should be viewed, at least in part, as activist responses to the film's lack of commercial availability is obvious from the majority of their titles and user-composed descriptions, which range from the declamatory ("Release this film now!") to the depressed ("So sad that this film can't be seen . . ."). However, at the same time that numerous gay-identified fans were pushing for the film's belated commercial release, they were ensuring the free availability of online paratexts that relied on entire scenes from *Phillip Morris,* uploading them in their entirety to YouTube and other video-sharing sites, and suggesting some of the contradictions at the center of "celebratory" fan production. To "celebrate" *Phillip Morris* has long been to "steal" its audiovisual content—to mobilize fair-use claims at the expense of commercial support, and as a means of exposing both the "hotness" as well as the "believability" of a film that more than one distributor has seemingly misunderstood.

Correctional Paratexts: *Phillip Morris* as "Honest" Prison Film

The depiction of gay "prison sex" in *I Love You Phillip Morris* might represent a first in film history: it shows not simply that such sex can be tender (so did Héctor Babenco's 1985 drama *Kiss of the Spider Woman*) but also that it needn't compete with any spoken or implied form of homophobia—something that no other film has, to my knowledge, quite achieved. (Even Jules Mann-Stewart's 2012 drama *K-11,* which depicts the "LGBT section" of a Los Angeles prison, features many a homophobic remark and unfolds from the perspective of a straight male prisoner mistakenly lumped together with "the gays.") Several contemporary prison films, including those set in juvenile detention facilities, do, however, similarly depict same-sex eroticism as unexpectedly and idiosyncratically central to prison life (perhaps in keeping with longstanding cultural stereotypes). These films may not efface homophobia, but they join *Phillip Morris* in rejecting both soap jokes—the kinds of comic bits in which shower sex is the source of considerable humor even as it evokes abject fear—and also the notion (so central to mainstream narrative cinema and media history, from *Sex in Chains* [William Dieterle, 1928] to *Oz* [1997–2003] and beyond) that male inmates use rape strictly to establish authority, or fuck solely as a result of a lack of available women. Several contemporary queer films argue, by contrast, that rape may be motivated by bona fide erotic desire (rather than by some abstracted, Foucauldian form of disciplinary autoeroticism). Furthermore, some queer films work to subvert the popular stereotype that governs mainstream depictions of prison, and that so often presents same-sex eroticism as a substitute for straight relations.[29]

Of the online, gay-identified fan practices that rely upon the iconography of *I Love You Phillip Morris,* some caption their GIFs, photomontages, and video mashups with scholarly claims about the gay-specific legitimacy of prison sex. One such example, a GIF that appeared on the "sassy" gossip blog Oh No They Didn't!, was tagged "film" and "LGBTQ rights," and suggested the combined erotic and political appeal of one of the film's showpiece sex scenes (in which Ewan McGregor's character, having outlined his explicitly gay craving, sucks the cock of the Jim Carrey character while both are behind bars).[30] The digital fan practices explored in the previous chapter sought to construct an unashamed eroticism from the relatively chaste audiovisual elements of *Howl,* partly for the purpose of establishing the centrality of sexual pleasure to gay biography (in keeping with the techniques of James Franco's own biopics *Sal* and *The Broken Tower,* and with the fan-produced digital creations surrounding them). The practices explored in the present chapter, which center on *I Love You Phillip Morris,* are somewhat different, in that they extract and extend the film's already-pronounced carnality, partly for the purpose of emphasizing that Steven Jay Russell, the film's biographical subject, was and remains "actively" gay (in contrast to the television programs that uphold him as a model of "post-gay" pathology).[31] They also mine *Phillip Morris* in order to posit that prison sex is sometimes consensual, openly and proudly gay-identified, and even quite hot, to boot.

In celebrating the gay specificity of consensual prison sex, such fan productions appear to confer a certain documentary legitimacy upon *Phillip Morris*—precisely the sort of legitimacy that similar fan productions found to be rather ironically absent from the overtly documentary-style *Howl.* What is perhaps most surprising about these two types of derivative fan productions is that, whatever their surface differences, they demonstrate equivalent conceptions of documentary "truth"—of a veracity that can only be located in open expressions of gay sexual specificities. Viewed from this perspective, the sexless yet documentary-dependent *Howl* is a fiction in need of correcting (hence the video mashups that generate satisfying sex from the film's manifestly dissatisfying scraps), while the flashy, formally audacious, star-studded *Phillip Morris,* with its erudite attention to the sociology of contemporary American prisons and its unashamed evocation of the precise mechanics of multiple erotic acts, has a *verité* authority tailor-made for YouTube's more "informational" pages (such as those that place *Phillip Morris* on a continuum of threaded videos showing "gay sex," all of which, in order to be watched, require users to sign in to the site to confirm that they are in fact over eighteen years of age). A YouTube video series entitled "Men Kissing Men in Gay-Themed Films," created by gay-identified user marfalej ecere in 2012, prominently includes numerous clips from *Phillip Morris,* all of them captioned with the user's own, experientially grounded "gay endorsement," as well as with his warnings to those who would bully him online: "MY CHANNEL ARE [sic] NOT FOR

THE HOMOPHOBIC PRICKS . . . DO NOT WANDER HERE AND WATCH MY UPLOADS." Tied to this caption is a disclaimer: "I do not own any part of these video clips . . . no copyright infringement intended . . . just promoting gay-themed films."[32] A similar YouTube video series, which contains a nearly identical disclaimer pointing to the importance of recasting piracy as fair use, relies upon *Phillip Morris* for the express purpose of "proving" that the gay-specific "realism" of its sex scenes is "singular." Titled "Gay Hot Kissing," and created by gay-identified user Ellis Jake, this particular video series suggests that, in keeping with its title, a majority of mainstream, gay-themed films rely upon the "hotness" of lip locking, while *Phillip Morris,* included here via a mashup of its sex scenes, suggests a welcome rarity, an erotic adventurousness on the order of softcore gay pornography.[33]

Perhaps unsurprisingly, such gay-identified fan productions must compete with structurally similar yet overtly anti-gay video creations. Take, for instance, a video that was uploaded to YouTube in the fall of 2010, shortly before the embarrassingly belated theatrical release of *Phillip Morris.* Titled "Cum in my ass! Jim Carrey," this roughly thirty-second video pivots around Carrey's famous "topping" scene, included here it in its entirety.[34] The scene may be intact, but it isn't untouched: straight-identified user Behind You!! Lookout.. opted to transform it through various digital filters (in psychedelic fashion, the image exhibits a range of saturated colors, especially green and yellow), an added thrash-metal soundtrack (featuring the fast tempo and aggressive strains of an Anthrax song, replacing the considerably calmer soundtrack of the original), and an "ending"—a tacked-on "follow-up" shot—selected from a scene that occurs much later in the film, in which Carrey's character vomits (thus suggesting a causal connection between gay sex and extreme nausea). In this instance, digital manipulation converts the film into an advertisement for gay pathology. "Cum in my ass! Jim Carrey" is thus the opposite of "allen & neal (gay romantic scene)": the latter manipulates the audiovisual elements of *Howl* in order to create a scene of sexual fulfillment, precisely in contrast to the original film's sexless irresolution. That *Phillip Morris* is manipulable within various digital fields is not, in itself, noteworthy, given the centrality of such manipulability to digitization in general and to YouTube-friendly editing software in particular.[35] What remains remarkable about *Phillip Morris* is that the film's gay-identified fans often claim to find evidence of its gay-specific verisimilitude even in encounters with anti-gay paratexts, of which there are numerous on YouTube. The much-viewed "Cum in my ass! Jim Carrey" may be seamless in its out-of-context stitching of two unrelated scenes together, creating an inescapable cause-and-effect quality with images of anal sex and of physical sickness, and its other manipulations may seem equally believable (the added soundtrack is, in fact, so convincingly matched to the *Phillip Morris* footage that I found myself needing to return to the original film in order to confirm its user-generated status). However, even this video, with its bombasti-cally anti-gay trappings, has inspired various irate commenters to "confirm" the documentary legitimacy of those *Phillip Morris* images that it co-opts. In "deal-ing" with the distortions of "Cum in my ass! Jim Carrey," numerous gay-identified YouTube users have claimed that they can see through these distortions to the "honesty" of the video's source—*Phillip Morris* itself, a film that some pointedly define as "documentary-like" in its "honest" depiction of gay sexuality and cul-ture. Describing the film's respect for the gay-identified erotic praxis that "Cum in my ass! Jim Carrey" cannot possibly obscure, even with its expertly achieved homophobic alterations, gay-identified users have thus demonstrated the signifi-cance of the YouTube comment section as a lens through which to examine queer cinema reception on the internet.[36]

AIDS in the Age of Irony: The Erotic Politics of Contemporary Prison Films

I Love You Phillip Morris is carefully structured to suggest that Russell's crimes, rather than constituting gay-specific mishaps, in fact reflect the general failures of the state of Texas—a state whose elected leaders are, the film suggests, not only actively, acutely homophobic in the familiar evangelical manner but also unin-terested in their own constituents. Nobody bothers to mold Russell into a pro-ductive citizen, and the film culminates in a muckraking analysis of the criminal inadequacies of "the leaders of Texas"—including and especially George W. Bush, who was governor at the time of the events depicted in the film, and who, in an end title, is identified as an embarrassment. The queer politics of *Phillip Morris* are thus inseparable from the film's fury over the incompetence of authority figures; from its focus on the perversions of justice made possible by the perva-sive homophobia of state officials; and, finally, from its willingness to position George W. Bush as the butt of a big, gay-friendly joke. But how, exactly, is ho-mophobia to blame for Russell's continued capacity to evade the law? According to the film, it prevented prison doctors from testing Russell's blood after he had forged a document identifying himself as HIV-positive, and it prevented prison officials from later mandating just such a test. In this instance, simply taking Rus-sell at his word was a matter not of suddenly trusting a man whose mendacious ways had long been in evidence but of assuming, under a rubric of homophobia, that the phrase "gay man with AIDS" is practically a redundancy. As Carrey's Russell says in his voice-over commentary, no one "thought twice" about his HIV status, and so he was admitted into specialized care despite the fact that his weight loss was attributable only to diet and excessive laxative use.

If *Phillip Morris* appears to be dangerously, perhaps even "irresponsibly" ir-reverent by using HIV/AIDS in so casually comedic a manner, then it is important to point out that the film includes a sequence of "sincere" suffering in which Russell's first partner, played by Rodrigo Santoro, lies dying. It is this sequence that most directly suggests the longstanding, conventionally mournful manner in which death by AIDS has been rendered in queer cinema; with its slowly expiring victim and tearful bedside boyfriend, it evokes, of course, *Philadelphia* (Jonathan Demme, 1993), but also *Longtime Companion* (Norman René, 1990) and the TV movie *An Early Frost* (John Erman, 1985). It is not, however, the only representational tactic that conceivably guards against charges that the film is, with respect to Russell's "most daring ploy," potentially offensively capricious. Another is the film's aforementioned focus on the way in which homophobia conditions people (including gay men) to assume unreservedly that AIDS and homosexuality are synonymous. Where the film might still seem egregiously insensitive, however, is in its initial refusal to inform the spectator of Russell's decision to "fake" the late-stage depredations of AIDS. Indeed, the film initially presents Russell as he publicly presents himself—as, that is, an "authentic" AIDS patient—only to slowly let us in on this sickest of jokes. But if at first we believe Russell, citing only his weight loss and all-too-forgeable admittance forms, then perhaps we, too, can be included among those who (like the bureaucratic villains of the film) unquestioningly capitulate to a cultural stereotype.

Despite or perhaps because of its brazen assimilation of a range of clichés, *I Love You Phillip Morris* represents a unique entry in the canon of queer cinema, and one that uses these cultural clichés (of gayness especially, but also of "Big Texas") to paint a fresh portrait of post-Stonewall (and pre–*Lawrence and Garner v. Texas*) forms of homophobia—a portrait whose believability is rooted not simply in the film's status as a biopic (with all the claims to cultural authority that the genre so often makes) but also in the lingering fatigue and disgust engendered by the George W. Bush years (at least for some Americans). A key difference between *Catch Me If You Can* (an early cinematic entry in the Bush presidency) and *Phillip Morris* (a post-Bush release) is not the latter's queerness but rather the way in which that queerness works to evoke a violently assimilationist culture. *Phillip Morris* lays the groundwork for this particular approach in its opening sequences, which are devoted to Russell's efforts to become, as he says, "a model citizen." They show him "taking a wife," "making babies," and generally enjoying the perks that a heterosexist society provides to its obliging members. Russell is, of course, a closeted gay man—but that doesn't mean that he's meek, or sexually repressed. Indeed, the film's first scene of gay sex has received considerable critical attention, presumably in part because its "dom top" is portrayed by Jim Carrey, "pounding ass" with utter abandon. The moment, notably, is as visually revealing as it is verbally explicit, with Russell declaring—quite loudly—his desire to come and his partner eagerly acquiescing, shouting, "Come in my ass! Come in my ass!" One couldn't ask for a more direct engagement with the mechanics of anal sex—the top's angle of entry, the bottom's position on the bed, the attendant efforts at spoken communication that help to ensure the success of "doggie style"—and such legibility has lent itself to various online versions of the scene. These include YouTube, Vimeo, and Dailymotion uploads whose titles identify the range of sexual terms and techniques explicated in the scene, and that zero in on the twice repeated command of the "bossy bottom" who tells his top what to do. That the term "bossy bottom" is not audible in the scene does not mean that it is unavailable to those who have chosen to upload this scene as an exemplar of gay erotic specificity in contemporary queer cinema. In contrast to fan uploads of *Howl* scenes that work assiduously to recut and effectively recontextualize those scenes, the better to suggest an erotic satisfaction that is in fact withheld from *Howl*'s gay characters, the majority of currently accessible fan uploads of this particular *Phillip Morris* sex scene suggest not that the scene is inadequate or incomplete, but rather that there are numerous terms to which it is relevant—gay vernacular terms that gay-identified users are well equipped to provide. The unauthorized uploading of entire scenes from contemporary queer films can thus contribute to a particular process of accretion, whereby the affirmative, gay-identified eroticism of certain works can be wedded to the parlance of their fans, thus demonstrating the importance of user-generated meanings even in the presence of direct representations of gay sex.

Filmic "Truth" Versus Television "Lies": *Phillip Morris* as Cinematic "Corrective"

As numerous fans have made clear through various video mashups, *I Love You Phillip Morris* can profitably be linked to thematically similar entries in other media, particularly television, and in so doing may help to demonstrate the importance of transmedia analyses to the question of queer representation. Indeed, the queer politics of *Phillip Morris* become considerably clearer when the film is viewed as the second of three popular cultural renderings of Russell's crimes—as the intervening cinematic stream in a series of cultural forces. The first of these is a 2005 episode of the Discovery Channel series *On the Run*. Titled "King of Cons," the episode presents Steven Russell as a prodigy of sorts—"a career con man with a genius IQ of 160" who managed to "outwit" authorities. ("He's smarter than they are," a talking-head expert calmly says of Russell's relationship to the feds.) Just as *Brokeback Mountain* was reading the American West (including Texas) through a consciously queer lens, "King of Cons" was striving to suggest that Texas—what the program's voice-over narrator terms, with apparent admiration, America's "biggest and baddest state"—can seem no match for queer chicanery. After all, the state's top lawmen were consistently unable to bring to justice a man who made little effort to mask his sexuality. However, whether those lawmen harbored homophobic motivations, and whether they were aware of the full extent of Russell's romantic maneuverings, are questions that the episode fails to ask. In fact, it fails even to introduce its central figure—the titular king of cons—as gay, instead opting to position him as "simply" chameleonic. Such a self-consciously post-gay approach evokes, however, a longstanding gay stereotype—akin to the kind of cliché that aligns queerness with criminality. Indeed, a chameleonic capacity—a flair for altering one's own appearance and identity—is part and parcel of popular renderings of gay pathology, including those that insist upon the sheer illegality of gayness. At the level of exposition, "King of Cons" plays no such psychologizing game, but it does, in using words like "chameleon," "genius," "prodigy," and "supernatural," suggest that there is something extraordinary—and perhaps extraordinarily pathological—about Steven Jay Russell.

Where "King of Cons" equivocates, arguing that there is simply "something different" about Russell, *I Love You Phillip Morris* opts for direct expressions of the man's sexual drives and eccentric sensibilities, showing him to be both a self-consciously stereotypical gay man and an exultant anti-state activist—an anarchist whose refusal to respect authority is bound up with his awareness of the twin terrors of heterosexism and homophobia. Surprisingly, however, the film is as casual about Russell's queer martyrdom as it is about his specific sexual practices. No special pleading takes place, and the substance of Russell's fuck-you to the straight establishment is as succinct and immediately obvious as the pleasure this "dom top" takes in a "tight ass." Throughout its ninety-eight minutes (to cite the running time of the final cut, as of this writing the only commercially available version of the film), *Phillip Morris* makes admirably clear that Russell is a mendacious, mercenary gay man, and it refuses to delve too deeply into his psyche, possibly for fear of evoking some platitude concerning the "inherent" pathology of homosexuality. That does not mean, however, that the film seems egregiously evasive. In fact, its telegraphic style—its reliance on epigrams and freeze-frames, its facility in offering a clear compendium of queer self-descriptions—militates against obfuscation.

"King of Cons," by contrast, is circumspect, and in a way that suggests a certain queasiness regarding the subject of homosexuality—a regressive reticence to address Russell's erotic identity. The dangers of taking a post-gay approach to clearly queer subject matter are amply evident in this episode, which refrains from emphasizing Russell's sexual orientation identity, sidestepping the matter in so forced, so strained a manner as to seem classically homophobic. The program takes such pains to establish Texas as "big" and as "bad" that one begins to suspect that it is going to openly celebrate a gay man's capacity to undermine the state's grandiloquent identity—which is precisely what Steven Jay Russell managed to do through his singular crimes (at least according to *I Love You Phillip*

Morris). However, in order for "King of Cons" to seem remotely interested in advocating queerness as a mode of iconoclasm, the program's viewer needs to imbue it with her own, extratextual knowledge of the case. For instance, if one knows that Russell was openly gay at the time that he committed his crimes, and partnered with a man whom he had protected in prison, then it is entirely possible to view the episode's early sequences as building toward some acknowledgement of Russell's gay-specific fuck-you to the straight establishment. Considered from this privileged perspective, the sequences seem cheeky—not only pro-Russell but also emphatically queer-positive. And yet the first reference to Russell's sexual orientation identity arrives some ten minutes into "King of Cons," and after the episode has expended considerable energy positioning Russell as "special," "sneaky," "extraordinary," and "unusual." It has, in other words, offered just about every euphemistic substitution for "gay," and in ways that, though clearly intended to establish that homosexuality is "not the issue"—not the cause of Russell's criminality—ironically evoke the old Hays Code strategies of "discreetly" identifying the love that dare not speak its name.

Much to the apparent delight of numerous YouTube users, however, *Phillip Morris* can serve to "correct" the "tasteful" strategies of "King of Cons," which is equally pirated across the internet—equally available on various video-sharing websites. When considered as a companion piece to Ficarra and Requa's film—as on the YouTube channel Gay-Themed Movies, which excerpts *Phillip Morris* and explains its "place" among an assortment of queer media texts—"King of Cons" seems an embarrassment, a relic of an earlier, constipated period of cultural production. By contrast, *I Love You Phillip Morris,* which is almost exactly contemporaneous with "King of Cons," makes no attempt to echo the outmoded style of "discretion" that the television program follows almost to the letter, and that lets words like "lover" and "friend" stand in for the more forceful phrases "fuck buddy" and "life partner" that the film favors. That "King of Cons" was beholden to certain restrictions is obvious; the "family-friendly" mandates of its network, however, do not excuse the episode's refusal to engage with the subject of homosexuality.

The producers of "King of Cons" cannot, perhaps, be blamed for statements made by their talking-head witnesses, each of whom seems strangely reluctant to spell out the self-identified queerness of the criminal they know only too well. It is, however, impossible to ignore the fact that the program's glib voice-over narration omits mention of Russell's struggles with institutionalized heterosexism and homophobia—struggles that led him to wed a woman, father children, and fib in a manner that only a closet case could possibly comprehend. If "King of Cons" is so concerned with presenting Texas as a hyperbolic psychic space—a strangely excessive "state of mind"—then why does the program refrain from mentioning that one of the state's exaggerated claims has been to criminalize sodomy past the point at which the majority of its fellow states struck down such laws? (At the time of *Lawrence and Garner v. Texas*, in 2003, it was one of only thirteen-and-a-half states to still enforce criminal laws centralizing the "degeneracy" of non-procreative erotic acts.) In refraining from highlighting Russell's homosexuality, "King of Cons" presents the man's criminality in a way that may be consistent with the genre to which the program belongs—the sort of reenactment-dependent, true-crime cable descendant of *Unsolved Mysteries* (1987–2010) and *America's Most Wanted* (1988–2012)—but the effect is to void the story of any social insight. Abstracted through language that positions him as a somewhat supernatural force, Russell's crimes become fodder for a forced suspense narrative ("Will the king of cons make a fool out of the toughest cops in America?"), leaving little room for a more expansive (and possibly empathic) biographical engagement. What's worse is the shockingly mocking voice-over commentary—the male-identified narrator who, in cheekily conspiratorial tones, describes Russell's "very . . . *special* client—his lover, Phillip Morris."

Refusing to accept that the true-crime television genre provides an airtight alibi for the adumbrations of "King of Cons"—for the episode's somewhat surprising (and self-consciously "post-gay") willingness to dance around the subject of homosexuality—is hardly nitpicking. It is, in fact, a stance that finds considerable support in one of the genre's other entries: an episode of the Investigation Discovery series *I (Almost) Got Away with It* entitled "Got a Boyfriend to Support," which, tellingly, premiered two years after the delayed release of *I Love You Phillip Morris*. The ninth episode of the series' third season, "Got a Boyfriend to Support" forcefully inserts the reality of same-sex romanticism into its standardized mandate for episode titles, all of which begin with the word "got" ("Got to Rob Vacation Homes," "Got to Rap," "Got to Run with My Brother"). The syntax is significant not merely for centralizing the word "boyfriend" but for the way in which it differs from that of most of the other titles in the series. For instance, the three titles parenthesized above, which represent especially popular episodes of *I (Almost) Got Away With It*, all emphasize compulsion—a person's pathological need to perform a particular act ("got to," of course, being in this context synonymous with "must"). By contrast, "Got a Boyfriend to Support" at least *potentially* suggests something far less compulsive and far less judgmental—something a bit more casual, a bit more accepting.

It is a title that the episode's structure both substantiates and transcends: yes, Steven Jay Russell had a boyfriend—a fact that the program openly and consistently acknowledges, in contrast to its televisual predecessor's occasional, seemingly reluctant reliance on regressive euphemisms (or diminutions) like "lover" and "friend"—but he hardly had to *support* him in the sense suggested by the title. He may have wanted to lavish his partner with gifts, but his principal motivation, as he himself points out in the episode, was to combat the heterosexist prejudice that surrounded him, and that prevented him from holding on to "legit" jobs after his employers discovered that his "significant other" was, in fact, a man. Even more so than *Phillip Morris*, "Got a Boyfriend to Support" shows how Steven Russell's crimes can be viewed through the rubric of queer rebellion—as, that is, reflective of a liberationist anti-state struggle. After all, the authority figures who failed consistently to catch this man were often openly reliant upon some of the most upsetting stereotypes of male homosexuality, such as the typically strict, allegedly airtight association between gayness and AIDS—an association that leads, as *Philip Morris* makes clear, to a homophobic reluctance to retest Russell, whose forged hospital admittance forms read "HIV positive." Unlike "King of Cons," which barely mentions AIDS (and which permits its talking heads to use words like "disease" and the deeply erroneous "virus" to describe the syndrome, and which fails to furnish appropriately corrective language in its voice-over commentary), "Got a Boyfriend to Support" acknowledges the all-too-believable asininity of those who reflexively responded to Russell's sudden weight loss with a stereotyping diagnostic flair.

Crucially, Russell himself is on hand in this episode to describe his bitterness at being persecuted by the straight, anti-gay establishment—at being fired, at being shamed, at being made the object of moralizing condemnation. So, he claims, he gave that establishment a "better"—a more "understandable"—reason to denounce him: he started breaking the law, and not (merely) by engaging in "sodomitic" acts. "Got a Boyfriend to Support" offers Russell the chance to describe his crimes in his own words. It uses the man as one of many talking-head "authorities," and while one might balk at having to engage with the statements of a seeming sociopath, it is clearly a coup for queer representation that this man is on hand to identify homophobia as the all too familiar—and therefore all too believable—force behind his actions. According to the Russell of "Got a Boyfriend to Support" (whose title alone should go a long way in indicating its allegiance to the cause of queer visibility, as well as its productive deviation from "King of Cons"), his criminality was precipitated by an awareness of anti-gay prejudice, and sustained through frequent confrontations with bigotry.

How two so contrasting television depictions of the same biographical subject can have been produced in such relatively quick succession—and on sister networks, no less—has much to do with tensions between what we might call assimilationist media on the one hand and aggressively "open" formats on the other. While there is no excuse for the disparaging tone of the "King of Cons" commentary, or for the program's careless use of inaccuracies regarding HIV/AIDS, it is clear that its intermittent and indirect references to homosexuality are what some might consider sufficient, particularly within the post-gay framework that the program appears to promote. *I Love You Phillip Morris* manages, in its own way, to expose the peculiarly unproductive manner in which "King of Cons" positions Texas. The television program routinely refers to the state as a "giant," and offers a series of long shots of the arid landscape, but why? For what possible thematic purpose? Is it simply to align Steven Russell's habitual criminality with the general hyperbole of Texas? "King of Cons" appears to present Texas as "grand" simply because it has no other way of describing it—has no recourse other than to the basic braggadocio of the place where "everything is bigger." But it is precisely this clichéd valorization of Texas as "big" and "tough" that contributes to the cultural impact of *Phillip Morris,* which matches its dispassionate approach to homosexuality with an equally cool take on Texas as a state of utter ridiculousness ("Fucking Texas" being Russell's dismissive phrase of choice). By pooh-poohing the reputation of Texas, *Phillip Morris* provides yet another implicit corrective to "King of Cons," in the process strengthening its queer credentials.

The film implicitly interrogates more than just a Discovery Channel series, however; its critical interventions extend unmistakably to queer cinema history—particularly to those films that address male-male prison sex. In the iconic *Kiss of the Spider Woman,* William Hurt's gay-identified character is referred to as a "fucking fag," and his capacity to attract his straight-identified cellmate is presented as a function not of sexual desirability but of mere kindness. "You're so kind to me," says Hurt's Molina to Raul Julia's Valentin, who replies, "No. You are kind to me." Both are political prisoners—Molina more "accidentally" so than Valentin, since it was Molina's "natural" and "inescapable" sexuality (as opposed to Valentin's deliberately violent activism) that landed him behind bars. Both men bring their cultural suppositions into the prison setting—their various hang-ups about race, masculinity, nationality, class, sex, and gender. To Molina, Valentin is a brute—but therein lies his appeal. (He's both sexually attractive to Molina and, as an evocation of "uncultured" rough trade, a fascinating sociological example.) Valentin, however, can reap no such sexual or intellectual benefits from being locked up alongside Molina, whom he believes to be his physical and psychological opposite. Initially, Valentin's homophobia shows in ways both obvious and subtle, but he slowly warms to Molina the raconteur, who regales him with tales of the titular Spider Woman—star of a film that the gay man recalls with luxuriant fondness.

As in the earlier *Midnight Cowboy* and the later *Brokeback Mountain,* the sequestering of two men in an unusual and perhaps hazardous physical space leads first to a grudging acceptance and later to full-blown love. Valentin not only enjoys the stories that Molina tells, he also appreciates what he believes to be the unadulterated generosity that led to their telling. (He's too lacking in sophistication to see that narrating is not necessarily a charitable practice—that it is often self-satisfying, a strategy by which to strengthen one's own memory and rhetorical skills, and to satisfy a personal, privately stoked nostalgia.) Believing Molina to be the kindest of men, Valentin returns the favor by fucking him—and the film, at this moment, offers a bizarre combination of Code-era visual "discretion" and sexually explicit post-Code sounds. After an enamored Molina falls upon his prison bed, and after Valentin removes his tattered white t-shirt in preparation for fucking, the camera pans to the candle that sits atop a tiny table in the corner, its flame flickering. Valentin blows out the candle, thus creating a shadowy mise-en-scène, as well as the impression that this 1985 film is rather unnecessarily (and therefore perhaps homophobically) unwilling to *directly* depict a same-sex erotic act—to place this act within the camera's frame. Of course, such discretion extended even to connubial unions in classical Hollywood cinema, the extinguishing of a candle so often serving as a signal of incipient sexual contact. In this case, however, sexual scrimping is restricted to the film's visual field. Its soundscape, by contrast, contains some rather surprising noises—not the grunts that one might expect but, instead, the kinds of complaints that, coming from Molina, serve largely instructive purposes. While staring at a screen that is almost completely black, the spectator hears a gay character telling his straight comrade, who has just offered a mercy fuck, that anal sex simply isn't easy.

"Wait—I'm squeezed against the wall!" cries Molina—as, presumably, the inexperienced and brutish top crashes down on him. Molina's second complaint-cum-instruction—"No, wait, let me lift my legs!"—leaves little doubt that Valentin simply doesn't know what he's doing. It also provides a sexual stereotype that, exactly twenty years later, *Brokeback Mountain* would counter, albeit somewhat unbelievably: the notion that no straight man—that is, no man previously accustomed to fucking only women—can possibly know, his first time at bat for a bottom, that entering an ass requires . . . *work*. While *Brokeback*'s nearly silent sex scene offers saliva (and not much of it, at that) as an impossibly effective lubricant, *Kiss of the Spider Woman* reveals, rather starkly, the centrality of spoken negotiation to anal sex. Approaching the film in a generous mood, one might say that its use of an almost embarrassingly antiquated signifier of sexual contact—the extinguished candle—creates precisely the sort of audiovisual circumstances in which paying close attention to spoken instructions is just about all the spectator can do. Hearing Molina's words requires a close consideration of how verbal communication—as opposed to, say, Jake Gyllenhaal's primal groan—is often essential to the execution of even vanilla forms of gay fucking.

Whatever the film's instructive intentions vis-à-vis gay sex, it is clear that *Kiss of the Spider Woman* travels smoothly across the quaintly queer-conscious bridge of prison films—the bridge that *Phillip Morris* obliterates, and without the aid of violent homophobia. In fact, it is altogether remarkable that the latter film portrays the grunge of prison life—the irrational and rapidly escalating fights, the moments stolen for masturbating, the downright Rabelaisian mealtime experiences—without feeling the need to assign it any anti-gay sentiments. The "fucking fag" of *Spider Woman* is missing here (and is, if anything, replaced by Russell's "fucking Texas" as the disgusted, reductive phrase of choice). When Russell and Morris share a fulsome prison kiss, it is while seated behind a man who masturbates furiously while staring at the communal television set. Throughout many of the prison sequences, the film foregrounds the collaborations among Russell, Morris, and a black prisoner who plays, on his own cherished tape deck, the queer couple's recording of Johnny Mathis singing "Chances Are." Surprisingly, given the clichéd equations between blackness and whiteness that I have described as offensively characteristic of contemporary queer cinema, the film's depiction of the black prisoner never comes close to suggesting servitude—never even intimates that this prisoner is assisting a pair of white men out of a sense of obligation or because he recognizes that they, too, "know struggle." Instead, he is presented as raucously willing to go along with a gay scheme—even (perhaps especially) if it means upsetting the guards who stalk the halls, and who eventually attack him for blasting Johnny Mathis.

Phillip Morris may function, in part, to suggest (however fancifully) that prison is a place where the pervasiveness of anal sex effectively precludes homophobia, but it is virtually alone among contemporary queer films in situating gay fucking amid a loud and lively social landscape. In the film, the wild world of the prison does not stop spinning so that Steven and Phillip can fuck; it spins on, chaotic as ever, its cacophony providing a unique and multidirectional accompaniment to anal sex. By contrast, *Kiss of the Spider Woman* erases everything that surrounds the erotic engagements of its same-sex pair, creating a cinematic space that suggests the hushed, minimalist stage of a two-character play. It isn't simply that, in *Spider Woman,* the screen has been rendered black by the blown-out candle—that there is nothing much to see beyond a crack in the wall that a tiny sliver of moonlight has illuminated. It is that the world has—improbably—fallen silent for this sex scene. We hear no nightingale, no car screeching by, no bailiff coming in from the nearby courtroom, noisy new prisoner in tow. We hear only Molina's voice—only his stylized "gay" speech acts.

As if to confirm his willingness to view the Valentin-Molina union as a sacred sexual convergence, director Héctor Babenco pans to the barred window, which comprises the first shot of the film's post-coital sequence. It is now daylight, and the sky is a bright blue with few clouds. We hear some background bustle, but not much. Mostly, we hear Molina speaking of how happy he feels—of how he doesn't want to "ruin" or otherwise sully the previous evening's experience with mere words. And yet, ever the chatty queen, he continues to speak, and the film, as if to confirm his failure to function within the prison environment, cuts to a flash-forward in which the man who will kill Molina is calling him a "shitfaced motherfuck." Molina's erotic dreams may have come true momentarily, but he is no match for a penitentiary that trades in homophobia, and that will surely forgive the straight Valentin for his sexual slumming.

If the political force of *Phillip Morris* derives, in part, from the film's presentation of gay sex as not just complexly pleasurable but also as a practice that cannot possibly faze the penal community (or even a Christian mother, as played by Leslie Mann), then that force gains a certain legitimacy from the film's ultimate association with what has been referred to as "Bush fatigue." Defined as the sense of exhaustion that descends upon a person whenever she is confronted with the legacy of a man whose presidency, as Jack Halberstam puts it, "deserves to enter the annals of history under the category of failure," Bush fatigue affects *Phillip Morris* in multiple ways, often leading it to omit mention of the man—until, of course, the end title, which succinctly associates him with sheer embarrassment.[37] *Phillip Morris* is a period piece: set in Texas in the 1990s, at a time when "Dubya" was governor, it shows the state—and, by implication, its chief executive—to be criminally incompetent. It also further besmirches Bush's governorship by outlining not simply the lack of effectiveness of his staunchly anti-gay positions, which fail to shame any gay-identified characters, but also their glaring lack of relevance even to the Christian conservatism of Texas (as embodied by the Leslie Mann character, who quickly becomes happily habituated to her husband's homosexuality). While I am not quite inclined to agree with the film that Texans, however "stupid" or "senseless," were generally accepting of homosexuality even during the reign of anti-sodomy statutes, I appreciate the film's fantasy elements, and also the way that they show local "tolerance" of homosexuality to be dependent not on a disavowal of eroticism but on an acknowledgement that sex is central (instead of, as per the post-gay approach, "incidental") to a gay male identity. It is precisely this acknowledgment that I look for online, returning again and again to those understudied pockets of the internet where queer cinema thrives—not simply as a series of pirated videos but also as fodder for a range of complex, contentious, and libidinous practices whose gay identifications are worthy of serious attention.

The real-life gay subject of *I Love You Phillip Morris* may have inspired a series of biographical film, television, and new-media representations—a veritable explosion of narrative approaches to his life story, a cycle centered on his specifically gay identity and its relationship to his much-publicized crimes. The star-studded *Phillip Morris* is, however, by far the most alert to the sociopolitical significance of Russell's sexuality, showing him to be a kind of gay crusader against the general incompetence of the straight establishment, as well as a vanguard against the inanities of "Big Texas." But the film's status as just one Russell-themed media product among many—its offering the gayest Russell of the bunch—does not necessarily mean that it is invulnerable to critiques of its inherent "straightness," particularly given its use of emphatically straight-identified film stars. When considered as a traditional star text, rather than as an exclusively gay one, *I Love You Phillip Morris* might easily be tossed onto a de-eroticized pile that includes such other Jim Carrey and Ewan McGregor films as *Mr. Popper's Penguins* (Mark Waters, 2011) and *Salmon Fishing in the Yemen* (Lasse Hallström, 2012). Enter the animated GIF, the user-generated, mobile frame grab that *Phillip Morris* fans have, in staggering numbers, used to underscore the film's gay-specific eroticism. Enter as well the art of fanfiction, and the equally innumerable fan-authored narratives devoted to extending the film's gay romance—to keeping it alive as a specifically gay experience. The story of *Phillip Morris* is thus—and perhaps inevitably—the story of the feature film's threatened loss of cultural hegemony in an era of convergent media texts, of transmedia storytelling and "boutique" cable networks, dedicated YouTube pages, and original streaming programs. Within this dynamic environment, fans of emphatically gay films, and of self-identified gay filmmakers, are adding to and shaping this rapid accretion of media by isolating, praising, and reproducing the label "gay"—even, occasionally, at the explicit expense of "queer."

What happens, however, when efforts to market to gay men precede the federal implementation of *any* gay-rights provisions, let alone of a distinctly privileged post-gay plan? How do gay-identified films, marketing campaigns, and digital paratexts function in countries that continue to criminalize homosexuality—even to the point of denying its humanity? In Nigeria, where homosexuality remains illegal—and punishable by death in Muslim states operating under Sharia law—there has been a veritable explosion of gay representations in the country's most prolific, largely Lagos-based movie industry, known as Nollywood. There is also, significantly—and, for some commentators, surprisingly—an abundance of Nigerian-authored online responses to these representations, which run the gamut from the vehemently anti-gay to the exultantly libidinous, raising key questions about understudied non-Western, web-enabled spectators of queer cinema. Thomas Elsaesser has identified the phrase "don't follow the flag, follow the tag" as one of globalization's key commands, particularly with respect to digital networked technologies: "Just as commodities, trade and labor no longer 'respect' the boundaries of the nation-state," so tags "easily cross borders and even continents."[38] In the following chapter, I examine how Nollywood-specific, African-produced digital paratexts, with their occasionally derivative tags, function largely to affirm that the gay African was, as such, "always there"—and always a fan as well as a subject of Nigeria's queer cinema.

5 "Nollywood Goes Homo"

Gay Identifications on the Nigerian Internet

Contemporary African cultures now offer more: sex is not only being put into words, but also into images . . . Both pleasure and voyeurism appear to reign now in Africa. In films, sex seems to have become trivial, or in any case not taboo anymore. Not only is it now *seen*, whether live or on the screen, but it has also become an important indicator of transformations that contemporary African cultures now experience.

> Alexie Tcheuyap, "African Cinema and Representations of (Homo)Sexuality"

[I]t is imperative that Nigerians insist on, and that their leaders honor, freedom of public expression. The media are not perfect, but they provide a necessary space for cultivating a genuine sense of national belonging . . . A free Nigerian media sphere has the potential to nourish the ecumenical, cosmopolitan leanings of [many Nigerian citizens], whose perspectives and contributions will all be crucial if Nigeria is ever to realize its promise as the Giant of Africa.

> Rudi Gaudio, "A View from the Ground"

IN APRIL 2013, Nigerian YouTube user 234 pulse, whose channel is devoted almost entirely to pirated footage of real and simulated sexual acts—footage lifted from sources as diverse as private smartphone recordings, porn websites, satellite telecasts, and commercial DVDs—uploaded a clip of a key scene from the Nollywood film *Pregnant Hawkers* (Patrick Hogan and Okechukwu Ifeanyi, 2013), in which a beautiful young man anally penetrates another. Like many of the user's other videos, the clip from *Pregnant Hawkers* is visibly the product of piracy: captured at a canted angle and within a shaky frame, on an apparently handheld recording device, the video's central cinematic images are encircled by the interface of the subscription website where *Pregnant Hawkers* may be watched with commercial interruption—Nigeria's OgaMadamTV, one of several sites that legally stream Nollywood films.[1] Uploaded to YouTube, the *Pregnant Hawkers* sex scene instantly acquired a compelling screen-within-a-screen-within-a-screen aesthetic. Bounded by the dissimilar interfaces of YouTube and OgaMadamTV, it tells more than just the story of modern media piracy, complicated as that story may be. It also provides a powerful reminder of the difficulty of suppressing evocations of gay subjectivity on interactive platforms—whatever the post-gay protestations those platforms may be asked to uphold. 234 pulse does not identify *Pregnant Hawkers* as a "gay" film, presumably preferring a post-gay system of classification, whereby the abovementioned images of anal intercourse become part of what is simply a "sex scene" as erotic as any other. YouTube's particular interface, however, provides for a preponderance of gay-specific alternatives to such an equalizing strategy—one that Brett Farmer, in his book *Spectacular Passions*, critiques as an "acritical pluralism wherein the differences that structure sexual subjectivities are all flattened out into a postmodern vision of democratic pan-sexuality," a sort of "libidinal utopianism."[2] Like social media platforms in general, YouTube's terms of use tend to militate against the sustained discursive production of a post-gay position, precisely by inviting "democratic" participation; it is practically impossible, in other words, for the post-gay sentiments of, say, a James Collard or a Bert Archer to be maintained, without gay-specific interruption, on a participatory site like YouTube. If gayness is under erasure in the writings of Collard and Archer, it is consistently re-inscribed on social media, whether through corporate practices that continue to position gay men as privileged consumers or through more personal, potentially resistant strategies. On YouTube in particular, gay specificity is bound to emerge even in relation to videos whose official descriptions reject "sexual labeling." In fact, such specificity *does* emerge in relation to the *Pregnant Hawkers* clip that 234 pulse, eschewing the word "gay" (and even the word "queer") while isolating a scene of same-sex erotic contact, uploaded in 2013. Whether in the form of prominently "recommended" videos that happen to be explicitly gay-themed or of user comments that tout *Pregnant Hawkers* as inescapably gay, resistance to a "label-free" ethos of uploading represents a powerful and prevalent mode of online reception. 234 pulse may prefer a video description that is free of the word "gay," and that refuses to invite sexually specific identifications, but in sharing a scene of same-sex eroticism, this semi-anonymous YouTube user enters into a site-specific contract that accommodates, even compels, reception practices that position *Pregnant Hawkers* as an emphatically gay affair.

It is also a Nigerian film, and Nigeria is widely believed to be—to quote the *Economist*—"no country for gay men."[3] Indeed, if the Nigerian federal government is currently committed to criminalizing homosexuality as an erotic practice (much to the chagrin of citizens who would plainly prefer a government capable of tackling widespread concerns about housing, water, electricity, and security), then it is also working to criminalize a wide range of gay identifications, including those allegedly "created" through media consumption. In other words, there is now a price to be paid for engaging with *Pregnant Hawkers* as a specifically gay film, that price being increased state surveillance and, potentially, a protracted prison sentence for Nigerian citizens. Nigeria's official governmental assumption is not necessarily that *Pregnant Hawkers,* with its direct representation of anal sex, might "inspire" one to self-identify as gay. It is, rather, that the film, if widely believed to be "about" gay men, might make purchasing a copy of it tantamount to acquiring "gay paraphernalia"—one of the consumer actions banned in Nigeria as of January 2014.[4] Since the country's political climate is, at present, so hostile to gay men in particular, filmmakers who have traded in gay representations have lately been forced to "rebrand" those representations, either as emphatically anti-gay documents or, in familiar post-gay fashion, as "not actually gay at all"—as, that is, far removed from the pitfalls of identity politics.

From the exultant way in which they engage in anal sex, the gay men of *Pregnant Hawkers* would seem to promote homosexuality as an intensely pleasurable practice. What's more, they are strikingly physically attractive, to the extent of inspiring spectatorial objectification. Indeed, the Nigerian blogosphere abounds with entries acclaiming the sex appeal of the two men—of the top in particular, whose "perfect" body and beautifully chiseled face suggest a familiarly "flattering" stereotype of male homosexuality—and *Pregnant Hawkers* would seem to have contributed to this reception tactic through the framing of this sex scene, which captures anal intercourse from distinctly favorable angles. As a consequence of this shooting style, and of its gay-specific object, the producers of *Pregnant Hawkers* have had to "correct" the film in ways that would appear to comply with newly expansive Nigerian laws, but that leave some Nigerian spectators perplexed at the suppression of a text that, in its onetime capacity as an advertisement for anal sex, served also as an advertisement for advances in the Nollywood film industry. There remains, in today's Nigeria, considerable tension between federal anti-gay laws and certain aspirations for Nollywood as a source of sophisticated "adult" representations—aspirations that often dovetail with the goals of local telecommunications providers to increase and improve internet access for Nigerians, thereby turning the country into an innovative "information society." Globacom, a Nigerian corporation that is currently West Africa's top "locally grown" telecommunications provider (and a major competitor of powerful foreign entities like China's StarTimes and South Africa's MTN), is on a much-publicized mission to give "everybody" access to the internet.[5] But surely this unbelievable "everybody" does not include the kind of citizen so roundly demonized—and so rigidly criminalized—in Nigeria's anti-gay laws. In addressing gay-identified online practices—those that, for instance, position *Pregnant Hawkers* as a pleasurable gay film—it is important to look beyond contexts where the surveillance of gay men's online activities is mostly commercially motivated (as in the construction of American gay men as both "majority queers" and ideal consumers). In today's Nigeria, gay men are under renewed pressure to refrain from expressing their subjectivities on the internet, even as their country's most prolific film industry is committed to producing gay-themed melodramas, and even as local officials are joining forces with telecommunications providers to promote Nigeria as a tech-savvy West African information hub. The rapidly expanding purview of Nigeria's anti-gay legislation does not mean that gay identifications have disappeared from local digital productions—quite the opposite, in fact, as this chapter is committed to detailing, turning to the multivalent online reception of what is now known as "Gay Nollywood."

That this category exists at all owes much to the fact that its filmic entries are, for the most part, unambiguously anti-gay, and thus in tune with certain state-sanctioned aspirations for Nollywood, an industry whose pedagogic potential has received considerable government attention in recent years. Two of the Nollywood films at the center of this chapter—2010's *Men in Love* and 2013's *Pregnant Hawkers*—are not nearly as denunciatory as their counterparts, however, and they have given rise to a wide range of gay-specific online reception practices, from the creation of Tumblrs that tout *Men in Love* as a sophisticated investigation of gender and sexuality to the blog-based composition of complaints about the homophobic suppression of *Pregnant Hawkers*. A film with the unique misfortune of having been produced on the eve of passage of new, astonishingly far-reaching anti-gay legislation, *Pregnant Hawkers* has undergone its own forced transformations across multiple media platforms. Swiftly removed even from legal streaming sites—including OgaMadamTV—the film would soon return under a new title, *Desperate Hawkers,* and with the aforementioned sex scene excised. Viewed through the lens of Nigerian political suppression, then, the video that 234 pulse uploaded to YouTube represents less a standard, shoddy, user-generated production—a casual product of "clip culture"—than a vital, even precious document: a record not simply of a single gay sex scene but also of its onetime availability on a site for streaming movies. Since the unique interface of OgaMadamTV remains visible within the frame of this pirated YouTube video, it serves the not insignificant purpose of proving that *Pregnant Hawkers* once had an online life—under that particular title and with a nearly two-minute scene of anal sex—before its state-sanctioned "revision." For those who, like me, clearly remember watching *Pregnant Hawkers* on OgaMadamTV in the early months of 2013, the film's disappearance from this and other sites has seemed a surreal suppression, especially since a similarly titled and almost identical film has since appeared in its place.

After January 2014, to Google "Pregnant Hawkers" has been to find a plethora of online entries identifying *Desperate Hawkers* but bearing no sign of the gay sex that—without actually describing it as such—234 pulse helpfully pirated and uploaded to YouTube. I have written elsewhere of the ways that title changes work to simulate product differentiation in an industry that, while famously productive, is often wrongly critiqued, even condemned, for offering homogenous melodramas.[6] It is important to point out that the industrial process by which, say, the film *Sharon Stone* (Adim Williams, 2003) became *Sharon Stone in Abuja* when broadcast on the continent-wide satellite channel Africa Magic—a process that has provided a semblance of change, of newness, in the excavation and exhibition of "old" Nollywood films on "new" platforms—is *not* the panicked, homophobic process by which *Pregnant Hawkers,* a film with a two-minute gay sex scene, has become *Desperate Hawkers,* a film stripped of all references to homosexuality. The latter case, and the gay-identified online practices that it has inspired, suggest two salient points that are at the heart of this chapter: viral, gay-identified paratexts are hardly limited to exclusively Western contexts of production and consumption, and in Nigeria, taking Nollywood as their object, they tend to resist more than just the privileges and limitations of a post-gay perspective, preferring to question both the anti-gay assumptions of the Nigerian political system and the notion that internet access is apolitical—uncritical, even "unthinking"—in the global South. In reality, the online practices that, in Nigeria, rise up around Gay Nollywood—practices that include blogging, vlogging, and commenting on a wide range of websites and via a diversity of apps—frequently contest the blind assumptions both of Nigerian law and of Western popular discourse, even as they reproduce certain imported queer theories and reflect an abiding awareness of "official" Nigerian forms of heterosexism and homophobia. As Neda Atanasoski argues in *Humanitarian Violence,* recent forms of U.S. imperialism depend upon—indeed, produce—an image of the global South as uniformly homophobic, and it is in express opposition to this image that locally produced online paratexts often function. In this chapter, I begin with an account of internet use in Nigeria that takes stock of a wide range of efforts to address male homosexuality and to categorize Gay Nollywood—efforts that complicate current scholarly understandings of fans and fan cultures, and that have important consequences for the theorization of online spectatorship. In the second half of the chapter, I turn to close readings of the Nollywood film *Men in Love* (Moses Ebere, 2010) and its digital paratexts, which include a dazzling array of online productions that resist any easy explanations for the film's narrative focus on gay male culture and sexuality. Essentialist renderings of the anti-gay African would suggest that Nollywood is only interested in representing homosexuality to the extent that such representations can be recuperated as denunciatory—as proof of the "deviance" of gay men and of gay sexual practices. If *Men in Love* makes us look closer, then so does its prominent, multivalent online presence.

Exhuming African Texts: Media Archaeology, Federal Regulation, and Gay Nollywood Online

> [L]et's be honest: We simply don't know if the availability of [the internet] is going to help the long-term prospects of gay rights in Nigeria. After all, changing social attitudes on such charged issues would require a series of painful political, legal, and social reforms and sacrifices, which may or may not have been made easier by the Internet.
>
> —Evgeny Morozov, *The Net Delusion*

> Although scholars have noted the rising potentials for democracy in Africa as a result of increased use of digital media and mobile technologies, there seems to be a disregard or disavowal of queerness as part of that growing democratic space, as well as a related tendency to regard African culture solely in terms of mainstream writing and journalism.
>
> —Evan Mwangi, "Queer Agency in Kenya's Digital Media"

If media archaeology can illuminate key aspects of the online reception of gay-themed films, then some of the central tools of the discipline—including topos analysis—can help to uncover a complicated history of media production and consumption that, in Nigeria, remains officially contentious, even dangerous. In relation to Gay Nollywood, it is essential to examine the twin topoi of homophobic condemnation and affirmative recuperation—equally recurrent ways of using digital forms to endorse or resist Nigeria's anti-gay laws, to reflect both a renewed state homophobia and an emergent homoprotectionism. Demonstrating that the gay identifications that emerge through the online reception of contemporary queer cinema are inevitably multivalent—neither exclusively empathic nor strictly denunciatory—the analyses that follow attempt to paint a portrait of how Nigerians of many different backgrounds are using the internet to define Gay Nollywood. Whatever else they reveal, such uses serve the indispensable purpose of archiving and annotating films whose gay-positive themes remain literally unspeakable in the Nigerian public sphere, and whose images and sounds have, in some cases, similarly been stricken from official records. The film *Pregnant Hawkers* may, according to the mandates of Nigeria's most recent anti-gay laws, have been "rebranded" as an emphatically straight vehicle, one containing no vestiges of gay sexuality or culture, but its original version has left seemingly innumerable traces online. Furthermore, the websites that now stream the revised, retitled version of the film contain obligatory comment sections that, perhaps inevitably, offer reflections on the version that is no longer available—the one that opened with a stunning gay sex scene. On iROKOtv.com, arguably the most popular source for streaming Nollywood films, the *Desperate Hawkers* page, whose "official" description has been stripped of all allusions to the film's first, gay-inclusive version, nevertheless features user comments that insist on the onetime existence and availability of *Pregnant Hawkers,* highlighting that version's erotic "gay content." In February 2014, iROKOtv subscriber fav.nik complained that *Desperate Hawkers* was missing crucial gay characters—that "scenes where nude gays were having live sex were cut" from the film.[7] While it is unclear what this user means by "live sex"—whether the phrase reflects an assumption that the actors, rather than simply simulating anal intercourse, were in fact "actually fucking" on screen—it is obvious that clear, gay-conscious memories of *Pregnant Hawkers* frequently inform the online reception of its heterosexualized successor, indicating the persistence of user-generated resistance to Nigeria's anti-gay proscriptions.

That this resistance originates *with* Nigerians, and in many cases *in* Nigeria, counters prevalent Western assumptions about internet use in Africa. As decades of postcolonial scholarship have revealed, Africa is often seen—particularly in the "enlightened" global North—as a purely pre-modern site of utter illiteracy; indeed, Tavia Nyong'o argues that, through queer-conscious Western platforms, Africans are habitually identified with a fear or ignorance of the internet and of the complex subjectivities that this relatively new medium can coax into being. For Nyong'o, such condescending claims function in a manner familiar from the operations of racism, in this case shoring up gay whiteness as a privileged locus for "open" cultural and sexual expressions, and emboldening gay-identified, white Western activists to rue, say, Africans' alleged inability to access Grindr—as if that app, seemingly de rigueur for the erotically active gay man, were also a potentially transcontinental ambassador of queerness. Africans, then, are typically "depicted through the metaphor of the closet, globally and transhistorically construed and, through that metaphor, placed at a prior point in a historical development that the West has already progressed through."[8] This representational technique stands in stark contrast to the way that African internet users are commonly depicted on the African continent. In Nigeria in particular, recent anti-gay laws derive directly from the conviction that openly gay Africans are behaviorally "infectious"—and that they are, according to a stereotype of male homosexuality that is no less available in Nigeria than in the United States, more apt than others to access the internet in the pursuit of their erotic and cultural goals. Hence the renewed efforts of the Nigerian government to censor and monitor those citizens suspected of being gay—a state of affairs that renders risky indeed the very reception practices at the center of this book.

In Nigeria, state homophobia is increasingly dependent upon digital sophistication. Since 2014, the Nigerian government's surveillance of Manjam, a social networking service that uses GPS technology to connect gay-identified men, has steadily intensified with the cooperation of several telecommunications companies—part of the ongoing backlash against Western political efforts to inspire the repeal of African anti-gay laws. Nigeria's close (and, in some senses, unique) association with anti-gay ordinances is relatively new: when then-president Olusegun Obasanjo tried to push an anti-gay bill in 2005, he failed, owing in part to widespread apathy regarding vestigial colonial laws, particularly those that call for the criminalization of same-sex erotic contact. Nearly a decade later, however—after Hillary Rodham Clinton's 2011 International Human Rights Day speech and Barack Obama's 2012 statement of support for same-sex marriage—Obasanjo's bill seemed to come back from the dead; it passed unanimously in 2013, a measure of Nigeria's sudden resistance to Western invocations of "gay rights."[9] Deploying homophobia in a fashion that is all too familiar in African politics, the Nigerian state has since worked to deflect public attention away from some of the seismic economic, social, and cultural shifts occasioned by its ongoing capitulation to structural adjustment—to neoliberal pressures to privatize and eliminate all manner of regulatory frameworks (except, of course, for those pertaining to expressions of same-sex loving, which remain heavily policed). In constructing the figure of the tech-savvy, internet-loving gay man, the Nigerian state not only invents a new domestic culprit—a distractingly fresh source of national problems, including of the pederasty increasingly associated with Boko Haram—but also cajoles citizens into seeing Nigeria as a bona fide information society (without, of course, apprising them of the imperialist circuits that are making mobile internet use so famously prevalent in the country). Rather than promoting awareness of the plainly neocolonial role of Facebook (with its plans to beam internet access from drones) or of StarTimes (the Chinese corporation that has won major government contracts in the realm of digital media distribution), the Nigerian state prefers to present the hypothetical gay blogger as a Western-influenced source of local economic woes.

Submarine cables coursing into Nigeria have dramatically expanded and improved internet access there, at the same time that the Nigerian state has intensified its anti-gay regulations, resulting in a complex and contradictory cultural, social, political, and corporate landscape, one in which groundbreaking modes of media access are mixed with a reactionary response to male homosexuality. Instructively, the internet-specific proscriptions written into 2014's Same-Sex Marriage Prohibition Act were partly the result of Western press coverage of Nigeria's "online gays." Of particular concern to Nigerian officials was a 2010 article in the *Economist* that suggested that gay fellowship was "flourishing online" in response to the violent homophobia of federal law and of mainstream churches. Rather flippantly titled "Homosexuality in Nigeria: Go Online if You're Glad to Be Gay," the article naively endorsed the internet as a safe haven for gay Nigerian men, omitting mention of a then-thriving state surveillance apparatus that rendered gay-identified online activity dangerous indeed—and that, partly as a result of the viral popularity of the article, gained strength in 2014.[10] At first glance, there would appear to be something distinctly Foucauldian about the Nigerian government's fear of the generative potential of new social practices—a fear that, of course, assumes a far different guise in digital media theory, both in Nigeria and abroad. "Interactivity goes both ways," writes Lisa Nakamura. "Web sites create users who can interact with them, just as texts create their readers."[11] If the original *Pregnant Hawkers*—pregnant, as it were, with an opening scene of same-sex eroticism—is capable of "creating" gay spectators, then so too, perhaps, are the websites where Nollywood fandom flourishes. Unfortunately for Nigerian lawmakers, these sites may be too plentiful—and too, in digital-media terms, difficult to decipher—to be policed the way that a single film such as *Pregnant Hawkers* has been policed (and suppressed, and "revised").

The importance of highlighting the online activities of populations previously identified with digital illiteracy cannot be overstated. As Nakamura notes, the popular "figuration of cyberculture as white by default tends to demonize people of color as unsophisticated, uneducated, and stuck in a pretechnological past."[12] Here, Nakamura echoes Anne McClintock's notion of "panoptical time"— what Nyong'o has described as "an optical effect that produces a fantasy of the other as somehow occupying a different order of time."[13] It is precisely this effect— this way of envisioning Africa as internet-illiterate, as "stuck in the past"—that Nigerian political and corporate cultures are currently combating through the implementation of new measures for boosting local media industries, while simultaneously, and contradictorily, reaching as far back as the colonial era for the justifications and rhetoric of contemporary anti-gay legislation. Indeed, just as the U.S. Supreme Court decision on *Bowers v. Hardwick* (1986) invoked sixteenth-century English sodomy statutes, anti-gay laws in former British colonies like Nigeria and Uganda employ language, and impose criminalization procedures, that derive directly from the British penal codes of the late nineteenth and early twentieth centuries, and it is difficult to imagine a more retrograde legislative movement than that which seeks to widely pathologize identity-based homosexuality in sub-Saharan Africa.

However, just as certain utopian, post-gay aspirations for digital media cannot eclipse the simultaneously inspiring and troubling survival of gay specificity online, the anti-gay actions of African legislatures shouldn't stand in for the practices of African internet users. As a growing number of scholars are demonstrating, Africans approach the internet in ways that exceed both local and global assumptions. If, for Nakamura, "the study of Asian American online practices throws a much-needed wrench in the overly simplistic rhetoric of the digital divide," then so too does the study of Nigerians' online responses to Nollywood's gay-themed films—responses that, precisely because they run the ideological gamut in describing gayness, complicate facile assumptions about the transformative, indeed remedial, effects of internet access.[14] If millions more Nigerians were "web-enabled" when *Pregnant Hawkers* was first released than when, say, the lesbian-themed Nollywood classic *Emotional Crack* came out in 2003, that does not mean that they had become sufficiently more accepting of screen depictions of homosexuality to uphold *Pregnant Hawkers* as a valuable or even remotely morally acceptable film. It is not my intention to suggest that increased internet access has boosted support for same-sex loving in Nigeria, or that Nigerians' Nollywood-focused online practices reflect a uniform affection for a film like *Pregnant Hawkers,* with its direct depiction of same-sex erotic contact. Rather, I attempt to map some of the online strategies by which male homosexuality has been inscribed in Nollywood fandom, and to argue for the media archaeological relevance of these strategies while resisting utopian claims that, coming from a Western site of enunciation, would inevitably seem condescending—or worse.

It is important to point out that despite local and global suspicions to the contrary, there is in fact a complex, apparently populous, and rarely acknowl-edged network of internet users who identify as both gay and Nigerian—a net-work that spans gay dating sites, film-focused message boards, video-sharing platforms, and perhaps especially Facebook and Twitter. In December 2011, sev-eral self-identified gay Nigerians created a Facebook community page devoted to raising public awareness about then-imminent anti-gay legislation—legislation that, now very much established, expressly forbids all forms of "gay organizing," including protest via social media, thereby defining such sites as Facebook and Twitter as extensions of the Nigerian public sphere. Contributing to the maintenance of the aforementioned Facebook page, whose precise identifying information I am not furnishing here (for reasons that should be obvious), one self-identified gay Nigerian man publicly shared his name and contact information—along with a heartrending plea to visitors to refrain from assuming that the site is a stereotypical Nigerian scam—in the hope of combatting then-looming anti-gay laws. Such an action—brave self-identification in the face of identity-denying or -denouncing public policies—provides a powerful indica-tion of the importance of excavating expressions of gay male subjectivity through the tools of media archaeology. The Facebook page in question provides, in retro-spect, one of the most complex of political and affective timestamps—one whose poignancy lies in its reflection of a period, not too long ago, when it was still possible to imagine that certain Nigerian senators would fail in their bid to ban "gay meetings" along with all manner of gay identifications. It is, of course, diffi-cult to look back upon this Facebook page—frozen for posterity by the infa-mously retentive mechanisms of Facebook itself—without wondering if the Ni-gerian citizen who left his name and contact information in 2011 was in fact apprehended in 2014, when anti-gay hate crimes became newly permissible, as he worried they would.

In his account of Western queer activism and its typically pitied and misrepresented African object, Tavia Nyong'o rightly cautions against seeing Facebook as promoting anything other than a liberal "fantasy of participation": "We leap too quickly to the assumption that information and communications technologies are extending 'peer-to-peer' contact with other people across the globe, deepening our ability to intervene positively in their lives."[15] Simply engaging with the aforementioned Facebook page—as numerous Western-identified users have done, leaving comments pledging support for "gay rights" in Nigeria—represents at best a symbolic gesture. At worst, however, it might serve the unintended purpose of prompting government surveillance of the Nigerian citizens whose contact information appears on the page, precisely by driving up traffic and attracting notice. There remains, on the internet, an exceedingly fine line between protection and policing, between celebration and surveillance, particularly with respect to gay identifications. Consider, for instance, the gay dating site RealJock .com, which, as I have detailed elsewhere, archives information about physical fitness, global travel, and even military service.[16] By the summer of 2014, the website had apparently acquired so many Nigerian users that it created a portlet devoted to the country—a place where visitors can "browse gay men in Nigeria." Like an increasing number of gay-identified websites, RealJock.com employs monitoring software, offering a real-time traffic feed—a live listing of visitors from around the world, including Nigeria—that is indistinguishable, in semiotic terms, from even the most homophobic of internet surveillance methods. Indeed, there is something inescapably disciplinary—something potentially shaming, especially for vulnerable sexual minorities—about a live traffic feed that lists the exact location from which one is accessing a website, and it is difficult to reconcile the RealJock mantra of global inclusiveness with a monitoring process that might facilitate state reprisals. In its "Nigerian section," RealJock.com lists no fewer than thirty-seven Nigerian cities from which users have accessed the website. What for some visitors might seem an emboldening index of the website's worldliness might for others constitute a clear justification for geographically specific anti-gay surveillance—including the sort that has led to violent raids on the homes of suspected gay men in Nigeria, locations from which the men in question were said to have expressed their homosexuality online.

If the practices explored in this book's previous chapters work to distance contemporary gay fandom from earlier, excessively abstract forms of cybertheory—specifically by reintroducing embodied, gay-specific subjectivities into discourses of "web empowerment"—then there is perhaps no more sobering rebuke to the old modes of analysis, with their utopian "predilection for the disembodied image," than the material contexts of contemporary Nigeria, where the physical body of the individual gay-identified internet user is not only "relevant" but also, as a rule, at risk.[17] Furthermore, as Nakamura notes, debates about posthumanism have tended to elide the global persistence of material forms of oppression as well as to ignore the importance of embodied access to the internet, especially in the global South: "Online practices of visualizing bodies have, far from defining users as 'posthuman,' come to constitute part of the everyday material activity of information seeking and communicating that defines membership in the information society"—a society that the Nigerian government, in particular, presently upholds as metonymic of the nation.[18] It is perhaps precisely for this reason that the Nigerian government has recently increased efforts to monitor, curb, and criminalize gay men's use of the internet: if male homosexuality is "un-African," then it threatens to infect an African national identity that, in the most optimistic of corporatized terms, is increasingly inseparable from computational culture. Nakamura's comment about "visualizing bodies" holds a special relevance for any study of online production in and about Nigeria, especially since the reception of Gay Nollywood is increasingly generative of images of individual male homosexuals, from fictional film characters to actors and directors rumored to be gay.

A vast number of Nigerian websites ask, for instance, whether the actors in *Pregnant Hawkers* are "actually gay"—whether a viewer could or should distinguish, in this case, between performer and role. Despite the sophistication of Nollywood's star system, and of the public and private reception practices that it has inspired over the past two decades, some fans seem distinctly unwilling to believe that a man who "plays gay" is not himself "actually gay"—or, at the very least, that he does not "approve" of the homosexuality that he has been asked to enact on screen. Prominently coexisting with those online productions that uphold, say, *Pregnant Hawkers* as a "gay film" are anecdotes about the actors said to have turned down "gay roles" on the grounds of a "personal resistance" to homosexuality. Few online explorations of the gay-themed Nollywood film *Law 58* (Dickson Iroegbu, 2010) are without references to the two stars—Mike Ezuruonye and Desmond Elliot—who reportedly rejected roles in the project, "shunning" it on the basis of its gay themes.[19] The persistence of this twofold reception tactic, in which a user-generated online production both identifies a Nollywood film as "gay" and outlines its offensiveness to a Nollywood star understood to be homophobic, conceivably contributes to the widespread suspicion that actors who play gay characters are themselves homosexual (or at least illicitly supportive of homosexuality). Far from reflective of a lack of spectatorial sophistication, then, the gay-specific conflation of actor and role would seem to represent a keen awareness of Nigerian social policy: the Ghanaian blogger Ameyaw Debrah, who often covers Nollywood projects, upholds *Pregnant Hawkers* as a "daring gay film" that flies in the face of Nigerian law, thus making sense of the careful refusal of major stars to appear in it—and raising questions about the little-known actors who play its gay lovers.[20] If, Debrah suggests, these men are not so supportive of their country's anti-gay laws as to refuse to appear in a gay-themed film, then they must be politically opposed to any attempt to criminalize homosexuality—and must, moreover, be gay themselves. The epistemological operations at work here would seem to suggest that there is little *legal* difference between voicing resistance to anti-gay legislation and offering an emphatically gay self-identification: both modes of enunciation are, in fact, equally criminal in Nigeria, and have been since January 2014, when President Goodluck Jonathan signed into law new ways of suppressing pro-gay activism—and new justifications for aligning such activism, in juridical terms, with the "open expression" of one's homosexuality. Simply put, to support gay rights is to *be* gay—and thus doubly "criminal."[21]

Exploring this conundrum, the Nigerian blogs Ajetun, Naija Hottest Spot, and All Around Gist, in their coverage of gay-themed Nollywood films, mobilize the particular logic of reception that sees any actor portraying a gay role as himself being gay by default—a logic that is, ultimately, both dubious and dangerous. Other sites, however, trade in rumors that they present as such—as, that is, unsubstantiated, often salacious "bits of gossip." Consider, for instance, the blog 234 Pulse, whose creator was responsible for uploading the *Pregnant Hawkers* sex scene to YouTube, and who often examines the "gay rumors" surrounding Nollywood's male stars. In September 2013, the blogger posted a few paragraphs about the strenuous effort with which certain stars will guard against such rumors. Rather cynically titled "Nollywood Actor Uti Nwanchukwu [sic] Continues His 'I Am Not Gay Tour,' See the FINE A$$ Chick He Posed With," the blog post provides alleged photographic evidence of a Nollywood star's acquisition of a "beard"—a woman assigned to provide him with a semblance of heterosexuality. Uti Nwachukwu, the star in question, is in fact widely believed—not merely "rumored"—to be gay, as indicated in the calm certainty with which such Nigerian blogs and social networks as Gist Mania, Naija Pals, Bella Naija, and That 1960 Chick! evoke his alleged homosexuality.[22] In early 2013, Gist Mania even went so far as to casually refer to the young model and actor Alexx Ekubo as Nwachukwu's "gay partner," thus employing the kind of "progressive" language that, in under a year, would plainly be verboten in Nigerian federal law, motivating a wide range of local website administrators to replace the word "homosexual" with the stylized "homos3xual" in an effort to evade government surveillance—to sail beyond the radar of certain, state-supported search engines.[23]

Instructively, such online "outing" tactics have not abated since the implementation in January 2014 of a ban—somewhat misleadingly named the Same-Sex Marriage Prohibition Act—designed to radically limit references to homosexuality in Nigeria. While the online persistence of efforts to "out" Nollywood stars may say more about internet cultures in general than about Nigerian users in particular, it also signals some of the dangers of gay-themed digital productions in certain sub-Saharan African countries, where it is both difficult and profoundly unethical to attempt to verify an individual's homosexuality—verification being, as Sharon Cumberland suggests, one of the most magnetic yet dubious of goals for "conventional" (i.e., Western-focused) studies of online fan cultures, wherein efforts to "authenticate identity" often inspire, if not demand, "face-to-face" interaction.[24] A major reason for focusing on gay formations rather than gay users—for examining gay-identified digital *productions* rather than gay-identified digital *producers*—is that, in places where the consequences of "coming out" remain remarkably dire, the likelihood of finding publicly expressed gay identity claims is relatively low, despite the plentiful examples cited above. It is not my intention to "prove" that there are millions of gay-identified Nigerians, or that "gayness," broadly understood, is anything but a Western exportation that stands in complicated contrast to longstanding local conceptions of same-sex loving. Rather, I hope to suggest that gay formations—those that focus equally on gay male sexuality and culture, or that alternate between erotic and "artistic" representations—are increasingly central to Nollywood films and to Nollywood fandom. Southern Nigeria's flourishing film industry thus offers a compelling case study in the way that queer cinema, in the twenty-first century, both inspires and competes with user-generated online productions.

Especially relevant here is the familiar Foucauldian notion that censorship generates sociocultural practices—including, in the case of today's Nigeria, the online circulation of information about Gay Nollywood. That such information is often offered in the guise of an anti-gay proclamation is almost beside the point. The digital visual capital that accrues to gay-identified online productions, in Nigeria as in the United States, often exceeds the discursive intentions of individual users, complicating their polemical accounts of male homosexuality. If a post-gay film or public persona, originating and circulating in privileged, "humanitarian" Western contexts, almost invariably relies upon gay-specific representational codes (if only as obstacles to be surmounted), then online productions often seize upon those very codes precisely to quench the continued thirst for representation of gay-identified users and to demonstrate the inanity—the irrelevance—of a post-gay position. Similarly, and in a perhaps more familiar Foucauldian fashion, an anti-gay position, defining itself in express opposition to gayness, often trades in the kinds of gay representations—offered as evidence of "deviance"—that are in fact quite indistinguishable from invitations to performative duplication and even libidinal enjoyment. "The language and law that regulates the establishment of heterosexuality as both an identity and an institution, both a practice and a system," writes Diana Fuss, "is the language and law of defense and protection: heterosexuality secures its self-identity and shores up its ontological boundaries by protecting itself from what it sees as the continual predatory encroachments of its contaminated other, homosexuality."[25] However, as remains all but incontestable from the standpoint of cultural studies, even the most virulently anti-gay invocation is, at least potentially, an invitation to a resistant or "oppositional" reading (in Stuart Hall's terms)—a reception practice that should not be underestimated, even if it has inspired understandable skepticism about its capacity to reflect or inspire social and institutional change.

If it is tempting to overvalue the "negotiated" readings produced by particular internet users, then that is partly because participation in globalized networks raises challenging questions about multiple, increasingly covert forms of imperialism. When users in sub-Saharan Africa access such Western-owned websites as YouTube, Facebook, and Twitter, they often generate the kind of content that strengthens corporate bottom lines—however much it may "empower" them as individuated users of the internet.[26] According to Western humanitarian cliché, the so-called digital divide—the line allegedly separating the web-enabled "haves" from the internet-illiterate "have-nots"—is a problem in need of remediation through corporate intervention. In recent years, however, numerous digital media theorists have countered this simplistic approach, exposing the commercial goals that undergird it. Like the open-source software advocate Rishab Aiyer Ghosh, Lisa Nakamura critiques familiar political interpretations of the digital divide as "a problem to be 'fixed' by giving everyone access to technology."[27] Indeed, the corporate ambitions of Facebook, which prominently include plans to introduce drones to geographically hostile portions of Africa (including northern Nigeria), have lately called into question the site's relationship to certain modes of neocolonialism, thus recalling Ziauddin Sardar's concept of the internet as a tool of imperialism—a guarantor of continued Western domination.[28] In Nigeria, local resistance to Facebook has most famously assumed the form of a moralizing fear, particularly of the site's alleged inability to prevent its users from uploading and sharing nude pictures, despite the website's policy prohibiting such actions. As a 2014 Nigerian newspaper article suggests, "such concerns are not surprising" in today's Nigeria, amid federal reminders of the sexualized "dangers" of internet use.[29]

The popular association of Facebook with illicit online activity—and with new, allegedly "non-Nigerian" social practices more generally—has not prevented some Nigerians, including Nollywood filmmakers, from taking to the site in order to critique the very homosexuality that they see as being equally Western (and equally "evil"). In January 2014, Dickson Iroegbu, who directed one of Nollywood's most controversial depictions of male homosexuality—the heavily anti-gay Law 58—took to Facebook in order to express his support for the expansive anti-gay bill that had just been signed into law in Nigeria. He didn't stop there, however. In a status update of over two hundred words, Iroegbu directly addressed hypothetical gay Nigerians, calling them "crazy" and highlighting their inability to reproduce—to "make babies"—with one another. Upholding their non-procreative sexual practices as evidence not merely of their immorality but also of their extreme distance from standard Nigerian definitions of marriage (with their rootedness in a generalized African ethic of procreation), Iroegbu's message managed to undermine the very legislation that it purported to endorse. It did this by using Facebook to invite responses from its gay male addressees—an invitation that flew in the face of Nigeria's then-new prohibitions on gay self-identification. Perhaps Iroegbu intended to "expose" rather than interact with gay male Facebook users—to crudely assist the Nigerian government's anti-gay surveillance measures—but his message included two particularly curious statements. One was that, in Nigeria, gay men are "free to do gay shit" behind closed doors, in the privacy of their own homes—a statement dramatically and almost immediately contradicted by a series of hate crimes in which anti-gay vigilante groups entered and damaged the homes of suspected gay men, even going so far as to abuse and murder the men themselves, with the tacit support of federal and state governments.[30] The other was Iroegbu's challenge, couched in the Pidgin-inflected rhetoric of a childish dare, in which he called upon gay men to stage naked protests in the public sphere—a patently unlikely scenario, owing not merely to the mandated nudity but also to the general illegality of gay-themed public remarks. However much Iroegbu might believe his anti-gay use of Facebook to be a means of supporting his country's "righteous" stance on homosexuality, and however much he might view it as a way of critiquing the "liberal," Western-identified Facebook "from the inside," it is obvious that his relationship to the social networking service is broadly, and necessarily, supportive.[31] As Tavia Nyong'o notes, "the productions of nationally or globally conscious individuals increasingly flow through the same channels—Skype, Facebook, AT&T, Blogger.com—that any other lifestyle, interest, purchase, or interpersonal relation takes. A gay activist in Berlin can post an irate comment on the Facebook page of a homophobic journalist half a world away." Such "furious, contestatory activity, while registering [to some] as political action, is registering to Facebook, and so forth, as 'user-generated content.'"[32] The same, of course, might be said of Nigerian uses of YouTube, another Western-owned site whose globalizing tendencies have extended all the way to Nigeria, enabling users to extract, circulate, and annotate audiovisual evidence of Gay Nollywood.

If prominent digital paratexts tend to parse contemporary queer cinema in ways that generate visual economies of gay male sexuality and subjectivity, then such parsing is perhaps even more economical in today's Nigeria, where the relative scarcity of stable, bandwidth-heavy access to the internet, coupled with what Brian Larkin has referred to as the general inevitability of "breakdown and failure" in Nigeria's precise postcolonial circumstances, necessarily leads to the creation of the kinds of online productions that rely on clarity and brevity—that are more apt to communicate a monolithic gayness than an expansive queerness.[33] Of all platforms for user-created video, YouTube remains the most popular in

Nigeria, for reasons relating to the site's specific conditions of use. Emerging in 2005 and a key means of securing the precisely contemporaneous *Brokeback Mountain* (Ang Lee, 2005) as a film about gay rather than, say, bisexual or broadly queer men, YouTube imposes standard fifteen-minute 2GB limits on uploaded content—limits that can be exceeded only through relatively time-consuming, multiply contingent processes of request and verification. (A mobile phone, for instance, is required for those wishing to "prove" both their embodied existence and their "legitimate" need for expanded uploading rights.) As Jean Burgess and Joshua Green argue in their book on YouTube, the site has effectively conditioned users to provide "short 'quotes' of content—snippets of material [they] share to draw attention to the most significant portion" of a film or television series, thus militating against the production of a protean reading or subject-position.[34] As a "mediated cultural system," rather than a "neutral" platform for video sharing, YouTube retains a redactional relationship to media content—editing it for readily communicable meanings, rather than exploring, over time, its potential resistance to monolithic interpretations. A sustained personal video blog might gradually become popular, producing more and more facets of an individual online persona and slowly acquiring more and more subscribers, but it is not representative of the way in which users tend to parse contemporary queer films on YouTube. Far more emblematic is the work of 234 pulse, who powerfully demonstrates that Nollywood is now amenable to graphic depictions of same-sex erotic contact. Short "quotes" of media content—like the *Pregnant Hawkers* clip that runs just under one minute, and that offers a readily readable representation of anal intercourse as a gay sexual practice—are seemingly preferable to extended engagements, not merely because YouTube users have, presumably like internet users in general, become habituated to ever quicker, more concise productions, but also because such quotes can seem to serve properly promotional purposes, remaining relatively safe from corporate opprobrium—relatively suggestive of "fair use."

In Nigeria, however, particular *material* conditions of access to the internet are perhaps more decisive factors than taste and habit. As Alessandro Jedlowski points out, Nigeria may boast one of the highest rates of internet use in Africa, but "the quality of the connection rarely allows people to access bandwidth-heavy content like [feature-length streaming] video."[35] Like a growing number of Nollywood scholars, Jedlowski goes on to stress that "most Internet viewing of Nollywood films . . . occurs in the diaspora," but he has in mind a model of spectatorial engagement that centralizes *entire* feature films, rather than the kinds of clips that remain so popular on YouTube—even (perhaps especially) in Nigeria. In 2012, the number of YouTube views in Nigeria grew by 125 percent, launching Nigeria to the top of the list of sub-Saharan African countries with local YouTube domains. "Despite broadband limitations and network interruptions, YouTube has warmed its way into the hearts of Nigerians," claimed the blog Technesstivity, deploying the rhetoric by which, as Brenton Malin argues, "media technologies have been given a great responsibility for human emotion," acquiring an anthropomorphized "aura" that often eclipses—and just as often determines—the desires of individual users.[36] However, instead of viewing YouTube as a source of "warmth"—as a humanized mechanism that has sought and "won" Nigerian users—it is important to address some basic political, economic, and infrastructural considerations, such as those that militate against video-sharing alternatives to YouTube in sub-Saharan Africa. In 2013, Taiwo Kola-Ogunlade, Google's Communications and Public Affairs Manager for West Africa, announced, "Nigerians have embraced YouTube, creating and watching locally." He went on, "They are part of a highly connected global community that uploads 72 hours of video every minute and watches 4 billion hours of video a month."[37] The reasons for YouTube's success in Nigeria, however, likely have more to do with local, political and technological limitations on internet use than with the website's allegedly unique affective dimensions. Simply put, YouTube is, in Nigeria, currently more viable than, say, Netflix as an online video service, for some of the reasons outlined above—including and especially the website's privileging of "short 'quotes'" of media content. (There is also, of course, the matter of the international availability of certain subscription websites; for instance, Netflix did not become accessible in Nigeria until early 2016.) Since, as Burgess and Green argue, YouTube manages to retain its functionality "within the technological constraints of standard browser software and relatively modest bandwidth," it has proved uniquely amenable to the practical, material limitations of internet access in Nigeria.[38]

A number of Nigerian entrepreneurs have recently attempted to expand local uses of YouTube beyond the temporal, discursive, and affective confines of "clip culture"—with varying degrees of success. In 2008, just three years after YouTube was founded, Nigerian tech mogul Jason Njoku created Nollywood Love, a company devoted to obtaining official licenses for the uploading of thousands of Nollywood films to a dedicated YouTube channel (also called Nollywood Love).[39] Available in sponsor-supported segments, Nollywood films continue to enjoy a prominent place on YouTube (both YouTube.com and YouTube.ng, the website's localized Nigerian version) that is not unlike their presence on iROKOtv .com, a website that Njoku created in 2010. Offering thousands of Nollywood films as early as 2011, Njoku later developed a fee-based subscription site— iROKOtv PLUS—for users willing to pay to avoid commercial interruptions. (Today, iROKOtv.com is completely commercial-free—a subscription-only website on the order of Netflix.) Diasporic views of entire feature films on both Nollywood Love and iROKOtv far exceed those in Nigeria, as Jedlowski makes clear. However, as a site for what Burgess and Green call "short 'quotes,'" and as evidenced in its annual roundups of most-watched videos, YouTube remains a key means for Nigerians to directly engage with brief clips of individual Nollywood films—including and especially those that address male homosexuality by confining it to a few "fuck scenes." Furthermore, as Nigerian-based Nollywood fandom attests, YouTube videos often enjoy broad lives beyond the site itself. Henry Jenkins points out that the website's "distinctive technical affordances make posting YouTube content elsewhere a trivial matter of copying and pasting code, allowing videos to be inserted into diverse cultural economies and social ecologies."[40] Indeed, the video "SCENE FROM NOLLYWOOD MOVIE 'PREGNANT HAWKERS'"—uploaded to YouTube by 234 pulse in April 2013—has since appeared on a number of Nigerian websites, from personal blogs to Nollywood-themed Tumblr accounts and beyond. A nearly minute-long clip, it does not require the kind of bandwidth-heavy internet connection that remains relatively scarce in Nigeria. As a technically accessible short quote, the video reduces two gay characters to the anal intercourse that they mutually enjoy—but so, for the most part, does *Pregnant Hawkers* itself, thus complicating any claims about its pirated YouTube paratext representing a misleading extraction.

"Is that all there is?" asked one Nigerian-identified viewer of "SCENE FROM NOLLYWOOD MOVIE 'PREGNANT HAWKERS'"—to which a fellow commenter might rightly reply in the affirmative. Except for a few brief scenes in which the two male lovers exchange spoken endearments, and in which one cruelly betrays the other, *Pregnant Hawkers* is a strictly heterocentric affair.[41] Indeed, a later moment in this film that is largely devoted to heterosexual intrigue features the self-identified gay characters enjoying a quietly romantic evening, complete with a fancy meal, fine wine, and even a kiss that seems, at first, to seal their status as "soul mates." These characters are barely a part of *Pregnant Hawkers,* however, making the pirated YouTube clip seem an attempt less to actively "limit" the film's gayness to hardcore sexuality than to accurately reflect its narrative constraints. Conceivably, 234 pulse could have uploaded the brief dinner scene as a means of suggesting how gay characters operate socially (at least part of the time) in *Pregnant Hawkers,* but such a scene would surely not have generated as many views as that which offers the apparent shock value of a Nollywood film "going gay"—and in a big way, with a direct depiction of anal intercourse. If Pink 2.0, as a complex cultural interface, functions to condense queerness into limited conceptions of gay male sexuality and culture, then that is partly due to the explicit and unspoken mandates by which media become "spreadable"—mandates that result, in part, from the systematic conditioning of internet users to recognize the viral potential of sexual imagery.

The persistent online presence of *Pregnant Hawkers* is attributable to more than just a principled distaste for the kind of covert censorship that turned the film into the "gay-free" *Desperate Hawkers.* It is also a function of forms of state homophobia that, in Nigeria, are finding more and more outlets online—and that increasingly require audiovisual evidence of just how "raunchy" gay representations can be. NaijaRules.com, a Nigerian message board devoted to Nollywood fandom, contains a prominent, popular NSFW thread (created by a member whose handle is Village-Boi) that positions *Pregnant Hawkers* as a "sex film"—and one whose objectionable, "disgusting" status derives from its depiction of gay men; via a hyperlink, Village-Boi offers the YouTube video "SCENE FROM NOLLYWOOD MOVIE 'PREGNANT HAWKERS,'" thus confirming Henry Jenkins's comments about the extreme and inherent "spreadability" of YouTube content.[42] By contrast, the Nigerian Tumblr site Wadup Naija (wadup .com.ng) describes *Pregnant Hawkers* as a "gay pornographic movie," and provides, as support for this classification, a screenshot of its opening sex scene—albeit one derived directly from the aforementioned YouTube video. Retaining the visual details that would seem to prove that practices of piracy enabled 234 pulse to acquire and upload the video—details that include the unmistakable interface of OgaMadamTV, with its color-coded (i.e., green-and-white) evocation of a Nigerian national identity—the Wadup Naija post confidently asserts that *Pregnant Hawkers* is both gay and pornographic. On the basis of a single YouTube video, and of the visual semiotics that it freezes via a screenshot, Wadup Naija makes a case for the gayness of an entire film, rather than of two of its minor characters—a reading that it imposes on "SCENE FROM NOLLYWOOD MOVIE 'PREGNANT HAWKERS,'" whose bland title alone suggests that 234 pulse is not playing the same game of sexual taxonomy.[43]

(VIDEO Viewers discretion advised) (+18) OMG Nollywood goes Porn: Watch Nollywood Gay Porn Movie.

OMG .....What is happening to Nollywood? I'm shocked seeing such sence in a movie! Going nude and having live sex is now in vogue in Nollywood. God pls help us. **NO BE SMALL THING!**

Video after the cut.........please viewers discretion is seriously advised!! +18

Figure 5.1. In contrast to the strategies of YouTube user 234 pulse, the majority of Nollywood-themed Nigerian blogs identify *Pregnant Hawkers* (Patrick Hogan and Okechukwu Ifeanyi, 2013) as a "gay movie," with No Be Small Thing going so far as to call it "gay porn" (2013).

While 234 pulse refrains from attaching a gay label to the pirated clip from *Pregnant Hawkers,* preferring instead to call it simply a "scene from a Nollywood movie," the YouTube user comments collected beneath the video—and almost impossible to ignore when I watched it for the first time in early 2014—tell a different, emphatically gay story, one furnishing the polar declarations of homophobia ("disgusting gayness") and affirmation ("the best part of the movie was this gay scene"). By the time 234 pulse uploaded the video, *Pregnant Hawkers* had already earned a reputation as "gay porn," albeit on the basis of this single sex scene, which culminates with the men being discovered, in flagrante delicto, by a middle-aged woman, who, at the sight of anal intercourse, employs a "silent scream" worthy of Brecht's Berliner Ensemble (or, for that matter, Rod Steiger in *The Pawnbroker* [Sidney Lumet, 1965]). In *Pregnant Hawkers,* the love that dare not speak its name in a Nigeria that abounds with increasingly stringent anti-gay laws is repurposed as a love that generates great, mutually satisfying sex: when the grinning top (played by Nollywood heartthrob Khing Bassey) proudly calls himself a "bad boy," the moaning bottom delightedly concurs. It is only the homophobic interloper who is unable to utter a word, her disgusted response to gay sex rendered ridiculous through her soundless scream. One could hardly ask for a hotter, more approving presentation of same-sex erotic contact, or for a more denigrating depiction of the near-comic idiocy of knee-jerk homophobic revulsion. The scene's embodied contours are ambiguous, however: are these men— these salaried actors—actually fucking? While the frontal nudity of the actor who portrays the avid bottom becomes visible toward the end of the scene, as his exposure to an unannounced guest compels him to rise to his feet and pull up his pants, the nudity of the top is tantalizingly partial, and utterly unclear as an index of the actors' precise physical actions. While the top's pubic hair is visible as he "plows away," the question of whether penetration actually occurred during the shooting of this scene has inspired a range of reflections across the Nigerian blogosphere—reflections that, whatever their ideological differences, serve the shared purpose of positioning *Pregnant Hawkers* as a gay film, and Nigeria as the national home of millions of gay men.

At first glance, these two claims might seem equally spurious, and it is important to emphasize that *Pregnant Hawkers,* far from being a sustained piece of queer-positive filmmaking, focuses almost entirely upon the cultural and sexual practices of a series of straight-identified characters. Despite the fact that it begins with the sex scene described above, which rather misleadingly suggests that it is going to privilege the experiences of the men whose lovemaking is interrupted by a most homophobic encroacher, *Pregnant Hawkers* follows four straight characters whose dramas derive directly from their heterosexual passions: an unhappily engaged young woman lusts after, and eventually attempts to seduce, her fiancé's best friend, who, for his part, hopes to convince his girlfriend that his loyalty to her is unlikely to lapse. If the film's gay lovers, who deliver its first lines, quickly fade into the background, becoming subsumed under some distinctly heterosexist narrative mandates, then they are perhaps the perfect filmic embodiments of the ephemerality of gay identities in today's Nigeria. The Same-Sex Marriage Prohibition Act, signed into law by President Goodluck Jonathan in January 2014, a year after the release of *Pregnant Hawkers,* provides a variety of punitive measures (including a fourteen-year prison term) for those who publicly self-identify as gay, attend gay-themed meetings, patronize or operate a "gay organization," purchase material copies of a gay-themed film, or, of course, engage in "gay sex" (narrowly defined, according to the British colonial penal code that continues to structure the criminalization of homosexuality in Nigeria, as anal sex—precisely the kind of "sodomitical" sex so directly represented in the opening scene of *Pregnant Hawkers*).[44] If a Nigerian citizen can circumvent federal law in order to leave gay-identified traces online, then so too can the officially suppressed *Pregnant Hawkers,* albeit through processes that are perhaps less "personalized." The former may bravely engage with any one of a number of gay-centered websites still operating locally (though under constant threat of state reprisal), and he may well pursue access to various circumvention technologies, including virtual private networks that "allow users in a repressively censored place . . . to 'proxy' the connections through a computer in a more open place"— although such access is, of course, multiply contingent, and unlikely to be feasible for the vast majority of Nigerian gay men hoping to make "gay use" of the internet.[45] For its part, *Pregnant Hawkers* has been the beneficiary of considerable audience interest, and it provides a useful reminder of why the tools of media archaeology are so crucial to the study of queer texts, especially in emergent information societies that continue to criminalize homosexuality.

Before leaving the topic of *Pregnant Hawkers,* I would like to consider a viral image, generated in Nigeria by a Nigerian internet user, that encapsulates one of my broader points about Pink 2.0—namely, that this complex cultural interface works to ensure the online survival of gay-themed films despite the official and informal circuits of censorship that seek to suppress them. My argument here is not so much that the internet alone facilitates the survival of media texts and of their contested reception—that it inevitably circumvents and supersedes state censorship—but that the diversity of online uses to which "gay images" may be put, particularly in Nigeria, ensures that audiences will remain aware of *Pregnant Hawkers* even as they are confronted with its comparably chaste, "gay-free," state-sanctioned replacement. In October 2012, Nigerian actor Khing Bassey, who plays the sexy, gay-identified "dom top" in *Pregnant Hawkers,* was severely injured in a motorcycle accident, having defied the Lagos State government's ban on the use of motorcycles on local highways. During his complicated convalescence, Bassey tweeted a "selfie"—a digital self-portrait—showing his facial bandages, stitches, and scars.[46] That the image soon went viral is perhaps unsurprising. After all, it offers gruesome, iconographic evidence of the mere humanity of a flesh-and-blood movie star—of the vulnerable physicality of a particular star's body—and conceivably satisfies multiple modes of fandom, from the sadistic to the empathic. What happens, however, when images of the actor's injuries are read in relation to his gay-identified film character? Star-centered schadenfreude assumes telling valences when the gay-identified *Pregnant Hawkers* is inserted, however retroactively, into the equation of Bassey's personal pain and recovery. Shot several months after Bassey had completed his convalescence, the film for which he "went gay" is occasionally upheld as an explanation for the still-circulating images of his facial wounds. Not content with a single image, Bassey in fact took and tweeted numerous selfies from different stages of his recuperation. Not one of these images shows a smiling or remotely buoyant Bassey; all of them suggest a physically painful, emotionally upsetting recovery, and thus lend themselves to a certain iconography of gay victimhood. Semiotically, they evoke the growing number of viral images of the bloody results of anti-gay hate crimes—images that present the puffy eyelids, bleedings cheeks, and cracked lips of various gay-identified victims, and that tend to galvanize the users of social networking services, compelling them to address the persistence of particularly violent forms of homophobia. The equally viral online presence of Bassey's *Pregnant Hawkers* sex scene makes it close to impossible for some users to refrain from reading the star's grim selfies according to some of the potentially brutal consequences of "coming out" in Nigeria—and, for that matter, anywhere in the world. What's more, the particular illegality that in fact led to Bassey's facial scarring—the actor's decision to sidestep state prohibitions against motorcycle use on Lagos highways—makes a handy stand-in for the illegality of homosexuality in Nigeria. The knowledge that Bassey broke the law, and the lingering online evidence of the bloody repercussions of this crime, conspires to substitute gay sex for motorcycle use—especially when YouTube clips of *Pregnant Hawkers* can so easily be embedded beneath Bassey's selfies, as they are on numerous Nigerian websites. Whether illicitly riding a motorcycle or "topping" another man, Bassey suggests the kind of law-flouting risk-taking that can end a career—and even a life.

Those online productions that do not explicitly present Bassey's bloody selfies as evidence that his on-screen "deviance" has been punished—that do not attempt to suggest that he was beaten for portraying a sexually active gay man in *Pregnant Hawkers*—still position these selfies within a broadly anti-gay backlash. In a post entitled "Double Whammy," the blog 234 Pulse argues that the "uglification" of Bassey's face—the alleged loss of his "pretty-boy" looks in a motorcycle accident—is inseparable from the "uglification" of his star persona that he achieved by appearing in a "gay movie scene." While the blog itself does not appear to adopt a moral stance on Bassey's gay-receptivity, preferring instead to explain, in relatively dispassionate terms, the twin reasons why his star has been fading—why the Nollywood film industry has allegedly "abandoned" him—it still mobilizes a gay-specific taxonomy in a way that it does not on a different online platform.[47] On YouTube—still operating pseudonymously as 234 pulse—the blogger manages to suggest that *Pregnant Hawkers* defies sexual categorization. Taken together, the discursively discrepant yet intimately connected blog and YouTube channel indicate that gay specificity may be inscribed online only when it is under threat—of erasure or, worse still, of violent, state-sanctioned retaliation, as the political contexts of contemporary Nigeria make all too clear.

Beyond *Pregnant Hawkers:* Iroegbu's *Law 58*

With its direct depiction of the pleasures of anal sex, *Pregnant Hawkers* would seem an extreme case of Nollywood "going gay"—a film that ups the erotic ante considerably on such classic industry depictions of male homosexuality as Kenneth Nnebue's *End Time* (1999), in which the gayness of a pair of minor characters is established primarily through tame dialogue exchanges, and Emem Isong's *Reloaded* (2009), which relies on certain cultural stereotypes in order to self-consciously communicate the human diversity of southern Nigeria. Both *End Time* and *Reloaded* were produced before the passage, in 2013, of sweeping anti-gay legislation; so were the 2010 films *Hideous Affair* (whose title alone should signal its compliance with Nigeria's federal, state, and local policies of pathologizing male homosexuality), *Dirty Secret* (ditto), and *Men in Love,* a far more complicated case that I examine in greater detail below. Because these films, to varying degrees, reflect the federally sanctioned sentiment that homosexuality is "un-African," and because they do not feature hardcore (or even softcore) sex scenes, they have not been subjected to the sort of censorship measures that have "heterosexualized" *Pregnant Hawkers* since its initial release in early 2013—that have mandated, among other changes, the excision of the aforementioned depiction of anal sex.

The poorly timed production of *Pregnant Hawkers* had, however, a crucial precursor in *Law 58,* a film whose planned release date of 2010 was pushed back by nearly two years, owing to the objections of the Nigerian Film & Video Censors Board—an outfit that, as Lindsey Green-Simms and Unoma Azuah suggest, functions not unlike Hollywood's erstwhile Production Code Administration, particularly with respect to representations of "sex perversion."[48] According to director Dickson Iroegbu, the Abuja Censors Board refused to certify the movie—that is, pass it for commercial release in Nigeria—"on the grounds that it dwells on an issue that is not allowed" in the country. That "issue" being male homosexuality, Iroegbu was forced to shorten *Law 58,* removing scenes that could be construed as "humanizing" gay characters, and adding an opening crawl explaining the film's political stance.[49] "This is a true life story," the text begins, thus suggesting that truth telling, however upsetting, offers its own instructive alibi—a documentary justification in the face of federal homophobia. Iroegbu, who wrote the exculpating crawl, claims that his intention in making *Law 58* was to represent, not normalize or valorize, sexual practices and identities that "do exist" in Nigeria—a claim that has been echoed by many a Nollywood filmmaker responsible for having generated "gay images," from producer Emem Isong (whose 2003 film *Emotional Crack* is said to be based on her own experience of receiving unwanted "lesbian attention") to director Theodore Anyanji (who, in defending his *Dirty Secret* against charges of moral degeneracy, claimed that it simply reflects a particularly "distasteful reality").[50] Iroegbu's crawl continues, "The Nigerian society by its laws frowns against the act of homosexuality, hence the need to tell this story . . . The aim is to help present the general view [and] the natural laws guiding true Africans' perception of the inordinate act, and not highlight or promote it." Familiar from a whole host of anti-gay ordinances presently "active" in sub-Saharan Africa, the alignment of homophobia with "true African-ness" renders homosexuality a fictive identity—a deviant erotic practice that doesn't deserve analysis beyond its association with "sodomy." Iroegbu, like his Nollywood counterparts, thus provides an explanation for his film's depiction of same-sex eroticism—a justification for opening scenes in which two shirtless men share a passionate embrace, and in which they kiss in close-up.

As if to further cement the film's anti-gay stance, *Law 58* features a theme song that spells out the "sin" of homosexuality. Written and performed by Austine Erowele, one of Nollywood's most prolific composers, the song offers hysterically anti-gay sentiments verging on camp: "A man to love another? No, no, no, no, no! This stain is on me, I wish my life to be right! Take me away from this—this shame is on me!" The "me," in this instance, refers to Charles (Mac Maurice Ndubueze), a young man who "experiments" with homosexuality, having succumbed to the enticements of a venerable elder, Chief Douglas (played by the legendary actor Kanayo O. Kanayo), who euphemistically runs a "club" for gay men, and who represents "the evangelical scourge of the gay seducer."[51] Chief Douglas quickly becomes the film's sole pro-gay mouthpiece, but *Law 58* takes pains to present his sentiments as both "sick" and singularly actionable: when he confronts the conflicted Charles about the young man's persistent desire to become a "normal" husband and father, the chief stands before the gates of his Lagos compound, the tall metal bars overwhelmingly suggesting those of a prison. "Take a good look at me," the chief instructs Charles. "At my age, I lack nothing! What do you need a family for? We"—meaning gay men—"rule the world!" Again, the association of gay men with worldliness threatens to present Nigeria, and by extension all of sub-Saharan Africa, as disconnected from global

Figure 5.2. Dickson Iroegbu's *Law 58* (2010).

trends, and thus as powerless in all but the most Christian (and, for that matter, Muslim) of arenas.

When the chief suggests that "it's how much you've enjoyed [your life] that matters"—that self-fulfillment, "getting what you desire," is "what really counts"— he sounds as reasonable as any inspirational elder. But when he issues his belief that Lagos will one day become the gay capital of the world, he is meant to seem the strangest and least convincing of mentors. "The plan," he says, sounding much like a stock villain with designs on global domination, "is to have our homes and our streets filled with homophiles! On that day, a fag can conveniently marry another." By the end of the film, however, that day has not come—nor will it ever, according to the Christian characters who close *Law 58* with some passionate anti-gay sermonizing, suggesting that gay marriage is "beyond an abomination" in the eyes of God. Erowele's theme song echoes this conviction by equating gay marriage—what the Nigerian senate proudly defined, in 2013, as "an eternal impossibility" in the country—with sheer obscenity. If the song suggests that male homosexuality "makes you wonder what the world is turning to," then so does a televangelist who, late in the film, extricates Africa from an "international scene" that has unaccountably "gone gay." The sheer continental chauvinism of her remarks represents the inverse of a commonly expressed Western mode of global gay rights activism, which, as Tavia Nyong'o argues, often "pities" an Africa positioned as inexplicable, thus contributing to the maintenance of neocolonialist stereotypes that mystify the continent in order to "manage" it, and that mobilize "compassion" as a mode of control.[52] Asking her viewers to accept "African-ness as godliness," the Nigerian televangelist also asks them to "take sides" in the global struggle to define male homosexuality. Produced with the participation of Christ the King Catholic Church, *Law 58* offers some striking and seemingly unassailable religious credentials, ensuring that, unlike *Pregnant Hawkers,* it will remain free of federal interference. For however much Nigeria's newest anti-gay laws might signal a fear of the potentially pro-gay effects of film spectatorship—of the "contagiousness" of gay representation, and, in particular, of a certain homophile affect—there remains a pronounced industrial investment in the ability of attractive Christian characters to outshine "deviance," even when that deviance is enacted by so beloved and charismatic a star as Kanayo O. Kanayo.

Moses Ebere's *Men in Love*

Like *Law 58,* the Nollywood film *Men in Love* culminates in an embrace of "Christian values"—the kind that can "crush" homosexuality, and stop deviance "dead in its tracks." The narrative and thematic paths by which the film arrives as this rote, eleventh-hour Christian recuperation, however, are not what might be expected. Indeed, the film challenges conventional conceptions of Nollywood in ways that have inspired multivalent online responses. Throughout its first hour, *Men in Love* struggles to construct a dichotomy between the "essential" promiscuity of straight men and the equally entrenched monogamy of their gay-identified counterparts. In this sense, it represents both an endorsement and a denunciation of certain patterns of sexual stereotyping, exaggerating the extent to which, as one character avers, "straight men cheat," while at the same time denying a corresponding promiscuity among gay men, who emerge, at least initially, as more interested in love than in sex, and as opposed to acquiring multiple partners simultaneously. According to various posts on the Facebook page of the Black Gay Men's Blog, a key site for the global, networked reception of *Men in Love,* the "believability" of the film's presentation of straight male promiscuity—of a married man who simply "can't help himself"—lends credence to its high-minded depiction of an idealized, "monogamy-minded" gay man, a rebuke to the sort of stereotype that, even in Nollywood films, has frequently positioned homosexuality as synonymous with erotic avidity, and as uniquely open to polyamorous pursuits.[53] Consider, for instance, Nollywood's cycle of "campus cult" films, which includes both lesbian- and gay-identified entries, and in which same-sex erotic contact is frequently a group affair: *Beautiful Faces* (Kabat Esosa Egbon,

2004), for instance, features a sorority whose lesbian leader (played by Stephanie Okereke) wreaks havoc on campus, sleeping with countless girls and acquiring a reputation as a "homo whore," while *Women's Affair* (Andy Chukwu, 2003), starring Genevieve Nnaji, even more explicitly positions gender segregation as generative not just of lesbianism but also of "group sex." Lindsey Green-Simms and Unoma Azuah argue that such films "reflect a certain discourse within Nigeria that sees homo-social environments as dangerous and retrograde, as disruptive to a modern and orderly heteronormativity."[54] *Men in Love* deviates from this schema by aligning its gay male protagonist with "women's experiences," and by suggesting that he "gets along with girls" on the basis of his feminine identification. In other words, the film replaces one stereotype—that of the misogynist gay man—with another. At the same time, as a means of cultivating spectatorial trust, *Men in Love* carefully outlines the "ugly" yet "unsurprising" sexual promiscuity of its straight male protagonist, couching it in (specious) statistics: like "the majority" of straight men, the married Charles (John Dumelo) is powerless to resist the sexual advances of the women who surround him. Having struggled to establish its realist credentials in the realm of sexual representation—including by having one character quote actual psychiatric responses to straight male promiscuity, and by confronting "the ugly truth" of spousal cheating—the film proceeds to outline some of the virtues associated with gay men as "model citizens," as well as the legitimacy of homosexuality as an involuntary identity category, an "essence" that one acquires "at birth."

Men in Love lingers on straight male promiscuity in a manner that is entirely in tune with Nollywood's typical approaches to spousal cheating, but that departs dramatically from standard narrative practice by presenting it as a negative counterpoint to gay men's "essential fidelity." In fact, the film's first hour strategically juxtaposes the serial adultery of its straight protagonist with the loyalty of his gay friend, suggesting a case of special pleading on behalf of gay virtue, one that depends upon the careful concealment of the gay man's character flaws, which emerge only in the film's second hour. As if to promise a narrative entirely devoted to the heterosexual sources of marital conflict, the film's opening sequence is set in a hotel room where Whitney (Tonto Dikeh) finds her husband, Charles, carrying out a steamy affair with his secretary—a scenario of discovery that, for the characters in question, is painfully recurrent. ("You're always doing this!" Whitney shouts at her husband, who concedes sheepishly that he has "a problem," one that waxes and wanes but "never really goes away.") In the first indication that *Men in Love* is going to depart from Nollywood's typical representational protocol, Whitney proceeds to employ a variety of expletives in denouncing her cheating husband, as well as his "tarty" mistress. "Why are you fucking your secretary, Charles?" Whitney asks, and, as if to emphasize the diegetic as well as industrial transgression of her "dirty" word choice—rare in a Nollywood that remains generally beholden to a relatively expletive-averse censorship board—she repeats it several times, until it acquires an incantatory power, eventually transforming into a gerund: "I came to catch your lying fucking ass! To see your cheating fucking!" Finally, Whitney directs her rage at Charles's secretary, who cowers in a corner as she receives Whitney's insults, and who screams in pain as the other woman, having kicked her repeatedly, finally smashes a wine bottle over her head.

Whitney's "rage problem," as one character calls it, becomes an object of analysis in the next scene, which is set in the living room of Whitney's friends Flora (Halima Abubakar) and Rina (Ejinne), two women whose cohabitation is quickly explained—even "excused"—as a cost-saving measure, rather than a reflection of "lesbian intent." Calmly if somewhat condescendingly explaining that "it's in a man's nature to cheat," Rina attempts to excuse Charles's behavior by offering an essentialist understanding of male heterosexuality. Whitney rejects Rina's remarks, however, arguing, "There are men today in Nigeria who would rather give up their right arms than cheat on their wives. Why can't my own just be like that? Why can't I have the perfect love, the perfect marriage?" Reminding her unattached, childless friends that she is in fact "lucky enough to have a son," Whitney vows to take the boy far away from his father, should Charles ever cheat again. Citing the high incidence of "repeat offenses" among "male cheaters"— an incidence that, she claims, "has confounded even the most acclaimed of psychologists"—Rina reminds Whitney that Charles is unlikely to curb his erotic appetite, to limit it to sexual encounters with his wife. At this mention of sex with Charles, Whitney sighs. "I can't deny that I miss my husband in a certain kind of way," she says, to which Rina responds, "Don't look a gift horse in the mouth!"— meaning that if Charles satisfies Whitney sexually, then such satisfaction is worth her awareness of the man's chronic infidelity.

After reconciling with her husband—and apologizing for sending his mistress to the hospital—Whitney asks Charles to fuck her in their spousal bed. He does—so violently that the fitted sheets detach from the mattress, revealing a bare box spring that shudders with every thrust. Rare in a Nollywood film, this direct depiction of penetrative sex suggests that *Men in Love* is alert to erotic details— to some of the material consequences of intercourse, which here include the near mutilation of a well-made bed. Later, Whitney claims that this "makeup sex" was transformative: it "was the best, and felt like the first," restoring her to a condition of virginity, and to the experience of "defilement," which also, of course, suggests that she bled—that Charles's jabbing, thrusting sexual actions were painful as well as pleasurable (or pleasurable because painful). This evocation of erotic defilement is a foreshadowing device: it anticipates the scene in which Charles loses *his* virginity—anally, and underneath another man. That man is Alex (the late Muna Obiekwe), the manager of a resort hotel who, in his spare time, organizes fashion shows. When he first appears in the film, Alex is standing in the lobby of Clear Networks, the Lagos-based telecommunications company that Charles owns. Alex hopes to enlist the company as a sponsor of his latest fashion show, but first he must convince a skeptical secretary to submit his written request to those who might be able to honor it. She looks at him askance, however, and with a distinctly homophobic frown: Alex is not a "real" man, nor a "proper Nigerian," if a fashion show is his forte.

Even before Alex comes out as gay, *Men in Love* toys with the stereotyped equation between male homosexuality and effeminacy, between "being a fag" and "looking fabulous." Numerous characters, including the Clear Networks secretary who serves as the company's gatekeeper, appear to suspect Alex of being gay on the basis of his self-confessed "interest in fashion." Imploring the secretary to consider his plan to acquire the sponsorship of Clear Networks, Alex is reduced to the role of a beggar—of a solicitous outsider whose lowly status is signaled not merely by his anguished pleading but also by the fact that he's barred from entering the central offices of a major company. Banished to an anteroom, Alex is first aligned with the company's all-female secretarial force, and then further diminished by the head secretary's dismissive response to his request that she submit his paperwork "to the men." It is only when Charles appears, and recognizes Alex as a former schoolmate, that the fashion-obsessed supplicant is permitted to enter an "inner room"—Charles's vast office, where the two men discuss their University of Ibadan football team, the Dragons, on which Alex served as the goalkeeper. "You are looking *fantastic*," Alex tells Charles, a bit too enthusiastically to mask his libidinous interest in the other man. Close-ups of Alex's face, revealing the shine in his eyes, make clear his sexual desire for an old "football buddy," who, for his part, is polite but reserved. It seems that memories of their time as teammates are hazier for Charles than for Alex, who has obviously been carrying a torch for the Clear Networks CEO, a man whose marriage remains in peril, despite his recent, well-received sexual performance.

Eager to convince Whitney that he has changed—that his cheating is "a thing of the past"—Charles takes his wife to a resort hotel that, unbeknownst to him, is under Alex's management. Flirting their way through a game of pool in the hotel lobby, Charles and Whitney finally crawl atop the table in order to fuck, but Alex interrupts them. Visibly disappointed to find Charles in flagrante delicto with a woman, Alex asks him to explain his choice of this particular hotel for his assignations, as if operating under the assumption that Charles had wanted to rub the gay Alex's nose in his heterosexual prowess. But Charles does not, at this point in the film, know that Alex is gay. During their previous meeting, Alex had relied exclusively upon a series of queer codes in his conversation with Charles—upon the erotically charged evocation of an erstwhile athletic "brotherhood," a schoolboy bond that predated their university experiences. Suddenly, in the hotel that he manages, Alex is forced to confront the possibility—indeed, the likelihood—that Charles does not share his sexual orientation identity.

Explaining that he is engaged not in a furtive affair but in a last-ditch effort to mend his marriage, Charles takes Whitney by the hand and introduces her to Alex. At this point, in Nollywood's familiar melodramatic fashion, a young, scantily clad woman shows up out of nowhere, sidling into the pool hall and announcing that Charles is the love of her life—that he once fucked her, then failed to return her calls. An apoplectic Whitney chooses not to break a pool cue on the young woman's body—violence against essentialized "sluts" being her typical response to her husband's infidelities—and instead storms off, inspiring the ever-solicitous Alex to chase after her, but to no avail: the wronged wife holes up in her hotel room, asking that no man be permitted to enter. Later, over drinks in the hotel bar, Alex tells a despondent Charles that Whitney will "come around," but that she needs Alex to "talk some sense into her." At first, it seems as if Alex's status as the hotel's manager makes him exceptional—the only kind of man who might be allowed to enter Whitney's hotel room. However, upon closer consideration, it becomes clear that Alex is viewing Charles through Whitney's eyes, empathizing with the woman whose lust is at odds with her pride. In fact, Alex's feminine identification is nowhere more pronounced than during these scenes, in which he refers to himself as a sounding board and sob sister—the sort of person who understands the inner workings of a woman's mind, and who holds the key to her recuperation. Like Flora and Rina, Alex comprehends "the woman's side of the story"—a factor that clearly contributes to the film's conflation of male homosexuality and gender inversion. What's worse, Alex's determination to mend the marriage makes him the queerest kind of connubial catalyst—a gay go-between whose principal skill is to interpret femininity for the bewildered Charles.

Men in Love mobilizes another gay male stereotype in the scenes that follow, in which Alex attempts to convince Whitney that Charles is "in love" with his wife and "wants to make things work"—despite the fact that he has made no such claims, having instead preferred to wallow in a certain self-pity, one that pivots around the melodramatically bad timing of his ex-lover's appearance in the pool hall. Evoking the stereotyped figure of the mendacious gay man, Alex exaggerates Charles's compunction, inflating it to operatic proportions and even providing a few florid details. "He was almost crying," Alex lies, leaving Whitney to assume that her husband is, as Alex argues, "a new man," one more willing to show emotion (especially remorse). His plan to mend the marriage having succeeded—due in large part to his gay-coded performance skills, his facility with tall tales and emotional manipulation—Alex invites Charles to dinner to celebrate a pair of victories: not only has Whitney agreed to take Charles back, but Charles, in appreciation, has rewarded Alex with a Clear Networks contract to support his forthcoming fashion show.

After signing the contract, Alex and Charles shake hands, sealing the formality of the occasion. Alex, however, has a hard time letting go, gripping Charles's hand long after the requisite seconds have passed, the conventional motions completed. Charles, though he is visibly perplexed, and perhaps even alarmed, refrains from questioning Alex's unusual gesture, and the two men repair to a fancy restaurant where, as Charles declares, "the food is off the hook." "I haven't had such good food in a long time," he confides to Alex, who, ever attuned to "women's feelings," says, "I hope you're not trying to discredit Whitney." Then, indicating that he is capable of moving beyond—or merely complicating—his feminine identification, Alex responds to the question of whether he knows how to cook by saying, "I know better than most women." Emphasizing a point at which he deviates from "most women," Alex nevertheless, and perhaps paradoxically, manages to align himself with a "feminine" pursuit—"home cooking"—that, by a certain stereotyping logic, is not unlike orchestrating fashion shows (Alex's other, allegedly gender-deviant talent). He also demonstrates a certain resistance to the "very Nigerian" notion that, while a man may be married or single, he is necessarily straight—or else he wouldn't be a man at all. When Charles says that he pities the wife of the restaurant's chef—an imagined woman who must, he maintains, respond to her husband's culinary talents with considerable envy—Alex asks, "What makes you think he's married?" "Well, he's a handsome chap," Charles confesses, suggesting that he is not as blind to "male appeal" as he has previously maintained. "I've studied his face and physique."

At this sign that Charles may not, after all, be blindly heteronormative—that he may in fact understand some of the scopic components of male homosexuality, the libidinous pleasures to be found in scrutinizing a man's "face and physique"— Alex decides to enlighten his friend regarding the chef in question. "He's what we call a confirmed bachelor," Alex declares. Then, as if suspecting the insufficiency of this coded reference to the man's homosexuality, he adds, "Even if he wanted to get married in this country, it wouldn't be possible. You see . . . he's gay." Charles, in response, looks shocked—and more than a bit sickened. "Is the idea of someone being gay repulsive to you?" asks Alex. "No, not at all," replies Charles. "It's just that I find it surprising that anyone would want to be gay. I mean, what's the point? What do you stand to gain?" By way of answering these questions, Alex, who has not yet come out to Charles, offers anecdotal evidence of homosexuality's "perks," which include the impossibility of "unwanted pregnancies" among "exclusive" lesbians, as well as the close-knit underground networks that thrive amid an awareness of Nigeria's anti-gay laws. Alex then suggests that if Charles were bisexual—willing to satisfy his extramarital impulses with men only—he "would not be having problems with Whitney," since same-sex erotic

Figure 5.3. Hungry eyes: Alex (Muna Obiekwe) fixes his gaze on Charles (John Dumelo) in Moses Ebere's *Men in Love* (2010).

contact requires considerably more careful planning than does straight spousal cheating, simply because it constitutes a criminal act in Nigeria. The chronically unfaithful Charles perks up at this mention of "cheating without consequences," asking if it would truly "be easier to cheat on one's wife with a male lover." Answering in the affirmative, Alex notes that hermetic secrecy is a requirement of life "on the down-low"—to which Charles can only respond by referring to the Bible, which, he says, "frowns on the *act*" of homosexuality.

By emphasizing the word "act"—by suggesting that same-sex erotic contact can be disarticulated from a gay identity—Charles opens the door for a queer disquisition from Alex, who takes the opportunity to come out as gay. At this point, the film cuts to a seemingly countervailing space—that of the Lagos living room where Whitney sits with her son, Charles Jr., and waits in vain for her husband to return at a reasonable hour. The abrupt juxtaposition of shots suggests a moralizing dimension—specifically, that the quaint domestic setting, flush with the human evidence of a successful, properly procreative marriage, is where Charles should be at this very moment. Instead of enjoying a quiet evening with his wife and son, Charles is out discussing homosexuality with one gay man while eating the "fabulous" food prepared by another; as a consequence of neglecting his spousal and parental duties, he is doubly exposed to the "sin" of homosexuality. However, in a measure of the film's queer sophistication, *Men in Love* offers a nominally normative domestic space that nevertheless evinces a coded queerness, encapsulated in the rainbow Lego collection of Charles Jr. Arranged on a table and the focus of a close-up, the collection clearly supports Alex's argument that the cultural components of queerness—some of the modes and styles of expression—are everywhere in Nigeria, even in a seeming stronghold of heteronormativity. Reinforcing this point, the film will later provide a visual rhyme that links the Legos to a rainbow bracelet proudly worn by Bobby (Promise Amadi), Alex's openly gay, defiantly "mincing" ex-boyfriend, who isn't afraid of his country's criminalization of homosexuality, and who adopts gay-liberationist symbols at every opportunity (pink, for instance, is his preferred shirt color, the triangle his favorite shape).[55] Whatever concessions to homophobic convention follow in the film—and there are certainly more than a few—*Men in Love* manages, by cutting directly from Alex's gay self-identification to a queerly multicolored tableau, to suggest that gay cultural symbols are far more visible, and far more palatable, than Nigerian custom would concede, extending even into the sphere of child's play.

A handful of prominent online commentators have taken the film's rainbow iconography as evidence of its "gay credentials," and Nollywood Love, the Nigerian company that licensed the film for viewing on its dedicated YouTube channel, even offers a rainbow-colored thumbnail as an illustrated product description (thus anticipating the way that rainbow filters would appear to predominate online, and especially on YouTube and Facebook, in the wake of the 2015 U.S. Supreme Court ruling that made same-sex marriage a nationwide right guaranteed by the Constitution).[56] Similarly, the YouTube channel Gay-Themed Movies, which streams a wide range of shorts and features, once offered a brief, rainbow-centered clip of *Men in Love* as part of a playlist that also included such queer films as *Fortune and Men's Eyes* (Harvey Hart, 1971) and *The Laramie Project* (Moisés Kaufman, 2002).[57] Clearly, *Men in Love* has enjoyed an online life that hasn't simply extended Nollywood spectatorship to web-enabled fans the world over, but that has also witnessed the extraction and celebration of its queerest images. In June 2011, Gay-Themed Movies managed to highlight the gay specificity of *Men in Love* while also categorizing it alongside some bona fide queer classics, despite both the snobbish suspicion that a Nollywood product isn't a "real film" and the equally condescending, racist claim that there is no such thing as a black African consciousness of "authentic" gay cultural and sexual practices. In this Western misreading, Africa is generalized as "overly susceptible to pernicious 'fervor'"—whether that of a primitivism that rejects the legitimacy of "expert knowledge" or of a Western-derived Pentecostalism so panicked over the thought of homosexuality that it suppresses all reason.[58]

Viral media texts have powerfully contributed to this Western suspicion of Africans' "gay knowledge"—to the distinctly primitivist notion that a black African will only exaggerate or misinterpret homosexuality as a consequence of barbarism. Consider, for instance, "Eat Da Poo-Poo," a wildly successful series of video remixes whose shared source is a brief clip from a 2010 Current TV documentary entitled *Missionaries of Hate*. In the clip, Ugandan pastor Martin Ssempa, addressing a crowd of reporters and parishioners, confidently describes a variety of "common" gay male sexual practices, including feces eating. In May 2010, YouTube user dudeuter uploaded a clip of Ssempa's absurd, shit-centered declaration, launching weeks of video remixes ranging from the politically dialectical to the cheekily musicalized: Ray William Johnson's much-watched "You be Nasty!!," which intercut the Current TV footage with a Barack Obama ad, suggested that Obama's "rational" support for gay marriage was a function of his "American-ness" and alleged estrangement from his Kenyan heritage, while BartBaKer's equally viral Auto-Tune remix transformed Ssempa's words into a funky musical refrain.[59] At the same time, a Ssempa-quoting Reddit thread reached that website's front page—an indication of its popularity among users—and drew critical attention to the essentialist Western conviction that Ssempa's remarks reflected a mindless "African-ness," one uniquely generative of Western comic pleasure.[60]

Prominent among those who contributed to this ethnocentric conviction was the gay blogger Perez Hilton, who reposted the video that dudeuter had initially uploaded, along with a few enraged remarks about the persistence of "misrepresentation," particularly of gay men, in Africa—remarks that Hilton tempered by acknowledging the video's comedic value.[61] However, as Tavia Nyong'o points out, such condescending Western accounts are themselves flagrant misrepresentations, not just of Africans in general but of Ssempa in particular: positioning the pastor as a relic of the pre-internet age—as a man who has not yet "seen the light" through peer-to-peer contact with "advanced" populations—these accounts fail to observe that Ssempa, in the footage culled from Current TV, "carries around his up-to-date Apple laptop to show graphic pictures of homosexuality"—still and moving images that were themselves downloaded from a range of gay porn sites, including some "homegrown" African ones.[62] In other words, the popular, indeed viral digital paratexts that mock Ssempa—and, by extension, "ignorant" and "internet-illiterate" Africans—are all predicated on a Western failure (or racist refusal) to recognize the pastor's web-enabled position, his facility with digital technologies, and his awareness of the production of gay pornography in the West as well as in Africa. Rather than the spoken offshoot of an essentialized African barbarism, the "cartoonish explicitness with which [Ssempa] claimed to represent gay male sex" may suggest some of the residual effects of an exaggerated gay pornography—a reflection, in other words, of Ssempa's exposure to the kinds of websites that consistently attempt to up the ante on the performance of same-sex eroticism, occasionally by embracing hyperbolic, even coprophagic fetishes that resemble those in Ssempa's descriptions. In fact, the pastor's apparent willingness to accept gay porn as evocative of "actual," "real-life" gay sexual practices points to the now-axiomatic notion that pornography, because so pervasive and so easily accessed online, produces rather than merely "supplements" embodied eroticism, particularly among young gay men.

Far from being utterly unaware of online media, as many of his Western critics have claimed, Martin Ssempa is perhaps too "plugged in"—even to the extent of blurring the lines between online representations and offline experiences. While such a reading runs the risk of encouraging yet another racist stereotype— that of the rabid African unable to distinguish fantasy from reality—it suggests the importance of recognizing the extent to which Africa has been subjected, in the contexts of neoliberalism and deregulation, to the distortions of viral media texts, which in turn lampoon or otherwise critique the victims of their hegemony, especially when those victims are from sub-Saharan Africa, rather than a comparatively privileged northern region whose inhabitants are increasingly essentialized, in the wake of the often misrepresented Arab Spring, as supremely, even "defiantly" media-literate. As Nyong'o suggests, the Western discursive production of "the uncanny specter of the supposedly atavistic African with a Facebook profile" represents a preventative measure, a way of foreclosing direct engagements with the material conditions of African internet access and with the political, psychic, and even physical effects of Western media imperialism—a method, moreover, through which Western queer activists can justify their interventionism, since it constructs the black African as a pre-conscious, media-illiterate cipher in need of rescuing from the clutches of a pernicious Pentecostalism.[63] Despite the conclusiveness with which Western memes position it, Martin Ssempa's symbolic relationship to discourses of male homosexuality remains ambiguous—complex and eminently contestable. Ssempa is not, as Perez Hilton would have it, benighted by virtue of his citizenship in the "internet-free" global South; he is, instead, a demonstrably web-enabled public figure whose limiting, laughable beliefs grow partly out of his engagement with gay-identified digital productions—including and especially the equally limiting, equally laughable porn clips that he screened to a shocked audience in Uganda.

If it is difficult for many Westerners to imagine an African accessing, let alone parsing, a gay porn site, then it is perhaps even more difficult for them to concede the existence both of gay-identified African fans and of gay-themed African films, as if the allegedly backward continent had not yet witnessed the invention of homosexuality. The defiantly forthcoming *Men in Love*—a film that resists the proscriptions of the Nigerian Film and Video Censors Board, which often militates against the suggestion that homosexuality represents an identity category, rather than simply an "evil act"—suggests the pronounced significance of Nollywood in the global online reception of contemporary queer cinema. As suggested by the multiple, often critical modes of gay fandom that serve to annotate it, *Men in Love* marks a sustained effort to address biologically based theories of homosexuality, as well as the notion that gay men can be identified through their patterns of cultural production and consumption. Alex, for instance, is appalled to discover Whitney's ignorance of gay culture—her inability to pick up on "the signs" of his homosexuality, which to him seem clearly comprehensible. Having failed to "accurately" interpret Alex's culinary skills, fashion sense, and symbolic investment in the rainbow design schemes that characterize his resort hotel, Whitney hastens to introduce him to her single girlfriends, in the hope that either Rina or Flora will "fall for him." Informing Charles of her matchmaking aspirations, Whitney is unaware of the fact that Alex has recently come out to her husband, who, in response to her erroneous assumption that Alex is straight, becomes increasingly and uncharacteristically passive, to the point of prompting Whitney to aggressively seduce him. In dramatic contrast to his earlier role as violently penetrative, Charles is now unable to "take control" of his wife's body, as if the mere knowledge of Alex's homosexuality were profoundly enfeebling. Another, less pathologizing interpretation is available, however—one that would position Charles as remarkably sympathetic to the plight of gay men in federally homophobic Nigeria: it is entirely possible that, in response to Whitney's false and heterocentrist assumption, and given his new awareness of Alex's criminalized identity, Charles is unable to enjoy a privilege that he has previously taken for granted—unable, that is, to act upon his own, state-sanctioned, marriage-cemented erotic prerogatives. As a consequence, Whitney must adopt a distinctly non-normative sexual role, one that reverses her typically subservient position and, in the process, runs the risk of "feminizing" her husband: not only does she suck on Charles's nipples, but she spanks him, too, turning the tables on what was previously a male-initiated form of foreplay—one in which *Whitney's* nipples were the ones sucked, *her* ass the one spanked. Suddenly, against the backdrop of diegetic debates about sexual stereotypes, Whitney evokes the specter of gender inversion—much to Charles's visible dismay.

Whitney's ignorance of the "true meanings" of certain codes and practices is not, however, representative of the responses of all Nigerian women to gay cultural expressions—a point that *Men in Love* emphasizes through depictions of diverse female characters. When Alex finally meets Rina and Flora, it is at a dinner that Whitney and Charles are hosting, but for which Alex has provided the "fabulous" food. While the bold, flirtatious Rina, who seems desperate to seduce Alex, is deaf to his attempts to communicate his gayness through innuendo and metaphor, the more subdued, observant, contemplative Flora is not. Only Flora raises a knowing eyebrow at Alex's mention of being "different" from most men, and she will later need to instruct Whitney in the "obviousness" of Alex's homosexuality—an obviousness that, for her and for others, extends well beyond his perceptible sexual attraction to Charles. If Whitney, in contrast to the clear-eyed Flora, remains confused for most of the film, then so, it seems, does Alex himself: he claims that he is estranged from other gay men—that he only has eyes for Charles—shortly before he attends his own birthday party, which a dozen of his closest gay friends have organized. Held in a private home, the party evokes the conditions of the closet, which here include the maintenance of an "underground" network of gay men—a communitarian conception of gay life in Nigeria, one involving a collective if temporary detachment from the public sphere as well as the cultivation of psychic tools for negotiating the boundaries between "inside" and "outside," between "gay pride" and pervasive forms of heterosexism and homophobia. It is to this particular party, however, that Alex will bring a representative of the "outside world": the straight Charles, who, upon arrival, will recoil at the sight of so many gay men sequestered within one physical space—much like the Don Murray character in Otto Preminger's *Advise and Consent* (1962), who stumbles into a gay bar and, shocked and appalled at what he sees, struggles simply to remain standing. Prior to Charles's arrival, the party has consisted of multiple modes of male bonding, and *Men in Love* has lingered on these images of gay fellowship, suggesting an anthropological approach that is not without its own Hollywood precedents, such as Robert Aldrich's *The Killing of Sister George* (1968), which famously offers documentary-style shots of the denizens of a lesbian bar in London. (In both films, the camerawork becomes conspicuously handheld upon the penetration of "gay space.") Turning an ethnographic eye on Alex's birthday party, director Moses Ebere details the styles of cultural expression that the party privileges: the color pink, for instance, predominates, and several men wear ornate jewelry, sport diamond-studded designer sunglasses, and sip fancy cocktails, suggesting a distinctly bourgeois model of gay affiliation. Indeed, Western brand names—especially Burberry—are more visible here than in any other scenes in the film, powerfully contributing to its implicit argument that membership in *any* gay community, even an "underground" one that resists the heterocentrist summonses of Nigerian public life, requires purchase power, as well as the acquisition of what one character calls "the right styles."

Burberry isn't the only Western import at work in *Men in Love*, however; another is queer theory, particularly as adapted from American historical experiences like the Stonewall riots, *Bowers v. Hardwick,* and the formation of ACT-UP. The problems inherent in exporting Western theories to Africa have inspired a wide range of academic analyses, from Oyèrónké Oyěwùmí's *The Invention of Women* (1997), which considers the imperialist function of a Western feminism that willfully ignores the particularities of Yorùbá culture, to Nyong'o's more recent account of the ways that Facebook, Twitter, and other social networking sites are transforming Africa into "a kind of projection screen" on which to map strictly Western theoretical and activist concerns.[64] If, as numerous scholars have argued, Nollywood represents "an archive of worldliness," then *Men in Love,* one of the industry's most controversial and polysemic films, reflects a certain awareness of the potency and transportability of Western queer theory, which inspires some characters—especially Alex and Bobby—while forcing others to cynically question its allegedly emancipatory applicability in a country that continues to criminalize gay identities.[65] Of course, as Alex understands it, Western queer theory can help to combat state-sanctioned denialism by demonstrating not that homosexuality is biologically based but that it is socially constructed, thus throwing into stark relief the performative aspects of *all* gendered categories, *all* sexual orientation identities—even officially "acceptable" ones. As he suggests at one point, amending the gender essentialism of Rina and Flora (who both believe in the inevitability of sexual infidelity among straight men), Charles's chronic cheating is as much the result of his libido as of gendered expectations—of assumptions that, because articulated so often and with such confidence, are indistinguishable from social commands. Charles is, in other words, "performing" his masculinity as well as his heterosexuality by cheating on Whitney, but he might just as easily "perform" femininity and homosexuality, particularly with the queer Alex as his guide.

If *Men in Love* appears, initially, to endorse Western queer theory by showing its positive effects on Alex, it also, eventually, critiques it as dogmatic—oppressively, even violently so. What at first seems a breezy agreement with Judith Butler's theories of gender performativity quickly becomes a way for Alex to justify his self-described "obsession" with Charles. On more than one occasion, Charles affirms his "exclusive" sexual interest in women—only to hear Alex proclaim that the *performance* of homosexuality in fact *produces* homosexuality, actions constituting identities in this social constructionist conception. When an exasperated Charles argues that Alex's theories have little to do with life in Nigeria, *Men in Love* begins to suggest a certain resistance to Western imports, which doubles, in this instance, as a denunciation of homosexuality: in the film, only gay characters peddle Western theories, and their Western commodity products—from T-shirts to sunglasses—are by far the most conspicuous. It is as if gay men are not merely, in the parlance of Nigeria's anti-gay laws, "un-African," but also blindly supportive of Western "fashions"—from the discursive to the material. Perhaps recognizing some of the unsavory connotations of the social constructionist position—its historical impediments to political mobilization, to identitarian activism—Alex suddenly adopts a more "understandable," universalist, biologically based approach, arguing that homosexuality is "inherent" in some humans, rather than an "option" or a "performance." Hoping to dissuade Charles from thinking that gayness represents a voluntary sexual orientation identity—a mere "lifestyle choice"—Alex suddenly announces that he's been in love with him "since school," that this overpowering love "still lives," and that it is as immune to suppression as Charles's desire to cheat on his wife with a wide range of women. "I'm gay," Alex says. "I can't do anything about it. It's who I am." Having appropriated Charles's own self-justifying language—his own eagerness to excuse infidelity as biologically motivated, as "inherent"—Alex proceeds to suggest that both men are "sinners," and that neither can judge the other. Charles agrees, acknowledging that gay men "really exist" in Nigeria and that Alex is helplessly in love with him, but finally and firmly concluding that he cannot return a gay man's affections. For if Alex is "inherently" gay, then Charles is "inherently" straight. "I wish you all the best in your life," Charles says to Alex. "I'm just not going to be a part of it."

Having failed to queerly co-opt the object of his intense affection, the hopelessly enamored Alex must devise a new plan of action. The social constructionist position may not have worked, but neither did the universalist alternative, which served the unintended purpose of affirming Charles's heterosexuality. Alex is thus left to question the various terms on which he has long understood his own identity. Ultimately, he will choose a non-Western—and distinctly Nollywoodian—paradigm for promoting homosexuality, filtering Butler's theories of performativity through local modes of the occult, and marshaling some juju to, as he says, "get the job done." If Charles will not deign to perform homosexuality for Alex's erotic pleasure, then the infectious, transformative juju, which Alex apparently has the power to mobilize, will perform it for him. Before Alex casts a spell on his "dream man," turning Charles into an effeminate bottom at his beck and call, he must reconcile his own worldliness with the alleged limitations of life in Nigeria—must, in other words, rehearse some of the terms of Western gay activism, and attempt to apply them to local sociopolitical conditions. In extended sequences devoted to the subject of identity politics, *Men in Love* offers several lines of dialogue that evince Alex's awareness of some of the central rhetorical strategies of gay liberation—strategies that are transcultural and transhistorical, inasmuch as they rely upon familiar, universalist discourses of self-knowledge and self-acceptance: "I believe that everyone should be proud of who they are, and what they do," says Alex, who claims that such a belief is part and parcel of a "universal" liberationism. Later, however, the complexities of Alex's character begin to emerge, and soon threaten to spill over into the downright contradictory, as he meets with his gay male friends—one of whom, Bobby, is a former lover—and announces that he is "obsessed" with a straight man. To his friends, Alex's passion for the married Charles suggests a painful stereotype—that of the sad and self-defeating gay man, the sort of "silly queen" who sets himself up for failure by targeting the unattainable. Bobby, who wears a rainbow bracelet—a symbol of his own gay pride—as well as a tight white t-shirt and trendy knit scarf, suggests that Alex is delusional: "This guy does not return your feelings. And, most importantly, he's not gay!" Alex, however, clings to the fantasy of a "contagious" homosexuality, believing himself capable of "converting" Charles. "It isn't until you've experienced being gay that you can call yourself gay," he says, adding that if he could only fuck the object of his lust, then Charles would suddenly, as a consequence, "come out." Such a suggestion not only rankles Alex's friends, evoking as it does the offensive figure of the predatory gay man; it also contradicts Alex's earlier conviction that gayness is as much cultural as sexual—that it is present "at birth" and thus "immediately" available as an identity category. Like Bobby, Alex's friend Cain (Ndu Ogochukwu) is dubious—unwilling to accept that Alex is in any way justified in pursuing a married straight man. It seems that Alex is confused to the point of dementia, and his gay friends, recognizing this disturbing development, attempt to rehabilitate him.

Perhaps the most compelling scenes in *Men in Love* are those devoted to gay friendships, and to raging debates about the "sources" and "contours" of homosexuality, which, rather than reflecting a stereotyped African "time lag" in relation to studies of sexual diversity (wherein Africa dramatically "lags behind" the West in comprehending queerness), in fact demonstrate the lasting significance of questions of sexual orientation and gender identity—questions upon which queer theory plainly rests. Whatever else it offers in the way of a melodramatic and religiously sanctioned heterosexism and homophobia, *Men in Love* furnishes the kinds of gay representations on which digital paratexts thrive. These paratexts may take pro-gay or anti-gay form, but such is the range of expressions within Gay Nollywood, as Green-Simms and Azuah have argued: some Nollywood filmmakers "make gay-themed films to acknowledge the reality of homosexuality in Nigeria, some make them to denounce that reality, and others are simply looking to profit from a theme that has proven to sell well."[66] Similarly, some fans produce paratexts that, using *Men in Love* as their source, seek to confirm the accuracy of the film's depiction of gay men, at the same time arguing that homosexuality "really exists" in Nigeria; others are content to accept the film's apparent endorsement of homophobia, attempting to further ratify it through paratexts that deny the emergence of queer activism in West Africa; and still others neither embrace nor denounce homosexuality, and rather openly adopt the film's explicit imagery as a means of generating "hits"—of increasing traffic to their websites. After all, "sex sells," as one Nigerian blogger puts it—a clichéd statement that applies to films as much as to the websites that parse them. That this particular blogger uploads Nollywood's "straight" as well as "gay" sex scenes, and offers them as evidence of the industry's "pornographic turn," suggests less an interest in anti-gay moralizing than an investment in taking erotic stock of contemporary African media. After all, he offers no qualitative distinctions between Nollywood's "straight" and "gay" entries: "sex is sex," whether anal play or procreative activity.[67]

By contrast, as a commercial project subject to the Nigerian Censors Board, *Men in Love* must take a definite stand on the issue of male homosexuality, eventually condemning the "practice" as "sinful"—as an "erotic evil"—even as it excuses Charles's chronic infidelity. As Green-Simms and Azuah make clear, the vehemently anti-gay strains of a renewed Pentecostalism require Nollywood filmmakers to clearly condemn homosexuality, since Pentecostal audiences represent a key, lucrative target market for the industry.[68] As a means of appeasing these audiences, even seemingly pro-queer or otherwise thematically sophisticated films like *Men in Love* must offer an eleventh-hour "righting of wrongs"—a last-minute denunciation of homosexuality as "ungodly." Thus *Men in Love,* which begins with a proud and political gay man, ends with his transformation into a rapist, self-serving sorcerer, and convicted criminal. Nevertheless, for the discerning, queer-conscious spectator, there remains that rainbow-colored rhyming device—the presence throughout this ostensibly anti-gay film of a powerfully affirmative iconography, and of an alternative to "homophobic rhetoric on both state and religious fronts."[69] If Martin Ssempa's infamous speech should not be reduced to his ludicrous claim that gay men "eat da poo-poo," since a wider-ranging engagement with his words would surely reveal a sophisticated parsing of various online artifacts (including global gay pornography), then *Men in Love,* which similarly trades in absurdly anti-gay complaints, must not be limited to its eleventh-hour capitulation to Pentecostalism—and not merely because it contains so many rich representations of gay male cultural and sexual identities in today's Nigeria. Respecting the narrative, thematic, and formal diversity of *Men in Love* offers a way of understanding the discrepant online practices that have parsed the film, and that are hardly reflective (as a familiar Western interpretation would have it) of a stereotyped African "madness"—of an unskilled, preconscious co-optation of digital networked technologies. *Men in Love* is a remarkably complicated, even ambivalent film, and so, of course, is the role of the internet in "officially" anti-gay Nigeria.

After celebrating his birthday, Alex manages to drug Charles, carry him into his bedroom, and fuck him. The film presents anal penetration as so painful that it can awaken even the narcotized: Charles, drugged into an artificial sleep yet sufficiently conscious to respond to what is happening to his body, twists his face in agony as Alex rapes him. He is unable to fight back, of course, due to a combination of narcotics and the near-Herculean, juju-fueled strength of Alex at the moment of penetration. Indeed, Alex's superhuman qualities become even clearer in the scenes that follow, in which he reveals himself to be in close contact with the occult—and to have spiked Charles's drink with more than just a "rape drug." Indeed, Alex is an agent of juju—the ancient West African occult that often manifests as a motivating force in Nollywood films—and he is able to "possess" Charles, in the process transforming him into a gay man. Here, however, juju works slowly, giving Charles a chance to comprehend the full horror of what has happened to him before he is subsumed under a new social and sexual identity. When he finally regains complete consciousness, early the next morning, Charles immediately accuses Alex of having raped him. He suspects, from symptoms that include persistent anal pain, that Alex has "entered" him—an accusation that is even more accurate than Charles realizes. "You drugged me so you could have your evil way with me!" Charles shouts at Alex, who claims, in cruelly euphemistic terms, that "what happened" was a function of his "burning desire." "I just couldn't help myself!" Alex says, having once again adopted Charles's own sanitizing, self-justifying language—Charles's own self-exculpating take on spousal cheating—turning it against Charles in the cruelest of ways. Charles, in response, punches Alex.

The juju soon takes effect, however, and Charles becomes instantly enamored of Alex, eager to let the other man assume control of his life. Indeed, Charles quickly and giddily capitulates to Alex's desire to see him dress "like a gay man," which means that the two are soon wearing matching outfits—much to the dismay of Whitney, who remains perplexed at the sudden presence of Alex in her home. When Alex buys Charles a car—just as Charles had once bought Whitney a car—he demonstrates his capacity to fulfill "the husband function," effectively defining Charles as a wife and goading Whitney into feeling as if "the world has turned upside-down." Charles hasn't exactly replaced Whitney, however—nor has Whitney resigned herself to third billing in what is now a three-adult household. (Charles Jr. remains conveniently offscreen, his role rendered temporarily superfluous.) Indeed, as Green-Simms and Azuah suggest, Alex and Whitney become competitors in attempting to care for Charles, and director Moses Ebere manages to indicate that it is Whitney's "aggressive streak"—her eagerness to beat Alex, to "top him" in showering her husband with affection—that prevents her from seeing what to others appears painfully obvious: that Alex and Charles are lovers.[70] It is only when the two men "go public" with their relationship that Whitney is forced to confront its sexual underpinnings. Attending a fashion show at which a bubbly emcee introduces them as a couple, Alex and Charles proudly hold hands while walking the event's red carpet. A confused Whitney watches from the sidelines; flanked by Flora and Rina, who have long understood that Charles has "gone gay," Whitney clearly requires some clarifications. It is up to the sophisticated Flora to explain that Charles is now "with Alex"—and that he suddenly identifies as gay. Later, an enraged Whitney confronts Charles: "You have defiled our marriage vows in the worst way!" she screams. "Do I not fuck you in the right way?" Failing to receive an illuminating answer from her husband, Whitney visits Pastor Mrs. Mike (Becky Ogbuefi), who shares her prophetic vision of sexual "deviance": "I saw your husband tied in chains," she claims, "and subject to the sinful wishes of another young man, who only seeks to destroy him." Weeping uncontrollably, Whitney vows to marshal the forces of "god and the law." Determined to learn more about the criminalization of homosexuality in her country, Whitney hits the books, studying the language of Nigeria's anti-gay legislation and later bringing her new knowledge to Alex. "Homosexuality caught in the act in this country—in Nigeria—is a crime, and all criminals must go to jail!" she screams at him. "By the time I am through with you, the next male bod that passes your sights—you will puke on it!" Whitney thus demonstrates not merely that she supports her country's anti-gay laws but that she believes in their curative potential. After all, she promises both that Alex will go to jail and that, thus criminalized, he will cease to see other men as being remotely sexually attractive. Nigeria's official anti-gay stance is thus a purgative ("you will puke"), but one that requires the assistance of "competent citizens" like the formerly naïve Whitney, who now knows what Alex "is"—and who calls on two police officers to take him away. Alex now in prison, the film ends with Pastor Mrs. Mike and other Pentecostalists speaking in tongues as they attempt to "cure" Charles of his juju-induced homosexuality—to exorcize the "gay demon" inside of him. Standing in Charles's living room as Whitney and Charles Jr. look on anxiously, the exorcists eventually succeed. Charles is "cured," the family is reunited, and the film fades to black.

To note that *Men in Love* lingers online, in a variety of iterations, is perhaps to state the obvious. Nollywood films, however, are often believed to be uniquely ephemeral—"sloppily" produced and thus exceedingly disposable—and that is why it is important to emphasize their online survival. Whatever becomes of their material editions—whatever happens to the cheap discs that flood the markets of West Africa and the diaspora—individual Nollywood films persist through video-sharing and streaming platforms like Netflix, YouTube, OgaMadamTV, iROKOtv, iBAKAtv, and Dobox, as well as through blogs, Instagram accounts, Twitter feeds, and Facebook pages that parse particular entries, keeping them alive despite (or perhaps because of) the constant deluge of new titles, the constant activity of a famously prolific industry. The online prominence of *Men in Love,* like that of the *Pregnant Hawkers* sex scene I described earlier, is very much a function of Nollywood's growing erotic sophistication—of the industry's openness to the kinds of risqué representations that, whatever Nigeria's moral laws and systems of surveillance, seem ripe for multiple modes of internet reception.

In *Men in Love,* the depiction of anal sex is hardly simplistic. While an unequivocal example of rape, Alex's penetration of Charles carries challenging gendered dimensions—ones that the Nigerian blogosphere has steadily been debating since the film's release, indicating the importance of a media archaeological approach to online articulations of gayness in a Nigeria whose anti-gay laws have become increasingly oppressive. If a media archaeology of Gay Nollywood can prove that *Pregnant Hawkers* lives on—specifically as a gay-identified, sexually explicit film—despite seemingly effective censorship measures, then so too can it prove the importance of *Men in Love* to local efforts to comprehend the vicissitudes of same-sex eroticism and the law. If Alex's assumption of the "aggressive," insertive position in anal sex suggests a dramatic deviation from his feminine identification—a surprising development given his erstwhile status as a largely passive, "fashion-obsessed" and thus "feminized" gay man—then it is also positioned as a requirement of the rape scenario. In order to successfully "steal" Charles's "gay virginity," Alex must not only drug the other man, but provide his own erection as well—must, that is, enter Charles anally, the better to "show him something new." Implicit in this evocation of "newness" is, of course, the notion that a man "becomes" gay only by being anally penetrated—a notion whose genealogy is traceable to ancient Greek thought, as Foucault notes, and whose discursive nodes continue to oppose a "passive" bottoming with an "active" topping.[71] Here, Alex seizes a newly masculine identity by topping, and confers upon Charles a new identity as a gay man—or so he insists.

Numerous Nigerian blogs have debated the gendered aspects of this scene, suggesting its centrality not simply to the narrative of *Men in Love* but also to the emergent genre known as Gay Nollywood. It is tempting, in fact, to refer to Alex's rape of Charles as the genre's primal scene, for while it isn't the first to directly depict male same-sex eroticism—or even to detail the process of anal penetration—it confronts the spectator with an especially traumatizing sight, with an act that is doubly, even triply deviant: not only do two Nigerian men flout their country's longstanding criminalization of homosexuality—a criminalization that was freshly intensified, via a senate-authored injunction, at the time of the film's production—but their sexual contact is also unprotected, and the product of rape. The triple specter of male-male erotic contact, barebacking, and sexual assault lends the scene a singularity—gives it a special status—even within a proliferation of Nollywood representations of gay sexuality.

In an entry entitled "Nollywood Gone Wrong," the Nigerian blog The Zone provides a detailed account of *Men in Love* that, in addition to rejecting the film as a valueless commercial product, also critiques its efforts to present Alex as a stereotype-shattering "man's man"—as, that is, the consistently "aggressive" top to Charles's frequently enfeebled bottom.[72] Using screenshots that he obtained from the film's YouTube trailer as visual evidence, the blog's creator illustrates the persistent conflation of masculinity and sexual aggression in *Men in Love*. Beneath a screenshot showing Alex poised to penetrate Charles, the blogger writes that the two characters are "about to get busy": "Obviously Muna [Obiekwe, who plays Alex] is the man in this relationship, as John [Dumelo, who plays Charles] looks quite helpless." Beneath a screenshot showing a scene from the film's second part, in which a naked Alex approaches a fully conscious, now gay-identified Charles from behind, the blogger writes, "Just as I thought. Muna's the man"—a caption that can be read in two ways, both as a confirmation of the film's conflation of insertive sexuality and masculinity and as a celebration of Alex's role as a "power top." Alex is both "a man"—masculinized via the assumption of the aggressive, insertive sexual position—and "*the* man," by virtue of his capacity to "take charge" of Charles, to "show him who's boss."

Apart from offering a thoughtful, relatively technologically sophisticated engagement with the sexual politics of *Men in Love,* The Zone also demonstrates the persistent importance of YouTube in a regional context where reliable streaming video remains relatively scarce. As the well-illustrated entries devoted to the rape scene attest, YouTube trailers represent convenient sources of screenshots— ways for Nollywood fans to parse the gay-specific representations of individual films, to upload and annotate images, and to construct illustrated guides across a variety of websites, from Facebook pages to WordPress blogs and beyond. A mere trailer—a two-to-three-minute condensation of a much longer film—would seem to suggest a severe limitation, a meager source of audiovisual materials. Viewed from this perspective, and with an awareness of the homophobic censorship practices that abound on YouTube (where, notoriously, representations of male-male eroticism are among the most likely to be age-restricted, even when the eroticism in question is limited to kissing), a YouTube trailer would seem to be an improbable source of "gay content," as would just about any mainstream movie trailer. Nollywood trailers are not, however, Hollywood trailers, and in an indication of the growing salability of Gay Nollywood, they have a tendency to foreground specifically gay content, further enabling spectators (whatever their own identifications) to construct online monuments to gay subjectivities.

If contemporary "clip culture" threatens to reduce complex representations of queerness to the essentialized dimensions of gay sexuality, as the viral life of Martin Ssempa makes all too clear—and as Pink 2.0 proves more generally—then resistance may appear in the least likely of places. In Lisa Nakamura's words, "visual cultures of movement and signification," as opposed to text, are not only attractive to those with diminished attention spans.[73] They are also, in some instances, *necessary* in places where literacy rates remain low, and where a diversity of spoken languages often precludes mutual communication—places like Nigeria, whose eventual emergence as an information society has been predicated on the capacity of the graphical internet to bridge gaps among more than 250 ethnic groups and over 500 languages. "The internet has tremendous potential for challenging colonial regimes of power, particularly those that privilege access to the written word," writes Nakamura.[74] One way of understanding how such challenges may operate is by contrasting Nigerian blog accounts of *Men in Love* with Western (particularly American) ones. Where the latter tend to be witheringly dismissive—to reject Gay Nollywood as "opportunistic," and to condemn the genre as patently absurd and offensive in the face of Nigeria's anti-gay laws—the former often adopt a more measured approach, as The Zone, with its carefully selected and revelatory screenshots, makes so brilliantly clear. A gay-identified Western blog like the popular Towleroad, whose white gay administrator, Andy Towle, angrily tracks Nigeria's human rights offenses, enacts the process by which the West habitually absolves itself of blame for criminalization measures that, in Nigeria and Uganda (among other African countries), are rooted in a penal code imposed by colonial Britain and enforced with the support of powerful American evangelicals—all while didactically circumscribing the "outrageous" viral images from *Men in Love* and *Pregnant Hawkers* in ways that align them with Ssempa's popular "eat da poo-poo" sound bite.[75]

The visual practices that predominate on, say, The Zone—unlike those that, on Towleroad, juxtapose stock images and impassioned anti-Nigeria prose, and that constantly incorporate ads that target (and feature) white gay men—may in fact inspire close readings of Gay Nollywood, promoting rather than preempting sophisticated interpretation. While The Zone uses text to question the gendered implications of the sex scenes in *Men in Love*, several other Nigerian sites trade exclusively in images of anal eroticism, thus raising the question of what happens when the written word is entirely excluded from efforts to parse Gay Nollywood. Image-only productions—those that do not explain that the same-sex contact in *Men in Love* is the product of rape or juju, and that refrain from pointing out that *Pregnant Hawkers* effectively turns its back on its gay characters—hold the potential to transform such films into more gay-positive texts, ones whose visual pleasures needn't be limited by written disclaimers, whether about Nigeria's lasting anti-gay laws or about personal, religiously inflected opposition to homosexuality. If viral images of anal sex stand in for a *Pregnant Hawkers* that exhibits more than a bit of homophobia, and that has been suppressed since the passage of the Same-Sex Marriage Prohibition Act—if, that is, the gay-positive part exceeds and supplants the homophobic whole—then that may be a good, generative thing.

Conclusion

Antiviral

Technics can by itself promote authoritarianism as well as liberty, scarcity as well as abundance, the extension as well as the abolition of toil.

Herbert Marcuse, "Some Social Implications of Modern Technology"

The unobtrusive grayness of so many types of media practice, from system administration to data gathering or the control and verification of all sorts of qualities and attributes, calls for a kind of suspicious attentiveness, the cultivation of a sensibility able to detect minor shifts of nuance, hints of a contrast where flatness would otherwise be the rule.

Matthew Fuller and Andrew Goffey, *Evil Media*

Taste the full spectrum of LGBT experiences," exhorts an ad on LogoTV .com. Encircling the ad, and dominating the website's interface at the time of writing, is an image of a white man "fellating" a peeled banana. If the plenitude that the first ad promises is not necessarily belied by the rather stale, constricting visual joke of the second, still it suggests a queer confidence that Logo TV cannot possibly support—and that isn't even queer in the theoretical sense, considering that the term "full spectrum" presupposes a set number of subject-positions and affective engagements, and certainly not "a literary critical category of an almost inevitable definitional elasticity," or "a site of permanent becoming."[1] Both queer theory and affect theory have complicated facile conceptions of a "full spectrum of experiences," the former by considering sexuality "as something more than sex"—and sex as something more than, and even something profoundly different from, the mechanisms of genital relations—and the latter by addressing, in addition to mundane emotions, the forces that function beyond cognition, producing unaccountable physical responses and demanding, in Bruno Latour's terms, attention to the human body as an interface whose readability increases with experience, and irrespective of the social categories that seek to contain it.[2] The organizing principles that inhere in an acronym like "LGBT," and particularly in its explicit deployment as a bounded "spectrum" whose elements are separable—digital—suggest the very constriction that affect theory endeavors to escape. Similarly, scholars working in the digital humanities are asking how we might rethink the relationship between embodied subjects and new technologies without reverting to some of the more fanciful premises of posthumanism. N. Katherine Hayles, in recognizing that meaning, which has been so central to the humanities, in fact "has no meaning for the cognitive unconscious," asks, "What exists beyond meaning, beyond interpretation, beyond hermeneutics?"[3]

Several films take up Hayles's challenge in depicting queerly computational operations as, ultimately, unknowable, and particularly in relation to human sexuality. The 2014 Alan Turing biopic *The Imitation Game,* for instance, presents modern computing not merely as Turing's brainchild but also, and even more provocatively, as a function of his homosexuality. Whether computing thus reflects and reproduces the experience of a socially transgressive eroticism or of the violent suppression and connotative encoding of such eroticism remains an open question—though *The Imitation Game,* in one of the film's most mawkish fabrications, has Turing naming his code-breaking machine "Christopher," after his childhood crush, and eventually finding a kind of tragic romance in interactivity. Other films are far less sentimental in imagining what digital networked technologies might mean in terms of human eroticism. Terry Gilliam's *The Zero Theorem* (2013) gestures toward the notion of a normalizing algorithm with its depiction of a fictional corporation called Mancom, which generates a cultural interface that is, in several crucial respects, the heterocentric counterpart to Pink 2.0. Early in the film, an advertisement hails Mancom as a system designed to "create order from disorder," largely by directing individuals to the "best" among an overwhelming sea of new options. That none of these options are explicitly identified only makes the ad more chilling; Mancom's mission is to distill cultural models based exclusively upon the stereotyped desires of straight white men. The film is full of advertising images consisting of such clichéd sexual fantasies as the blonde, blue-eyed, big-breasted nurse or the blonde, blue-eyed, big-breasted delivery girl, which suggest the dystopian consequences of algorithmic streamlining—a sort of digital Darwinism. Gilliam's satirical take on the aptly named Mancom—which, we're repeatedly told, works with "entities," not numbers—suggests the many ways that algorithms presently function to limit possibility in the name of consumer comfort. Regrettably, however, the film falls victim to the very homogenizing tendencies that it critiques, offering an early queer cameo—a brief appearance by the gay actor Ben Wishaw, playing a bitchy, swishy doctor who believes that death begins at birth—and then reneging on its implied promise to provide an imaginative alternative to algorithmic standardization. It is one thing to create a cookie-cutter world premised on the networked manipulations of a major corporation; it is quite another to reduce the female lead (played by Mélanie Thierry) to the dichotomous dimensions of Madonna and whore. To be sure, there is often a fine line between satirical critique and downright endorsement; *The Zero Theorem* suggests that such a line may well be indistinct, as least for Terry Gilliam.

For all its maddening ambiguities, however, Gilliam's film is instructive in the way that it imagines some of the physical, psychic, social, and sexual consequences of algorithmic streamlining. Simply put, *The Zero Theorem* suggests that algorithms don't just interpellate us during the moments we spend online; the film also depicts the frightening possibility that we may begin to look like them, think like them, act like them, and almost certainly fuck like them. In short, we will *become* our algorithms, perhaps without even knowing it. And yet, time and again, we are told to embrace algorithms as readily readable, even flattering reflections of our own idiosyncrasies. In those instances in which algorithms can be aligned with "tolerance"—with the inclusion of queer subjects under capitalism—we are told even more: that algorithms, far from limited and homogenizing, in fact "naturally" radiate from and "naturally" respond to the demands of a diverse citizenry. Such is the ongoing conundrum of visibility politics, as Eric O. Clarke so memorably argues in his book *Virtuous Vice:* activist organizations "demand not only that mainstream media present 'positive' queer images, but also that queers themselves conform to the restrictive terms defining such images"—by, for starters, finding their respective places on that "full spectrum" of commercially sanctioned identities and experiences, but also, in today's terms, by understanding algorithms as profoundly *personalized*.[4] Clarke helpfully explains how this prosthetic understanding—this manufactured feeling—acquires political capital: "While predicated on the extraction of value in the form of profit margins and market share, commercial publicity has nevertheless come to function as if it were a form of political representation that democratically recognizes and equitably circulates a constituency's civic value."[5] To put it in more contemporary terms, if a digital networked technology permits male homosexuality to rise algorithmically without ever gesturing toward queer alternatives, it is bound to have "statistics" to fall back upon—the allegedly higher incidence of gay men online, and their "qualitatively different" skills, consumer habits, and social, cultural, sexual, and political needs.

For evidence of some of the real, material effects of such formulations, one need only consider the intensity of the ongoing backlash against Logo's showpiece reality series *RuPaul's Drag Race,* which rests on the impression that the series promotes transphobia. For some of its most conspicuous critics, *RuPaul's Drag Race* reflects an outmoded or at least limited understanding of gender identity and performance, one that privileges the camp sensibilities of emphatically gay-identified men and thus permits the displacement of trans experiences, even as the series incorporates trans contestants (most notably Monica Beverly Hillz). One of the most streamed series on Logo's website, *RuPaul's Drag Race* is perhaps emblematic of the way that, in the digital age, even a seemingly expansive queerness can serve to smuggle in representations of and for gay men—a process reinforced through commercial advertising, both on television and online. (Consider, for instance, the proliferation of ads touting products and services for gay men on Logo's cable and satellite channel, or ones that presuppose insertive, ejaculatory sex and thus HIV risk among queer consumers, marking the sponsor-supported interface of Logo's website as a forum not merely for Big Pharma but also for phallic eroticism.) When RuPaul, taking to Twitter to defend the series that bears his name, referred to the backlash as the result of a "gay movement" gone berserk, he seemed to underscore what was, and what remains, at the heart of critiques: the sublimation of trans realities to emphatically gay-identified fantasies.[6]

The *Drag Race* controversy represents only the tip of the transphobic iceberg, however, and RuPaul is no more responsible for the operations of Pink 2.0 than any other internet user. (In fact, he remains one of the smartest and savviest of queer commentators on contemporary politics and popular culture, despite the occasional, perhaps unintentionally transphobic faux pas.) If, as Jasbir Puar suggests, it is impossible to stand outside of homonationalism—to consider it a mere character trait that one can overcome through education and social action—then Pink 2.0 is equally impossible to evade or preempt on an individual level. It is what the internet is made of—is as essential to its operations as environmental degradation is to the mechanisms of advanced capitalism. However we may feel about the value of gay-identified drag as a queer cultural form, it is necessary to stress that, even if *RuPaul's Drag Race* could possibly satisfy the expectations of all queers, it would still, as a heavily networked media product, enter the matrix of Pink 2.0, with startling results. We shouldn't assume, then, that assimilation is anathema to interactivity. Clarke provides a powerful caution in this regard: "For oppositional queer resources to inform a more general publicness requires moving beyond the lie of liberal pluralism—the lie that a supposedly neutral state apparatus and a capitalized media can fully accommodate competing political visions and ways of life."[7] The German media theorist Wolfgang Ernst might be describing the intersections of queer cinema and a confining cultural interface when he writes that, in the digital age, "two different regimes clash as human performativity is confronted with technological or algorithmical operations."[8] Yet Ernst poses the provocative question of whether it is our analytic framework—our all too human methodology—that imposes various restrictions on computer programs, in the process defining and decrying their technological features as limitations. To extend Ernst's argument, perhaps it is we who, with our own discursive shortcomings, effectively prevent recognition of queerness in digital networked technologies. Such failure needn't be feared or, more to the point, denied the label of queer. In *Epistemology of the Closet*, Eve Kosofsky Sedgwick writes of the sexual-political significance of "particular opacities"—even of "a plethora of *ignorances*," an erotics of unthinking that might facilitate queer subject-positions.[9]

Maybe, then, the truly queer is already here, albeit operating beneath or beyond our perception; maybe computer design—not as humans narrativize it, but on its own, indecipherable technological terms—is queer. The problem with such an approach, however, is that it runs the risk of returning to familiar narratives of posthumanism that have been so roundly (and so rightly) critiqued. Is it possible to invest in the notion of a computational queerness that remains inaccessible to humans when such an approach has long enabled ignorance of embodied realities, and in particular the effects of racism, classism, imperialism, misogyny, and various forms of queerphobia?

When GLAAD, the non-governmental media-monitoring organization based in the United States, discontinued its annual Network Responsibility Index in 2015, it cited the "changed landscape" of contemporary popular culture, particularly with respect to representations of trans characters; what had once reflected a systematic effort to police negative portrayals and inspire positive ones was suddenly, in GLAAD's view, unnecessary.[10] To some, the emergence of such films and television programs as *Tangerine* (Sean Baker, 2015), *About Ray* (Gaby Dellal, 2015), *The Danish Girl* (Tom Hooper, 2015), *Transparent* (2014–), and *I Am Cait* (2015–) suggests a shift in focus for queer representations in audiovisual media—a veritable "trans moment" whose cultural prominence might appear to eclipse considerations of gay men and lesbians. But the precise production methods and textual strategies of the above works (from the casting of cis performers in trans roles in *About Ray*, *The Danish Girl*, and *Transparent* to the persistent reduction of trans identity to certain sartorial practices and patterns of conspicuous consumption), coupled with their foundational relationships to such insidiously queer-conscious corporate superpowers as Apple, Amazon, and NBCUniversal, tell a more complicated story. Furthermore, the *Transparent* that—to this viewer, at least—so often seems a strategic forum on lesbianism recalls Chris Straayer's account of coming-out narratives, which tend, for Straayer, to suggest that "lesbian survival" requires "a constant readiness to identify with heterosexuals."[11] Extending Straayer's analysis into the terrain of contemporary transgender representation, it seems reasonable to suggest that the recent spate of trans-identified coming-out narratives has required, both diegetically and via various modes of extratextual publicity, the production of transgender identity as proximate to—even definitionally analogous to—homosexuality, offering an all too familiar conflation of gender and sexuality that often serves to sustain the discursive power and sheer queer hegemony of gay masculinity. While the coming-out narrative of *Transparent*'s Maura Pfefferman (Jeffrey Tambor) is tied to those of her daughters Ali (Gaby Hoffmann) and Sarah (Amy Landecker), both of whom explore the complexities of same-sex erotic attraction (including by, in Ali's case, studying early-twentieth-century sexology under the influence of a famous lesbian feminist), *The Danish Girl* features a protagonist who "clarifies" her transgender identity by firmly hailing a male character (played by Ben Wishaw) as "a homosexual." Thus even in those rare instances in which gender and sexuality are *not* conflated, lesbianism and gayness emerge as essential to the depiction of trans characters—even to the point of subsuming those characters, as on the second, ludicrously ambitious, altogether pretentious season of *Transparent*, which purports to uncover transcultural and transhistorical forms of Jewishness, gender "deviance," and homosexuality, which, in turn, overdetermine the Pfefferman family's neuroses.

Such strained intersections between gender and sexuality are so abundantly available online that one critic could casually refer to the emergence of *Tangerine* as "the transgender equivalent of what happened for gay men" with the production of the equally exuberant *The Adventures of Priscilla, Queen of the Desert* (Stephan Elliott, 1994)—a film that is hardly reducible to depictions of gay men (its protagonist, played by Terrence Stamp, identifies as a woman) but that, as its original theatrical trailer makes painfully clear, has long been promoted as "the story of three guys."[12] Trans journalist and playwright Leela Ginelle, in her essay "A Case Study in Transmisogyny: Film Reviews of 'Tangerine,'" exposes the endurance of such limited, downright offensive rhetorical strategies, particularly online, where, Ginelle concludes, such posts as her own will remain necessary as long as cissexism continues to condition internet use, whether through cultural determinations or material affordances.[13] For her part, Morgan Collado, a trans woman of color, recounted "the trauma of *Tangerine*" on the website Autostraddle, where she scrutinized the film's authorship and outlined its ultimate function as a white male fantasy of abjection, despite the creative contributions of its trans stars, Mya Taylor and Kitana Kiki Rodriguez.[14] What strikes me as particularly relevant to *Pink 2.0* is the way this white male fantasy is tied to, indeed dependent on, a certain mastery of new technologies, such that *Tangerine* serves as a feature-length advertisement for the iPhone 5S on which it was shot.

In his book *So You've Been Publicly Shamed*, Jon Ronson argues that restrictive online designs, coupled with phobic public responses to anything that appears to exceed them, are "creating a world where the smartest way to survive is to be bland."[15] The concept of Pink 2.0, as I have developed it in this book, is relevant to Ronson's argument insofar as it functions to uphold homonormativity, which rises algorithmically in ways that often seem poisonously bland, as in memes in which male homosexuality is reduced to sartorial expertise ("Fashion Is Gay"), or in advertising images in which a man's mouth surrounding a ripe banana represents the height of queer wit. In *Status Update*, Alice E. Marwick suggests that, on the internet, "what is acceptable to create and disseminate has been increasingly circumscribed by what is safe," and what is "safe" is a certain "normative ideal" associated with the tech community's ubiquitous white male entrepreneur.[16] That the gayness of this figure is frequently strategically deployed should scarcely seem surprising. As David Valentine argues, "mainstream gay and lesbian politics has been shaped by a concern that is at root a (white, middle-class) gay male concern," thus influencing a wide range of cultural and social theories and practices, particularly those related to digital networked technologies that demand a kind of conformity.[17]

The very repetitions that enable a digital text to "go viral" are what militate against the accessibility of queer subject-positions online, particularly when corporations set and monitor the terms of a text's circulation. That is why it is so important to look beyond the viral, beyond the trending, beyond the "buzz-worthy." Perhaps, then, Erkki Huhtamo's model of topos analysis, however useful for media archaeology in general, is not a productive framework for investigating queer inscriptions online. After all, queerness as a counterhegemonic project is *supposed* to resist sameness and repetition—the rhetoric of reproduction that derives from distinctly heterosexist frameworks. In other words, either queerness, as distinct from homonormativity, cannot be distilled on the internet, or we are looking in the wrong places, through the wrong portals, and using the wrong search tools. A hashtag, for example, cannot be queer; a hashtag can only be corporate. For even if deployed in the service of an explicitly anti-corporate project, the hashtag helps Twitter's bottom line—and can, in its own way, contribute to the ongoing valuation and rewarding of white gay men as "majority queers" capable of dramatically boosting a site's data assets. Facebook, for its part, continues to honor white gay men in ways that may be invisible to other queer users but that may also directly affect them, particularly as Facebook works with banks to determine who is "deserving" of loans. Unsurprisingly, the clichéd equation between gay masculinity and conspicuous consumption—an equation that is increasingly manufactured through social media analytics—returns again and again, and potentially to the material detriment of queer users who, however "accommodated" through Facebook's openness to a diversity of self-identifications, may lack, and consistently fail to receive, the benefits associated with white gay men. In acknowledging such disturbing realities, queer theorists of the internet must confront the limitations of language, which include, of course, the limitations of interfaces and algorithms. We must search for new historiographic approaches, and for new forms of evidence. If we attempt to write the history of queer cinema's online reception, then our very methods must be queer. We must attend to sites that themselves queer archival criteria, even if they provide gay-identified images of white cis men—sites like foot-fetish blogs, which, in some cases, archive queer cinema not by conventional design but according to fetishistic idiosyncrasies.

That is where to find queerness online—a queerness of form that precludes widespread adoption, through practices that are either illegal, all but illegible, or simply "too specific." Squeamishness about "niche" or otherwise minoritized erotic practices is such that fetish blogs are reasonably resistant to corporate co-optation (to the extent that *any* cultural formation can be considered resistant to corporate co-optation). Obscure, film-focused fetish websites often shed light upon the queer formal strategies of what might otherwise seem bland, assimilationist texts. Even those sites that evince a comparably "vanilla" eroticism, and that celebrate the two white dudes who fuck in *I Want Your Love,* or the two white dudes who fuck in *I Love You Phillip Morris,* explode homonormative conceptions of queer cinema by classifying the category's entries alongside amateur and commercial pornography, subverting the plainly assimilationist claims of such cultural arbiters as film directors, film distributors, and film critics for the *New York Times.*

I have tried to suggest some of the limitations of both a purely utopian and a strictly dismissive approach to the internet as a platform for contemporary queer cinema, revealing the contradictions and compromises inherent even in seemingly inclusive gestures, as well as the complex and multidirectional effects of ostensibly confining online artifacts. For if the internet's "inherent queerness" is a mirage, then the notion that there are no online alternatives to homonormativity is perhaps equally mythical. Perpetual threats to net neutrality, however, demand vigilance—a sense of how internet service providers might, in an environment of extreme deregulation, "restrict traffic emanating from various websites, or to specific users."[18] Given some of the corporate histories that this book recounts, it isn't difficult to imagine that the discriminatory activities of ISPs might end up "rewarding" white gay men while continuing to prevent, or at least inhibit, access to alternative constructions of queerness. Content creation is, of course, only half the battle, begging the question of what happens when an admirably, expansively queer text "can't" be delivered to audiences—when ISPs, perhaps reflecting the abiding corporate conviction that queers of color are invariably poor while white gay men are invariably wealthy and willing to spend more for enhanced "convenience," limit their allegedly queer-friendly "express lanes" to and for various homonormative formations. Pink 2.0 has an unsettlingly bright future in a climate of continuing deregulation, and we must meet threats to net neutrality with more than just connection speeds in mind. We must make queer theory a central tool in our efforts to problematize digital networked technologies, even as we use those technologies for innumerable professional, emotional, and erotic ends.

Notes

A Note on Scope and Terminology

1. Paul Dourish, "Protocols, Packets, and Proximity," 198.

2. Gustavo Cardoso, Guo Liang, and Tiago Lapa, "Cross-National Comparative Perspectives From the World Internet Project," 217. For a strictly infrastructural approach to defining the internet—to understanding it as, specifically, a "global system of networked computers, servers, and routers"—see Nicole B. Ellison and Danah M. Boyd, "Sociality Through Social Network Sites," 151–172. Definitions that emphasize interpersonal exchanges, offering up the internet as "a social medium that is used to facilitate communication with others through a number of different modalities," can be found in Barrie Gunter, "The Study of Online Relationships and Dating," 173–194.

3. Dourish, 199.

4. Ibid., 199–200.

5. Bad Object-Choices, "Introduction," in *How Do I Look?*, 24.

6. Allied with the internet in this respect (as well as in many others) is the advertising industry. Adrian Martin has considered the resurgence of firm, even inflexible identitarian claims amid a generalized techno-utopianism: "Today, the target audience has returned, but in a new form mixing identity politics, market-speak, and the type of 'data analysis' which universities now go crazy for: demographics." Martin examines the persistent "idea that who we are in social terms is so fixed and exact that it can be mapped onto a precise taste in films and a specific 'worldview'"—an idea that is plainly far removed from the foundations of queer theory. Adrian Martin, "Transcendence," De Filmkrant, January 2016, http://filmkrant.nl/world_wide_angle

7. Manuel Castells, *Communication Power*, 26.

8. Such is the strategy of The Karpel Group, a specialty market-outreach firm that I discuss in the introduction. The Karpel Group managed the "queer" marketing campaigns of all of the films listed here, among many others.

9. See also: Travis Bryant, Jack Merridew, Mark E. Miller, Calvin Bremer, the Rhodes Bros, and many other successful, gay-identified bloggers.

10. Jack Linchuan Qiu, "Network Societies and Internet Studies," 109.

11. Ibid., 112–113.

12. This may change: in April 2016, the Associated Press announced that it would stop calling for the capitalization of "internet." See Dante D'Orazio, "The Associated Press Style Guide Will No Longer Capitalize 'Internet,'" April 2, 2016, http://www.theverge.com/2016/4/2/11352744/ap-style-guide-will-no-longer-capitalize-internet

13. David Silver, "Introduction: Where Is Internet Studies?" 8. For more on closed hypertext environments, see Brian Massumi, *Parables for the Virtual*. For more on the transition to a primarily app-driven from a primarily browser-driven experience of networked activity, see Hye Jin Lee and Mark Andrejevic, "Second-Screen Theory," 40–61.

Introduction

1. Deborah Netburn, "Brendan Eich's Prop. 8 Contribution Gets Twittersphere Buzzing."

2. "Mozilla Developer Hampton Catlin On Brendan Eich Stand Down," BBC News, April 4, 2012. Accessed July 24, 2015. http://www.bbc.com/news/technology-26888579.

3. OkCupid expanded dropdown options for users' gender and sexual orientation identities in November 2014, nine months after Facebook famously shifted to a more "open" interface, adopting fifty-six possible "custom genders" for its users—a shift that many critics saw as a means simply of selling more (and more focused) advertising space. "[L]et's not pretend the decision was free of the desire to increase Facebook's revenues and profitability," wrote Sean Davis. Davis, "Facebook Cares More About Targeting Ads Than Affirming Your Gender Identity."

4. In *Online a Lot of the Time*, Ken Hillis helpfully historicizes this stereotype, considering gay men as "early adopters" of the internet, and focusing on personal webcam sites that "form part of a history of claims to visibility made by gay/queer men understanding themselves as very much part of an emergent and cosmopolitan digital visual culture." Ken Hillis, *Online a Lot of the Time*, 36.

5. The phrase "some queers are better than others" comes from Jasbir K. Puar, Terrorist Assemblages 48.

6. Thomas Waugh, "Films by Gays For Gays," in *The Fruit Machine*, 18.

7. Alice E. Marwick, *Status Update*, 233.

8. See Sarah Schulman, *Israel/Palestine and the Queer International*; Hillary Rodham Clinton, "Remarks in Recognition of International Human Rights Day," December 6, 2011, http://www.state.gov/secretary/20092013clinton/rm/2011/12/178368.htm

9. Petit Fours, "Why Gay People Love the Internet: Four Reasons."

10. In his queer history of computing, Jacob Gaboury considers the life, career, computational legacy, and cultural reverberations of Turing, "the father of computer science." The subject of Morten Tyldum's 2014 film *The Imitation Game*, Turing occupies a prominent place in Gaboury's history "not simply for the visibility of his difference, but [also] for the fundamental role he played in defining the limits of computation." Gaboury goes on to emphasize the need "to look beyond those limits"—which are as much cultural as technological—"in identifying a queer history of computing." Gaboury readily admits that, in mobilizing the term "queer," he is "applying it to a group of men who may better fit its historically pejorative definition . . . than its contemporary transgressive one," but his subsequent work in this area considers queerness as a far more capacious category than Turing's biography might imply. Jacob Gaboury, "A Queer History of Computing."

11. Even the otherwise heterosexualized Sandra Bullock film *The Net* (Irwin Winkler, 1995), one of Hollywood's first depictions of the commercial internet, addresses this connection between new technologies and the politics of male homosexuality. The film's narrative unfolds against the backdrop of AIDS activism; a framing device involves the internalized homophobia of the United States Secretary of Defense (played by Ken Howard), who commits suicide after being misdiagnosed as HIV-positive, while a climactic scene features gay male marchers chanting, "Out of the closets and into the streets!"

12. Fredric Jameson, "Class and Allegory in Contemporary Mass Culture," 851.

13. Puar notes that these "divergent gendered relationships to mobility, space, place, and nation" are "rarely commented on by industry frontrunners." Puar, *Terrorist Assemblages*, 66.

14. This figuration is, of course, identical to the "ideal tourist" of Puar's investigation. Puar, *Terrorist Assemblages*, 63.

15. Ozon offered these remarks during an interview with the now-defunct website AfterElton, whose "replacement" website, The Backlot (tagline: "The Corner of Hollywood and Gay"), has not archived the conversation.

16. Nick Davis, The Desiring-Image, 10.

17. Quoted in ibid., 11.

18. Davis, for his part, suggests that such distributors favor "the kinds of aesthetically modest, thematically safe, frequently flesh-flaunting entertainments that serve as objects of derision in many Y2K-era laments for the more stylized and politicized queer cinema of the 1990s." Ibid, 162.

19. I am reminded of Parker Tyler's account of *Pink Narcissus* in his groundbreaking book *Screening the Sexes*: for Parker, *Pink* represents "mainly only ultrarich faggot fudge, ludicrously embarrassing, but the truth is that the erotic effects and the camera work occasionally, aided by music, become the vehicles of genuine plastic imagination and true poetic mood." Tyler, *Screening the Sexes*, 181.

20. David Pendleton, "Out of the Ghetto," 48.

21. See Brad Epps, "The Fetish of Fluidity" and Jasbir Puar, *Terrorist Assemblages*.

22. As of this writing, for example, Netflix's "Gay & Lesbian" section features 91 "gay" entries and 48 "lesbian" ones, with a mere 13—including *Boys Don't Cry* and *Transamerica*—potentially classifiable along different axes, albeit ones that are not rhetorically available on this particular platform (or, for that matter, on Hulu, Amazon, iTunes, and others).

23. David Pendleton, "Out of the Ghetto," 49.

24. See Amy Taubin's critique of the New Queer Cinema, "Beyond the Sons of Scorsese," 37. See also José Esteban Muñoz, "Dead White," 127–138. In the words of Harry M. Benshoff, the (allegedly) "increasing divergence of queer types on screen is still limited by the structures of white patriarchal capitalism; queer women and people of color are not represented in these texts as regularly as are white gay men" (194). Harry M. Benshoff, "(Broke) Back to the Mainstream," 192–213. Numerous scholars stress the indebtedness of digital media to the constraints of the cultural practices that have preceded them. "If you don't like what you find on the Web," writes T. V. Reed, "don't just blame the online world. Blame the offline world out of which it came" (21). T. V. Reed, *Digitized Lives*.

25. Lauren Berlant and Elizabeth Freeman, "Queer Nationality," 215.

26. Robert McChesney, *Corporate Media and the Threat to Democracy*, 34. Indeed, "new devices may most often just reinforce the same old existing patterns of communication and interaction," in the words of T. V. Reed. Reed, *Digitized Lives*, 28. Similarly, Ken Hillis suggests that some of the more prominent "queer" uses of digital networked technologies have tended to reproduce familiar modes of self-expression: "Men using personal webcams to transmit images of sexual desire and identity claims may seek new forms of sexual equality online that build on preexisting and somewhat naturalized assumptions about gay/queer socialities and sexualities and the goals, desires, and practices organized around them." Hillis, *Online a Lot of the Time*, 35.

27. See Gaboury's 2014 presentation "On Uncomputable Numbers: Toward a Queer History of Computing," which he delivered at the Cranbrook Academy of Art. The presentation can be viewed in its entirety on the institution's YouTube channel: https://www.youtube.com/watch?v=LfsvRemAnCM.

28. Jean-François Lyotard, *The Postmodern Condition*, 4. Lyotard's views on the computationally determined obsolescence of knowledge have had a tremendous impact on digital media theory, as has Gilles Deleuze's notion that machines "express those social forces capable of generating them and using them" ("Postscript on the Societies of Control," 6). N. Katherine Hayles, for example, would seem to be invoking Lyotard when she writes, "Indeterminate

data—data that are not known or otherwise elude the boundaries of the preestablished categories—must either be represented through a null value or not be represented at all." Hayles, *How We Think*, 178. As Matthew Fuller and Andrew Goffey argue in *Evil Media*, "Everything is already understood, predefined; one is always already a consumer; what one wants is only a function, a combinatorial variant of what is already on offer, the corporation deciding in advance the reality within which the consumer will then exercise his or her sovereignty" (99). Tim Unwin, in his essay "The Internet and Development," argues that "the expansion of the Internet serves very specific capitalist interests" and, barring major interventions, "will only replicate and reinforce existing structures of dominance and control" (531). Finally, Gene I. Rochlin, in a book published in the mid-1990s, writes of "the roughness of the human-machine interface and the inherent inability of preprogrammed, automated systems, however clever, to deal effectively with the variety and unpredictability of human beings." Rochlin also stresses how computers subordinate our "flexibility and range of choice"—how we are constrained by "arbitrary but firmly programmed rules": "The more powerful a data management program, the greater the requirement that data be entered in certain specific and structured ways; what does not fit must be reshaped or discarded. The more structured the data entry, the more confining the rules and possibilities for searching. The larger and more established the database and its rules, the more difficult to modify or extend them. Eventually, the machine's rules reign." Gene I. Rochlin, *Trapped in the Net*, 3–4.

29. Elizabeth Grosz, quoted in *The Routledge Queer Studies Reader*, 205.

30. Jaron Lanier, You Are Not a Gadget, 7.

31. Matias Viegener, "'The Only Haircut That Makes Sense Anymore,'" 127.

32. Quoted in David Valentine, *Imagining Transgender*, 45.

33. Mark D. Jordan, "Making the Homophile Manifest," in *Swinging Single*, 181.

34. Writing in the early 1990s, Alexander Doty suggested that the chief obstacle facing reception studies was the very concept of "the audience"—a category already configured (even in the period just prior to the massification of the internet in the United States) as "fragmented, polymorphous, contradictory, and 'nomadic,' whether in the form of individual or group subjects." Alexander Doty, "There's Something Queer Here," 71.

35. Davis, *The Desiring-Image*, 11.

36. Ibid., 26. Ken Hillis, addressing the terms "gay" and "queer," writes of "the truly ironic emergence of a dyadic relationship between them even as the latter term was designed to move beyond homo/hetero binaries while not abandoning the interests of those who desire members of the same sex." Hillis, *Online a Lot of the Time*, 212. Similarly, David M. Halperin cautions against the impulse to "despecify the lesbian, gay, bisexual, transgender, or transgressive content of queerness, thereby abstracting queer and turning it into a generic badge of subversiveness, a more trendy version of 'liberal.'" Halperin, "The Normalization of Queer Theory," 341. Finally, in their introduction to "Queer Bonds," a special issue of the journal *GLQ*, Joshua J. Weiner and Damon Young ask, "[C]an we be so sure—today, when assimilation and homonormativity have become such viable and complexly articulated possibilities—that queer will reliably name a category that has successfully distanced itself from 'normative' gayness and lesbianism?" Joshua J. Weiner and Damon Young, "Introduction: Queer Bonds," 229–230. For her part, Elizabeth Grosz cautions against an uncritical embrace of the capaciousness of "queer," noting the term's capacity to accommodate the kinds of straight-identified subject-positions that, while "kinky" and "perverse" and thus far removed from majoritarian ideals, may nevertheless consolidate patriarchal power or perpetuate misogyny. There are, of course, no easy solutions to these conundrums, and I gesture toward them even as I offer an understanding of "queer" as broadly and powerfully counterhegemonic. See Elizabeth Grosz, "Experimental Desire," 209n1.

37. Ken Hillis echoes David Halperin's allegation that queer theory has often been abstracted from everyday experiences, limiting recognition of embodied realities. Hillis suggests that "within academic contexts 'queer' has been so appropriated by theory" as to retain little use-value for gay men, even as he recognizes that "the term continues to be used in other"—that is, nontheoretical, nondogmatic—"ways both on the street and on the Web." Hillis argues that the term "gay/queer," as he employs it, "does not deny difference between men identifying as gay or as queer, but neither does it hold them apart; instead, it acknowledges and performs an attempt at the necessary ongoing dialogue among the overdetermined realities for which the terms are stand ins" (212). Hillis uses "gay/queer" not simply because it reflects actual online designations in his sample group but also because he finds it "valuable in its richness as a term that bridges generational differences and that acknowledges the various cultural and political realities of men who desire men, whether gay, queer, or both at once": "The '/' can be read not as separating but as introducing a conjoining betweenness, as well as a recognition of the shifts in the ways that [internet] sites and operators are described (and self-describe) as alternately gay, queer, and gay/queer." I don't agree that "gay/queer" amounts to "a requeering of queer"—that it should be seen as "defamiliarizing or making it strange once again" (214). Thus I maintain the necessary separation of "gay" and "queer" when opposing homonormativity to non- or antinormative politics. That is not to say, however, that I intend "queer cinema" to exclude films by, about, and/or "for" gay men. Queer cinema represents a potentially capacious project that, regrettably, often reflects the racialized, gendered, class-specific, and erotic limitations of "gay" as a category of consumer capitalism.

38. Kara Keeling, "Queer OS," 153. Keeling thus echoes Lev Manovich's understanding of "the logic of a computer" as shaping a vast array of cultural practices and materials. Manovich, *The Language of New Media*, 63.

39. T. V. Reed defines the digital native as "an individual who grew from infancy in a technology-rich environment," and the digital immigrant as "a person who began interacting with high-tech devices later in life." Reed, *Digitized Lives*, 220.

40. Teresa de Lauretis, "Queer Texts, Bad Habits, and the Issue of a Future," 243.

41. Keeling, "Queer OS," 153.

42. Puar, *Terrorist Assemblages*, 230n9.

43. Ibid., 22.

44. As far back as the early 1990s, Alexander Doty was already advocating a balanced approach to the concept of "queer"—an approach that would acknowledge precisely these kinds of compromises while also allowing for expansive interpretive and affective engagements: "I don't want to suggest that there is a queer utopia that unproblematically and apolitically unites straights and queers (or even all queers) in some mass culture reception area in the sky. Queer reception doesn't stand outside personal and cultural histories; it is part of the articulation of these histories." Alexander Doty, "There's Something Queer Here," 83.

45. Quoted in Thomas Waugh, *The Romance of Transgression in Canada*, 9.

46. Gay European Tourism Association, "GETA Is Here to Help." Accessed July 24, 2015. http://www.geta-europe.org.

47. The term "prosumer" comes from Alvin Toffler in *The Third Wave*. "Produser" is Axel Bruns's term, which Bruns defines in his 2007 essay "Produsage: Towards a Broader Framework for User-Led Content Creation." For a discussion of the distinctions between the two terms, see Susan Murray, "Amateur Auteurs?" 264.

48. As Puar notes in *Terrorist Assemblages*, Community Marketing, Simmons Marketing Research Bureau, and Overlooked Opinions are among the marketing research firms that have reproduced this dubious consensus. For an exploration of this phenomenon as it unfolded just prior to the massification of the internet, see M. V. Lee Badgett, "Beyond Biased Samples." For

a later account, see Fred Fejes and Ron Lennon, "Defining the Lesbian/Gay Community?" For more on Harris Interactive in relation to "gay polling," see Katherine Sender, *Business, Not Politics*, 152–153. Sender suggests some of the corporate mechanisms by which the gay male consumer became a cultural cliché in the United States, and her meticulous analysis covers internet advertising and various modes of online surveillance.

49. Frank Pasquale, *The Black Box Society*, 25. Quoting an MIT study that concludes that gay men "'can be identified by their Facebook friends,'" Pasquale notes that "plenty of characterizations are indisputably damaging or sensitive in any context"—even the allegedly inclusive United States. Pasquale, *The Black Box Society*, 25–26. The popular construction of Facebook as a gay haven far preferable (because whiter and "classier") than MySpace serves also to efface MySpace's remarkable history of marketing queer cinema. While virtually all commentators remark upon MySpace's lasting utility for musicians, no scholar has acknowledged the site's singularity as a venue for marketing queer-themed short films. In many cases, MySpace has acted as the *only* such venue—as, for instance, for the short film *Purple Haze* (Dan Fry, 2012). That *Purple Haze* later appeared on YouTube, Vimeo, and other video-sharing sites should not diminish the significance of MySpace as the inaugural venue for its promotion.

50. Jack Glascott, "How the Internet Made Us Gay," *The Huffington Post*, February 23, 2015, http://www.huffingtonpost.com/jack-glascott/how-the-internet-made-us-gay_b_6726840 .html

51. Guy Hocquenghem, *Homosexual Desire*, 132.

52. Ibid, 138.

53. Dwight A. McBride, *Why I Hate Abercrombie & Fitch*, 101.

54. Michael Bronski, *Culture Clash*. See also Stuart Elliott, "Absolut Celebrates Its 30 Years of Marketing to Gay Consumers."

55. Erik Piepenburg, "'Magic Mike' Is Big Draw for Gay Men."

56. Noah Tsika, "Magic Matt Bomer," *Huffington Post*, July 18, 2012. Accessed July 24, 2015. http://www.huffingtonpost.com/noah-tsika/magic-matt-bomer_b_1681549.html.

57. Kara Keeling, "Queer OS," 154.

58. Sara Ahmed, *The Cultural Politics of Emotion*, 165, italics in the original.

59. For Lisa Duggan, homonormativity "does not contest dominant heteronormative assumptions and institutions but upholds and sustains them, while promising the possibility of a demobilized gay constituency and a privatized, depoliticized gay culture anchored in domesticity and consumption." Duggan, "The New Homonormativity," 179. For more on the concept of homonationalism, see Puar, *Terrorist Assemblages*.

60. Piepenburg, "'Magic Mike' Is Big Draw for Gay Men."

61. "Shadenmoure," "Magic Mike gay scene," YouTube, January 18, 2014. Accessed July 24, 2015. http://www.youtube.com/watch?v=E3GN5HIIBe0.

62. Originally uploaded in 2005, the video was soon removed on the grounds that it violated copyright; re-uploaded (by YouTube user "lilo kim") in February 2009, the video remains available at the time of writing (summer 2015). Accessed July 24, 2015. http://www.youtube.com /watch?v=GMLBFA7wuh4.

63. Gerard Genette, *Paratexts*, 1.

64. Ibid.

65. Ibid.

66. Diana Fuss, "Inside/Out," 1.

67. Eve Kosofsky Sedgwick, *Epistemology of the Closet*, 3.

68. Ibid.

69. Lisa Parks, "Flexible Microcasting," 133. Tim O'Reilly, "What Is Web 2.0."

70. David Halperin, *How to Be Gay*, 124–125.

71. Sedgwick, Epistemology of the Closet, 16, 32.

72. Lee Edelman, "Unnamed."

73. My use of "spreadable" here is indebted to the anthology *Spreadable Media,* edited by Henry Jenkins, Sam Ford, and Joshua Green.

74. For more on this type of "technological imaginary," see T. V. Reed, *Digitized Lives,* 37–38.

75. According to Alice E. Marwick, "One of the reasons Web 2.0 was so successful is because it both revived and revitalized long-held techno-utopian beliefs," signifying for many "a return to the early web as an exciting space of creativity and innovation." Marwick, *Status Update,* 65.

76. Henry Jenkins, *Textual Poachers;* Mel Stanfill, "'The Fan' as/in Industry Discourse"; Kristina Busse, in Louisa Stein, "Online Roundtable on *Spreadable Media,*" 159. Alexis Lothian usefully defines fan studies as offering "a range of models for relating to popular culture and digital media that centralize affective connections and ways of being that cannot be reduced to the economic, even as they inevitably become forms of exploited labor." Lothian, "A Different Kind of Love Song," 143.

77. Quoted in Pasquale, *The Black Box Society,* 72.

78. See Philip Bump, "What Google's Algorithms Will Tell Voters About the 2016 Candidates," *Washington Post,* February 18, 2015. http://www.washingtonpost.com/blogs/the-fix/wp/2015/02/18/heres-what-you-get-when-you-google-the-2016-presidential-candidates/.

79. Some artists and scholars have used the term "perverse archives" to describe both the sheer obscenity of colonial archiving practices and the ironic postcolonial/subaltern appropriation of those practices. See, for instance, Rosanne Kennedy's "Indigenous Australian Arts of Return." I am using the term somewhat differently here.

80. Wendy Robinson, "Catching the Waves," 64.

81. Tim Dean, "Introduction: Pornography, Technology, Archive," 11.

82. In deploying this understanding of queerness, I invoke earlier claims for queer theory as "a site for inquiry into many kinds of sexual non-conformity" and a means of illuminating "various sexual subcultural practices." Henry Abelove, Michèle Aina Barale, and David M. Halperin, "Introduction," xvii; Donald E. Hall and Annamarie Jagose, "Introduction," *The Routledge Queer Studies Reader,* xvi.

83. My strategies here recall various critiques of *heteronormative* cartographies of the body, as in Foucault's *The History of Sexuality* and Judith Butler's *Gender Trouble.* See also Puar, *Terrorist Assemblages,* 112.

84. Quoted in Tim Dean, "Lacan Meets Queer Theory," 157.

85. Ibid.

86. In investigating foot and crush fetishism, I am in queer solidarity with Helen Hok-Sze Leung, who writes that she is "led by a queer impulse to pervert the boundaries of queer theory—now respectably distant from its scandalous origin—by attending to precisely what appears to be outside its proper domain." Leung goes on to ask, "[H]ow may our understanding of 'what counts as theory'—what constitutes theoretical efforts—be transformed by queering the generic boundaries of a recently institutionalized field of knowledge?" Helen Hok-Sze Leung, "Archiving Queer Feelings in Hong Kong," 400. Similarly, Donald E. Hall and Annamarie Jagose see queer studies as "arguing for the validity and significance of various marginalized sexual identities and practices"; in their words, "queer studies attempts to clear a space for thinking differently about the relations presumed to pertain between sex/gender and sex/sexuality, between sexual identities and erotic behaviors, between practices of pleasure and systems of sexual knowledge." Hall and Jagose, "Introduction," xvi.

87. Dean, "Introduction," 6, 7.

88. Epps, "The Fetish of Fluidity," 413. Consider, as well, the racism and homophobia so central to hacktivist practices, particularly online. Indeed, various discourses of white supremacy,

coupled with clichéd constructions of male homosexuality, remain conspicuous in the rhetoric of hacktivists (see, for instance, the prominent hacktivist group The Gay Nigger Association of America, as well as the prevalence of the word "faggot" in hacktivist identities, policies, and practices).

89. Alexander R. Galloway, "Anti-Determinism," *Culture and Communication*, December 18, 2015, http://cultureandcommunication.org/galloway/anti-determinism

90. For more on the identification of "targets" and "waste," see Joseph Turow, *The Daily You.*

91. Marwick, *Status Update*, 18.

92. Such vids abound within the YouTube-specific parameters of *Dorian Gray* fandom, turning Ben Barnes into a standard music-video heartthrob by sourcing shots in which he appears shirtless or sprucely dressed and setting those shots to romantic pop songs. Henry Jenkins notes that the romantic conservatism of such vids constitutes "a form of fan fiction to draw out aspects of the emotional lives of the characters or otherwise get inside their heads." Henry Jenkins, "Quentin Tarantino's *Star Wars*?" 224.

93. Keeling, "Queer OS," 154.

94. Tim Dean, "Stumped," 433.

95. Huhtamo, "Dismantling the Fairy Engine," 28.

96. Ibid.

97. Leung, "Archiving Queer Feelings in Hong Kong," 400.

98. Tyler, *Screening the Sexes*, x.

99. As David Halperin notes, queer theory was founded "first and foremost by an impulse to transform what could count as knowledge." David M. Halperin, "The Normalization of Queer Theory," 343. Sedgwick, for her part, views queer theory as offering a series of promises: "promises to make invisible desires and possibilities visible; to make the tacit things explicit; to smuggle queer representation in where it must be smuggled and . . . to challenge queer-eradicating impulses frontally where they are to be so challenged." Eve Kosofsky Sedgwick, "Queer and Now," 5.

100. Again, the phrase "some queers are better than others" comes from Puar, *Terrorist Assemblages*, 48.

1. Digitizing Gay Fandom

1. Grindr. Accessed July 24, 2015. http://grindr.com/learn-more.

2. Several scholars have considered the queer significance of the network as a conceptual model. Kate Thomas, in her work on the Victorian postal system, suggests the usefulness of queer theory for "explaining the ways that networks simultaneously bind us and also show us divergent pathways, help us understand ourselves as both linked and dispersed, reveal the contrapuntal, often erotic relationships between fiction and counterfiction." Thomas underscores the importance of recognizing "that a consequence of a universal communication system is quirk and miscellany. As soon as you invoke 'everyone' and incorporate them into a network designed to mix and connect everyone, communication interfaces (the term is not of our Internet era but is actually Victorian) become queer." Kate Thomas, "Post Sex," 70.

3. See Michael O'Loughlin, "Get Your Salvation Via Hookup App?" The Advocate, April 23, 2014. Accessed July 24, 2015. http://www.advocate.com/politics/religion/2014/04/23/get-your-salvation-hookup-app.

4. This post-gay/post-racial position has long been promoted through popular media—particularly cinematic representations of computing. Barry Levinson's 1994 film *Disclosure* is perhaps paradigmatic in this regard, as when Demi Moore's character, an executive at the fic-

tional technology company DigiCom, proclaims, "What we're selling is freedom. We offer through technology what religion and revolution have promised but never delivered: freedom from the physical body; freedom from race and gender, from nationality and personality, from place and time." She concludes that "we can [now] relate to each other as pure consciousness"—a preposterous assertion that is perhaps the essence of post-gay/post-racial rhetoric.

5. See Jasbir Puar, "Homonationalism Gone Viral."

6. See Liam Stack, "Activist Removed After Heckling Obama at L.G.B.T. Event at White House." Note the headline's unquestioning use of the term "heckling" to describe Gutiérrez's intervention.

7. Queerty, "Watch Obama Shut Down Heckler at LGBT Pride Event: 'You're In My House.'" http://www.queerty.com/watch-obama-shut-down-heckler-at-lgbt-pride-event-youre -in-my-house-20150624. It is through the invocation of the gay tourism industry that this case further recalls Puar's observations, particularly the opening chapter of *Terrorist Assemblages*.

8. Zachary Small, "A Game Where You Host Corporate-Sponsored Pride Parades," Hyper-allergic.com, February 23, 2016, http://hyperallergic.com/277844/a-game-where-you-host -corporate-sponsored-pride-parades/

9. A. Aneesh, *Virtual Migration*.

10. Sherry Turkle, *Alone Together*.

11. Eric Herhuth, "Life, Love, and Programming," 65.

12. For more on this aspect of Facebook, see Tavia Nyong'o, "Queer Africa and the Fantasy of Virtual Participation." See also Ulises A. Mejias, "The Limits of Networks as Models for Organizing the Social," and Evgeny Morozov, *The Net Delusion*. What at first was a means of differentiating Facebook from the radicalized "ghetto" of MySpace (the assumption being that people of color couldn't possibly be gay, and that white gay men couldn't possibly be poor) is now a way of maintaining, acting upon, and extensively benefiting from notions of exclusivity even as Facebook accommodates a range of gender identifications. Like so many other online power players, Facebook continues to find ways of "rewarding" white gay men.

13. Jennicet Gutiérrez, "EXCLUSIVE: I Interrupted Obama Because We Need to Be Heard," *Washington Blade*, June 25, 2015. Accessed October 3, 2015. http://www.washingtonblade.com /2015/06/25/exclusive-i-interrupted-obama-because-we-need-to-be-heard/.

14. For more on the concept of "waste," see Joseph Turow, *The Daily You*.

15. Quoted in Chris Straayer, *Deviant Eyes, Deviant Bodies*, 174.

16. David J. Phillips, "Cyberstudies and the Politics of Visibility," 222.

17. Ibid., 223.

18. Ibid.

19. In a presentation entitled "Homonationalism Gone Viral: Discipline, Control, and the Affective Politics of Sensation," Puar notes that homonationalism, despite increasingly popular deployments of the term, "is not an accusation, it's not a problematic subject-positioning, it's not something that you can necessarily stand outside of . . . it is, rather, an assemblage . . . of state practices, of bodily practices, of neoliberal economic forces, and various kinds of global discourses." See https://www.youtube.com/watch?v=6aoDkn3SnWM, accessed October 4, 2015.

20. Scholarship on the internet has, since the early 2000s, sought to demystify the medium by calling attention to its corporatization as well as to dramatic global discrepancies in access and digital literacy. "When the internet first emerged as a tool for the relatively inexpensive mass dissemination of information and images," writes Giselle Fahimian, "some scholars embraced it as a potential harbinger of semiotic democracy, a society in which all persons are able to participate in the generation and circulation of cultural meaning-making. However, it quickly became apparent that the true power of meaning-making actually remained concentrated in the

hands of the relatively few goliaths of the corporate world." Fahimian, "How the IP Guerrillas Won," 132. Joke Hermes has outlined many of the pitfalls associated with a utopian approach to digital networked technologies: "The technical availability of Web 2.0 and cheap media technology does not mean that either technological skills or a sense of ownership and self-assurance in the face of these new possibilities are an everyday reality, let alone real ownership of new possibilities and technologies. A naïve belief in Web 2.0 technology . . . may well be our worst enemy." Hermes, "The Scary Promise of Technology," 197. For her part, Elizabeth Losh draws attention to what she terms "the myth of democratizing media," arguing that "it is important to question the uncritical celebration that has often attended the arrival of what seems to be an era of user-generated content and user-friendly interfaces." Elizabeth Losh, "The Myth of Democratizing Media," 208. Nevertheless, grandiose language persists as a means of describing internet searches, as in Thomas Elsaesser's rather quixotic comments about pursuing certain tags; doing so, for Elsaesser, "started off several other chain reactions, which opened up wholly unexpected avenues, in a wonderful efflorescence of rhizomatic profusion, beckoning in all directions and sending one on a most wonderful journey of discovery, more stupendous than Faust and Mephisto on their Magic Carpet in F. W. Murnau's *Faust,* and more recursive, reflexive, and self-referential than the Marx Brothers' *Duck Soup* or Buñuel's *The Phantom of Liberty.*" Elsaesser, "Tales of Epiphany and Entropy," 162. With this rather florid description, Elsaesser seems not to have heeded Lev Manovich's famous warnings about the "myth of interactivity." Memorably, Manovich claims that "interactive media ask us to identify with someone else's mental structure." Offering a trenchant critique of hyperlinking, he notes that "to click on a highlighted sentence to go to another sentence" is in fact "to follow pre-programmed, objectively existing associations." Lev Manovich, *The Language of New Media,* 61.

21. Matthew Tinkcom, "Perceptions of Place."

22. Shaukat examines the "desi-queer" (a term that he uses "to denote a gay South Asian understanding of homosexuality") "who has been disguised, erased, and heterosexualized for decades, most recently through new-media platforms." Usman Shaukat, "Sufi Homoerotic Authorship and Its Heterosexualization in Pakistan," 105.

23. The term "algorithmic architectures" comes from Patricia Ticineto Clough, Karen Gregory, Benjamin Haber, and R. Joshua Scannell, "The Datalogical Turn." For more on neoliberalism's relation to these issues, see William Davies, "Neoliberalism and the Revenge of the 'Social.'"

24. In this imagined Nigerian homonationalist scenario, and in keeping with Puar's theoretical framework, the cultivation of "properly homo" Nigerians would depend, at least in part, upon the depiction of the Muslim members of Boko Haram as queerly deviant—a depiction that is already available in and beyond Nigeria, as in coverage of the kidnapped Chibok schoolgirls. Puar, *Terrorist Assemblages.*

25. Lauren Berlant and Elizabeth Freeman, "Queer Nationality," 215.

26. Nguyen Tan Hoang, "New Approaches to Pornography," a workshop at the 2015 Society for Cinema and Media Studies Conference in Montreal.

27. Judith (Jack) Halberstam, *The Queer Art of Failure.* Throughout this book, I refer to Halberstam as "Jack," in keeping with one of Halberstam's own practices of self-identification; see http://www.jackhalberstam.com/on-pronouns/. Jacob Gaboury examines some of the connections—affective and otherwise—between Halberstam's arguments and the queer history of computing that he is compiling. See Gaboury, "On Uncomputable Numbers." Other scholars have suggested that failure, while not necessarily queer, is at least generative of new ideas: Gregory Turner-Rahman, building on Alan Singer's essay "Beautiful Errors," claims that "error, in its cognitive role, makes explicit alternative potentialities." In addition, he considers

the "surprising aesthetic potential" of computer glitches. Turner-Rahman, "Abductive Authorship of the New Media Artifact," 154, 156. For his part, Thomas Elsaesser writes of "the structural value of 'failure': not as a negative feature that needs to be eliminated, but as the very point where potential failure can be seen to become productive." Elsaesser, "Tales of Epiphany and Entropy," 155. Perhaps most provocatively, Kara Keeling describes her imagined "Queer OS" as "a malfunction within technologies," but a malfunction "with a capacity to reorder things" and "make what was legible soar into unpredictable relations." Keeling, "Queer OS," 157.

28. Pasquale, *The Black Box Society*, 25.

29. William Uricchio, "The Algorithmic Turn," 21.

30. Eve Kosofsky Sedgwick, *Epistemology of the Closet*, 12, italics in the original.

31. Lee Edelman, "Unnamed." What Edelman does not point out, however, is that Sedgwick, in her book *Tendencies,* acknowledges—even queers—this seemingly contradictory attachment to "a kind of formalism," characterizing it as "a visceral near-identification with the writing I cared for, at the level of sentence structure, metrical pattern, rhyme" (3). Sedgwick thus suggests that, far from signaling a betrayal of a non-algorithmic impulse, reading algorithmically can in fact represent "one way of trying to appropriate . . . the numinous and resistant power of the chosen objects" of scholarly analysis. Sedgwick writes, "For me, this strong formalist investment didn't imply (as formalism is generally taken to imply) an evacuation of interest from the passional, the imagistic, the ethical dimensions of the text, but quite the contrary" (4).

32. Virgina Eubanks, "The Policy Machine." http://www.slate.com/articles/technology /future_tense/2015/04/the_dangers_of_letting_algorithms_enforce_policy.html.

33. Uricchio, "The Algorithmic Turn," 32.

34. Eubanks, "The Policy Machine."

35. In her introduction to the "Queer Theory" issue of *differences* (1991), Teresa De Lauretis notes that the term "gay and lesbian," which initially emerged as a means of designating "distinct kinds of life-styles, sexualities, sexual practices, communities, issues, publications, and discourses," later became "standard currency," crowding out "queer" and making it difficult to "avoid all of these fine distinctions in our discursive protocols, not to adhere to any one of the given terms, not to assume their ideological liabilities, but instead to both transgress and transcend them—or at the very least problematize them" (v). Digital technologies, I argue, only exacerbate this dilemma, "locking in" the term "gay & lesbian." In the words of Elizabeth Grosz, this term has "a pre-designated and readily assumed constituency, and a correlative set of identities. And with it, a series of easy presumptions and ready-made political answers." Grosz, "Experimental Desire," 209, n1.

36. O'Reilly, "What Is Web 2.0," 38.

37. Donna Minkowitz, "Love Hurts," *Village Voice*, April 19, 1994. For more on the activist responses to Minkowitz's article, see David Valentine, *Imagining Transgender*, 224.

38. In 2014, after years of evasions and tone-deaf rebuttals (including on the pages of *The Village Voice*), Minkowitz issued an apology for misgendering Brandon Teena. See David-Elijah Nahmod, "Journalist Apologizes for Misgendering Brandon Teena," *The Bay Area Reporter*, October 23, 2014, http://bayareareporter.org/news/article.php?sec=news&article=70112

39. In 2010, Jordan Rubenstein resisted this logic, starting a Change.org petition entitled "Ask Netflix: Change Transphobic Summary of 'Boys Don't Cry.'" Citing the use of "she" and "her" in Netflix's official description of the film's protagonist, Rubenstein's petition garnered a mere 119 supporters—sufficient to receive a response from Netflix, which revised its description of *Boys Don't Cry* (replacing "she" and "her" with "he" and "him"). See https://www.change .org/p/ask-netflix-change-transphobic-summary-of-boys-don-t-cry. As of this writing, however, Netflix has not altered its algorithmic operations to prevent the film from being classified

as "lesbian." Wherever one accesses it, the site still categorizes *Boys Don't Cry* according to the following genres: "Drama, Gay & Lesbian, Social Issue Dramas, Gay & Lesbian Romance, Gay & Lesbian Dramas, Indie Dramas, Lesbian."

40. See Rusty Barrett, "The Emergence of the Unmarked," 219.

41. See Thomas Vander Wal, "Folksonomy Coinage and Definition." http://www.vanderwal.net/folksonomy.html.

42. Elizabeth Van Couvering, "Search Engines in Practice," 118. "The myth of egalitarian interactivity needs to be scrutinized on a number of levels," writes T. V. Reed. "Most importantly, it is key to recognize that new, alternative cultural forms are always up against deeply entrenched, fabulously well-funded existing cultural production monopolies." Indeed, "the power of an individual not working for a large media corporation to disseminate cultural offerings to the Net's audience pales alongside Viacom's ability to do so." Reed, Digitized Lives, 44.

43. According to Van Couvering, search engine bias "give[s] a particular slant to the web," ensuring that the "results retrieved for a given query [will] represent only a portion of the potentially searchable web and [will] over-represent popular sites, commercial sites and American sites." Van Couvering, "Search Engines in Practice," 119.

44. Ibid., 118.

45. Valentine, *Imagining Transgender*, 254.

46. Ibid, 203.

47. Jenkins, *Textual Poachers*, 190.

48. Abigail De Kosnik, "*Fifty Shades* and the Archive of Women's Culture," 122.

49. Alexis Lothian, "A Different Kind of Love Song," 144. Instructively, Joshua J. Weiner and Damon Young characterize queer studies in terms of an "isometric tension between queer world-making and world-shattering," suggesting that the obviously liberating dimensions of fan labor do not represent our only queer entrée into fan-driven platforms. Joshua J. Weiner and Damon Young, "Queer Bonds," 223–224.

50. For more on these sites, and on the monetization of fan labor, see Karen Hellekson, "Making Use Of."

51. Ibid., 130.

52. Describing what they call "the politics of algorithmic culture," Alexander Galloway and Eugene Thacker distinguish freedom of use from freedom of expression, defining the latter as an obsolete concept—painfully inapplicable to contemporary technocultures in which obstacles to access include multiple and multiplying constraints on programming. Alexander Galloway and Eugene Thacker, "The Metaphysics of Networks," 149, 151.

53. British journalist Mark Simpson coined the term "metrosexual" in 1994, and later, in 2014, coined the term "spornosexual," which combines "sport" and "porn" and ostensibly describes straight men who obsessively maintain a body type befitting an athlete or porn star. See Meredith Engel, "What Is a 'Spornosexual'?" The term "stromo" (or "straight homo") became popular around the theatrical release of *Magic Mike XXL* and is said to describe that film's star, Channing Tatum, as well as Ryan Gosling, Adam Levine, and other celebrities. See Merle Ginsberg, "Introducing the Stromo!"

54. Judith Halberstam, "Automating Gender," 444.

55. I hope to evoke Eve Kosofsky Sedgwick's definition of sexuality as "the array of acts, expectations, narratives, pleasures, identity-formations, and knowledges . . . that tends to cluster most densely around certain genital sensations but is not adequately defined by them." Sedgwick, *Epistemology of the Closet*, 29.

56. For more on content-identification software, see Toby Miller, "Being 'Accountable,'" 95.

57. Lauren Berlant, "Cruel Optimism," 100.

58. Andrew Solomon, "Honey Maid and the Business of Love."

59. Ibid.

60. In Nakamura, *Digitizing Race,* 176.

61. Elsaesser, "Tales of Epiphany and Entropy," 166.

62. Jenkins, *Textual Poachers,* 192.

63. Stuart Hall, "Encoding/Decoding."

64. As the video migrated across various platforms, its title—perhaps inevitably—changed, acquiring new grammatical and typographic contours ("rules of attraction gay," "Gay *rules attraction,*" "Paul Denton GAY SCENES," "The Rules of Attraction is GAY," etc.) but never jettisoning the qualifier "gay." While I am here using the title of the video that I first encountered in the fall of 2002, I recognize the difficulty of identifying an "authentic" or "original" title for an unauthorized extractive work whose dizzying circulation and reclassification is perhaps characteristic of Web 2.0. Searching for "rules of attraction" and "gay" on YouTube yields an assortment of instructive descendants—part of a topos that takes inventory of the gay credentials of a queer feature film.

65. Sean Griffin, *Tinker Belles and Evil Queens,* 69.

66. In *The Language of New Media,* Lev Manovich describes the digital construction of a personal reality as an "efficient representation" of the self, further aligning Web 2.0 with a sense of "efficiency"—and also with an unmistakable (if suspect) epistemological certainty. Might there be a way of theorizing gay men's relationship to digital media as a profoundly productive process designed to efficiently communicate the sexual and cultural identities of gay users, as well as of the queer films that so often serve as subjects and as sources of their shared digital creations? "Pink 2.0" describes this new (if imagined) gay subjectivity, as well as a new approach to queer cinema reception on the internet.

67. In Manovich, *The Language of New Media,* 70.

68. Halperin proposes that it is possible to "speak about gay male subjectivity," to "inquire into its specificity, and maybe even define the particular ways of feeling that constitute it, without worrying about whether our conclusions would make gay subjectivity look normal or abnormal, healthy or diseased." But what about the kind of queer expansiveness that a privileging of gay subjectivity might preclude? Halperin, *How to Be Gay,* 15.

69. Manovich, *The Language of New Media,* 129.

70. Ibid., 63.

71. Ibid., 64.

72. Ibid., 63.

73. Acland, "Introduction," in *Residual Media,* xiii.

74. Hoberman and Rosenbaum, *Midnight Movies,* 43.

75. Ernst, *Digital Memory and the Archive,* 81.

76. Again, I am indebted here to the anthology *Spreadable Media.*

77. Jacob Gaboury, "A Queer History of Computing: Part 2."

78. Gaboury, "A Queer History of Computing: Part 3."

79. Ibid. For a vivid depiction—and a rather startling endorsement—of the gender essentialism of the Turing Test, see Alex Garland's 2015 film *Ex Machina.* Its plot set in motion by a fresh, twenty-first-century deployment of the Turing Test, the film features much discussion of Turing and his methods, and even offers a character who critiques the way that normative notions of gender and sexuality continue to be embedded in "thinking machines." However, even as it gestures toward a queer condemnation of the Turing Test, *Ex Machina* embraces a certain gender essentialism, culminating in the creation of a female-identified form of artificial

intelligence that, "being female" (and programmed to express and, to a certain extent, "experience" heterosexuality), seduces and betrays a series of men, à la the typical femme fatale of film noir.

80. Kate Thomas, "Post Sex," 74; Lauren Berlant, "Cruel Optimism," 94.

81. For more on this "lesbian gaze," see Judith Halberstam, "The Transgender Gaze in *Boys Don't Cry*," 294–298.

82. Quoted in Steven D. Brown and Ian Tucker, "Eff the Ineffable," 232.

83. For a stimulating analysis of Deleuze's conception of "desire" as a counterpoint to Foucault's conception of "pleasure," see Steve D. Brown and Paul Stenner, *Psychology Without Foundations*, 193.

84. Quoted in ibid.

85. José Esteban Muñoz, *Cruising Utopia*, 94.

86. Ibid., 185.

2. Epistemology of the Blogosphere

1. Stephen Holden, "NewFest Is Coming Out of the Margins"; Linda Williams, *Screening Sex*, 265. In Holden's view, Mathews is able to "show comfortable, nonperformance-oriented lovemaking among men who have genuine affection for one another."

2. Mathews is also the creator of *In Their Room,* which he describes as "an ongoing multi-city documentary series about gay men, bedrooms, and intimacy"—as well as a project that evolved "out of a frustration of seeing so few representations in movies of gay life that felt relevant to my life as a gay man." Calling *In Their Room* "very modern, very relevant, and also very uncensored," in 2012 Mathews launched a Kickstarter campaign to raise money for the series' London episode, exhorting gay fans to fund "authentic" representations of gay sexuality and culture. In his four-minute Kickstarter video, Mathews explains that his intention is to record the private spaces and daily practices of "different twentysomething [and] thirtysomething gay guys." As Mathews's voice touts the importance of difference, we see (relative) sameness: white hipsters fondling their commodities, from DVDs to vinyl records. Lest footage of a bearded man applying lipstick and false eyelashes be construed to represent an expansive queerness, a voice intrudes to discredit identity play and to tout gay male exclusivity: "I'd rather see . . . gay guys who want to be sleeping with other gay guys." This stated preference vividly recalls Holden's take on Mathews's *I Want Your Love,* which for Holden offers an "authentic" same-sex eroticism in contrast to the flagrant fakery of gay-for-pay schemes. But where *In Their Room* is a documentary series in which human subjects self-identify as gay men within an articulated rubric of gay representation, *I Want Your Love* is a narrative fiction film whose actors' identity claims are unavailable to the spectator—except, of course, when spectatorship occurs online. The films' actors may portray "out and proud" characters, but they cannot, during the duration of *I Want Your Love,* exceed the diegesis by providing the kinds of pronouncements that are peppered throughout *In Their Room* (whose title alone promises a penetrating exploration of gay subjectivities). It is only through online spectatorship that certain identity-based juxtapositions become available to the experience of continuous spectatorship, as when *I Want Your Love* appeared, in late 2012, within a Vimeo interface bounded by information about the gay men who appear in the movie. The multilayered Vimeo interface thus provides plenty of gay identifications, aiding certain modes of spectatorship and reception.

3. Daniel Robichaud, "*I Want Your Love*: Film Review." According to Linda Williams, pornography is perhaps best described as "a genre intent on the maximum visibility of sexual function with the accompanying intent to arouse." Williams, *Screening Sex,* 266. Describing

Michael Winterbottom's *Nine Songs* (2004), however, she suggests that it is "graphic . . . without being pornographic": "Despite its undoubted display of graphic sex, and despite the fact that its display might arouse, it never focuses on the plumbing details of hard-core involuntary display." It is well choreographed, in other words—like a musical.

4. http://www.nytimes.com/2012/07/27/movies/newfest-gay-themed-films-at-lincoln-center.html?pagewanted=all.

5. Nakamura suggests that such digital coexistence is inevitable, stressing increased literacy and accessibility: "One technological innovation does not replace another . . . but rather occupies different forms and communicative spaces, thus affording 'ordinary' users the opportunity to create digital signatures without needing to own expensive software or advanced graphical skills." Nakamura, *Digitizing Race,* 65.

6. Dean, "Introduction," 11.

7. For his part, Wolfgang Ernst calls the internet "a dynamic archive, the essence of which is permanent updating." Ernst, *Digital Memory and the Archive,* 84.

8. Shujen Wang, "'Dreaming with BRICs?'" 102–103.

9. For more on the American Film Institute's conception of the "success" of *Queer Eye* in contradistinction to the "problem" of piracy, see Steven Cohan, "Queer Eye for the Straight Guise," 178.

10. For more, see Margret Grebowicz, *Why Internet Porn Matters.*

11. Chuck Kleinhans, "The Change From Film to Video Pornography," 161.

12. Linda Williams, *Hard Core,* 121.

13. Quoted in Linda Williams, *Screening Sex,* 325.

14. For more on these and other conventional archives, see Alison Trope, *Stardust Monuments.*

15. Rich Cante and Angelo Restivo, "The Cultural-Aesthetic Specificities of All-male Moving-Image Pornography," 147.

16. Zabet Patterson, "Going On-line," 106.

17. Ibid., 107. Thomas Waugh has helpfully described this process in terms of "the entrenchment of homosocial male eroticism in the marketplace of the commodified sexual revolution." Thomas Waugh, "Homosociality in the Classical American Stag Film," 139.

18. See GayPornBlog.com.

19. This quotation comes from Naked Sword's official, Mathews-approved description of the film. See www.iwantyourlovethemovie.com.

20. www.nakedsword.com.

21. In their book *Evil Media,* Matthew Fuller and Andrew Goffey complain of those "large swaths of the internet consisting of pornographic landfill, the approach of which is largely to grow and occupy space" (63)—a representative description that suggests that, for these authors as for their fellow media studies scholars, such pockets of the internet function like parasites or fungi, spreading unthinkingly and without any input from users. It is precisely this myopic prejudice that needs to be overcome in order for the field of film and media studies to more thoroughly and more convincingly address cultural production on the internet.

22. The Australian Classification Board cited "prolonged scenes of actual explicit sexual activity" as a reason for the ban. See Don Groves, "Australian Ratings Board Stands By 'I Want Your Love' Ban," Deadline.com, March 5, 2013, http://deadline.com/2013/03/australian-ratings-board-stands-by-i-want-your-love-ban-446565/. For the Change.org petition, see Grant Scicluna, "Australian Classification Board: Overturn the 'Refused Exemption' Status of the Film *I Want Your Love,*" http://www.change.org/en-AU/petitions/australian-classification-board-overturn-the-refused-exemption-status-of-the-film-i-want-your-love.

23. Lucas Hilderbrand, *Inherent Vice.*

24. B. Ruby Rich, *New Queer Cinema*, 267; Linda Williams, *Screening Sex*, 322.

25. Peter Lehman, "Revelations about Pornography," 87.

26. http://www.buzzfeed.com/louispeitzman/the-hottest-zac-efron-gifs-from-the-paperboy#.taglL2BXVg.

27. *SNL* in fact generated what is widely believed to be the first YouTube sensation—the first *pirated* video to go viral: the now-legendary "Lazy Sunday." See Jean Burgess and Joshua Green, *YouTube*, 3. Other examples of pirated *SNL* videos quickly going viral on YouTube are, of course, "Dick in a Box" and "Mother Lover"—two music-video parodies that are remarkably gay-receptive, albeit in coded and quirky ways. Perhaps the "lesson" to be derived from this history is that queerness is widely tolerable when subtle and subtextual; a direct representation of gay desire—and of a gay fetishistic practice—may well be contrastingly verboten, as the case of "Foot Rub" suggests.

28. "Why Did NBC Yank Zac Efron's Foot-Fetish SNL Clip?" Oh No They Didn't!, April 15, 2009. Accessed July 24, 2015. http://ohnotheydidnt.livejournal.com/34189568.html?page=6.

29. Matt Baume, "Why Did David Letterman Refuse to Shake Hands With John Cameron Mitchell?" Queerty, May 24, 2014. Accessed July 24, 2015, http://www.queerty.com/why-did-david-letterman-refuse-to-shake-hands-with-john-cameron-mitchell-20140524.

30. This phrase is, in fact, the name of the site: see www.tastyboysoles.tumblr.com.

31. Eddie Scarry, "7 Things You Better Know Before Seeing (Or Not Seeing) 'The Paperboy.'" FishbowlDC, October 2, 2012. Accessed July 24, 2015, http://www.adweek.com/fishbowldc/the-paperboy-screening-7-things/86117.

32. Waugh, "Homosociality in the Classical American Stag Film," 139. Evoking Eve Kosofsky Sedgwick's concept of the "homosocial continuum," Waugh argues that stag films are "tenaciously engaged with the homosocial core of masculinity as constructed within American society," 128.

33. Heather Love, *Feeling Backward*, 15.

34. Williams famously argues that "pornography's closest genre affiliation is the musical in which the lyrical choreography of song and dance numbers resemble the rhythms of bodies in the sex act." Linda Williams, *Screening Sex*, 266. "Clip culture" substantiates her claim by crafting a kind of online equivalence between musicals and pornography—excerpting "big numbers" in the case of the former, and cum shots in the case of the latter.

35. Roland Barthes, "The Third Meaning," 63. See also Franklin Melendez's account of the "sublimity" of pornography in "Video Pornography, Visual Pleasure, and the Return of the Sublime."

36. See Patricia White, *Uninvited*, 53–58.

37. Hilderbrand, *Inherent Vice*.

38. http://www.youtube.com/watch?v=uMPaZif99wU.

39. See Linda Williams, *Hard Core*, 38. Nakamura, for her part, describes several connections between AIM buddy icons and early cinema, mentioning Muybridge: "[A] knowledge and grounding of early cinema might be helpful in understanding the culture of animated GIFs (a common feature of amateur digital signatures and homemade AIM buddies)." Nakamura, *Digitizing Race*, 31–32.

40. Linda Williams, *Hard Core*, 39.

41. Ibid., 3.

42. Straayer, *Deviant Eyes, Deviant Bodies*, 189.

43. Sandra Lee Bartky, *Femininity and Domination*, 59.

44. Straayer, *Deviant Eyes, Deviant Bodies*, 193.

45. Nakamura, *Digitizing Race*, 65.

46. There is yet another connection between "The Zesty Guy" and gayness: the conservative protest group One Million Moms has highlighted his on-screen performance, aligning it with the kind of "gay display" that they are (in)famously committed to condemning; arguing that the Kraft ad is just as objectionable as any direct and approving representation of gay men, One Million Moms makes clear that it is readably oriented to more than just "the ladies." See "Shame on Kraft," http://onemillionmoms.com/issues/shame-on-kraft-for-not-fully-covering -their-models/.

47. https://www.facebook.com/StrangerByTheLake.

48. Halperin, *How to Be Gay*, 75.

49. http://en.wikipedia.org/wiki/Sal_Mineo.

50. Linda Williams, *Screening Sex*.

51. "Lars von Trier Brings Dogma Approach to Gay Porn," The Advocate, September 29, 2004. Accessed July 24, 2015. http://www.advocate.com/arts-entertainment/entertainment -news/2004/09/29/lars-von-trier-brings-dogma-approach-gay-porn-13849. See also Madonna Nation, "Lars von Trier Reinvents Gay Porn," September 29, 2004. Accessed July 24, 2015. http://z3.invisionfree.com/Madonna_Dot_Refugees/ar/t8369.htm.

52. https://twitter.com/LarsvonNympho, May 30, 2014.

53. Boyd Van Hoeij, "The 'Nymphomaniac' Cheat Sheet: Everything You Need to Know About Lars von Trier's Epic Study of Sexual Obsession." Indiewire, December 24, 2013. Accessed July 24, 2015. http://www.indiewire.com/article/the-nymphomaniac-cheat-sheet -everything-you-need-to-know-about-lars-von-triers-epic-study-of-sexual-obsession.

54. In a discussion of the film, the erotic blog Adult Mag acknowledges this connection between *Corbin Fisher/Falcon Studios* and Trier's *Nymphomaniac,* suggesting that it is simply par for the course—an inevitability—in the digital age. See Gabe Gonzalez, "Nymphomaniac: It Blew." Adult Mag, April 9, 2014. Accessed July 24, 2015. http://adult-mag.com/nymphomaniac -panel-lars-von-trier/.

55. Straayer, *Deviant Eyes, Deviant Bodies*, 230.

56. White, *Uninvited*, xv.

57. In *Interior. Leather Bar.,* Mathews seems to follow what Linda Williams says of Nagisa Oshima—that "not to speak sex in the realistic way of which cinema alone is capable is to leave out an enormous chunk of human life." However, Williams's medium-specific claim seems to endorse the documentary necessity of on-screen sex at the same time that it implicitly denies the evidentiary function of internet pornography—a point that she explores in greater detail in her conclusion to *Screening Sex,* in which she confesses that she would prefer to occupy a position "in a public place before [a] big screen." Williams, *Screening Sex,* 322.

58. White, *Uninvited*, xv.

59. See John Fiske, *Television Culture*.

60. Weiss, "Reacting to Miley."

3. Franco, Ginsberg, Kerouac & Co.

1. In Fred Topel, "Exclusive Interview: Rob Epstein and Jeffrey Friedman on Lovelace." Crave Online, August 6, 2013. Accessed July 24, 2015. http://www.craveonline.com/entertainment /film/interviews/547993-exclusive-interview-rob-epstein-jeffrey-friedman-on-lovelace/2.

2. Other poorly reviewed examples include Noah Buschel's 2007 biopic *Neal Cassady,* in which Glenn Fitzgerald plays Kerouac as a smug seducer and altogether selfish success, as well as Gary Walkow's 2000 drama *Beat,* with Ron Livingston as an especially gentle, manipulable Ginsberg.

3. Rich, *New Queer Cinema*, 249.

4. Hall, "Encoding/Decoding," 51–61.

5. "Acting with James Franco," Episode 1: "Sense Memory." Funny Or Die, March 12, 2008. Accessed July 24, 2015. http://www.funnyordie.com/videos/f12ee4dfcf/acting-with-james-franco-episode-1-sense-memory-from-james-franco-judd-apatow-dave-franco-and-cohenobrien.

6. Franco, of course, has to compete with perhaps the greatest of all interpreters of Ginsberg: the redoubtable David Cross, who in another queer film of the twenty-first century, Todd Haynes's *I'm Not There* (2007), whizzes by Bob Dylan's car on a motorcycle from which he offers bits of hard-won poetic wisdom (much to the infectious delight of Dylan, played here by a beautifully, boyishly reverent Cate Blanchett).

7. Dan Avery, "Get Full-Frontal Gay James Franco Assault At The IFC Center's FrancoFest," NewNowNext, March 6, 2014. Accessed July 24, 2015. http://www.newnownext.com/get-full-frontal-james-franco-assault-at-the-ifc-centers-francofest/03/2014/. Dellie Mack, "16 Reasons Why James Franco Might Be Gay!" Oh My GAHH, January 6, 2013. Accessed July 24, 2015. http://www.ohmygahh.com/2013/01/06/16-reasons-why-james-franco-might-be-gay/.

8. http://www.youtube.com/watch?v=JUICq86zJYI.

9. Ginsberg's many filmic avatars cannot seem to catch a single sexual break: in 2013's *Kill Your Darlings*, Daniel Radcliffe's Ginsberg is kissing the kid of his dreams, Dane DeHaan's Lucien Carr, when Jack Huston's Jack Kerouac interrupts, prompting Carr to run off and leave Ginsberg alone.

10. Ted Casablanca and Taryn Ryder, "Hotties Franco and Hamm Fired Up Over Prop 8!" E! Online, January 22, 2010. Accessed July 24, 2015. http://www.eonline.com/news/163531/hotties-franco-and-hamm-fired-up-over-prop-8; http://homobrute.tumblr.com.

11. In Stephen Battaglio, *David Susskind*, 46.

12. A. O. Scott, "Leaping Off the Page, a Beatnik's Poetic Rant."

13. Derek Paget, *No Other Way to Tell It*, 1.

14. J. Hoberman, "Nothing Is Holy (Holy! Holy!) in Howl," *Village Voice*, September 22, 2010, http://www.villagevoice.com/film/nothing-is-holy-holy-holy-in-howl-6394703.

15. Stanley Cavell, *The World Viewed*, 173.

16. Siobhan Somerville, *Queering the Color Line*, 165.

17. Kobena Mercer, "Skin Head Sex Thing," in *How Do I Look?*, 178.

18. Rich, "New Queer Cinema," 248. The connections between *Milk* and *Howl* are extensive. Each film introduces its biographical subject via a reminiscing series of self-descriptions captured on tape. Furthermore, *Milk* is *Howl*'s obvious forerunner, one of its obvious aesthetic inspirations as well as a likely commercial catalyst.

19. Hilderbrand, *Inherent Vice*, 104.

20. D. N. Rodowick, *The Virtual Life of Film*, 26.

21. Juan Antonio Suárez, *Pop Modernism*.

22. Scott, "Leaping Off the Page, a Beatnik's Poetic Rant."

23. See Richard Dyer, *The Matter of Images*.

4. Liberating Gayness

1. https://www.youtube.com/watch?v=LyHCznfiVdQ.

2. See Allegra Tepper, "'Blue is the Warmest Color' Can't Play Idaho Theater Due to 'Obscenity.'"

3. See Seth Abramovich, "NBA Owner Larry Miller Not Jazzed About 'Brokeback.'"

4. For more on these policies, see Burgess and Green, *YouTube.*

5. See Timothy Harper, "NBCUniversal's Rick Cotton Works to Combat Internet Piracy and Protect Content." *Super Lawyers*, September 2012. Accessed July 24, 2015. http://business .superlawyers.com/new-york-metro/article/The-Internet-Frontier/f4c84aa2-efb4-4727-aeoa -2b5bfe3d7254.html.

6. Ibid.

7. Hilderbrand, *Inherent Vice.*

8. See Marco Cerritos, "Was 'I Love You Phillip Morris' Too Gay for Hollywood?" First-Showing.net, December 10, 2010. Accessed July 24, 2015. http://www.firstshowing.net/2010 /editorial-was-i-love-you-phillip-morris-too-gay-for-hollywood/.

9. Susan Sontag, "Notes on 'Camp.' "

10. Matthew Tinckom, *Working Like a Homosexual*; Steve Cohan, *Incongruous Entertainment.*

11. Cohan, *Incongruous Entertainment*, 15.

12. Michael DeAngelis, *Gay Fandom and Crossover Stardom.* DeAngelis writes, "While some gay men's fantasies of the 'if only' limit themselves to constructions of scenarios under which 'unauthorized' sexual desire finds a safe place, other accounts are much more explicit in their descriptions and visualizations of sexual acts," 232.

13. Ibid., 121.

14. Inaugurated by the user tigershere, June 13, 2010. Accessed July 24, 2015. http:// survivorsucks.yuku.com/topic/71193/Jim-Carrey-I-can-haz-buttsecks#.Un6FQ825Yrw.

15. Ryan Tedder, "Jim Carrey is Giving this Muscle Daddy a Pounding," Queerty, June 8, 2010. Accessed July 24, 2015. http://www.queerty.com/jim-carrey-is-giving-this-muscle-daddy -a-pounding-20100608.

16. http://tinypic.com/view.php?pic=1263301&s=6.

17. Michael Musto, "Jim Carrey Movie 'Too Gay' for Release?"

18. See Michael Fleming, "Carrey Lights Up 'Phillip Morris.' " *Variety,* June 3, 2007. Accessed July 24, 2015. http://variety.com/2007/film/markets-festivals/carrey-lights-up-phillip -morris-1117966194/.

19. See ibid.

20. Andy Towle, "This Is What a Jim Carrey-Ewan McGregor Kiss Looks Like." Towleroad, December 5, 2009. Accessed July 24, 2015. http://www.towleroad.com/2008/12/this-is-what-a/.

21. In some cases, the fan-driven digital manipulation of queer media ends up generating products that appear to be more popular than their sources; consider, for instance, the astonishingly high number of YouTube views of fan videos featuring Luke and Noah, the gay couple portrayed by actors Van Hansis and Jake Silbermann on the CBS daytime drama *As the World Turns*, which seemed (to say the least) in excess of the soap's own viewership—a disappointingly low viewership that led to the program's cancellation in 2009. See, for instance, "Just So You Know," a so-called "NUKE" (or "Noah and Luke") fan video uploaded by kittylynch in 2008. Accessed July 24, 2015. http://www.youtube.com/watch?v=GNgpTJFaiws.

22. Rodowick, *The Virtual Life of Film*, 97.

23. For an account of this history, see Mike Fleming, Jr., "Jim Carrey Film 'I Love You Phillip Morris' Finds Buyer and Gets December 3 Release," *Deadline,* August 26, 2010. Accessed July 24, 2015. http://deadline.com/2010/08/jim-carrey-film-i-love-you-phillip-morris -finds-buyer-and-gets-december-3-release-63088/.

24. See ibid.

25. See Toby McDonald, "McGregor Gay Film Too Risqué for Cinema," *Sunday Times* (London), March 15, 2009. Accessed July 24, 2015. http://www.thesundaytimes.co.uk/sto/news/uk _news/article156075.ece.

26. Ibid.

27. http://www.impawards.com/2010/i_love_you_phillip_morris.html.

28. http://www.movieposteraddict.com/2009/07/08/i-love-you-phillip-morris/.

29. These include *Locked Up* (Jörg Andreas, 2004) and *A Jihad for Love* (Parvez Sharma, 2007).

30. Oh No They Didn't! "'I Love You Phillip Morris' Gets a Release Date, FINALLY," August 26, 2010. Accessed July 24, 2015. http://ohnotheydidnt.livejournal.com/50370183.html?page=2.

31. These include "King of Cons," a 2005 episode of the Discovery Channel series *On the Run*. As a reenactment-dependent television documentary, "King of Cons" purports to be more invested in what its voice-over narrator refers to as "the facts" than in any nuanced interpretation of psychology or sexuality. But facts, of course, include sexual practices—complex erotic acts—and it fell to Russell himself, in a high-profile *Esquire* interview, to explain the centrality of gay specificity to his story—that is, until *Phillip Morris* came around. See Alex Hannaford, "The Great Escapee," 89–93.

32. http://www.youtube.com/watch?v=WhnyKcEcz6w.

33. https://www.youtube.com/playlist?list=PLy2aU-4Si15wrfHGIuZXVPSyfcJn6k9Pw.

34. http://www.youtube.com/watch?v=JagzGOr5AhI.

35. For more on YouTube-friendly software, see Burgess and Green, *YouTube*.

36. See the comment section for "Cum in my ass! Jim Carrey," which has received over three million views as of this writing: http://www.youtube.com/watch?v=JagzGOr5AhI.

37. Halberstam, *The Queer Art of Failure*, 94.

38. Elsaesser, "Tales of Epiphany and Entropy," 165.

5. "Nollywood Goes Homo"

1. For more on these sites, see Moradewun Adejunmobi, "Evolving Nollywood Templates for Minor Transnational Film." *Black Camera* 5, no. 2 (Spring 2014): 74–94.

2. Farmer, *Spectacular Passions*, 16.

3. G.P., "No Country for Gay Men," *Economist*, January 14, 2014. Accessed October 18, 2015. http://www.economist.com/blogs/baobab/2014/01/nigeria. See also Michael Schultz, "Kleintje Pils to Play YMCA?" Accessed October 18, 2015. http://mikeschultz.org/2014/01/23/kleintje-pils-to-play-ymca/. Lindsey Green-Simms and Unoma Azuah point out that, in Nigeria, "public figures and the mainstream press won't seem to acknowledge that there is a desire to bring discussions of same-sex romance into the public sphere"—that Nigerians are capable of articulating homosexuality beyond the rhetoric federal anti-gay laws (48). Lindsey Green-Simms and Unoma Azuah, "The Video Closet," 48.

4. This ban is part of the so-called Jail the Gays bill—officially (if misleadingly) known as the Same-Sex Marriage Prohibition Act. For more, see Rick Gladstone, "Nigerian President Signs Ban on Same-Sex Relationships." See also Alexis Okeowo, "A Rising Tide of Anti-Gay Sentiment in Africa," NewYorker.com, February 18, 2014, http://www.newyorker.com/news/news-desk/a-rising-tide-of-anti-gay-sentiment-in-africa. When the actress Goldie Hawn posted a selfie on Twitter that showed her happily shaking hands with President Goodluck Jonathan, she caused a minor controversy. Claiming she didn't know about Jonathan's anti-gay views when she met him, Hawn later tweeted an apology—and a denunciation of Jonathan's presidency. See John M. Becker, "Goldie Hawn Apologizes After Photo With Nigerian Pres," Bilerico Project, January 23, 2014. Accessed July 24, 2015. http://www.bilerico.com/2014/01/goldie_hawn_apologizes_after_photo_with_nigerian_p.php.

5. For more on Globacom, see the corporation's website: http://www.gloworld.com.

6. Noah Tsika, "A Lagosian Lady Gaga. See also Jane Bryce, "Signs of Femininity, Symptoms of Malaise."

7. http://irokotv.com/video/5352/desperate-hawkers.

8. Nyong'o, "Queer Africa and the Fantasy of Virtual Participation," 50.

9. For more on this history, see Norimitsu Onishi, "U.S. Support of Gay Rights in Africa May Have Done More Harm Than Good," nytimes.com, December 20, 2015, http://www .nytimes.com/2015/12/21/world/africa/us-support-of-gay-rights-in-africa-may-have-done -more-harm-than-good.html?hp&action=click&pgtype=Homepage&clickSource=story -heading&module=first-column-region&region=top-news&WT.nav=top-news

10. "Homosexuality in Nigeria: Go Online if You're Glad to Be Gay," *Economist*, February 11, 2010. Accessed October 18, 2015. http://www.economist.com/node/15503420. For more, see Morozov, *The Net Delusion*, 201.

11. Nakamura, *Digitizing Race*, 86.

12. Ibid.

13. Nyong'o, "Queer Africa and the Fantasy of Virtual Participation," 50. Nakamura describes this phenomenon in terms of a "violated temporality," which she ties to the disorienting recognition that racism persists in an allegedly (and increasingly "officially") "postracial" West. Nakamura, *Digitizing Race*, 195.

14. Nakamura, *Digitizing Race*, 86. Nakamura argues that "the rush to bridge the digital divide participates in a dangerously paternalistic discourse of uplift and cultural imperialism that is compounded by the [internet's] intense attractiveness on both the cultural and economic levels." The internet has been "accorded the cachet formerly given to literacy"; "its early associations with research, education, and the written word, coupled with its increasing convergence with moving-image forms, give it a positive cultural valence that is hard to match"—a valence that, I would argue, extends to contemporary southern Nigeria. Nakamura, *Digitizing Race*, 94.

15. Nyong'o, "Queer Africa and the Fantasy of Virtual Participation," 44.

16. Noah Tsika, "'Compartmentalize Your Life,'" 230–244.

17. Carol Armstrong quoted in Nakamura, *Digitizing Race*, 7.

18. See Christopher Babatunde Ogunyemi and Joseph Ayo Babalola, "Digital Literacy and Space Technology in Nigeria," *Journal of Space Technology*, June 15, 2012. Accessed July 24, 2015. http://www.ist.edu.pk/jst/previous-issues/june-2012.

19. See, for instance, Joseph Ejiro, "Desmond Elliot, Mike Ezuruonye Turned Down Offer to Star in Upcoming Gay Movie 'Law 58,'" The Joseph Ejiro Blog. http://josephejiro.wordpress .com/2013/03/30/desmond-elliot-mike-ezuruonye-turned-down-offer-to-star-in-upcoming -gay-movie-law-58-producer-dickson-iroegbu/. See also "Desmond Elliot, Mike Ezuruonye Reject Gay Roles," *Nation* (Nigeria), February 4, 2012.

20. Ameyaw Debrah, "More Shocker From Nollywood: Watch Nigeria's Most Daring Gay Movie, 'Pregnant Hawkers,'" AmeyawDebrah.com, April 4, 2013. Accessed July 24, 2015. http:// www.ameyawdebrah.com/more-shocker-from-nollywood-watch-nigerias-most-daring-gay -movie-pregnant-hawkers/.

21. See Gladstone, "Nigerian President Signs Ban on Same-Sex Relationships."

22. http://www.234pulse.com/2013/09/nollywood-actor-uti-nwanchukwu-continues-his-i -am-not-gay-tour-see-the-fine-a-chick-he-posed-with/.

23. http://www.gistmania.com/talk/topic,134617.0.html.

24. Cumberland, "Private Uses of Cyberspace," 263.

25. Fuss, "Inside/Out," 2.

26. Indeed, in his essay "Virality, Infomatics, and Critique," Seb Franklin argues that any activist, potentially empowering video that goes viral, "while fulfilling a normatively good

objective of spreading awareness of political or economic injustice, contributes to the data mine and thus the bottom line of a company such as Google or Facebook." Franklin, "Virality, Informatics, and Critique," 161. In *Digitizing Race,* Nakamura writes, "The issue of a basically unthreatened material base for participation, unchanged technological protocols, unchallenged economic systems—in short, the pesky problem of protest within a system that one is nonetheless employing to frame the protest—continues to haunt the study of minority new media cultures," 205.

27. Nakamura, *Digitizing Race,* 87.

28. Ziauddin Sardar, *Postmodernism and the Other.*

29. Sam Olukoya, "Facebook Growing Fast in Nigeria," Deutsche Welle, April 2, 2014. Accessed July 24, 2015. http://www.dw.com/en/facebook-growing-fast-in-nigeria/a-17408466.

30. See Adam Nossiter, "Mob Attacks More Than a Dozen Gay Men in Nigeria's Capital," *New York Times,* February 14, 2014. http://www.nytimes.com/2014/02/16/world/africa/mob-attacks-gay-men-in-nigerias-capital.html.

31. https://www.facebook.com/dickson.iroegbu.1.

32. Nyong'o, "Queer Africa and the Fantasy of Virtual Participation," 53.

33. Brian Larkin, *Signal and Noise.*

34. Burgess and Green, *YouTube,* 49. Thomas Elsaesser offers a somewhat different conception of the site, one that aligns YouTube use with cinema spectatorship: "Not only is YouTube closest to the cinema, in that it shows visual segments extracted from different media (cinema, television, performances, home movies, advertisements, camcorder sessions, pop concerts), but also because YouTube suggests the illusion—like its owners, Google—of a kind of totality, a full universe: if you cannot find it on Google, many people now seem to think, it either doesn't exist, or is not worth knowing or having, and so increasingly (and equally surprisingly) with YouTube." Elsaesser, "Tales of Epiphany and Entropy," 153.

35. Alessandro Jedlowski, "From Nollywood to Nollyworld," 29.

36. Brenton Malin, *Feeling Mediated,* 5.

37. "Nigeria Records Second Highest YouTube Figures in Sub-Saharan Africa in 2012," *This Day* (Nigeria), March 1, 2013. Accessed July 24, 2015. http://allafrica.com/stories/201303011081.html.

38. Burgess and Green, *YouTube,* 1.

39. For more, see Adejunmobi, "Evolving Nollywood Templates for Minor Transnational Film."

40. Henry Jenkins, "What Happened Before YouTube," 116.

41. Comment by user bizbubba, http://www.youtube.com/watch?v=pXtdv_nuYN8.

42. Jenkins, "What Happened Before YouTube."

43. "Nollywood Releases Gay Pornographic Movie," Wad Up Online, April 6, 2013. http://waduponline.tumblr.com/post/47265116678/video-nollywood-releases-gay-pornographic-movie.

44. For more on this connection, see Nyong'o, "Queer Africa and the Fantasy of Virtual Participation."

45. Eric E. Schmidt and Jared Cohen, "The Future of Internet Freedom."

46. https://twitter.com/khingBassey.

47. "Double Whammy: Has Nollywood Abandoned Actor King [sic] Bassey Because of His Gay Movie Scene AND Accident That Affected His 'Pretty boy' Face?" 234 Pulse, May 18, 2013. Accessed July 24, 2015. http://www.234pulse.com/2013/05/double-whammy-photos-has-nollywood-abandoned-actor-king-bassey-because-of-his-gay-movie-scene-and-accident-that-affected-his-pretty-boyface/.

48. Green-Simms and Azuah, "The Video Closet."

49. Benjamin Njoku, "BOMBSHELL! Dickson Iroegbu Releases Gay Movie," *Vanguard* (Nigeria), January 28, 2012. Accessed July 24, 2015. http://www.vanguardngr.com/2012/01/bombshell-dickson-iroegbu-releases-gay-movie/.

50. See Green-Simms and Azuah, "The Video Closet."

51. Nyong'o, "Queer Africa and the Fantasy of Virtual Participation," 51.

52. See ibid.

53. See Green-Simms and Azuah, "The Video Closet."

54. Ibid, 42.

55. Alex, for his part, wears a beaded rainbow bracelet that recalls, of course, Charles Jr.'s rainbow Lego collection. Avoiding the Bobby who clearly continues to carry a torch for him, who comically fellates a chicken skewer, and who cries out colloquialisms like "gurl" and "whatevs," Alex focuses on Charles, hoping to reassure him that all gay men aren't like Bobby.

56. http://www.youtube.com/watch?v=B1EKOFHDsFQ.

57. http://www.youtube.com/channel/UCM7pevrRFVxu6jSCbS8i-lQ.

58. Nyong'o, "Queer Africa and the Fantasy of Virtual Participation," 46.

59. https://www.youtube.com/watch?v=Z_g8TSdaG-Q.

60. http://knowyourmeme.com/memes/eat-da-poo-poo.

61. http://perezhilton.com/2010-06-02-eat-da-poo-poo#.VbKv4qYXy_s.

62. Nyong'o, "Queer Africa and the Fantasy of Virtual Participation," 59.

63. Ibid, 56.

64. Ibid, 53.

65. See, for instance, the essays included in Carmela Garritano, "Close-Up: Nollywood."

66. Green-Simms and Azuah, "The Video Closet," 48.

67. http://ameyawdebrah.com/more-shocker-from-nollywood-watch-nigerias-most-daring-gay-movie-pregnant-hawkers/.

68. Green-Simms and Azuah, "The Video Closet," 48.

69. Ibid.

70. Ibid, 47.

71. See, for instance, Leo Bersani, "Gay Betrayals," in *Is the Rectum a Grave? And Other Essays*, 36–44.

72. http://thebex.tumblr.com/post/1661924111/nollywood-gone-wrong.

73. Nakamura, *Digitizing Race*, 89.

74. Ibid, 88.

75. See Nyong'o, "Queer Africa and the Fantasy of Virtual Participation."

Conclusion

1. Peter Dickinson, quoted in Thomas Waugh, *The Romance of Transgression in Canada*, 9; Annamarie Jagose, *Queer Theory*, 131.

2. Teresa De Lauretis, "Queer Texts, Bad Habits, and the Issue of a Future," 243. See also Bruno Latour, "How to Talk about the Body?"

3. Hayles posed this question during her 2013 presentation "Rethinking Thinking: Material Processes and the Cognitive Nonconscious" at the Western Humanities Alliance. See https://www.youtube.com/watch?v=7iDL9yDH4ko.

4. Eric O. Clarke, *Virtuous Vice*, 30.

5. Ibid., 30.

6. @RuPaul, May 24, 2014, 12:41 p.m.

7. Clarke, *Virtuous Vice*, 171.

8. Wolfgang Ernst, "Media Archaeography," 242–243.

9. Sedgwick, *Epistemology of the Closet*, 8, italics in the original.

10. See Kyle Turner, "LGBT Film: Still Suffering From Baby-Step Syndrome," February 16, 2016, https://psmag.com/lgbt-film-still-suffering-from-baby-step-syndrome-f76c1ad46050#.qbotz96pz

11. Straayer, *Deviant Eyes, Deviant Bodies*, 34.

12. Samuel Spencer, "Review: 'Tangerine,' A Film of Many Segments, All of Them Sweet," December 2, 2015, https://samuelspencerwrites.wordpress.com/2015/12/02/film-review-tangerine-sean-baker-2015/

13. Leela Ginelle, "A Case Study in Transmisogyny: Film Reviews of 'Tangerine,'" July 13, 2015, http://www.pqmonthly.com/a-case-study-in-transmisogyny-film-reviews-of-tangerine/23106

14. Morgan Collado, "A Trans Woman of Color Responds to the Trauma of *Tangerine*," Autostraddle, August 26, 2015, http://www.autostraddle.com/a-trans-woman-of-color-responds-to-the-trauma-of-tangerine-301607/

15. Jon Ronson, *So You've Been Publicly Shamed*, 266.

16. Marwick, *Status Update*, 277–278.

17. David Valentine, *Imagining Transgender*, 238.

18. Jennifer Holt, "Regulating Connected Viewing," 19.

Bibliography

Abate, Michelle Ann, and Kenneth Kidd. "Introduction." In *Over the Rainbow: Queer Children's and Young Adult Literature,* edited by Michelle Ann Abate and Kenneth Kidd, 1–14. Ann Arbor: University of Michigan Press, 2011.

Abelove, Henry, Michèle Aina Barale, and David M. Halperin. "Introduction." In *The Lesbian and Gay Studies Reader,* edited by Henry Abelove, Michèle Aina Barale, and David M. Halperin, xv–xviii. New York: Routledge, 1993.

Abramovich, Seth. "NBA Owner Larry Miller Not Jazzed About 'Brokeback.'" Gawker .com, January 12, 2006. Accessed July 24, 2015. http://gawker.com/148247/nba -owner-larry-miller-not-jazzed-about-brokeback.

Acland, Charles R., ed. *Residual Media.* Minneapolis: University of Minnesota Press, 2006.

Adejunmobi, Moradewun. "Evolving Nollywood Templates for Minor Transnational Film." *Black Camera* 5, no. 2 (Spring 2014): 74–94.

Ahmed, Sara. *The Cultural Politics of Emotion.* New York: Routledge, 2004.

———. "Happy Objects." In *The Affect Theory Reader,* edited by Melissa Gregg and Gregory J. Seigworth, 29–51. Durham, NC: Duke University Press, 2010.

———. "Queer Feelings." In *The Routledge Queer Studies Reader,* edited by Donald E. Hall and Annamarie Jagose, with Andrea Bebell and Susan Potter, 422–442. New York: Routledge, 2013.

Alt, Casey. "Objects of Our Affection: How Object Orientation Made Computers a Medium." In *Media Archaeology: Approaches, Applications, and Implications,* edited by Erkki Huhtamo and Jussi Parikka, 278–301. Berkeley: University of California Press, 2011.

Amato, Joe. "Endnotes for a Theory of Convergence." In *New Media: Theories and Practices of Digitextuality,* edited by Anna Everett and John T. Caldwell, 255–264. New York: Routledge, 2003.

Andrejevic, Mark. "Authoring User-Generated Content." In *Media Authorship,* edited by Cynthia Chris and David Gerstner, 123–136. New York: Routledge, 2012.

Aneesh, A. *Virtual Migration: The Programming of Globalization.* Durham, NC: Duke University Press, 2006.

Angelides, Steven. "The Queer Intervention." In *The Routledge Queer Studies Reader,* edited by Donald E. Hall and Annamarie Jagose, with Andrea Bebell and Susan Potter, 60–73. New York: Routledge, 2013.

Arata, Luis O. "Reflections on Interactivity." In *Rethinking Media Change: The Aesthetics of Transition,* edited by Henry Jenkins and David Thorburn, 217–226. Cambridge, MA: MIT Press, 2003.

Arzumanova, Inna, and Sarah Banet-Weiser. "Creative Authorship: Self-Actualizing Individuals and the Self-Brand." In *Media Authorship,* edited by Cynthia Chris and David Gerstner, 163–179. New York: Routledge, 2012.

Atanasoski, Neda. *Humanitarian Violence: The U.S. Deployment of Diversity*. Minneapolis: University of Minnesota Press, 2013.

Badgett, M. V. Lee. "Beyond Biased Samples: Challenging the Myths of the Economic Status of Lesbians and Gay Men." In *Homo Economics: Capitalism, Community, and Lesbian and Gay Life*, edited by Amy Gluckman and Betsy Reed, 73–86. New York: Routledge, 1997.

Bad Object-Choices, eds. *How Do I Look? Queer Film and Video*. Seattle: Bay Press, 1991.

Bakardjieva, Maria, and Georgia Gaden. "Web 2.0 Technologies of the Self." In *Cultural Technologies: The Shaping of Culture in Media and Society*, edited by Göran Bolin, 153–169. New York: Routledge, 2012.

Barker, Martin. "Fantasy Audiences Versus Fantasy Audiences." In *Film Theory and Contemporary Hollywood Movies*, edited by Warren Buckland, 286–309. New York and London: Routledge, 2009.

Barrett, Rusty. "The Emergence of the Unmarked: Queer Theory, Language Ideology, and Formal Linguistics." In *Queer Excursions: Retheorizing Binaries in Language, Gender, and Sexuality*, edited by Lal Zimman, Jenny L. Davis, and Joshua Raclaw. New York: Oxford University Press, 2014. 195–224.

Barthes, Roland. *Camera Lucida: Reflections on Photography*. Translated by Richard Howard. New York: Hill and Wang, 1980.

———. "The Third Meaning: Research Notes on Some Eisenstein Stills." In *Image-Music-Text*, translated by Stephen Heath, 52–68. New York: Hill and Wang, 1977.

Bartky, Sandra Lee. *Femininity and Domination: Studies in the Phenomenology of Oppression*. New York: Routledge, 1990.

Benshoff, Harry M. "(Broke) Back to the Mainstream: Queer Theory and Queer Cinemas Today." In *Film Theory and Contemporary Hollywood Movies*, edited by Warren Buckland, 192–213. New York: Routledge, 2009.

———. *Monsters in the Closet: Homosexuality and the Horror Film*. Manchester: Manchester University Press, 1997.

———. "Reception of a Queer Mainstream Film." In *New Queer Cinema: A Critical Reader*, edited by Michele Aaron, 172–186. New Brunswick: Rutgers University Press, 2004.

Benshoff, Harry M., and Sean Griffin. *Queer Images: A History of Gay and Lesbian Film in America*. Lanham: Rowman & Littlefield, 2006.

———, eds. *Queer Cinema: The Film Reader*. New York: Routledge, 2004.

Bergson, Henri. *Matter and Memory*. Cambridge, MA: Zone Books, 1990.

Berlant, Lauren. "Cruel Optimism." In *The Affect Theory Reader*, edited by Melissa Gregg and Gregory J. Seigworth, 93–117. Durham, NC: Duke University Press, 2010.

———. "Starved." In *After Sex? On Writing Since Queer Theory*, edited by Janet Halley and Andrew Parker, 79–90. Durham, NC: Duke University Press, 2011.

Berlant, Lauren, and Elizabeth Freeman. "Queer Nationality." In *Fear of a Queer Planet: Queer Politics and Social Theory*, edited by Michael Warner, 193–229. Minneapolis: University of Minnesota Press, 1993.

Berlant, Lauren, and Michael Warner. "Sex in Public." In *The Routledge Queer Studies Reader*, edited by Donald E. Hall and Annamarie Jagose, with Andrea Bebell and Susan Potter, 165–179. New York: Routledge, 2013.

Berry, Chris, Soyoung Kim, and Lynn Spigel, eds. *Electronic Elsewheres: Media, Technology, and the Experience of Social Space.* Minneapolis: University of Minnesota Press, 2009.

Bersani, Leo. *Is the Rectum a Grave? And Other Essays.* Chicago: University of Chicago Press, 2010.

———. "Shame On You." In *After Sex? On Writing Since Queer Theory,* edited by Janet Halley and Andrew Parker, 91–109. Durham, NC: Duke University Press, 2011.

Björkin, Mats. "Peer-to-Peer File-Sharing Systems: Files, Objects, Distribution." In *Cultural Technologies: The Shaping of Culture in Media and Society,* edited by Göran Bolin, 51–63. New York: Routledge, 2012.

Boddy, William. "Redefining the Home Screen: Technological Convergence as Trauma and Business Plan." In *Rethinking Media Change: The Aesthetics of Transition,* edited by Henry Jenkins and David Thorburn, 191–202. Cambridge, MA: MIT Press, 2003.

Bolin, Göran. "Introduction: Cultural Technologies in Cultures of Technology." In *Cultural Technologies: The Shaping of Culture in Media and Society,* edited by Göran Bolin, 1–18. New York: Routledge, 2012.

Bolton, Matthew. "The Ethics of Alterity: Adapting Queerness in *Brokeback Mountain.*" In *Queer Love in Film and Television: Critical Essays,* edited by Pamela Demory and Christopher Pullen, 257–268. London: Palgrave Macmillan, 2013.

Braman, Sandra. "Technology and Epistemology: Information Policy and Desire." In *Cultural Technologies: The Shaping of Culture in Media and Society,* edited by Göran Bolin, 133–152. New York: Routledge, 2012.

Bronski, Michael. *Culture Clash: The Making of Gay Sensibility.* Boston: South End Press, 1984.

———. *The Pleasure Principle: Sex, Backlash, and the Struggle for Gay Freedom.* New York: St. Martin's Press, 2000.

———. *A Queer History of the United States.* Boston: Beacon Press, 2012.

Brown, Steven D., and Ian Tucker. "Eff the Ineffable: Affect, Somatic Management, and Mental Health Service Users." In *The Affect Theory Reader,* edited by Melissa Gregg and Gregory J. Seigworth, 229–249. Durham, NC: Duke University Press, 2010.

Brown, Steven D., and Paul Stenner. *Psychology Without Foundations: History, Philosophy, and Psychosocial Theory.* London: Sage, 2009.

Bruns, Axel. "Produsage: Towards a Broader Framework for User-Led Content Creation." In *Creativity and Cognition: Proceedings of the 6th ACM SIGCHI Conference on Creativity & Cognition,* ACM, Washington, DC, 2007.

Bryce, Jane. "Signs of Femininity, Symptoms of Malaise: Contextualizing Figurations of 'Woman' in Nollywood." *Research in African Literatures* 43, no. 4 (Winter 2012): 71–87.

Burgess, Jean, and Joshua Green. *YouTube: Online Video and Participatory Culture.* Cambridge, MA: Polity Press, 2009.

Butler, Judith. *Bodies That Matter: On the Discursive Limits of "Sex."* New York: Routledge, 1993.

———. *Gender Trouble: Feminism and the Subversion of Identity.* New York: Routledge, 1990.

Buzzard, Karen S. F. "Net Ratings: Defining a New Medium by the Old, Measuring Internet Audiences." In *New Media: Theories and Practices of Digitextuality,* edited by Anna Everett and John T. Caldwell, 197–208. New York: Routledge, 2003.

Caldwell, John T. "Second-Shift Media Aesthetics: Programming, Interactivity, and User Flows." In *New Media: Theories and Practices of Digitextuality,* edited by Anna Everett and John T. Caldwell, 127–144. New York: Routledge, 2003.

Cante, Rich, and Angelo Restivo. "The Cultural-Aesthetic Specificities of All-male Moving-Image Pornography." In *Porn Studies,* edited by Linda Williams, 142–166. Durham, NC: Duke University Press, 2004.

Cardoso, Gustavo, Guo Liang, and Tiago Lapa. "Cross-National Comparative Perspectives From the World Internet Project." In *The Oxford Handbook of Internet Studies,* edited by William H. Dutton, 216–238. New York: Oxford, 2013..

Carroll, Hamilton. *Affirmative Reaction: New Formations of White Masculinity.* Durham, NC: Duke University Press, 2011.

Castells, Manuel. *Communication Power.* New York: Oxford University Press, 2009.

Cavell, Stanley. *The World Viewed: Reflections on the Ontology of Film.* Cambridge, MA: Harvard University Press, 1971.

Chan, Kenneth. "Bad Boys Need Love, Too: The Cinematic Negativity of Gay Romance in *I Love You Phillip Morris.*" In *Queer Love in Film and Television: Critical Essays,* edited by Pamela Demory and Christopher Pullen, 23–32. London: Palgrave Macmillan, 2013.

Chun, Wendy Hui Kyong. *Control and Freedom: Power and Paranoia in the Age of Fiber Optics.* Cambridge, MA: MIT Press, 2006.

———. "The Enduring Ephemeral, or The Future is a Memory." In *Media Archaeology: Approaches, Applications, and Implications,* edited by Erkki Huhtamo and Jussi Parikka, 184–206. Berkeley: University of California Press, 2011.

———. "Introduction: Race and/as Technology; or, How to Do Things to Race." *Camera Obscura* 70, vol. 24, no. 1 (2009): 7–35.

Cimino, Kenneth W. *Gay Conservatives: Group Consciousness and Assimilation.* New York: Routledge, 2006.

Clarke, Danae. "Commodity Lesbianism." In *The Lesbian and Gay Studies Reader,* edited by Henry Abelove, Michèle Aina Barale, and David M. Halperin, 186–201. New York: Routledge, 1993.

Clarke, Eric O. *Virtuous Vice: Homoeroticism and the Public Sphere.* Durham, NC: Duke University Press, 2000.

Clough, Patricia T. "The Affective Turn: Political Economy, Biomedia, and Bodies." In *The Affect Theory Reader,* edited by Melissa Gregg and Gregory J. Seigworth, 206–228. Durham, NC: Duke University Press, 2010.

Clough, Patricia Ticineto, Karen Gregory, Benjamin Haber, and R. Joshua Scannell. "The Datalogical Turn." In *Non-Representational Methodologies: Re-Envisioning Research,* edited by Phillip Vannini, 146–164. New York: Routledge, 2015.

Cohan, Steven. *Incongruous Entertainment: Camp, Cultural Value, and the MGM Musical.* Durham, NC: Duke University Press, 2005.

———. "Queer Eye for the Straight Guise: Camp, Postfeminism, and the Fab Five's Makeovers of Masculinity." In *Interrogating Postfeminism: Gender and the Politics of Popular Culture,* edited by Yvonne Tasker and Diane Negra, 176–200. Durham, NC: Duke University Press, 2007.

Coleman, E. Gabriella. "Phreaks, Hackers, and Trolls: The Politics of Transgression and Spectacle." In *The Social Media Reader,* edited by Michael Mandiberg, 99–119. New York: NYU Press, 2012.

Couldry, Nick. *Media, Society, World: Social Theory and Digital Media Practice.* Hoboken, NJ: Wiley, 2012.

———. *Why Voice Matters: Culture and Politics After Neoliberalism.* London: Sage, 2011.

Crary, Jonathan. *Techniques of the Observer: On Vision and Modernity in the 19th Century.* Cambridge, MA: MIT Press, 1990.

Crimp, Douglas. "The Boys in My Bedroom." In *The Lesbian and Gay Studies Reader,* edited by Henry Abelove, Michèle Aina Barale, and David M. Halperin, 344–349. New York: Routledge, 1993.

Cumberland, Sharon. "Private Uses of Cyberspace: Women, Desire, and Fan Culture." In *Rethinking Media Change: The Aesthetics of Transition,* edited by Henry Jenkins and David Thorburn, 261–280. Cambridge, MA: MIT Press, 2003.

Cvetkovich, Ann. *An Archive of Feelings: Trauma, Sexuality, and Lesbian Public Cultures.* Durham, NC: Duke University Press, 2003.

———. "Public Feelings." In *After Sex? On Writing Since Queer Theory,* edited by Janet Halley and Andrew Parker, 169–179. Durham, NC: Duke University Press, 2011.

Davies, William. "Neoliberalism and the Revenge of the 'Social.'" OpenDemocracy, July 16, 2013. Accessed July 24, 2015. https://www.opendemocracy.net/william -davies/neoliberalism-and-revenge-of-"social".

Davis, Nick. *The Desiring-Image: Gilles Deleuze and Contemporary Queer Cinema.* New York: Oxford University Press, 2013.

Davis, Sean. "Facebook Cares More About Targeting Ads Than Affirming Your Gender Identity." *Federalist,* February 13, 2014. Accessed July 24, 2015. http://thefederalist .com/2014/02/13/facebook-cares-more-about-targeting-ads-than-affirming-your -gender-identity/.

Davison, Patrick. "The Language of Internet Memes." In *The Social Media Reader,* edited by Michael Mandiberg, 120–136. New York: NYU Press, 2012.

Dean, Tim. "Introduction: Pornography, Technology, Archive." In *Porn Archives,* edited by Tim Dean, Steven Ruszczycky, and David Squires, 1–28. Durham, NC: Duke University Press, 2014.

———. "Lacan Meets Queer Theory." In *The Routledge Queer Studies Reader,* edited by Donald E. Hall and Annamarie Jagose, with Andrea Bebell and Susan Potter, 150–162. New York: Routledge, 2013.

———. "Stumped." In *Porn Archives,* edited by Tim Dean, Steven Ruszczycky, and David Squires, 420–440. Durham, NC: Duke University Press, 2014.

———. *Unlimited Intimacy: Reflections on the Subculture of Barebacking.* Chicago: University of Chicago Press, 2009.

Dean, Tim, Steven Ruszczycky, and David Squires, eds. *Porn Archives.* Durham, NC: Duke University Press, 2014.

DeAngelis, Michael. *Gay Fandom and Crossover Stardom: James Dean, Mel Gibson, and Keanu Reeves.* Durham, NC: Duke University Press, 2001.

D'Emilio, John. "Capitalism and Gay Identity." In *The Lesbian and Gay Studies Reader,* edited by Henry Abelove, Michèle Aina Barale, and David M. Halperin, 467–478. New York: Routledge, 1993.

De Kosnik, Abigail. "*Fifty Shades* and the Archive of Women's Culture." *Cinema Journal* 48, no. 4 (2009): 116–125.

Delany, Samuel. *The Motion of Light in Water: Sex and Science Fiction Writing in the East Village.* Minneapolis: University of Minnesota Press, 2004.

———. *Times Square Red, Times Square Blue.* New York: NYU Press, 1999.

De Lauretis, Teresa. "Queer Texts, Bad Habits, and the Issue of a Future." *GLQ: A Journal of Lesbian and Gay Studies* 17, no. 2–3 (2011): 243–263.

———. "Queer Theory: Lesbian and Gay Sexualities." *Differences: A Journal of Feminist Cultural Studies* 3, no. 3 (1991): iii–xviii.

Deleuze, Gilles. "Postscript on the Societies of Control." *October* 59 (Winter 1992): 3–7.

Denizet-Lewis, Benoit. "The Man Behind Abercrombie & Fitch." *Salon,* January 24, 2006. Accessed July 24, 2015. http://www.salon.com/2006/01/24/jeffries/.

Desjardins, Mary. "The Incredible Shrinking Star: Todd Haynes and the Case History of Karen Carpenter." *Camera Obscura* 57, vol. 19, no. 3 (2004): 23–55.

Dewhurst, Robert. "*Gay Sunshine,* Pornopoetic Collage, and Queer Archive." In *Porn Archives,* edited by Tim Dean, Steven Ruszczycky, and David Squires, 213–233. Durham, NC: Duke University Press, 2014.

DiCarlo, John. "The Gym Body and Heroic Myth." *Gay and Lesbian Review* (July/August 2001): 14–16.

Doty, Alexander. *Making Things Perfectly Queer: Interpreting Mass Culture.* Minneapolis: University of Minnesota Press, 1993.

———. "There's Something Queer Here." In *Out In Culture: Gay, Lesbian, and Queer Essays on Popular Culture,* edited by Corey K. Creekmur and Alexander Doty, 71–90. Durham, NC: Duke University Press, 1995.

Dourish, Paul. "Protocols, Packets, and Proximity." In *Signal Traffic: Critical Studies of Media Infrastructures,* edited by Lisa Parks and Nicole Starosielski, 183–204. Urbana: University of Illinois Press, 2015.

Drum, Gary. "He's In. He's Out. He's Post-Gay: The Misadventures of James Collard's Post-Gay Journey to America." Hardyboy.com, June 1, 2007. Accessed July 24, 2015. http://www.hardyboy.com/postgay.html.

Duggan, Lisa. "The New Homonormativity: The Sexual Politics of Neoliberalism." In *Materializing Democracy: Toward a Revitalized Cultural Politics,* edited by Russ Castronovo and Dana D. Nelson, 175–194. Durham, NC: Duke University Press, 2002.

———. "Queering the State." In *Sex Wars: Sexual Dissent and Political Culture,* edited by Lisa Duggan and Nan D. Hunter, 179–193. New York and London: Routledge, 1995.

———. *The Twilight of Equality? Neoliberalism, Cultural Politics, and the Attack on Democracy.* Boston: Beacon Press, 2003.

Dyer, Richard. *The Matter of Images: Essays on Representation.* London: Routledge, 1993.

Edelman, Lee. "Ever After: History, Negativity, and the Social." In *After Sex? On Writing Since Queer Theory,* edited by Janet Halley and Andrew Parker, 110–120. Durham, NC: Duke University Press, 2011.

———. *Homographesis: Essays in Gay Literary and Cultural Theory.* New York: Routledge, 1994.

———. *No Future: Queer Theory and the Death Drive.* Durham, NC: Duke University Press, 2004.

———. "Unnamed: Eve's *Epistemology.*" *Criticism* 52, no. 2 (Spring 2010) 185–190.

Elliott, Stuart. "Absolut Celebrates Its 30 Years of Marketing to Gay Consumers." *New York Times,* October 26, 2011. Accessed July 24, 2015. http://www.nytimes.com /2011/10/27/business/media/absolut-heralds-its-marketing-to-gay-consumers .html?_r=0.

Ellison, Nicole B., and Danah M. Boyd. "Sociality Through Social Network Sites." In *The Oxford Handbook of Internet Studies,* edited by William H. Dutton, 151–172. New York: Oxford University Press, 2013.

Elsaesser, Thomas. "Tales of Epiphany and Entropy: Paranarrative Worlds on YouTube." In *Film Theory and Contemporary Hollywood Movies,* edited by Warren Buckland, 150–172. New York: Routledge, 2009.

Eng, David L., Judith Halberstam, and José Esteban Muñoz. "Introduction: What's Queer about Queer Studies Now?" *Social Text,* nos. 84–85 (2005): 1–17.

Engel, Meredith. "What Is a 'Spornosexual'?" *New York Daily News,* June 12, 2014. Accessed July 24, 2015. http://www.nydailynews.com/life-style/health /spornosexual-article-1.1826983.

Epps, Brad. "The Fetish of Fluidity." In *Homosexuality and Psychoanalysis,* edited by Tim Dean and Christopher Lane, 412–431. Chicago: University of Chicago Press, 2001.

Ernst, Wolfgang. *Digital Memory and the Archive.* Edited and with an Introduction by Jussi Parikka. Minneapolis: University of Minnesota Press, 2013.

———. "Media Archaeography: Method and Machine Versus History and Narrative of Media." In *Media Archaeology: Approaches, Applications, and Implications,* edited by Erkki Huhtamo and Jussi Parikka, 239–255. Berkeley: University of California Press, 2011.

Eubanks, Virginia. "The Policy Machine." *Slate,* April 30, 2015. Accessed July 24, 2015. http://www.slate.com/articles/technology/future_tense/2015/04/the_dangers_of _letting_algorithms_enforce_policy.html.

Everett, Anna. "Digitextuality and Click Theory: Theses on Convergence Media in the Digital Age." In *New Media: Theories and Practices of Digitextuality,* edited by Anna Everett and John T. Caldwell, 3–28. New York: Routledge, 2003.

Everett, Anna, and John T. Caldwell. "Issues in the Theory and Practice of Media Convergence." In *New Media: Theories and Practices of Digitextuality,* edited by Anna Everett and John T. Caldwell, xi–xxx. New York: Routledge, 2003.

Fahimian, Giselle. "How the IP Guerrillas Won: ®™ARK, Adbusters, Negativland, and the 'Bullying Back' of Creative Freedom and Social Commentary." *In Censoring Culture: Contemporary Threats to Free Expression,* edited by Robert Atkins and Svetlana Mintcheva, 132–148. New York: New Press, 2006.

Farmer, Brett. *Spectacular Passions: Cinema, Fantasy, Gay Male Spectatorships.* Durham, NC: Duke University Press, 2000.

Fejes, Fred, and Ron Lennon. "Defining the Lesbian/Gay Community? Market Research and the Lesbian/Gay Press." *Journal of Homosexuality* 39, no. 1 (2000): 25–42.

Ferguson, Roderick A. *Aberrations in Black: Toward a Queer of Color Critique.* Minneapolis: University of Minnesota Press, 2004.

Fiske, John. *Television Culture.* London: Methuen & Co. Ltd., 1987.

Foucault, Michel. *The History of Sexuality.* Vol. 1, *An Introduction,* translated by Robert Hurley. London: Penguin, 1990.

———. *The History of Sexuality.* Vol. 2, *The Use of Pleasure,* translated by Robert Hurley. New York: Pantheon Books, 1985.

———. *The History of Sexuality.* Vol. 3, *The Care of the Self,* translated by Robert Hurley. New York: Pantheon Books, 1986.

Franklin, Seb. "Virality, Informatics, and Critique; or, Can There Be Such a Thing as Radical Computation?" *Women's Studies Quarterly* 40, no. 1/2 (Spring/Summer 2012): 153–170.

Freeman, Elizabeth. "Time Binds, or Queer Erotohistoriography." *Social Text,* nos. 84–85 (2005): 57–68.

Freud, Sigmund. *Three Essays on the Theory of Sexuality.* Translated and revised by James Strachey. Eastford, CT: Martino Fine Books. 2000 [1962].

Friedberg, Anne. "The Virtual Window." In *Rethinking Media Change: The Aesthetics of Transition,* edited by Henry Jenkins and David Thorburn, 337–354. Cambridge, MA: MIT Press, 2003.

Frye, Marilyn. "Some Reflections on Separatism and Power." In *The Lesbian and Gay Studies Reader,* edited by Henry Abelove, Michèle Aina Barale, and David M. Halperin, 91–98. New York: Routledge, 1993.

Fuller, Matthew and Andrew Goffey. *Evil Media.* Cambridge: MIT Press, 2012.

Fuss, Diana. "Inside/Out." In *Inside/Out: Lesbian Theories, Gay Theories,* edited by Diana Fuss, 1–12. New York: Routledge, 1991.

———, ed. *Inside/Out: Lesbian Theories, Gay Theories.* New York: Routledge, 1991.

Gaboury, Jacob. "Hidden Surface Problems: On the Digital Image as Material Object." *Journal of Visual Culture* 14, no. 1 (April 2015): 40–60.

———. "On Uncomputable Numbers: Toward a Queer History of Computing." YouTube .com, October 13, 2014. Accessed July 24, 2015. https://www.youtube.com/watch?v =LfsvRemAnCM.

———. "A Queer History of Computing." Rhizome.org, February 19, 2013. Accessed July 28, 2015. http://rhizome.org/editorial/2013/feb/19/queer-computing-1/.

Galloway, Alexander R. *The Interface Effect.* London: Polity, 2012.

Galloway, Alexander, and Eugene Thacker. "The Metaphysics of Networks." In *Censoring Culture: Contemporary Threats to Free Expression,* edited by Robert Atkins and Svetlana Mintcheva. New York: New Press, 2006.

Garritano, Carmela, ed. "Close-Up: Nollywood: A Worldly Creative Practice." *Black Camera* 5, no. 2 (Spring 2014).

Gaudio, Rudi. "A View From the Ground." In *Nigeria: What Is to Be Done?* edited by Ebenezer Obadare (free eBook, via Africa Is a Country, 2015), http:// africasacountry.com/2015/03/nigeria-what-is-to-be-done/. Accessed October 18, 2015.

Genette, Gerard. *Paratexts: Thresholds of Interpretation.* Cambridge: Cambridge University Press, 1997.

Gillespie, Tarleton. "The Stories Digital Tools Tells." In *New Media: Theories and Practices of Digitextuality,* edited by Anna Everett and John T. Caldwell, 107–206. New York: Routledge, 2003.

Ginsberg, Merle. "Introducing the Stromo! Why Straight Male Stars are Going Gay(ish)," *Hollywood Reporter,* June 25, 2015. Accessed July 24, 2015. http://www .hollywoodreporter.com/news/introducing-stromo-why-straight-male-804291.

Gitelman, Lisa. "How Users Define New Media: A History of the Amusement Phono-
graph." In *Rethinking Media Change: The Aesthetics of Transition,* edited by Henry
Jenkins and David Thorburn, 61–80. Cambridge, MA: MIT Press, 2003.

Gladstone, Rick. "Nigerian President Signs Ban on Same-Sex Relationships." *New York
Times,* January 13, 2014. Accessed July 24, 2015. http://www.nytimes.com/2014/01/14
/world/africa/nigerian-president-signs-ban-on-same-sex-relationships.html?_r=0.

Glass, Loren. "Up from Underground." In *Porn Archives,* edited by Tim Dean, Steven
Ruszczycky, and David Squires, 127–143. Durham, NC: Duke University Press,
2014.

Goldsmith, Kenneth. *Uncreative Writing: Managing Language in the Digital Age.* New
York: Columbia University Press, 2011.

Goodman, Paul. "The Politics of Being Queer." In *Nature Heals: The Psychological Essays
of Paul Goodman,* edited by Taylor Stoehr, 216–225. New York: Dutton, 1979 [1969].

Gray, Mary L. *Out in the Country: Youth, Media, and Queer Visibility in Rural America.*
New York: NYU Press, 2009.

Grebowicz, Margret. *Why Internet Porn Matters.* Stanford, CA: Stanford University
Press, 2013.

Greenberg, David F. *The Construction of Homosexuality.* Chicago: University of Chicago
Press, 1998.

Green-Simms, Lindsey, and Unoma Azuah. "The Video Closet: Nollywood's Gay-
Themed Movies." *Transition* 107 (2012): 32–49.

Greven, David. *Manhood in Hollywood from Bush to Bush.* Austin: University of Texas
Press, 2009.

———. *Men Beyond Desire: Manhood, Sex, and Violation in American Literature.*
London: Palgrave Macmillan, 2005.

Griffin, Hollis. "Debbie Downer Has a Facebook Problem: Regulating Affect on Social
Media Networks." *Flow* 14.01 (2011). Accessed July 28, 2015. http://flowtv.org/2011
/06/debbie-has-a-facebook-problem/.

———. *Feeling Normal: Media, Affect, and Queer Critique.* Bloomington: Indiana
University Press, forthcoming.

———. "Love Hurts: Intimacy in the Age of Pervasive Computing." *Flow* 19, no. 02
(2013). Accessed July 28, 2015. http://flowtv.org/2013/11/love-hurts-the-age-of
-pervasive-computing/.

———. "'Your Mom Is So Fat . . . ,' or Talking Politics on the Internet." *Flow* 19, no. 06
(2014). Accessed July 28, 2015. http://flowtv.org/2014/02/talking-politics-on-the
-internet/.

Griffin, Sean. *Tinker Belles and Evil Queens: The Walt Disney Company from the Inside
Out.* New York: NYU Press, 2000.

Grosz, Elizabeth. "Experimental Desire: Rethinking Queer Subjectivity." In *The
Routledge Queer Studies Reader,* edited by Donald E. Hall and Annamarie Jagose,
with Andrea Bebell and Susan Potter, 194–211. New York: Routledge, 2013.

———. *Space, Time, and Perversion: Essays on the Politics of Bodies.* New York: Routledge, 1995.

Gunter, Barrie. "The Study of Online Relationships and Dating." In *The Oxford Handbook of Internet Studies,* edited by William H. Dutton, 173–194. New York: Oxford
University Press, 2013.

Halberstam, Judith. "Automating Gender: Postmodern Feminism in the Age of the Intelligent Machine," *Feminist Studies* 17, no. 3 (Autumn, 1991): 439–460.

———. "The Politics of Negativity in Recent Queer Theory," in "Forum: Conference Debates. The Antisocial Thesis in Queer Theory," *PMLA* 121 (2006): 823–825.

———. *The Queer Art of Failure*. Durham, NC: Duke University Press, 2011.

———. "The Transgender Gaze in *Boys Don't Cry*." *Screen* 42, no. 3 (2001): 294–298.

———. "Who's Afraid of Queer Theory?" In *Class Issues*, edited by Amitava Kumar, 256–275. New York: NYU Press, 1997.

Hall, Donald E., and Annamarie Jagose. "Introduction." In *The Routledge Queer Studies Reader*, edited by Donald E. Hall and Annamarie Jagose, with Andrea Bebell and Susan Potter, xiv–xx. New York: Routledge, 2013.

Hall, Stuart. "Deviance, Politics, and the Media." In *The Lesbian and Gay Studies Reader*, edited by Henry Abelove, Michèle Aina Barale, and David M. Halperin, 62–90. New York: Routledge, 1993.

———. "Encoding/Decoding." In *Media Studies: A Reader*, edited by Paul Marris and Sue Thornham, 51–61. New York: NYU Press, 2004.

Halley, Janet, and Andrew Parker. "Introduction." In *After Sex? On Writing Since Queer Theory*, edited by Janet Halley and Andrew Parker, 1–16. Durham, NC: Duke University Press, 2011.

Halperin, David M. *How to Be Gay*. Cambridge, MA: Harvard University Press, 2012.

———. "How to Do the History of Male Homosexuality." In *The Routledge Queer Studies Reader*, edited by Donald E. Hall and Annamarie Jagose, with Andrea Bebell and Susan Potter, 262–286. New York: Routledge, 2013.

———. "The Normalization of Queer Theory." *Journal of Homosexuality* 45, vols. 2–4 (2003): 339–343.

———. *Saint Foucault: Towards a Gay Hagiography*. New York: Oxford University Press, 1997.

———. *What Do Gay Men Want? An Essay on Sex, Risk, and Subjectivity*. Ann Arbor: University of Michigan Press, 2007.

Halperin, David M., and Valerie Traub, eds. *Gay Shame*. Chicago: University of Chicago Press, 2009.

Hannaford, Alex. "The Great Escapee." *Esquire* (February 2010): 89–93.

Hansen, Mark B. N. *Bodies in Code: Interfaces with Digital Media*. New York: Routledge, 2012.

———. *New Philosophy for New Media*. Cambridge, MA: MIT Press, 2004.

Harper, Phillip Brian. "Eloquence and Epitaph: Black Nationalism and the Homophobic Impulse in Responses to the Death of Max Robinson." In *The Lesbian and Gay Studies Reader*, edited by Henry Abelove, Michèle Aina Barale, and David M. Halperin, 159–175. New York: Routledge, 1993.

———. "Gay Male Identities, Personal Privacy, and Relations of Public Exchange: Notes on Directions for Queer Culture." *Social Text* 52–53 (Fall/Winter 1997): 5–29.

Harris Interactive. "Gay and Lesbian Adults Are More Likely and More Frequent Blog Readers." PR Newswire, July 13, 2010. Accessed July 25, 2015. http://www.prnewswire.com/news-releases/gay-and-lesbian-adults-are-more-likely-and-more-frequent-blog-readers-98317299.html.

Harrison, Nate. "Appropriation Art, Subjectivism, Crisis: The Battle for Fair Uses." In *Media Authorship,* edited by Cynthia Chris and David Gerstner, 56–71. New York and London: Routledge, 2012.

Hawk, Byron, David M. Rieder, and Ollie Oviedo, eds. *Small Tech: The Culture of Digital Tools.* Minneapolis: University of Minnesota Press, 2007.

Hayes, Jarrod. "Queering Roots, Queering Diasporas." In *Rites of Return: Diaspora Poetics and the Politics of Memory,* edited by Marianne Hirsch and Nancy K. Miller, 72–87. New York: Columbia University Press, 2011.

Hayles, N. Katherine. *How We Think: Digital Media and Contemporary Technogenesis.* Chicago: University of Chicago Press, 2012.

Hellekson, Karen. "Making Use Of: The Gift, Commerce, and Fans." *Cinema Journal* 48, no. 4 (2009): 125–131.

Hennessy, Rosemary. "The Material of Sex." In *The Routledge Queer Studies Reader,* edited by Donald E. Hall and Annamarie Jagose, with Andrea Bebell and Susan Potter, 134–149. New York: Routledge, 2013.

Herhuth, Eric. "Life, Love, and Programming: the Culture and Politics of *WALL-E* and Pixar Computer Animation." *Cinema Journal* 53, no. 4 (Summer 2014): 53–75.

Hermes, Joke. "The Scary Promise of Technology: Developing New Forms of Audience Research." In *Cultural Technologies: The Shaping of Culture in Media and Society,* edited by Göran Bolin, 189–202. New York: Routledge, 2012.

Hilderbrand, Lucas. *Inherent Vice: Bootleg Histories of Videotape and Copyright.* Durham, NC: Duke University Press, 2009.

Hillis, Ken. *Digital Sensations: Space, Identity, and Embodiment in Virtual Reality.* Minneapolis: University of Minnesota Press, 1999.

———. *Online a Lot of the Time: Ritual, Fetish, Sign.* Durham, NC: Duke University Press, 2009.

Hoad, Neville. "Queer Theory Addiction." In *After Sex? On Writing Since Queer Theory,* edited by Janet Halley and Andrew Parker, 130–141. Durham, NC: Duke University Press, 2011.

Hoberman, J., and Jonathan Rosenbaum, *Midnight Movies.* Da Capo Press, 1983.

Hocquenghem, Guy. *Homosexual Desire.* Durham, NC: Duke University Press, 1993.

Holden, Stephen. "NewFest Is Coming Out of the Margins." *New York Times,* July 26, 2012. Accessed July 24, 2015. http://www.nytimes.com/2012/07/27/movies/newfest -gay-themed-films-at-lincoln-center.html?_r=0.

Holt, Jennifer. "Regulating Connected Viewing: Media Pipelines and Cloud Policy." In *Connected Viewing: Selling, Streaming, & Sharing Media in the Digital Age,* edited by Jennifer Holt and Kevin Sanson (New York: Routledge, 2014): 19–39.

Huhtamo, Erkki. "Dismantling the Fairy Engine: Media Archaeology as Topos Study," in *Media Archaeology: Approaches, Applications, and Implications,* edited by Erkki Huhtamo and Jussi Parikka, 27–47. Berkeley: University of California Press, 2011.

Huhtamo, Erkki, and Jussi Parikka, eds. *Media Archaeology: Approaches, Applications, and Implications.* Berkeley: University of California Press, 2011.

Hunsinger, Jeremy, Lisbeth Klastrup, and Matthew M. Allen, eds. *International Handbook of Internet Research.* New York: Springer, 2010.

Ihde, Don. *Bodies in Technology.* Minneapolis: University of Minnesota Press, 2001.

Jagose, Annamarie. *Queer Theory: An Introduction.* New York: NYU Press, 1996.

Jameson, Fredric. "Class and Allegory in Contemporary Mass Culture: *Dog Day Afternoon* as a Political Film." *College English* Vol. 38, No. 8 (April 1977): 843–859.
———. *Signatures of the Visible.* New York: Routledge, 2007 [1992].
Jedlowski, Alessandro. "From Nollywood to Nollyworld: Processes of Transnationalization in the Nigerian Video Film Industry." In *Global Nollywood: The Transnational Dimensions of an African Video Industry,* edited by Matthias Krings and Onookome Okome, 25–45. Bloomington: Indiana University Press, 2013.
Jenkins, Henry. *Convergence Culture: Where Old and New Media Collide.* New York: NYU Press, 2006.
———. *Fans, Bloggers, and Gamers: Media Consumers in a Digital Age.* New York: NYU Press, 2006.
———. "Quentin Tarantino's *Star Wars?* Digital Cinema, Media Convergence, and Participatory Culture." In *Rethinking Media Change: The Aesthetics of Transition,* edited by Henry Jenkins and David Thorburn, 281–314. Cambridge, MA: MIT Press, 2003.
———. "Quentin Tarantino's *Star Wars?* Grassroots Creativity Meets the Media Industry." In *The Social Media Reader,* edited by Michael Mandiberg, 203–235. New York: NYU Press, 2012.
———. *Textual Poachers: Television Fans and Participatory Culture.* New York: Routledge, 2013 [1992].
———. "What Happened Before YouTube." In *YouTube: Online Video and Participatory Culture,* edited by Jean Burgess and Joshua Green, 109–125. Cambridge, MA: Polity Press, 2009.
Jenkins, Henry, Sam Ford, and Joshua Green, eds. *Spreadable Media: Creating Value and Meaning in a Networked Culture.* New York: NYU Press, 2013.
Jenkins, Henry, and David Thorburn, eds. *Rethinking Media Change: The Aesthetics of Transition.* Cambridge, MA: MIT Press, 2003.
Jones, Adrian. "Playing with Himself: James Franco, Hollywood Queer." In *Queer Love in Film and Television: Critical Essays,* edited by Pamela Demory and Christopher Pullen, 193–206. London: Palgrave Macmillan, 2013.
Keeling, Kara. "Queer OS." *Cinema Journal* 53, no. 2 (Winter 2014): 152–157.
Kennedy, Rosanne. "Indigenous Australian Arts of Return: Mediating Perverse Archives." In *Rites of Return: Diaspora Poetics and the Politics of Memory,* edited by Marianne Hirsch and Nancy K. Miller, 88–104. New York: Columbia University Press, 2011.
King, Katie. *Networked Reenactments: Stories Transdisciplinary Knowledges Tell.* Durham, NC: Duke University Press, 2012.
Kleinhans, Chuck. "The Change from Film to Video Pornography: Implications for Analysis." In *Pornography: Film and Culture,* edited by Peter Lehman, 154–167. New Brunswick: Rutgers University Press, 2006.
Kolko, Beth, Lisa Nakamura, and Gilbert Rodman, eds. *Race in Cyberspace.* New York: Routledge, 2000.
Lacan, Jacques. *Seminar VII: The Ethics of Psychoanalysis.* Translated by Dennis Porter. London: Routledge, 1992.
Lanier, Jaron. *Who Owns the Future?* New York: Penguin, 2013.
———. *You Are Not a Gadget.* New York: Vintage Books, 2011.

Larkin, Brian. *Signal and Noise: Media, Infrastructure, and Urban Culture in Nigeria.* Durham, NC: Duke University Press, 2007.

Latour, Bruno. "How to Talk about the Body? The Normative Dimension of Science Studies." *Body and Society* 10, no. 2–3 (2004): 205–229.

Lee, Hye Jin, and Mark Andrejevic. "Second-Screen Theory: From the Democratic Surround to the Digital Enclosure." In *Connected Viewing: Selling, Streaming, & Sharing Media in the Digital Age,* edited by Jennifer Holt and Kevin Sanson, 40–61. New York: Routledge, 2014.

Lehman, Peter. "Revelations about Pornography." In *Pornography: Film and Culture,* edited by Peter Lehman, 87–98. New Brunswick: Rutgers University Press, 2006.

Lessard, Donovan. "A Critique of the 'Post-Gay' Thesis." *Z Magazine,* December 1, 2011. Accessed July 24, 2015. https://zcomm.org/zmagazine/a-critique-of-the-post-gay -thesis-by-donovan-lessard/.

Lessig, Lawrence. *The Future of Ideas: The Fate of the Commons in a Connected World.* New York: Random House, 2001.

———. "REMIX: How Creativity Is Being Strangled by the Law." In *The Social Media Reader,* edited by Michael Mandiberg, 155–169. New York: NYU Press, 2012.

Leung, Helen Hok-Sze. "Archiving Queer Feelings in Hong Kong." In *The Routledge Queer Studies Reader,* edited by Donald E. Hall and Annamarie Jagose, with Andrea Bebell and Susan Potter, 398–411. New York: Routledge, 2013.

Levinson, Paul. *New New Media.* London: Pearson, 2009.

Lorde, Audre. "The Uses of the Erotic: The Erotic as Power." In *The Lesbian and Gay Studies Reader,* edited by Henry Abelove, Michèle Aina Barale, and David M. Halperin, 339–343. New York: Routledge, 1993.

Losh, Elizabeth. "The Myth of Democratizing Media: Software-Specific Production Cultures." In *Media Authorship,* edited by Cynthia Chris and David Gerstner, 197–211. New York: Routledge, 2012.

Lothian, Alexis. "A Different Kind of Love Song: Vidding Fandom's Undercommons." *Cinema Journal* 48, no. 4 (2009): 138–145.

Lothian, Alexis, and Amanda Phillips. "Can Digital Humanities Mean Transformative Critique?" *Journal of e-Media Studies* 3, no. 1 (2013). Accessed July 29, 2015. http://journals.dartmouth.edu/cgi-bin/WebObjects/Journals.woa/xmlpage/4 /article/425.

Love, Heather. *Feeling Backward: Loss and the Politics of Queer History.* Cambridge, MA: Harvard University Press, 2007.

———. "Queers ____ This." In *After Sex? On Writing Since Queer Theory,* edited by Janet Halley and Andrew Parker, 180–191. Durham, NC: Duke University Press, 2011.

Ludlow, Peter, ed. *Crypto-Anarchy, Cyberstates, and Pirate Utopias.* Cambridge, MA: MIT Press, 2001.

Lunenfeld, Peter. "Space Invaders: Thoughts on Technology and the Production of Culture." In *New Media: Theories and Practices of Digitextuality,* edited by Anna Everett and John T. Caldwell, 63–74. New York: Routledge, 2003.

Lyotard, Jean-François. *The Postmodern Condition: A Report on Knowledge.* Translated by Geoff Bennington and Brian Massumi. Minneapolis: University of Minnesota Press, 1984.

Malin, Brenton. *Feeling Mediated: A History of Media Technology and Emotion in America.* New York: NYU Press, 2014.

Mamber, Stephen. "Narrative Mapping." In *New Media: Theories and Practices of Digitextuality*, edited by Anna Everett and John T. Caldwell, 145–158. New York: Routledge, 2003.

Mandiberg, Michael. "Introduction." In *The Social Media Reader*, edited by Michael Mandiberg, 1–12. New York: NYU Press, 2012.

———, ed. *The Social Media Reader*. New York: NYU Press, 2012.

Manovich, Lev. *The Language of New Media*. Cambridge, MA: MIT Press, 2001.

———. "The Poetics of Augmented Space." In *New Media: Theories and Practices of Digitextuality*, edited by Anna Everett and John T. Caldwell, 75–92. New York: Routledge, 2003.

Marcuse, Herbert. "Some Social Implications of Modern Technology." In *The Essential Frankfurt School Reader*, edited by Andrew Arato and Eike Gebhardt, 138–162. New York: Continuum, 1982.

Marks, Laura U. "Invisible Media." In *New Media: Theories and Practices of Digitextuality*, edited by Anna Everett and John T. Caldwell, 33–46. New York: Routledge, 2003.

Marwick, Alice E. *Status Update: Celebrity, Publicity, & Branding in the Social Media Age*. New Haven, CT: Yale University Press, 2013.

Massumi, Brian. *Parables for the Virtual: Movement, Affect, Sensation*. Durham, NC: Duke University Press, 2002.

McBride, Dwight A. *Why I Hate Abercrombie & Fitch: Essays on Race and Sexuality*. New York: NYU Press, 2005.

McChesney, Robert. *Corporate Media and the Threat to Democracy*. New York: Seven Stories Press, 1997.

McPherson, Tara. "US Operating Systems at Mid-Century: The Intertwining of Race and UNIX." In *Race after the Internet*, edited by Lisa Nakamura and Peter Chow-White, 21–37. New York: Routledge, 2011.

McRobbie, Angela. *The Aftermath of Feminism: Gender, Culture and Social Change*. London: SAGE, 2008.

McRuer, Robert. *Crip Theory: Cultural Signs of Queerness and Disability*. New York: NYU Press, 2006.

Medovoi, Leerom. *Rebels: Youth and the Cold War Origins of Identity*. Durham, NC: Duke University Press, 2005.

Mejias, Ulises A. "The Limits of Networks as Models for Organizing the Social." *New Media and Society* 12, no. 4 (2010): 603–617.

Melendez, Franklin. "Video Pornography, Visual Pleasure, and the Return of the Sublime." In *Porn Studies*, edited by Linda Williams, 401–430. Durham, NC: Duke University Press, 2004.

Mercer, Kobena. "Looking for Trouble." In *The Lesbian and Gay Studies Reader*, edited by Henry Abelove, Michèle Aina Barale, and David M. Halperin, 350–359. New York: Routledge, 1993.

———. "Skin Head Sex Thing: Racial Difference and the Homoerotic Imaginary." In *How Do I Look? Queer Film and Video*, edited by Bad Object-Choices, 169–210. Seattle: Bay Press, 1991.

Miller, D. A. *Place for Us: Essay on the Broadway Musical*. Cambridge, MA: Harvard University Press, 1998.

Miller, Toby. "Being 'Accountable': TV Audiences and Surveillance." In *Cultural Technologies: The Shaping of Culture in Media and Society,* edited by Göran Bolin, 87–102. New York: Routledge, 2012.

Moon, Michael. "Do You Smoke? Or, Is There Life? After Sex?" In *After Sex? On Writing Since Queer Theory,* edited by Janet Halley and Andrew Parker, 55–65. Durham, NC: Duke University Press, 2011.

Morozov, Evgeny. *The Net Delusion: The Dark Side of Internet Freedom.* New York: Public Affairs, 2012.

Muñoz, José Esteban. *Cruising Utopia: The Then and There of Queer Futurity.* New York: NYU Press, 2009.

———. "Dead White: Notes on the Whiteness of New Queer Cinema." *GLQ: A Journal of Lesbian and Gay Studies* 4, no. 1 (1998): 127–138.

———. *Disidentifications: Queers of Color and the Performance of Politics.* Minneapolis: University of Minnesota Press, 1999.

———. "Ephemera as Evidence: Introductory Notes to Queer Acts." *Women & Performance: A Journal of Feminist Theory* 8, no. 2 (1996): 5–15.

———. "The Sense of Watching Tony Sleep." In *After Sex? On Writing Since Queer Theory,* edited by Janet Halley and Andrew Parker, 142–150. Durham, NC: Duke University Press, 2011.

Murray, Susan. "Amateur Auteurs? The Cultivation of Online Video Partners and Creators." In *Media Authorship,* edited by Cynthia Chris and David Gerstner, 261–272. New York: Routledge, 2012.

Musto, Michael. "Jim Carrey Movie 'Too Gay' for Release?" *Village Voice,* March 24, 2009. Accessed July 24, 2015. http://www.villagevoice.com/blogs/jim-carrey-movie -too-gay-for-release-6375671.

Mwangi, Evan. "Queer Agency in Kenya's Digital Media." *African Studies Review* 57, no. 2 (September 2014): 93–113.

Nakamura, Lisa. *Cybertypes: Race, Ethnicity, and Identity on the Internet.* New York: Routledge, 2002.

———. *Digitizing Race: Visual Cultures of the Internet.* Minneapolis: University of Minnesota Press, 2007.

———. "Race In/For Cyberspace: Identity Tourism and Racial Passing on the Internet." *Works and Days: Essays in the Socio-Historical Dimensions of Literature & the Arts* 25/26 (Fall 1995, Winter 1996): 181–193.

Nakamura, Lisa, and Peter Chow-White, eds. *Race After the Internet.* New York: Routledge, 2011.

Netburn, Deborah. "Brendan Eich's Prop. 8 Contribution Gets Twittersphere Buzzing," *Los Angeles Times,* April 4, 2012. Accessed July 24, 2015. http://articles.latimes.com /2012/apr/04/business/la-fi-tn-brendan-eich-prop-8-contribution-20120404.

Nguyen, Tan Hoang. "The Opening of Kobena, Cecila, Robert, Linda, Juana, Hoang, and the Others." In *Porn Archives,* edited by Tim Dean, Steven Ruszczycky, and David Squires, 61–77. Durham, NC: Duke University Press, 2014.

———. *A View from the Bottom: Asian American Masculinity and Sexual Representation.* Durham, NC: Duke University Press, 2014.

Nossiter, Adam. "Mob Attacks More Than a Dozen Gay Men in Nigeria's Capital." *New York Times,* February 14, 2014. Accessed July 24, 2015. http://www.nytimes.com /2014/02/16/world/africa/mob-attacks-gay-men-in-nigerias-capital.html.

Nunes, Mark. *Cyberspaces of Everyday Life*. Minneapolis: University of Minnesota Press, 2006.

Nunokawa, Jeff. "Queer Theory: Postmortem." In *After Sex? On Writing Since Queer Theory*, edited by Janet Halley and Andrew Parker, 245–256. Durham, NC: Duke University Press, 2011.

Nyong'o, Tavia. "Queer Africa and the Fantasy of Virtual Participation." *WSQ: Women's Studies Quarterly* 40, no. 1 (2012): 40–63.

Ogas, Ogi, and Sai Gaddam. *A Billion Wicked Thoughts: What the World's Largest Experiment Reveals About Human Desire*. New York: Dutton, 2011.

O'Reilly, Tim. "What Is Web 2.0? Design Patterns and Business Models for the Next Generation of Software." In *The Social Media Reader*, edited by Michael Mandiberg, 32–52. New York: NYU Press, 2012.

O'Riordan, Kate, and David J. Phillips, eds. *Introduction to Queer Online: Media Technology & Sexuality*. New York: Peter Lang, 2007.

Osterweil, Ara. "Andy Warhol's *Blow Job*: Toward the Recognition of a Pornographic Avant-Garde." In *Porn Studies*, edited by Linda Williams, 431–460. Durham, NC: Duke University Press, 2004.

Page, Ruth, and Bronwen Thomas, eds. *New Narratives: Stories and Storytelling in the Digital Age*. Lincoln: University of Nebraska Press, 2011.

Paget, Derek. *No Other Way to Tell It: Dramadoc/Docudrama on Television*. Manchester: Manchester University Press, 1998.

Parks, Lisa. "Flexible Microcasting: Gender, Generation, and Television-Internet Convergence." In *Television After TV: Essays on a Medium in Transition*, edited by Lynn Spigel and Jan Olsson, 133–162. Durham, NC: Duke University Press, 2004.

———. "Technostruggles and the Satellite Dish: A Populist Approach to Infrastructure." In *Cultural Technologies: The Shaping of Culture in Media and Society*, edited by Göran Bolin, 64–86. New York: Routledge, 2012.

Pasquale, Frank. *The Black Box Society: The Secret Algorithms That Control Money and Information*. Cambridge, MA: Harvard University Press, 2015.

Patterson, Zabet. "Going On-line: Consuming Pornography in the Digital Era." In *Porn Studies*, edited by Linda Williams, 104–126. Durham, NC: Duke University Press, 2004.

Patton, Cindy. "From Nation to Family: Containing African AIDS." In *The Lesbian and Gay Studies Reader*, edited by Henry Abelove, Michèle Aina Barale, and David M. Halperin, 127–140. New York: Routledge, 1993.

Pendleton, David. "Out of the Ghetto: Queerness, Homosexual Desire and the Time-Image." *Strategies* 14, no. 1, 2001: 47–62.

Peters, Mischa. "Exit Meat: Digital Bodies in a Virtual World." In *New Media: Theories and Practices of Digitextuality*, edited by Anna Everett and John T. Caldwell, 47–62. New York: Routledge, 2003.

Petit Fours. "Why Gay People Love the Internet: Four Reasons." The Most Cake, July 19, 2010. Accessed July 24, 2015. http://themostcake.co.uk/culture/why-gay-people-love-the-internet-four-reasons/.

Phillips, David J. "Cyberstudies and the Politics of Visibility." In *Critical Cyberculture Studies*, edited by David Silver and Adrienne Massanari, 216–227. New York: NYU Press, 2006.

Piepenburg, Erik. "'Magic Mike' Is Big Draw for Gay Men." *New York Times,* July 4, 2012. Accessed July 24, 2015. http://www.nytimes.com/2012/07/05/movies/magic -mike-with-channing-tatum-draws-gay-men.html.

Poster, Mark. *What's the Matter with the Internet?* Minneapolis: University of Minnesota Press, 2001.

Puar, Jasbir K. "Homonationalism Gone Viral: Discipline, Control, and the Affective Politics of Sensation." Lecture, the Prince Alwaleed Bin Talal Bin Abdulaziz Alsaud Center for American Studies and Research, American University of Beirut, May 3, 2012. Accessed July 24, 2015. https://www.youtube.com/watch?v =6aoDkn3SnWM.

———. *Terrorist Assemblages: Homonationalism in Queer Times.* Durham, NC: Duke University Press, 2007.

Pullen, Christopher. "Ford's *A Single Man* and Bachardy's *Chris and Don:* The Aesthetic and Domestic Body of Isherwood." In *Queer Love in Film and Television: Critical Essays,* edited by Pamela Demory and Christopher Pullen, 233–244. London: Palgrave Macmillan, 2013.

Purvis, Tony. "Sexualities." In *Literary Theory and Criticism: An Oxford Guide,* edited by Patricia Waugh, 427–450. Oxford: Oxford University Press, 2006.

Qiu, Jack Linchuan. "Network Societies and Internet Studies: Rethinking Time, Space, and Class." In *The Oxford Handbook of Internet Studies,* edited by William H. Dutton, 109–128. New York: Oxford University Press, 2013.

Rambuss, Richard. "After Male Sex." In *After Sex? On Writing Since Queer Theory,* edited by Janet Halley and Andrew Parker, 192–206. Durham, NC: Duke University Press, 2011.

Reed, T. V. *Digitized Lives: Culture, Power, and Social Change in the Internet Era.* New York: Routledge, 2014.

Reuter, Donald F. *Gay-2-Zee: A Dictionary of Sex, Subtext, and the Sublime.* New York: St. Martin's Press, 2006.

Rich, Adrienne. "Compulsory Heterosexuality and Lesbian Existence." *Signs* 5 (1980): 631–660.

Rich, B. Ruby. "New Queer Cinema." *Sight and Sound,* September 2, 1992: 30–35.

———. *New Queer Cinema: The Director's Cut.* Durham, NC: Duke University Press, 2013.

Richter, Nicole. "Trans Love in New Trans Cinema." In *Queer Love in Film and Television: Critical Essays,* edited by Pamela Demory and Christopher Pullen, 161–168. London: Palgrave Macmillan, 2013.

Robichaud, Daniel. "*I Want Your Love:* Film Review." *Vancouver Weekly,* April 9, 2013. Accessed July 24, 2015. http://vancouverweekly.com/i-want-your-love-film-review -vancouver-queer-film-festival/.

Robinson, Wendy. "Catching the Waves: Considering Cyberculture, Technoculture, and Electronic Consumption." In *Critical Cyberculture Studies,* edited by David Silver and Adrienne Massanari, 55–67. New York: NYU Press, 2006.

Rochlin, Gene I. *Trapped in the Net: The Unanticipated Consequences of Computerization.* Princeton, NJ: Princeton University Press, 1997.

Rodowick, D. N. *The Virtual Life of Film.* Cambridge, MA: Harvard University Press, 2007.

Ronson, John. *So You've Been Publicly Shamed.* New York: Penguin, 2015.

Rosen, Jay. "The People Formerly Known as the Audience." In *The Social Media Reader,* edited by Michael Mandiberg, 13–16. New York: NYU Press, 2012.

Rubin, Gayle. "Thinking Sex: Notes for a Radical Theory of the Politics of Sexuality." In *Pleasure and Danger: Exploring Female Sexuality,* edited by Carole S. Vance, 267–293. London: Pandora, 1992.

Ruggill, Judd Ethan, and Ken S. McAllister. "Invention, Authorship, and Massively Collaborative Media." In *Media Authorship,* edited by Cynthia Chris and David Gerstner, 137–150. New York: Routledge, 2012.

San Filippo, Maria. *The B Word: Bisexuality in Contemporary Film and Television.* Bloomington: Indiana University Press, 2013.

———. "Before and After AfterEllen: Online Queer Cinephile Communities as Critical Counterpublics." In *Film Criticism in the Digital Age,* edited by Mattias Frey and Cecilia Sayad, 117–136. New Brunswick, NJ: Rutgers University Press, 2015.

Sardar, Ziauddin. *Postmodernism and the Other: The New Imperialism of Western Culture.* London: Pluto Press, 1997.

Schatz, Thomas. "New Hollywood, New Millennium." In *Film Theory and Contemporary Hollywood Movies,* edited by Warren Buckland, 19–46. New York: Routledge, 2009.

Schmidt, Eric E., and Jared Cohen. "The Future of Internet Freedom." *New York Times,* March 11, 2014. Accessed July 24, 2015. http://www.nytimes.com/2014/03/12/opinion/the-future-of-internet-freedom.html.

Schulman, Sarah. *Israel/Palestine and the Queer International.* Durham and London: Duke University Press, 2012.

Sconce, Jeffrey. "'Trashing' the Academy: Taste, Excess, and an Emerging Politics of Cinematic Style." *Screen* 36, no. 4 (1995): 371–393

———. "Tulip Theory." In *New Media: Theories and Practices of Digitextuality,* edited by Anna Everett and John T. Caldwell, 179–196. New York: Routledge, 2003.

Scott, A. O. "Leaping Off the Page, a Beatnik's Poetic Rant." *New York Times,* September 23, 2010. Accessed July 24, 2015. http://www.nytimes.com/2010/09/24/movies/24howl.html?_r=0.

Scott, D. Travers. "Fierce.net: Imagining a Faggoty Web." In *Why Are Faggots So Afraid of Faggots? Flaming Challenges to Masculinity, Objectification, and the Desire to Conform,* edited by Mattilda Bernstein Sycamore, 5–10. Oakland: AK Press, 2012.

Scott, Joan W. "The Evidence of Experience." *Critical Inquiry* 17 (1991): 773–797.

Sedgwick, Eve Kosofsky. *Between Men: English Literature and Male Homosocial Desire.* New York: Columbia, 1985.

———. *Epistemology of the Closet.* Berkeley: University of California Press, 1990.

———. "Melanie Klein and the Difference Affect Makes." In *After Sex? On Writing Since Queer Theory,* edited by Janet Halley and Andrew Parker, 283–302. Durham, NC: Duke University Press, 2011.

———. "Queer and Now." In *The Routledge Queer Studies Reader,* edited by Donald E. Hall and Annamarie Jagose, with Andrea Bebell and Susan Potter, 3–17. New York: Routledge, 2013.

———. *Tendencies.* Durham, N.C.: Duke University Press, 1993.

Seidman, Steven. "Identity and Politics in a 'Postmodern' Gay Culture: Some Historical and Conceptual Notes." In *Fear of a Queer Planet: Queer Politics and Social*

Theory, edited by Michael Warner, 105–142. Minneapolis: University of Minnesota Press, 1993.

Seigworth, Gregory J., and Melissa Gregg. "An Inventory of Shimmers." In *The Affect Theory Reader,* edited by Melissa Gregg and Gregory J. Seigworth, 1–28. Durham, NC: Duke University Press, 2010.

Sender, Katherine. *Business, Not Politics: The Making of the Gay Market.* New York: Columbia University Press, 2005.

Shaukat, Usman. "Sufi Homoerotic Authorship and Its Heterosexualization in Pakistan." In *Media Authorship,* edited by Cynthia Chris and David Gerstner, 105–120. New York: Routledge, 2012.

Shaviro, Steven. *Connected, or What It Means to Live in the Network Society.* Minneapolis: University of Minnesota Press, 2003.

Silver, David. "Introduction: Where Is Internet Studies?" In *Critical Cyberculture Studies,* edited by David Silver and Adrienne Massanari, 1–16. New York: NYU Press, 2006.

Sinfield, Alan. *Cultural Politics—Queer Reading.* Oxon: Routledge, 2005.

———. *Gay and After: Gender, Culture, and Consumption.* London: Serpent's Tail, 1998.

Snickars, Pelle, and Patrick Vonderau, eds. *Moving Data: The iPhone and the Future of Media.* New York: Columbia University Press, 2012.

Sobchack, Vivian. "Afterword: Media Archaeology and Re-presencing the Past." In *Media Archaeology: Approaches, Applications, and Implications,* edited by Erkki Huhtamo and Jussi Parikka, 323–334. Berkeley: University of California Press, 2011.

Solomon, Andrew. "Honey Maid and the Business of Love." *New Yorker,* April 5, 2014. Accessed July 24, 2015. http://www.newyorker.com/business/currency/honey-maid-and-the-business-of-love.

Somerville, Siobhan. *Queering the Color Line: Race and the Invention of Homosexuality in American Culture.* Durham, NC: Duke University Press, 2000.

Sontag, Susan. "Notes on 'Camp.'" In *Against Interpretation and Other Essays,* 275–292. New York: Picador, 2001.

Spillers, Hortense. "Mama's Baby, Papa's Maybe: An American Grammar Book." *Diacritics* 17, no. 2 (1987): 64–81.

Stack, Liam. "Activist Removed After Heckling Obama at L.G.B.T. Event at White House." *New York Times,* June 24, 2015. Accessed July 24, 2015. http://www.nytimes.com/2015/06/25/us/politics/activist-removed-after-heckling-obama-at-lgbt-event.html?_r=0.

Staiger, Janet. *Media Reception Studies.* New York: NYU Press, 2005.

Stalder, Felix. "Between Democracy and Spectacle: The Front-End and Back-End of the Social Web." In *The Social Media Reader,* edited by Michael Mandiberg, 242–256. New York: NYU Press, 2012.

Stanfill, Mel. "'The Fan' as/in Industry Discourse." Presentation at the Society for Cinema and Media Studies annual conference, Seattle, Washington, March 23, 2014. Accessed July 24, 2015. http://www.melstanfill.com/thefanasinindustrydiscourse/.

Stanley, Eric A. "Fugitive Flesh: Gender Self-Determination, Queer Abolition, and Trans Resistance." In *Captive Genders: Trans Embodiment and the Prison Industrial Complex,* edited by Eric A. Stanley and Nat Smith, 114. Oakland, CA: AK Press, 2011.

Stanley, Eric A., and Nat Smith, eds. *Captive Genders: Trans Embodiment and the Prison Industrial Complex*. Oakland, CA: AK Press, 2011

Stein, Louisa. "Online Roundtable on *Spreadable Media,* edited by Henry Jenkins, Sam Ford, and Joshua Green, with participants Paul Booth, Kristina Busse, Melissa Click, Sam Ford, Henry Jenkins, Xiaochang Li, and Sharon Ross." *Cinema Journal* 53, no. 3 (Spring 2014): 152–177.

Stone, Allucquére Rosanne. *The War of Desire and Technology at the Close of the Mechanical Age*. Cambridge, MA: MIT Press, 1995.

Straayer, Chris. *Deviant Eyes, Deviant Bodies: Sexual Re-Orientation in Film and Video*. New York: Columbia University Press, 1995.

———. "The Talented Poststructuralist: Heteromasculinity, Gay Artifice, and Class Passing." In *Masculinity: Bodies, Movies, Culture,* edited by in Peter Lehman, 115–132. New York: Routledge, 2001.

Stryker, Cole. *Epic Win for Anonymous: An Online Army Conquers the Media*. New York: Overlook Press, 2012.

Suárez, Juan Antonio. *Pop Modernism: Noise and the Reinvention of the Everyday*. Champaign: University of Illinois Press, 2007.

Sycamore, Matt (Mattilda) Bernstein, ed. *That's Revolting: Queer Strategies for Resisting Assimilation*. Brooklyn: Softskull, 2004.

Taubin, Amy. "Beyond the Sons of Scorsese." *Sight and Sound* 2, no. 5 (September 1992): 37.

Tcheuyap, Alexie. "African Cinema and Representations of (Homo)Sexuality." In *Body, Sexuality, and Gender: Versions and Subversions in African Literatures 1,* edited by Flora Veit-Wild and Dirk Naguschewski, 143–156. Amsterdam: Rodopi, 2005.

Tepper, Allegra. "'Blue is the Warmest Color' Can't Play Idaho Theater Due to 'Obscenity.'" *Variety,* October 10, 2013. Accessed July 24, 2015. http://variety.com/2013/film/news/blue-is-the-warmest-color-cant-play-idaho-arthouse-due-to-obscenity-1200712750/.

Thomas, Kate. "Post Sex: On Being Too Slow, Too Stupid, Too Soon." In *After Sex? On Writing Since Queer Theory,* edited by Janet Halley and Andrew Parker, 66–78. Durham, NC: Duke University Press, 2011.

Thorburn, David. "Web of Paradox." In *Rethinking Media Change: The Aesthetics of Transition,* edited by Henry Jenkins and David Thorburn, 19–22. Cambridge, MA: MIT Press, 2003.

Tinkcom, Matthew. "Perceptions of Place: The Nowhere and the Somewhere of Al Jazeera." In *Media Authorship,* edited by Cynthia Chris and David Gerstner, 247–260. New York: Routledge, 2012.

———. *Working Like a Homosexual: Camp, Capital, Cinema*. Durham, NC: Duke University Press, 2002.

Toffler, Alvin. *The Third Wave*. New York: Bantam, 1984.

Trope, Alison. *Stardust Monuments: The Saving and Selling of Hollywood*. Lebanon, NH: Dartmouth College Press, 2011.

Tsika, Noah. "'Be Wary of Working Boys': The Cultural Production of Queer Youth in Today's West Africa." In *Queer Youth and Media Cultures,* edited by Christopher Pullen, 239–250. London: Palgrave Macmillan, 2014.

———. "'Compartmentalize Your Life': Advising Army Men on RealJock.com." In *LGBT Identity and Online New Media,* edited by Christopher Pullen and Margaret Cooper, 230–244. New York: Routledge, 2010.

————. "A Lagosian Lady Gaga: Cross-Cultural Imitation in Nollywood's Anti-Biopic Cycle." In *Multiplicities: Cycles, Sequels, Remakes and Reboots in Film & Television,* edited by Amanda Ann Klein and R. Barton Palmer, 184–201. Austin: University of Texas Press, 2016.

————. "'One Dies, the Other Doesn't': *Brokeback* and the Blogosphere." In *The Brokeback Book: From Story to Cultural Phenomenon,* edited by William R. Handley, 205–228. Lincoln: University of Nebraska Press, 2011.

————. "The Queerness of Country: *Brokeback*'s Soundscape." In *Reading "Brokeback Mountain": Essays on the Story and the Film,* edited by Jim Stacy, 167–177. Jefferson, NC: McFarland, 2007.

Turkle, Sherry. *Alone Together: Why We Expect More from Technology and Less from Each Other.* New York: Basic Books, 2011.

Turner-Rahman, Gregory. "Abductive Authorship of the New Media Artifact." In *Media Authorship,* edited by Cynthia Chris and David Gerstner, 151–162. New York: Routledge, 2012.

Turow, Joseph. *The Daily You: How the New Advertising Industry Is Defining Your Identity and Your Worth.* New Haven, CT: Yale University Press, 2011.

Tyler, Parker. *Screening the Sexes: Homosexuality in the Movies.* New York: Holt, Rinehart, and Winston, 1972.

Unwin, Tim. "The Internet and Development: A Critical Perspective." In *The Oxford Handbook of Internet Studies,* edited by William H. Dutton, 531–554. New York: Oxford University Press, 2013.

Uricchio, William. "The Algorithmic Turn: Photosynth, Augmented Reality and the Changing Implications of the Image." In *Cultural Technologies: The Shaping of Culture in Media and Society,* edited by Göran Bolin, 19–35. New York: Routledge, 2012.

————. "Historicizing Media in Transition." In *Rethinking Media Change: The Aesthetics of Transition,* edited by Henry Jenkins and David Thorburn, 23–28. Cambridge, MA: MIT Press, 2003.

Valentine, David. *Imagining Transgender: An Ethnography of a Category.* Durham, NC: Duke University Press, 2007.

Van Couvering, Elizabeth. "Search Engines in Practice: Structure and Culture in Technical Development." In *Cultural Technologies: The Shaping of Culture in Media and Society,* edited by Göran Bolin, 118–132. New York: Routledge, 2012.

Vander Wal, Thomas. "Folksonomy Coinage and Definition." Vanderwal.net, February 2, 2007. Accessed July 24, 2015. http://www.vanderwal.net/folksonomy.html.

Viegener, Matias. "'The Only Haircut That Makes Sense Anymore': Queer Subculture and Gay Resistance." In *Queer Looks: Perspectives on Lesbian and Gay Film and Video,* edited by Martha Gever, John Greyson, and Pratibha Parmar, 116–133. New York: Routledge, 1993.

Wang, Shujen. "'Dreaming with BRICs?' On Piracy and Film Markets in Emerging Economies." In *Postcolonial Piracy: Media Distribution and Cultural Production in the Global South,* edited by Anja Schwarz and Lars Eckstein, 99–105. London: Bloomsbury Academic, 2014.

Wardrip-Fruin, Noah. "Digital Media Archaeology: Interpreting Computational Processes." In *Media Archaeology: Approaches, Applications, and Implications,* edited by Erkki Huhtamo and Jussi Parikka, 302–323. Berkeley: University of California Press, 2011.

Warner, Michael, ed. *Fear of a Queer Planet: Queer Politics and Social Theory.* Minneapolis: University of Minnesota Press, 1993.

———. *Publics and Counterpublics.* New York: Zone, 2002.

———. *The Trouble with Normal: Sex, Politics, and the Ethics of Queer Life.* Cambridge, MA: Harvard University Press, 1999.

Waugh, Thomas. "Films by Gays for Gays: *A Very Natural Thing, Word Is Out,* and *The Naked Civil Servant.*" In *The Fruit Machine: Twenty Years of Writings on Queer Cinema.* Durham, NC: Duke University Press, 2000.

———. "Homosociality in the Classical American Stag Film: Off-Screen, On-Screen." In *Porn Studies,* edited by Linda Williams, 127–141. Durham, NC: Duke University Press, 2004.

———. *Hard to Imagine: Gay Male Eroticism in Photography and Film from Their Beginnings to Stonewall.* New York: Columbia University Press, 1996.

———. *The Romance of Transgression in Canada: Queering Sexualities, Nations, Cinemas.* Montreal: McGill-Queen's University Press, 2006.

Weiner, Joshua J., and Damon Young. "Introduction: Queer Bonds." *GLQ: A Journal of Lesbian and Gay Studies* 17, no. 2–3 (2011): 223–241.

Weiss, Meredith L. and Michael J. Bosia, eds. *Global Homophobia: States, Movements, and the Politics of Oppression.* Urbana: University of Illinois Press, 2013.

Weiss, Sasha. "Reacting to Miley." *New Yorker,* August 30, 2013. Accessed July 24, 2015. http://www.newyorker.com/culture/culture-desk/reacting-to-miley.

White, Patricia. *Uninvited: Classical Hollywood Cinema and Lesbian Representability.* Bloomington: Indiana University Press, 1999.

Williams, Linda. *Hard Core: Power, Pleasure, and the "Frenzy of the Visible."* Berkeley: University of California Press, 1989.

———. "Pornography, Porno, Porn: Thoughts on a Weedy Field." In *Porn Archives,* edited by Tim Dean, Steven Ruszczycky, and David Squires, 29–43. Durham, NC: Duke University Press, 2014.

———, ed., *Porn Studies.* Durham, NC: Duke University Press, 2004.

———. *Screening Sex.* Durham, NC: Duke University Press, 2008.

Williams, Raymond. *Marxism and Literature.* Oxford: Oxford University Press, 1977.

Young, Damon R. "*The Living End,* or Love without a Future." In *Queer Love in Film and Television: Critical Essays,* edited by Pamela Demory and Christopher Pullen, 13–22. London: Palgrave Macmillan, 2013.

———. "Queer Seriousness." *World picture* 9 (Summer 2014): 1–17.

Zaslow, Jeffrey. "If TiVo Thinks You Are Gay, Here's How to Set It Straight." *Wall Street Journal,* A1, November 26, 2002.

Index

NOAH A. TSIKA is Assistant Professor of Media Studies at Queens College, City University of New York. He is the author of the books *Gods and Monsters: A Queer Film Classic* and *Nollywood Stars: Media and Migration in West Africa and the Diaspora* (IUP, 2015). His essays have appeared in *African Studies Review, Black Camera, Cineaste, Porn Studies, The Velvet Light Trap,* and *Women's Studies Quarterly,* as well as in numerous anthologies, including *LGBT Identity and Online New Media, The Brokeback Book, Reading Brokeback Mountain,* and *Queer Youth and Media Cultures.*

Lightning Source UK Ltd.
Milton Keynes UK
UKOW06f0832061016

284600UK00019B/105/P